OUTLINES OF

INDIAN PHILOSOPH

OUTLINES OF INDIAN PHILOSOPHY

Jadunath Sinha MA, PRS, PhD

New Central Book Agency (P) Ltd

LONDON

HYDERABAD ERNAKULAM BHUBANESWAR

NEW DELHI KOLKATA PUNE GUWAHATI

NCBA

REGD OFFICE

8/1 Chintamoni Das Lane, Kolkata 700 009, India
email: ncbapvtltd@eth.net

OVERSEAS

NCBA (UK) Ltd, 149 Park Avenue North, Northampton, NN3 2HY, UK
email: ncbauk@yahoo.com

EXPORT

NCBA Exports Pvt. Ltd, 212 Shahpur Jat, New Delhi 110 049
email: ncbaexports@ncbapvtltd.com

BRANCHES

2/27 Ansari Road, 1st Floor
Daryaganj, **New Delhi** 110 002
email: ncbadel@ncbapvtltd.com

House No. 3-1-315, 1st Floor
Nimboliadda, Kachiguda, **Hyderabad** 500 02
email: ncbahydb@ncbapvtltd.com

Shop Nos. 3 & 4, Vinayak Towers
681/B Budhwar Peth, Appa Balwant Chowk
Pune 411 002
email: ncbapune@ncbapvtltd.com

GSS Shopping Complex, 1st Floor
Opposite College Post Office, Convent Road
Ernakulam 682 035
0484-4021054/53

Shop No. 15, Bharati Towers, Ground Floor
Forest Park
Bhubaneswar 751 001
email: ncbabub@ncbapvtltd.com

Radhamayee Complex (Second Floor)
Opp. Axis Bank, Panbazar, Jaswanta Road
Guwahati 781 001
email: ncbaguwahati@ncbapvtltd.com

OUTLINES OF INDIAN PHILOSOPHY • Jadunath Sinha

Revised Second Edition: 1985
Reprinted: 1992, 1996, 1998, 2002, 2006
Reprinted: 2013, 2015, 2018, 2021

PUBLISHER : New Central Book Agency (P) Ltd
8/1 Chintamoni Das Lane, Kolkata 700 009

TYPESETTER : New Central Book Agency (P) Ltd
8/1 Chintamoni Das Lane, Kolkata 700 009

PRINTER : New Central Book Agency (P) Ltd
Web-Offset Division, Dhulagarh, Sankrail, Howrah

ISBN: 978 81 7381 203 4

Price: ₹ 385.00

Dedicated

To

My Grandfather

Sarveshwar Sinha

PREFACE TO SECOND EDITION

The book is an introduction to Indian Philosophy. It deals with the heterodox schools of the Carvaka, the Buddhist and the Jaina, and the orthodox schools of the Vaisesika, the Nyaya, the Samkhya, the Y9ga, the Mimamsa and the Vedanta. It deals with the Buddhist schools of the Vaibhasika, the Sautrantika, the Yogachara and the Madhyamika, the Mimamsa schools of Kumarila dnd Prabhakara, and the Vedanta schools of Samkara and Ramanuja, and also with their background, the philosophy of the Upanisads and the *Bhagwad Gita*. Madhva, Nimbarka, Vallabha, Krsnadasa Kauiraja (Chaitanya's philosophy) and Saivism and Saktism.

It treats of the main problems of epistemology, logic, ontology, ethics and theology, and of some problems of psychology. It discusses the nature and means of valid knowledge—'perception, inference, comparison, testimony, presumption and non-apprehension, intrinsic and extrinsic validity of knowledge, tests of truth, the nature and kinds of invalid knowlege, the nature of prakrti, matter, atoms, space, time, causality, creation, volution, medhanism and teleology, the nature and knowledge of the individual self, freedom of the will, bondage, liberation, pre-existence, future life and transmigration, the nature of God and His relation to the world and the individual self. It gives the proofs for the existence of prakrti, atoms, the individual self, and God advanced by the different systems.

It discusses, the Carvaka doctrines of materialism, naturalism, accidentalism, egoistic hedonism, and secularism, the Buddhist doctrines of phenomenalism, direct relism, indirect realism, subjective idealism, absolute idealism, realativism, nihilistic absolutism, ethics of ahimsa, and nirvana, and especially the Jaina doctrines of anekantavada, syadvada, saptabhanginyaya and nayavada.

It treats of the atheism of the Carvaka, the early Buddhists, the Jaina, the Samkhya and the Mimamsaka.

It deals with Samkara's Absolutism or monism and Ramanuja's qualified monism or objective idealism. It especially discusses the nature of the Absolute, God, maya, the empirical self, world-appearance, their interrelation, jnanayoga and realization of pure identity according to Samkara, and the nature of God, the individual self and the world, their reality and inseparable relation, refutation of maya, and niskama karma, devotion and knowledge as the means of the realization of community with God according to Ramanuja.

The book avoids superficiality and abstruseness. It is intended for advanced Graduate students of Indian and Foreign Universities. The Post-Graduate students will find it useful for mastering the essential systems of Indian philosophy.

My special thanks to my son Amiya Kumar Sinha, Executive Director, Jadunath Sinha Foundation for helping me in preparing the manuscript of the book.

39, S. R. Das Road
Calcutta-700 026
INDIA

Jadunath Sinha

CONTENTS

CHAPTER PAGE

ABBREVIATIONS

ADS.=Abhidhammāttasaṃgaha.
Ait.=Aitareya.
AK.=Abhidharmakoṣa.
AKV.=Abhidharmakoṣavyākhyā (edited by Narendra Nath Law, 1949, Calcutta, C.O.S., 31).
AMV.=Āptamīmāṃsāvṛtti.
AN.=Aṃguttaranikāya.
A.S.B.=Asiatic Society, Bengal.
ATV.=Ātmatattvaviveka (Udayana), B.I., 1939.
ATVP.=Ātmatattvavivekaprakāśaikā (Bhagīratha), (B.I., 1939).
BG.=Bhagavad Gītā.
B.I.=Bibliotheca Indica, A. S. B., Calcutta.
BhP.=Bhāṣāpariccheda (Viśvanātha), N.S.P., 1916.
Bṛ.=Bṛhadāraṇyaka.
Bṛ.=Bṛhati (Prabhākara) on S.Bh.
BS.=Brahma Sūtra.
B.S.S.=Benares Sanskrit Series.
Ch. S. S.=Chaukhāmbā Sanskrit Series.
Chand.=Chāndogya.
ChV.=Chāyāvyākhyā (Nāgeśa) on Yoga Sūtra.
C.O.S.=Calcutta Oriental Series, Calcutta.
C.U.=Calcutta University.
DN.=Dhīghanikāya.
DP.=Dhammapada.
DS.=Dravyasaṃgraha.
DSV.=Dravyasaṃgrahavṛtti.
E.H.=Ethics of the Hindus (Sushil Kumar maitra) C. U., Calcutta, 1925.
E.R.E.=Encyclopaedia of Religion and Ethics.
E.T.=English translation.
G.O.S.=Gaekwad Oriental Series, Bombay.
GTS.=Gammatasāra.
HIP.=History of Indian Philosophy (Jadunath Sinha) Vol. II, Calcutta, 1952; Vol. I, S.P.H., 1956.
IPC.=Indian Psychology : Cognition (Jadunath Sinha).
JK.=Jīvakāṇḍa.
Kaiṣ=Kaiṣitakī.
Kaṭh=Kaṭha.
KNR.=Kaṇādarahsya (Śaṃkara Miśra).
K.S.S.=Kāshī Sanskrit Series, Benares.
KV.=Kiraṇāvalī (Udayana) on PBh., Benares, Saṁvat 1941.

KVB.=Kiraṇāvalibhāskara (Padmanābha Miśra S.B.T., 1920).
KVP.=Kiraṇāvaliprakāśa (Vardhamāna), Benares, Saṁvat 1941.
L.S.=Laṅkāvatārasūtra (edited by B. Nanjio, Kyoto, 1935).
LV.=Laghuvṛtti on SDSm.
MB.=Mitabhāṣiṇī (Mādhava Sarasvatī) on SP., V: S. S., 1893.
MK.=Mādhyamikakārikā.
MKV.=Mādhyamikakārikāvṛtti.
MM.=Mānameyodaya (Madras) 1933).
MN.=Majjhimanikāya.
Māṇḍ. K.=Māṇḍukya Kārikā.
Māṇḍ=Māṇḍukya.
MP.=Milindapañha.
MPS.=Mahāparinibbānasutta.
MS.=Mīmāṁsā Sūtra (Jaimini).
Muṇḍ=Muṇḍaka.
NAV.=Nyāyāvatāravṛtti.
NBh.=Nyāyabhaṣya (Vātsyāyana). on NS., (Jīvananda, Calcutta, 1919).
NK.=Nyāyakandalī (Śrīdhara), V.S.S., 1895) on PBh.
NKL.=Nyāyakalikā (Jayanta Bhaṭṭa), S.B.T., 1925.
NKS.=Nyāyakusumāñjali (Udayana).
NKSB. =Nyāyakusumāñjalibodhinī (Varadarāja), (S.B.T., 1922).
NKSH.=Haridāsa's ṭīkā on NKS., Kārikā, Benares, 1913.
NKSM.=Nyāyakusumāñjalimakaranda (Rucidatta), Benares, 1912.
NKSP. =Nyāyakusumāñjaliprakāśa (Vardhamāna), Benares, 1912.
NM.=Nyāyamañjarī (Jayanta Bhaṭṭa), (V.S.S., 1895).
NNP.=Nyāyanibandhaprakāśa (Vardhamāna), on NVTP., (B. I., 1911).
NR.=Nyāyaratnākara (Pārthasārathi Miśra)on ŚV., (Ch. S.S., 1898-99).
NRM.=Nyāyaratnamālā (Parthaśarathi Miśra), (G.O.S., 1937).
NS.=Nyāyasūtra (Gautama), (Jivānanda, Calcutta, 1919).
NSA.=Nyāyasiddhāñjana (Veṅkaṭanātha Deśika).
NSār.=Nyāyasāra (Bhāsarvajña), B. I., 1910).
N.S.P.=Nirnay Sagar Press, Bombay.
NSV.=Nyāyasūtravṛtti (Viśvanātha) on NS., (Jivānanda, Calcutta, 1919).
NYR.=Nāyakāratna (Ramānujācārya) on NRM, (G.O.S., 1930).
NV.=Nyāyavārtika (Uddyotakara) on NBh., (B.I., 1887-1904).
NVTP. =Nyāyavārtikatātparyapariśuddhi (Udayana) on NVTT., (B.I., 1911).
NNTT. =Nyāyavārtikatātparyaṭīkā (Vācaspati Miśra), (V.S.S., 1898).
P.=Pañcāstikāyasamayaśara (Kundakundācarya).
PBh.=Praśastapādabhāṣya (V.S.S., 1895).
PI.=Introduction, E.T. of P.
PKM. =Prameyakamalamārtaṇḍa (Prabhācandra).
PMS.=Parīkṣāmukhasūtra.
PNT. =Pramāṇanayatattvālokālālaṃkāra.
Praś.=Praśna,

PSPM.=*The Prabhakara School of Purva Mimamsa* (Ganganath Jha).
RA.=Rāmāyaṇa (Vālmīki).
RBG.=Rāmānuja's Bhāṣya on BG.
RBS.=Rāmānuja's Śrībhāṣya on BS.
RK.=Ratnakrāvatārikā on PNT.
RM.=Rājamārtaṇḍa (Bhojadeva) on YS.
R.V.=Ṛg Veda.
RVS.=Rāmānuja's Vedāntasāra.
SAS.=Sarvārthasiddhi on TMK. (Venkaṭanatha Deśika).
SB.=Śaṁkara Bhāṣya.
SBE.=Sacred Books of the East.
SBG.=Śaṁkara Bhāṣya on BG.
SBS.=Saṁkara Bhāṣyc on BS.
ŚBh.=Śavarabhāṣya on MS.
ŚD.=Śāstradīpikā (Pārthasārathi Miśra), (Ch. S. S.)
S.B.T.=Sarasvatī Bhavan Text, Benares.
SDS.=Ṣaḍdarśanasaṁgraha (Mādhavācārya), Kalyan—Bombay, Saṁvat, 1982.
SDSm.=Ṣaḍdarśanasamuccaya (Haribhadra Sūri), Ch. S. S., No 95.
SGB.=Gauḍapāda-bhaṣya on SK.
SJM.=Jayamaṃgala on SK.
SK.=Sāṁkhyakārikā (Īśvarakṛṣṇa).
SM.=Siddhāntamuktāvali (Viśvanātha) on BhP., (N.S.P., 1916).
SMD.=Dinakarī on SM.
SN.=Saṁyuttanikāya.
SP.=Saptapadārthī (Śivāditya), V.S. S., 1893.
SPB.=Sāṁkhyapravacanabhāṣya (Vijñānabhikṣu), Benares, 1909, on SPS.
S.P.H.=Sinha Publishing House, Calcutta-26.
SPM.=Vedāntī Mahādeva's gloss on SPS.
SPS.=Sāṁkhyapravacanasūtra.
SS.=Sarvārthasiddhi.
SSBG.=Śrīdharasvāmī's bhāṣya on BG.
SSV.=Sāṁkhyasūtravṛtti (Aniruddha) on SPS., (BI).
STK.=Sāṁkhyatattvakaumudī (Vācaspati Miśra).
ŚV.=Ślokavārtika (Kumārila), Ch. S. S., 1898-99.
SVM.=Syādvādamañjarī (Hemacandra).
Śvet.=Śvetāśvatara.
Tait.=Taittirīya.
TBh.=Tarkabhāṣā (Keśava Miśra), Poona, 1924.
TCĪA.=Tattvacintāmaṇi, Īśvarānumāna (Gaṅgeśa), B. I.
TDTV.=Tātparyadīpikātātparyavṛtti on P.
TK.=Tarkakaumudī (Laugākṣi Bhāskara), N.S.P., 1914.
TMK.=Tattvamuktākalāpa (Vedāntadeśika).
TNR=Tantrarahasya (Rāmānujācārya), G.O.S., No 24.
TR.=Tārkikarakṣā (Varadarāja), Benares, 1903.

TRD=Tarkarahasyadīpikā on SDSm,, (BI.), 1914.
TRV.=Tattvarājavārtika.
TS.=Tattvasaṁgraha (Sāntarakṣita), G.O.S.
TSP.=Tattvasaṁgrahapañjikā (Kamalaśīla) on TS., G.O.S.
TSār.=Tattvārthādhigamasāra.
TSD.=Tarkasaṁgrahadīpikā.
TSN.=Nīlakaṇṭhī on TSG.
TSG. =Tarkasaṁgraha (Annambbhaṭṭa).
TSP.=Tarkasaṁgraha, Preface (Bodas).
TSV.=Tattvaślokavārtika.
TV.=Tattvavaiśāradī (Vācaspati Miśra) on YBh.
UÑC.=Uttaranaiṣadhacarita, B.I.
UNCT.=Tikā on UNC., B.I.
Up.=Upaniṣad.
VAS.=Vedārthasaṁgraha (Rāmānuja) on BS. Benares, 1894.
VD.=Vedāntadīpa (Rāmānuja) on BS. (B.S.S., 1904).
VP.=Vardhamāna Purāṇa.
VPB.=Vedāntaparibhāṣā (Dharmarājādhvarīndra).
VRS.=Vītarāgastuti on SVM.
VS.=Vaiśeṣika Sutra (Kaṇāda).
VSB.=Vaiśeṣikasūtra-Bhāṣya (Candrakānta Tarkālaṅkāra).
VSR.=Vedāntasāra (Sadānanda Yati).
V,S.S.=Vizianagram Sanskrit Series, Benares.
VSU.=Upaskāra (Śaṁkāra Miśra) on VS., (Gujgrati Press, Bombay, 1913).
VSV.=Vaiśeṣikasūtravivṛti (Jayanārāyaṇa) on VS. (,,).
VV.=Vyomavatī (Vyomaśivācārya) on VS., Ch. S.S., 1924.
YBh.=Bhāṣya (Vyāsa) on YS.
YMD.=Yotīndramatadīpikā.
YMP.=Yogamaṇiprabhā on YS.
YS.=Yogasūtra (Patañjali).
YSP.=Yuktisnehaprapūraṇī (Rāmakṛṣṇa Bhaṭṭa) on ŚD.
YV.=Yogovārtika (Vijñānabhikṣu) on YBh.
MBS. =Māhdvabhāṣya on Brahma Sūtra.
VPS. =Vivaraṇaprameyasaṁgraha.
ABS. =Anubhāṣya on Brahma Sūtra by Vallabha (BI).
PRK. =Prasthānaratnākara.
SAM. =Śuddhādvaitamārtaṇḍa.
SAMP. =Prakāśa on Śuddhādvaimārtaṇḍa.

CHAPTER I

THE COMMON IDEAS IN INDIAN PHILOSOPHY

THE SPIRITUAL BACKGROUND OF INDIAN PHILOSOPHY

The Upaniṣads are the foundation of Indian Philosophy, which teach spiritual monism and mysticism. The systems of Indian philosophy are systematic speculations on the nature of the Reality in harmony with the teachings of the Upaniṣads, which contain various aspects of the truth. They aim at the knowledge of the Reality with a view to transforming and spiritualizing human life. Philosophical knowledge does not aim at merely satisfying our theoretical and speculative interest, but also at realizing the highest truth in life.

Indian philosophy is essentially spiritual. Philosophy and religion are intimately connected with each other in India. Religion is not a system of dogmas, but a living experience. It is the practical realization of the spiritual truth. Philosophy is the theory of the Reality. It is an insight into the nature of the Reality, which leads to liberation. So Indian philosophy is not idle theorizing, but a spiritual quest.

Philosophy is called Darśana, which means vision. Philosophy is the vision of the Reality as a whole. It is an insight into the nature of the whole reality.

Indian philosophy is based on logical reason subordinate to the authority of the Vedas, which are believed to embody the intuitions of the seers of truth. The authority of the Vedas is that of intuition. Logical reason is subordinate to intuition. So Indian philosophy is based on rational speculation in harmony with the Vedas, and consciously aims at achieving the highest perfection (mokṣa) attainable in human life.

THE SCHOOLS OF INDIAN PHILOSOPHY

It is customary to divide the schools of Indian philosophy into two broad classes, *viz.*, orthodox (āstika) and heterodox (nāstika). The orthodox schools recognize the authority of the Vedas. The heterodox schools do not recognize their authority. The Cārvāka, the Bauddha, and the Jaina are the heterodox schools. They are called heterodox not because they are atheists, but because they reject the authority of the Vedas. The Nyāya, the Vaiśeṣika, the Sāṁkhya, the Yoga, the Mīmāṁsā, and the Vedānta are the orthodox schools. They believe in the authority of the Vedas. Among them the Sāṁkhya and the Mīmāṁsā are atheists. The Nyāya, the Vaiśeṣika, the Yoga, and the Vedānta are theists. The Sāṁkhya advocates dualism of prakṛti and puruṣas or individual selves. The Vedānta advocates spiritualistic monism, and recognizes the reality of Brahman or the Absolute. It regards the world and the individual selves as their appearances, or parts, or attributes, modes or accessories of Brahman. The Nyāya and the Vaiśeṣika advocate the reality of God, plurality of individual souls, and the world of diverse objects. They consider the world to be composed of the eternal atoms of earth, water, fire, and air existing in self-existent and eternal time and space. The Mīmāṁsā recognizes the reality of individual selves and the self-existent material world, and rejects the concept of God as the creator of the world. The Yoga grafts the notion of God on the Sāṁkhya dualism of prakṛti and puruṣas, and makes it theistic. So it is called the theistic Sāṁkhya.

The Nyāya emphasizes epistemology and logic, and discusses the nature, conditions, and validity of perception, inference, comparison and testimony. It especially deals with the nature, kinds, ground, and object of inference, and fallacies of inference. The other systems are largely indebted to it for their treatment of inference and fallacies.

The Vaiśeṣika emphasizes the seven categories : substance, quality, action, community, particularity, inherence, and negation. It discusses the nature of time, space, ether (ākāśa) and the different kinds of qualities and actions. It specializes in the philosophy of nature.

The Sāṁkhya advocates dualism, pluralism and atheism. It recognizes the reality of prakṛti and puruṣas or individual souls. Both are eternal. Prakṛti is unconscious. Puruṣas or souls are conscious. Prakṛti is active and mutable. Puruṣas are inactive and immutable. Prakṛti is composed of sattva, rajas and tamas, which are finer than atoms and modified into all physical, biological and psychical entities. The mind (manas), the intellect (buddhi) and egoism (ahaṁkāra) are modifications of prakṛti, which is the root-evolvent of matter, life and mind. Prakṛti evolves for the experience of puruṣas, and dissolves for their liberation. There is unconscious finality in its evolution and dissolution. The world is real and independent of the perceiving selves. The Sāṁkhya advocates spiritualistic pluralism, and rejects the notion of God as the creator of the world. Its atheism is antagonistic to the absolutism of the Upaniṣads.

The Yoga engrafts the concept of God upon the Sāṁkhya dualism of prakṛti and puruṣas, and makes it theistic. It is called the theistic Sāṁkhya. Prakṛti is eternal, unconscious and mutable. Puruṣas are eternal, conscious and immutable. God upsets the equilibrium of sattva, rajas and tamas by mere proximity, and starts the evolution of prakṛti. He directs its evolution as the efficient cause of the modifications of sattva, rajas and tamas into the various kinds of physical, biological and psychical entities by removing barriers to their production. He does not create prakṛti, the root-evolvent of the world. He merely removes obstacles to the modification of sattva, rajas and tamas into diverse effects. He does not create the individual souls. They can attain liberation without meditation on God, which is one of the means of attaining superconscious trance and liberation. He helps an aspirant practise the art of yoga by removing impediments to it. He is the supreme, omniscient, perfect person. The special feature of this system is comprehensive treatment of the art of yoga, which is assumed to be one of the methods of achieving mokṣa by some other systems.

The Mīmāṁsā is atheistic. It rejects the notion of God as the creator of the world. It admits the reality of the world and the finite souls. The world is self-existent and composed of the atoms of earth, water, fire, and air. The material objects are produced by their causes, and adapted to the enjoyments and sufferings of the individual souls according to the impersonal Law of Karma, which is not administered by God. Physical causation is subservient to moral causation. But it is not grounded in the will-causality of God. The individual souls are eternal spirits. They can attain liberation by action and knowledge. The Mīmāṁsā is called Karma-Mīmāṁsā because it lays stress on the performance of duties prescribed by the Vedas.

There are two schools of Mīmāṁsā founded by Prabhākara and Kumārila. There are essential differences in their epistemology and ontology. But both admit the self-validity of knowledge, eternity of the Vedas, and eternity of sounds, and reject the concept of God as the creator of the world and the composer of the Vedas. Prabhākara recognizes the categories of substance, quality, action, generality, subsistence or inherence, force, and similarity. He rejects the Vaiśeṣika categories of particularity and non-existence. Kumārila admits the categories of substance, quality, action, generality, and non-existence. He rejects the Vaiśeṣika categories of particularity and inherence. He rejects the categories of force and similarity recognized by Prabhākara. The Mīmāṁsā philosophy of nature resembles the Nyāya-Vaiśesika view.

The Vedānta deals with the nature and knowledge of Brahman. Its central concept is Brahman. It systematizes the teachings of the Upaniṣads. There are two main schools of the Vedānta : (1) the Advaita Vedānta founded by Śaṁkara and (2) the Viśiṣṭādvaita Vedānta founded by Rāmānuja. Śaṁkara advocates absolutism or spiritualistic monism. He regards the indeterminate Brahman or the Absolute as the ontological reality, and God, the individual souls and the world as phenomenal appearances which have only empirical reality. Brahman associated with Māyā or cosmic nescience is God (Īśvara), the creator, preserver and destroyer of the world, and the dispenser of the Law of Karma. Brahman limited by avidyā, a fragment of cosmic nescience, or its product, the psychophysical organism, is an individual self (jīva). The world-appearance is false ; it is a modification of Māyā which is neither existent nor non-existent, but indefinable. It projects the false appearance of the multiform world. It is a power of Īśvara who is not deluded by it. The finite self is identical with Brahman or Ātman, which is the eternal, undifferentiated, pure consciousness and bliss. It realizes its infinitude and absoluteness when it destroys ignorance (avidyā) and acquires intuition or vidyā. Knowledge is the means to liberation. Brahman is pure identity devoid of difference. Śaṁkara is a staunch advocate of pure monism. He believes in degrees of reality,—the ontological reality of Brahman or Ātman, the empirical reality of God, the individual souls and the world, and the illusory reality of dreams, reveries and illusions. He recognizes the empirical reality of morality and religion, which should be transcended by integral knowledge or intuition of Brahman as pure identity. He believes in progressive transcendence of empirical individuality, and intuitive realization of its identity with Brahman. He recognizes gradual release through the worship of God and the performance of the prescribed duties, and embodied release here and now through integral knowledge.

Rāmānuja is the founder of the Viśiṣṭādvaita Vedānta or qualified monism. He identifies Brahman with Īśvara,—the Absolute with God, and regards Him as the creator, preserver and destroyer of the world, and the Lord of the Law of Karma. He conceives of God as endowed with excellent qualities and devoid of impure qualities. He recognizes internal difference within Brahman. The conscious souls (cit) and the unconscious world (acit) are the attributes, modes, or accessories of Brahman, which are inseparably related to him. They constitute His body. Brahman is their soul. He is a unity-in-difference. There is a difference of attributes or modes in the unity of the divine substance. God is the efficient cause and the material cause of the world. It is a modification of prakṛti which is a power of God. Māyā is prakṛti which is real. It is composed of sattva, rajas and tamas which are divine powers. It is modified into the world which is real.

The individual souls are real and eternal. They have knowledge of external objects. They are knowers, and not pure consciousness. Knowledge without a knowing self and known objects is an unreal abstraction. Bondage is due to ignorance. Liberation is due to the triple method of disinterested actions, devotion, and knowledge of God. It is not identity but essential community with God. The finite souls, which are conscious monads, do not lose their integrity in Brahman in the state of release. The world, the finite souls and God are real and inseparably related to one another. The souls and the world are the attributes of Brahman, and cannot exist apart from Him. The divine substance also cannot exist apart from its attributes, conscious and unconscious. There is inseparable relation (apṛthaksiddhi) among them. The souls are irreducible to matter. Matter is irreducible to soul. Brahman is immanent in the finite souls and the world as their inner guide, and transcends them as their Lord. He harmonizes all differences within his all-embracing unity. He is the perfect person. He redeems the human souls from bondage by His grace. He advocates theism as distinguished from Śaṁkara's Absolutism.

Sometimes Mīmāṁsā is called Pūrva Mīmāṁsā because it deals with rituals whose performance is a propædeudic to the pursuit of the knowledge of Brahman. The Vedānta is called Uttara Mīmāṁsā because it deals with the nature of Brahman and the means of knowing Him. Dharma is the central concept of the Mīmāṁsā. Brahman is the central concept of the Vedānta.

The Cārvāka, the Buddhist, and the Jaina are the heterodox schools. They reject the authority of the Vedas and the concept of God. The Cārvāka advocates materialism, atheism, positivism, and hedonism. He admits the reality of the world only, composed of the gross elements of earth, water, fire, and air which are perceptible. He regards consciousness as an epiphenomenon of the body, and the self as the body endued with consciousness. He denies the existence of God and the permanent self, pre-existence and future life, heaven and hell, and transmigration and liberation. He condemns religion as priestcraft, and enjoins the pursuit of bodily pleasure. He denies the existence of all supersensible entities.

The Buddhists are phenomenalists. They regard change or becoming as the stuff of reality. Everything is impermanent. The Brahman of the Upaniṣads, that is eternal and unchanging, is a figment of the imagination. There is no permanent self. The self is an aggregate of changing bodily and mental processes. It is a series of momentary cognitions, feelings, volitions, and mental dispositions. The material objects are conglomerations of impermanent sensible qualities. The world is dynamic and subject to the law of causality. The Law of Karma governs the physical order, the biological order, and the moral order. The Buddhists believe in pre-existence, future life, transmigration, and liberation of the stream of consciousness. They lay stress on the conquest of passions and the cultivation of non-injury, good-will and love for mankind and sentient creatures.

The Hīnayāna Buddhists are realists, while the Mahāyāna Buddhists are idealists. The Vaibhāṣikas and the Sautrāntikas are Hīnayānists. The former advocate direct realism, and maintain that external objects are directly perceived. The latter advocate indirect realism, and maintain that impermanent external objects are inferred from their ideas in the mind. The Yogācāras and the Mādhyamikas are Mahāyānists. The former are generally subjective idealists (vijñānavādin), who deny the existence of external objects, and regard them as ideas. Some Yogācāras are absolute idealists, who regard the eternal, pure consciousness (vijñaptimātratā) as the absolute reality. It is transformed into the Ālayavijñāna, the cosmic mind, which generates empirical subjects and empirical objects. The Mādhyamikas regard the reality as void (śūnya) which is essenceless, predicateless, indefinable and incomprehensible, and look upon external objects and subjective ideas as mere appearances. They are called nihilists (śūnyavādin).

The Jainas are avowed atheists. They deny the existence of God as the creator of the world. They admit the reality of the world and the permanent souls. The world is material, while the souls are spiritual. Matter, the principle of motion (dharma), the principle of rest (adharma), space, and time constitute the non-soul (ajīva). The world is composed of homogeneous atoms. It is multiform and diverse, and contains an infinite number of substances with infinite qualities, modes and relations to one another. It contains being and becoming, permanence and change, unity and plurality, generality and particularity, and various other aspects. It is self-existent and not created by God. The souls are permanent spiritual entities endued with infinite knowledge, infinite perception, infinite bliss, and infinite power. They can realize these innate qualities, when they remove the crust of karma-matter on it by rigid moral discipline. Karmas are infra-atomic particles of matter produced by impure thoughts, emotions and actions, which encrust the souls and veil their innate powers. When they are completely destroyed, the souls shine forth in their innate glory, and become omniscient. They work out their own salvation by right faith, right knowledge, and right conduct. Matter and spirits constitute the reality, which are irreducible to each other. The Jainas advocate realism, dualism, spiritualistic pluralism, and atheism.

THE COMMON IDEAS IN THE SYSTEMS OF INDIAN PHILOSOPHY

1. The Reality of the World.—All schools of Indian philosophy recognize the reality of the world. The Cārvāka admits the reality of the world composed of the gross elements of earth, water, fire and air. The Buddhist realists maintain that the world is composed of atoms, which are combined into gross impermanent objects. The Vaibhāṣikas regard them as objects of direct perception. The Sautrāntikas regard them as objects of inference. The Jainas regard the world as composed of homogeneous atoms. The Nyāya and the Vaiśeṣika recognize the reality or the world in time and space, which is composed of heterogeneous atoms, governed by the law of causality, and subservient to the Law of Karma. The world is a physical order and a moral order. Physical causation is subservient to moral causation. The Mīmāṁsā also regards the world as formed out of atoms under the guidance of the Law of Karma. The Sāṁkhya, the Yoga, and the theistic Vedānta regard the world as evolved out of prakṛti consisting of sattva, rajas and tamas. Sattva is the principle of manifestation. Rajas is the principle of energy. Tamas is the principle of obstruction or inertia. The theistic Vedānta regards prakṛti as the power of God. The Yoga regards prakṛti as independent of God. The Sāṁkhya does not believe in God.

The Advaita Vedānta of Śaṁkara regards the world as a false appearance from the standpoint of the Absolute. But it recognizes the empirical reality of the world-appearance. It does not consider it to be an illusion. But it denies the ontological reality of the world. The Mādhyamika also recognizes the empirical reality of the world-appearance. The Yogācāra reduces the external objects to mere ideas of the perceiving mind. He does not recognize their extra-mental reality. The majority of the systems of Indian philosophy admit the reality of the world.

The world is a spatio-temporal and causal order. It exists in time and space, and is governed by causality. Time-relation, space-relation, and cause-effect-relation are constitutive of the cosmic order. Every finite positive entity is produced and destroyed. But atoms are indivisible and eternal. Causation is production or modification. An effect is a fresh emergence out of its cause or its modification. Causation is subject to a law. There is uniformity of causation. Particular causes produce particular effects at particular times, in particular places, and under particular circumstances. All events are governed by the law of causation. Physical causation is subordinate to moral causation. Diverse effects are adapted to enjoyments and sufferings of the individual souls. Periodic creation and dissolution of the world are generally admitted. The theory of cosmic evolution is clearly enunciated in the Sāṁkhya-Yoga literature. Every system of philosophy admits the reality of the world, at least as an appearance, accounts for its variety and multiplicity, and provides for the realization of our practical needs. It does not undermine our practical life.

2. **The Reality of the Self.**—The reality of the permanent self is generally admitted. Among the heterodox schools the Cārvāka denies the reality of the self, and identifies it with the body endued with consciousness. He regards consciousness as an epiphenomenon of the body. The Buddhist denies the reality of the permanent self, and regards it as a series of momentary ideas. Only the Jaina admits the reality of the permanent self as a knowing, feeling and active agent. All orthodox schools of Indian philosophy admit the reality of the Ātman or self as a permanent spiritual substance. The Nyāya and the Vaiśeṣika regard the self as an eternal substance endued with cognition, pleasure, pain, desire, aversion, volition, impression, merit and demerit. Consciousness is not its essence, but an adventitious quality. It acquires consciousness in conjunction with the body and the internal organ (manas). The Mīmāṁsā also holds the same view. Kumārila regards knowledge as a mode or activity of the self. Prabhākara regards it as a quality of the self. In dreamless sleep and release the self is devoid of consciousness. The Sāṁkhya and the Yoga regard the self as an eternal spirit whose essence is consciousness. Consciousness is its essential property, not an adventitious quality. Feeling and activity are qualities of the intellect (buddhi), which is a modification of prakṛti. But the self (puruṣa) is devoid of them ; it is feelingless and inactive ; it is only a knower of the modifications of prakṛti. The Nyāya-Vaiśeṣika, the Sāṁkhya-Yoga, and the Mīmāṁsā admit the plurality of selves to account for their variety of experiences, bondage and liberation. But the Advaita Vedānta admits the reality of one Self or Ātman, which is pure being, pure consciousness and pure bliss. It identifies the Ātman with Brahman. It regards the individual self (jīva) as the Ātman limited by ignorance (avidyā), or the mind-body-complex produced by it. It recognizes the empirical reality of the individual self and denies its ontological reality. The

Viśiṣṭādvaita Vedānta admits its ontological reality, and regards it as a part of Brahman.

The Sāṁkhya and the Mīmāṁsā deny the existence of God, but they admit the reality of the self, and its bondage and liberation. The Jaina also denies the existence of God, but admits the reality of permanent souls and their bondage and liberation.

3. **The Law of Karma.**—All schools of Indian philosophy except the Cārvāka believe in the Law of Karma. As we sow, so we reap. A right action inevitably produces a good consequence. A wrong action inevitably produces a bad consequence. Performance of a duty or a prescribed action produces a merit (puṇya) or virtue (dharma) in the soul. Violation of a duty or commission of a forbidden action produces a demerit (pāpa) or vice (adharma) in it. Merit or virtue produces happiness. Demerit or vice produces misery. Merit and demerit are unseen agencies (adṛṣṭa) which mature in course of time and bear fruits either in this life or in a future life. They are predisposing causes of happiness and misery while external objects are their exciting causes. There is no escape from the consequences of actions. Their fruits must be reaped in this life or in a future life. There is no destruction of the fruits of right and wrong actions (kṛtapraṇāṣa). One can never reap the fruits of actions undone (akṛtābhyāgama). The Law of Karma is the inexorable law of moral causation.

The Buddhist, the Jaina, the Sāṁkhya and the Mīmāṁsā believe in an impersonal Law of Karma which adjusts the realm of nature to the realm of spirits—the physical order to the moral order. It adjusts physical objects to the souls' happiness and misery in accordance with their merits and demerits. But the other systems believe in God who is the dispenser of the Law of Karma. He creates the physical objects out of atoms or prakṛti or His own nature and adjusts them to the unseen agencies in the individual souls.

Merits and demerits are called karmas. At a particular time we have accumulated karmas of the past births (prārabdha karma) and karmas which are being acquired in this birth (sañcīyamāna karma) to which will be added karmas which will be acquired in future (anārabdha karma). They determine the kind of birth, length of life, and enjoyments and sufferings. The Jaina regards karmas as infra-sensible particles of matter generated by passions and evil actions, which encrust the soul and obscure its innate qualities.

4. **Transmigration.**—Metempsychosis or transmigration of the soul is a corollary of the Law of Karma, which demands that right actions have good consequences and that wrong actions have bad consequences. Merits and demerits produced by right and wrong actions determine the kinds of birth. Excessive merits transport the souls to heaven, and make them celestial beings. Excessive demerits make them assume the bodies of beasts, birds and insects. Well-balanced merits and demerits make them transmigrate into human bodies. The souls are eternal. They are neither born nor destroyed. Their birth is association with bodies. Their death is dissociation from bodies. They survive the death of their bodies and assume other bodies, superhuman, human or subhuman, which are appropriate to the moral deserts acquired by them in the present births. They reincarnate in the bodies which will be the fit vehicles for enjoying the consequences of their actions in this life. The same soul continues through different births. Transmigration presupposes the permanence and continuity of the soul which assumes different bodies. All orthodox schools believe in the permanence and transmigration of the soul.

The Cārvākas do not admit the reality of the soul as distinct from the body, and so do not believe in its transmigration. The Bauddhas do not recognize the permanence of the soul. They regard it as a flux of ever-changing psychoses. But still they believe in its transmigration. The last psychosis embodying the dispositions of all past psychoses in the stream of consciousness assumes a body appropriate to it, and produces the initial consciousness in the new foetus. There is continuity of the same series of consciousness in its different births. There is 'transmigration of character' from the present birth to the future birth as Rhys Davids says. Though the Buddhists deny the permanence of the soul, they believe in the transmigration of the same series of cognitions. The Jainas recognize the reality of the permanent soul and its transmigration. The idea of transmigration is common to all systems of Indian philosophy except the Cārvāka school.

5. **Saṁsāra.**—Saṁsāra is a beginningless series of births and deaths. It is bondage (bandha) to embodied life in the spatio-temporal world. It is imprisonment of the eternal pure spirit in a destructible impure body. It is due to ignorance or false knowledge. The Sāṁkhya and the Yoga regard non-discrimination (aviveka) of the self (puruṣa) and prakṛti as the cause of bondage. The Nyāya, the Vaiśeṣika, the Mīmāṁsā and the Vedānta consider the soul to be eternal. When it is erroneously identified with the impermanent mind-body-complex, it is entangled in bondage. The Nyāya describes the cause of bondage thus : pain is due to birth ; birth is due to actions ; actions are due to faults ; faults are due to false knowledge.[1] Attachment, aversion and delusion are faults (doṣa) which are the springs of action. They are due to false knowledge of painful and transitory objects as pleasant and eternal. So bondage is due to false knowledge. Buddhism considers the self to be an impermanent aggregate of bodily and mental processes, and ascribes bondage to a false sense of individuality. The impermanent mind-body-complex is wrongly considered to be the permanent self. This false knowledge gives rise to bondage, which is terminated by true knowledge.

6. **Initial Pessimism and Ultimate Optimism.**—Indian philosophy is branded as pessimistic. Life abounds in suffering. Pain is the invariable accompaniment of embodied life. Saṁsāra is a beginningless series of births and deaths which are painful. The Buddha says : "Birth is painful, decay is painful ; disease is painful ; death is painful ; union with the unpleasant is painful ; separation from the pleasant is painful."

---

[1] NS., i, 1, 2.

Life is full of suffering. The world is a vale of tears. But the Buddha preaches the four noble truths: (1) there is suffering; (2) there is a cause of suffering; (3) there is cessation of suffering; (4) there is a way to stop suffering. Nirvāṇa is absolute extinction of suffering. The Sāṁkhya recognizes three kinds of pain: pain due to bodily diseases and mental troubles (ādhyātmika); pain due to other men and animals (ādhibhautika); and pain due to supernatural agencies (ādhidaivika). Embodied life full of suffering is bondage. Absolute negation of the three- fold suffering is release.[1] The Yoga admits three kinds of pain. The enjoyment of sensual pleasures gives rise to painful consequences. Thirst for them is intensified by enjoyment. The pain generated by the enjoyment of sensual pleasures is consequential (pariṇāmaduḥkha). Attachment to sensual pleasures involves aversion to those who thwart the desire for their enjoyment, which is painful (tāpaduḥkha). Feelings of pleasure and pain produce their dispositions (saṁskāra). They produce recollections of pleasure and pain, which produce actions. Actions produce merits and demerits, which produce pleasure and pain. The cycle of pain due to dispositions (saṁskāraduḥkha) continues. Release is complete destruction of these dispositions and absolute freedom of the self from the mind and its modes.[2] All kinds of pain are extirpated in the state of release. So Indian philosophy is characterized by initial pessimism and ultimate optimism.

7. **Liberation (mokṣa).**—The idea of liberation (mokṣa) is common to all systems of Indian philosophy. Only the Cārvāka materialist does not believe in it. He regards dependence as bondage, and independence as release. Buddhism regards complete extinction of suffering as nirvāṇa. Joy, sorrow, anger, fear, and lust are passions, which are compared to fire. Nirvāṇa is complete extinction of the fire of passions. Some Buddhists regard it as a state of positive bliss. Others regard it as an ineffable state beyond empirical pleasure and pain.

---

1 S P S., i,1.

2 YS., ii, 15.

The Jaina considers complete destruction of karma-matter investing the soul and realization of its infinite perception, infinite knowledge, infinite bliss and infinite power as release.

The Nyāya and the Vaiśeṣika look upon the existence of the self in its natural condition as liberation. It consists in absolute cessation of pain. It consists in complete destruction of the qualities of the soul,—cognition, pleasure, pain desire, aversion, volition, impression, merit and demerit. The Mīmāṁsā also considers complete destruction of merit and demerit and absolute extinction of pain as release. In release the self is divested of all experience, and remains in its pure essence. The Sāṁkhya considers absolute negation of threefold suffering as release. In the state of release there is complete isolation of the self from the mind-body-complex, which is a modification of prakṛti. There is complete destruction of mental functions and dispositions. The Yoga also considers complete isolation (kaivalya) of the self from the mind (buddhi) and its modes and dispositions as release. In the state of release the self abides in its essential nature, and realizes its intrinsic nature. The Advaita Vedānta regards the intuitive realization of identity of the individual self with Brahman as release which is a state of infinite bliss. The Viśiṣṭādvaita Vedānta regards similarity of the self with God in essence as release, which is a blissful state. So the idea of liberation is common to all systems of Indian philosophy.

8. The Means to Liberation.—The different systems of Indian philosophy lay down the means to the attainment of liberation. Yoga facilitates the attainment of true knowledge. It consists in sense-restraints, moral observances, bodily posture, breath-control, withdrawal of the sense-organs from their objects, fixation of mind, meditation, and trance. When the mind meditates on the self, and is absorbed in it, it dissolves, as it were, in the self, which manifests itself in its real nature. Yoga is a method of acquiring knowledge of the self, which is regarded as a means of release. Morality is an indispensable preliminary to meditation and trance. Non-injury, non-stealing, truthfulness, sex-restraint and non-covetousness are the restraints (yama). Purity of body and mind, contentment, penance, study of the scriptures, and meditation on God are the moral observances (niyama). They are included in the eightfold yoga. The Advaita Vedānta regards discrimination of the eternal and the non-eternal, dispassion for enjoyment of happiness on earth and in heaven, sense-control, mind-control, endurance, withdrawal of the senses from their objects, faith in the Ātman or Brahman, and desire for release as auxiliary to enquiry into the nature of Brahman. True knowledge depends upon the conquest of the lusts of the flesh and passions and desires of the mind, purity of body and mind, freedom from selfishness and egoism, tolerance of spirit, universal good-will and selflessness. Morality is an indispensable propaedeutic to the acquisition of true knowledge. Konwledge (jñāna) is considered to be the chief means of release. The Nyāya-Vaiśeṣika considers true knowledge of the reality the world, the self and God as the means of liberation. True knowledge destroys false knowledge, which generates attachment, aversion and delusion, which are the springs of action. The Sāṁkhya-Yoga regards discrimination of the self from the not-self or prakṛti and its modifications as the cause of release. The Advaita Vedānta considers the intuitive knowledge of identity of the jīva with Brahman as its cause. The knowledge of difference is ignorance (avidyā). The knowledge of identity is true knowledge (vidyā), which leads to life eternal. The Viśiṣṭādvaita Vedānta considers the disinterested performance of duties (niṣkāma karma), devotion and self-surrender to God, taking shelter in Him, and knowledge of the self's dependence on God as the means of release. It looks upon essential similarity with God as liberation. Mokṣa is a state of transcendental purity beyond empirical morality. There is complete transcendence of virtue and vice in it.

9. Pramāṇas.—Indian philosophy is not dogmatic and uncritical. Every system of philosophy is based on epistemology or theory of knowledge. The Cārvāka recognizes perception only as a means of valid knowledge (pramāṇa). The Bauddha and the Vaiśeṣika recognize perception and inference as pramāṇas.

The Sāṁkhya recognizes perception, inference and testimony as pramāṇas. The Nyāya recognizes perception, inference, comparison and testimony as pramāṇas. Prabhākara (Mīmāṁsā) recognizes perception, inference, comparison, testimony and presumption as pramāṇas. Kumārila (Mīmāṁsā) and the Advaita Vedānta recognize perception (pratyakṣa), inference (anumāna), comparison (upamāna), testimony (śabda), presumption (arthāpatti), and non-apprehension (anupalabdhi) as pramāṇas. They discuss the nature, object, conditions and grounds of valid knowledge.

10. The Authority of the Vedas.—All orthodox schools of philosophy recognize the authority of the Vedas. They cite the authority of the Upaniṣads in support of their views, and build up their systems of philosophy on rational speculation in harmony with the teachings of the Vedas. Reason cannot yield unquestionable certainty in respect of supersensible entities. Reason is overthrown by reason. It cannot land us in the solid foundation of truth. Reason is subordinated to the authority of the Vedas, which is regarded as the authority of intuition. Intuition is the immediate apprehension of the reality, which transcends discursive thought. It is supra-intellectual direct apprehension. Reason (tarka) is regarded as subordinate to intuition (anubhava). Intuition can override reason, but reason cannot overthrow intuition. Reasoning should be carried on under the guidance of intuition. But the different schools of Indian philosophy are not mere elaborations of the teachings of the Upaniṣads with the help of reason. They invent different theories of the Reality by systematic logical reasoning, appeal to those texts of the Upaniṣads which are in favour of their conclusions, and consider those opposed to their theories as spurious or explain them away. Even the different schools of the Vedānta build their theories of the Reality on logical reason and philosophical speculation, and endeavour to harmonize the relevant texts of the Upaniṣads with one another in the light of their preconceived theories. The Nyāya, the Vaiśeṣika, the Sāṁkhya, the Yoga, the Mīmāṁsā and the Vedānta widely diverge from one another in their philosophical speculations, though they all accept the authority of the Vedas.

They all regard consciousness as the ultimate court of appeal in knowing anything to be real.[1]

---

[1] PP., p. 22. HIP., Vol. I, Ch. VI.

CHAPTER II

THE PHILOSOPHY OF THE UPANIṢADS

THE PHILOSOPHY OF THE VEDAS

The orthodox schools of Indian phiosophy, the Nyāya, the Vaiśeṣika, the Sāṁkhya, the Yoga, the Mīmāṁsā, and the Vedānta believe in the authority of the Vedas. But the heterodox schools, the Cārvāka, the Buddhist and the Jaina reject their authority. The Upaniṣads contain the germs of the orthodox schools of Indian philosophy. They are parts of the Vedas. There are four Vedas, Ṛg Veda, Sāma Veda, Yajur Veda, and Atharva Veda. The first three constitute the triad, which are the original Vedas, and which enjoy higher authority. The Atharva Veda is a later addition. Each Veda has three divisions, *viz.*, the Saṁhitās, the Brāhmaṇas, and the Āraṇyakas. The Saṁhitās are mostly verses. The Brāhmaṇas are commentaries in prose. The Āraṇyakas are forest treatises. The Upaniṣads are mostly parts of the Āraṇyakas. The Sāma Veda contains the hymns of the Ṛg Veda, which are to be chanted in sacrifices. The Yajur Veda contains large portions of the Ṛg Veda. The Atharva Veda also contains many mantras of the Ṛg Veda, which is the earliest. The Vedas may be assigned latest to about 1500 B.C.

The Vedas represent different phases of religious thought. There are manifest signs of polytheism, organized polytheism, henotheism, monotheism, and monism. The grand, sublime, beautiful and useful aspects of nature are personified and deified. They are regarded as supernatural and superhuman spirits akin to human spirits. They are the deities presiding over the diverse phenomena of nature. They are not natural phenomena. They are pervasive supernatural entities, which govern the phenomena of nature, and which are benevolent to their worshippers, but terrific to their haters. They are mighty, invincible, wise, merciful, omniscient, pervasive, righteous, truthful and benevolent. They are easily propitiated by hymns, prayer, oblations, offerings and sacrifices. They give worldly prosperity, wisdom and moral qualities. They give victory in battles, wealth, long life, sons, grandsons, and happiness. The gods of fire (Agni), the sun (Sūrya), the dawn (Ūṣas), the earth (Pṛthivī), the sky (Dyaus), the bright sky and day (Mitra), the dark sky and evening (Varuṇa), the rain-cloud (Parjanya), the storms (Maruts), the winds (Vāyu, Vāta), the morning sun (Savitṛ) and the like are mentioned.

The different gods are personifications of the different powers of nature. They are sometimes worshipped individually. This phase of religious thought is not naturalism, but anthropomorphic polytheism. The gods are supernatural and superhuman powers, and endowed with spiritual qualities. They preside over particular phenomena of nature, but they are not confined to them. They pervade the whole of nature and beyond, or a considerable part of it, and are endowed with some qualities of the supreme god-head. This is the element of polytheism in the Vedas.

Sometimes the gods are invoked and worshipped in groups. Sometimes two gods, sometimes three, four, or more gods are invoked. Sometimes all gods (viśve devāḥ) are worshipped together, who are implicitly believed to be partial aspects of one supreme God. This phase of religious thought may be called organized polytheism.

The gods are gradually related to one another as the major and the minor, as dependent on one another, and as generating one another. Heaven and Earth are the mothers of Agni. Rudra is the father of the Maruts. Aditi is the mother of the Ādityas. The Aśvins are the brothers. Indra maintains the Earth and the Sky in their places. He is a major god and they are minor deities. The Maruts maintain the Sun, the Wind, and the Fire gods in the sky. They are superior to the three gods. Varuṇa, Mitra and Aryaman kindle Agni, and are glorious through him. They are interdependent on one another. This phase of religion is organized polytheism.

Among the multitude of gods any one is treated as the supreme god for the time being when he is worshipped.

Maxmüller calls this religion henotheism.[1] 'O Agni, thou art mighty Indra, the wide-ruling Viṣṇu, the king Varuṇa, the wondrous Mitra, Aryaman, the lord of beings. Thou art Rudra, the Maruts, the Winds, and Pūṣan. Thou art Savitṛ, a bestower of treasures, Bhaga, the lord of wealth, Ṛbhu, Aditi, Bhāratī, Iḍā and Sarasvatī. Thou art united with all gods, equal to them in strength, nay, thou surpassest them, when thy power has expanded over heaven and earth'[2] Here Agni is identified with many gods, and treated as superior to them. This phase of religious thought is called henotheism. It is a step from polytheism to monotheism.

The conception of Ṛta further harmonizes the gods with one another, and paves the way for monotheism. Ṛta is the physical order. It governs the uniformities of nature. Ṛta reigns everywhere, in the sky, in the sun, in the mountain, in the sacrifices, and in truth.[3] It is the natural order. The sacrifices should conform to Ṛta which is the law of rites. It is the law of truth, right, and justice. It is the moral law. Varuṇa is the custodian of the moral law or Ṛta. He adheres to the right, and punishes sins.[4] The gods follow the laws of Ṛta. It is the physical order and the moral order. It points to the existence of one supreme God, whose law is unalterable and inviolable. The conception of Ṛta prepares the way for monotheism, though it is an impersonal order, which upholds the gods and the world.

Hiraṇyagarbha or Prajāpati, Viśvakarmā, and Parama Puruṣa gradually take the place of one supreme God. Hiraṇyagarbha is Prajāpati, the Lord of all creatures. He arose in the beginning. He established the earth and heaven. He is the sole king of the entire universe. He rules over the mountains, the seas, and the rivers. He governs men and beasts. His commands are followed by other gods. He alone

[1] *The Six Systems of Indian Philosophy*, 1903, p. 40.

[2] Ṛ. V., ii, 1, 3-5. [3] Ṛ. V., iv, 40, 5.

[4] Ṛ. V., i, 65, 3 ; i, 68, 4 ; i, 79, 3 ; iii, 1, 11 ; iii, 2, 1 & 8 ; iii, 7, 2 ; iii, 10, 2 ; iv, 7, 7 ; i, 75, 5 ; i, 145, 5, i, 2, 8 ; iv, 85, 7-8.

is God above all gods. He may claim the rank of one supreme God.[1]

Viśvakarmā is the creator of the entire universe. He creates the sky and the earth. He is the world-architect. He is the seer of all. His eyes are everywhere. His face is everywhere. He is of all hands and feet. He is one God.[2]

There is a Cosmic Person who has a thousand heads, a thousand eyes, and a thousand feet. He pervades the entire universe and transcends it. Whatever exists, existed, and will exist is this Supreme Person. He is the Lord of immortality. He is not affected by the fruits of actions. The entire universe is only one-fourth of his being. The remaining three fourths remain in celestial immortality.[3] The Parama Puruṣa is both transcendent and immanent. He is immanent in the whole world. He transcends it, and remains beyond it in His immortal glory. The Puruṣa Sūkta teaches panentheism. These are the monotheistic tendencies in the Ṛg Veda.

Monotheism leads to monism. One Reality is conceived, which is manifested in diverse ways. 'There is one reality; sages call it by various names; they call it Agni, Yama, Mātariśvan'.[4] 'That One' is not personal; it is neither male nor female; it is neuter. It is an impersonal principle. There was nothing other than it.[5] The Nāsadīya Sūkta clearly brings out the monism of the Ṛg Veda. 'That One' was later identified with the Ātman or Brahman in the Upaniṣads.[6]

The monism adumbrated in the Ṛg Veda is developed into idealistic monism in the Upaniṣads, which regard Brahman, the infinite, eternal, omnipresent, omniscient, and pure Spirit as the ultimate reality. The temporal, spatial and causality-bound world is the manifestation of this infinite and eternal Spirit. It is permeated by Brahman, shines by its light and manifests the glory of Brahman. It is sometimes regarded as

---

[1] Ṛ. V., x, 121, 1-10. [2] Ṛ. V., x, 81, 2-4.
[3] Ṛ .V., x., 90, 1-3. [4] Ṛ.V., i., 164, 46. [5] Ṛ. V., x, 129, 1 & 2.
[6] HIP., Vol. II, pp. 418-24.

a mere appearance, a 'name and form'. It is a mere appearance of Brahman, which is one, non-dual, undifferentiated and pure consciousness. Brahman is non-temporal, non-spatial, and non-causal. It is imprersonal, transcendental, indefinable, incomprehensible and unknowable. Brahman is sometimes conceived as transcendent and immanent. Transcendent Brahman is acosmic, attributeless, or higher Brahman. Immanent Brahman is cosmic, or lower Brahman endowed with attributes and related to the world. Para Brahman is the impersonal and indeterminate Absolute, the ultimate reality. Apara Brahman is personal God (Īśvara), who is the creator, preserver, and destroyer of the world, the moral governor, and the inner controller of the world and the individual souls. Īśvara is the Lord of the Law of Karma. The individual souls are sometimes regarded as parts of Brahman, which are akin to Him, and guided by Him. They are sometimes regarded as Brahman limited by the adjunct of the mind-body-complex, which are identified with Para Brahman or Ātman, when their limiting adjuncts are destroyed.

UNQUALIFIED (NIRGUṆA) BRAHMAN OR THE ABSOLUTE

The Upaniṣads speak of Para Brahman or Absolute and Apara Brahman or God. The former is higher Brahman. The latter is lower Brahman. The former is indeterminate, unconditioned and devoid of attributes. The latter is determinate, conditioned and endowed with attributes. The former is unqualified and incomprehensible. The latter is qualified and comprehensible. The former is transcendent and non-phenomenal. The latter is immanent in the phenomenal world. The former is non-spatial, non-temporal, non-causal and acosmic. The latter is the Lord of the spatial and temporal world governed by causality. The former is the transcendental Being, Consciousness and Bliss which constitute its essence. The latter is the infinite, eternal, omnipresent, omniscient, and omnipotent creator, preserver, and destroyer of the universe, the moral governor, and the Lord of the Law of Karma. He is immanent in the world and the individual souls as their inner controller. He transcends them as their knower, governor and guide. Para Brahman and Apara Brahman are the two aspects of Brahman.[1] The higher Brahman is described by the method of negation. The lower Brahman is described by the method of affirmation. Para Brahman is described in neuter gender. It is impersonal and devoid of all sensible qualities. It is one and without any second. It is partless, inactive, calm, flawless, and taintless. It is devoid of sound, touch, colour, taste, and smell. It is neither air, nor ether, nor fire. It is neither any of the material elements nor any of the sensible qualities. It is devoid of all sense-organs, and yet possessed of the powers of all senses.[2]

Para Brahman is unborn, eternal, abiding, and ancient. It is infinite, beginningless, endless, ubiquitous, omnipresent, and immortal. It is pure, self-luminous, and immutable.[3] It is imperceptible, indefinable, ungrounded, and essenceless. It is invisible, unuasable, incomprehensible, indeterminate, indescribable, non-phenomenal, undifferentiated and good. It is one homogeneous consciousness. It is the Ātman or Self.[4]

Para Brahman is neither gross nor subtle, neither long nor short. It is greater than the greatest, and subtler than the subtlest. It is finer than the atoms. It is farther than the farthest, and nearer than the nearest. It is hidden here in the cavity of the heart. It is extremely subtle and present everywhere. It is ubiquitous and eternal.[5] It is spaceless and devoid of spatial characters, and yet the ground of the spatial order.

It is without beginning and end. It has nothing prior to it, and nothing posterior to it. It is devoid of temporal sequence. It transcends the past, the present, and the future,

---

1 Praś. Up., V. 2 ; Tait. Up., Brahmānandavallī, vi, 1.

2 Kaṭh. Up., i, 3, 15 ; Muṇḍ. Up., i, 1, 6 ; ii, 1, 2 ; iii, 1, 8 ; Chānd. Up., vi, 2, 1 ; Śvet. Up., vi, 16 ; Bṛ. Up., iii, 8, 8 ; Śvet. Up., iii, 17.

3 Kaṭh. Up., i, 2, 18.

4 Kaṭh. Up., i, 3, 15 ; ii, 1, 2 & 4 ; ii, 2, 8 & 15 ; ii, 3, 1 ; i, 2, 16.

5 Tait. Up., ii, 7.

which exist in the empirical world, and yet it is their ground. It is timeless and devoid of temporal characters, and yet the ground of the temporal order.[1] It is without inside and outside. It is the one, undifferentiated, homogeneous consciousness.[2]

It is self-caused, unborn, unageing, undying, imperishable, and immortal. It is devoid of origin and end. It is devoid of cause and effect. It is different from cause and effect.[3] It is neither becoming nor non-becoming. It is non-causal, and yet it is the ground of the empirical world governed by causality.

It is motionless, and yet it moves faster than the manas. It is unmoved, and yet it moves to a distant place. It is inactive, and yet it goes everywhere. It is the unmoved mover. Motion is change and mutation, which cannot affect the indeterminate Brahman, which is changeless and immutable. Modification is a mere word, a name, an appearance. It cannot affect Brahman, which is eternal, fixed and immobile.[4]

Para Brahman is one only and without any second. It is one, undivided, partless, and devoid of duality and plurality. It is the supreme reality. There is nothing higher than Brahman. There is nothing other than Brahman. Distinction, duality and plurality are appearances which have empirical reality. The indeterminate Brahman is one, non-dual, undifferentiated and distinctionless.[5]

Para Brahman is infinite and devoid of distinction of subject and object. None sees, none hears, and none knows, other than the Infinite Spirit.[6] In the finite there is a distinction between the knower and the known. The infinite is

---

[1] Māṇḍ. Up., 1, 7 ; Bṛ. Up., iii, 8, 8 ; Kaṭh. Up., i, 2, 20 ; Muṇḍ Up., iii, 1, 7 ; Muṇḍ. Up., i, 1, 6 ; Kaṭh. Up., i, 2, 14 ; ii, 1, 5, 12 & 13 ; Bṛ. Up., iv, 4, 15 & 16 ; iii, 8, 7 ; ii, 5, 19 ; Māṇḍ. Up, i, 1.

[2] Bṛ. Up., ii, 5, 19 ; Bṛ. Up., iv, 5, 13.

[3] Kaṭh. Up., i, 2, 14 ; Śvet. Up., vi, 9 ; Īśa Up., 12.

[4] Īśa Up., 4, 5 ; Kaṭh. Up., i. 2. 21 ; Chānd. Up., vi, 1, 14.

[5] Chānd. Up., vi, 2. 1 ; Śvet. Up., iii, 9 ; Bṛ. Up., ii, 4, 14 ; iv, 4, 19 ; Kaṭh. Up., ii, 1, 11.

[6] Chānd. Up, vii, 24, 1.

immortal. The finite is mortal. The infinite Brahman abides in its own glory.[1]

Though Para Brahman is indeterminate, unconditioned and attributeless, yet it has three essential characters. It is pure being, pure consciousness, and pure bliss. It is not empirical being determined by time, space, causality and forms. It is not empirical consciousness which involves the distinction of subject and object. It is subject-objectless transcendental consciousness, which is not determined by the intellectual categories of time, space and causality. It is infinite, eternal, universal and absolute consciousness. It is the foundational consciousness which is the ultimate ground of the universe and the finite selves. It is the pure self-luminous consciousness. It is the light of lights. The universe is illumined and manifested by its light. It is transcendental bliss which transcends pleasure and pain, joys and sorrows, which are due to the intercourse of of the senses and their objects. It is infinite, eternal, supreme and indefinable bliss. It is the infinite, eternal, supreme, transcendental being, consciousness and bliss.

Para Brahman is the truth of truth, the reality of reality. It is the infinite truth. It is the eternal reality in formed and formless beings. It is the transcendental reality in being and non-being. It is the supreme reality beyond empirical existence and non-existence. It is the trans-empirical reality beyond the temporal, spatial and causality-bound empirical world. It is the highest Being adored by all. It is the supreme goal of all finite beings. It is their highest good. It is to be realized by all.[2]

Para Brahman is the infinite truth, knowledge or consciousness. It is omniscient, all-knowing experience of the universe. The knowledge of the Ātman is eternal, sinçe it is never destroyed. It is the witness. It is conscious, detached and devoid of sattva, rajas and tamas. It is transcendental consciousness. It is one, infinite, eternal, non-dual, undifferentiated, subject-objectless conciousness. It is self-luminous.

---

1 Chānd. Up., vii, 24, 1.

2 Bṛ. Up., ii, 3, 6; Kaṭh. Up., ii, 2, 2; Praś. Up., ii, 5; Muṇḍ. Up., ii, 2, 1.

It illumines the entire universe, but it is not illumined by any thing. It is immeasurable and unfathomable, and yet it is certain and self-revealing. Self-revealing consciousness constitutes its essential nature.[1]

Para Brahman is transcendental bliss. Consciousness and bliss characterize the eternal being. Ānanda is bliss or freedom. It is the quintessence of love and joy (rasa). It reveals itself out of the fullness of joy. Eternal love, joy, or bliss is the source of self-revelation. It sustains the life of all finite beings. All creatures are animated and sustained by the eternal joy of Brahman. The finite souls attain bliss by attaining Brahman, which is eternal bliss. Brahman makes them blissful. They become fearless when they find their abode in Brahman. When they realize the bliss of Brahman, they are not afraid of any being.[2] All creatures spring from bliss, are sustained by bliss, and are absorbed in bliss. Brahman is the Self or Ātman. The Ātman is dearer than sons, dearer than wealth, dearer than all other things. Husband, wife, sons, wealth and other cherished objects are not dear for their own sake, but for the sake of the Ātman in them. There is bliss in the Infinite ; there is no bliss in the finite.[3]

Para Brahman is detached, pure, untainted, sinless, and free from attachment. It is beyond virtue and vice. It transcends empirical morality, and has supermoral transcendental purity. 'It is not this, not this'.[4] Determination is negation. Empirical attributes cannot be ascribed to it.

Para Brahman is the Ātman, the witness, the seer, and the knower. It is not an object. The conscious Self is the prius

---

[1] Tait. Up., ii, 1, 1 ; Mānd. Up., i, 7 ; Bṛ. Up., ii. 5, 19 ; iv, 4, 16 &20 ; iv, 3, 23 & 30 ; iii, 7, 23 ; iii, 8, 11 ; ii, 5, 19 ; Muṇḍ. Up., ii, 2, 10 & 11 ; i, 1, 9 ; ii, 2, 7 ; Kena Up., i, 4 ; iv, 5, 13 ; Kaṭh. Up., ii, 2, 15.

[2] Tait. Up., ii, 7 ; ii, 6, 1 ; Muṇḍ. Up., ii, 2, 8 ; Bṛ. Up., iii, 9, 28 ; iii, 7, 1.

[3] Bṛ. Up., i, 4, 8 ; ii. 4, 5 ; iv, 3, 32 ; Chānd. Up., vii, 13, 1 ; Tait. Up., iii, 6.

[4] Kaṭh. Up., i, 2, 14 ; Īśa Up., 8 ; Muṇḍ. Up., ii, 2, 10 ; Bṛ. Up., iv, 4, 22.

and presupposition of empirical objects. It cannot be derived from, and resolved into, objects. It is not manifested by words which are manifested by it. How can the Knower be known? It transcends the known and the unknown. Yet it is not unknowable. It is known by intuition which is above discursive intellect. It is not known by reason, but by intuition due to meditation.[1]

QUALIFIED (SAGUNA) BRAHMAN OR GOD (ĪŚVARA)

Para Brahman is the indeterminate Absolute. Apara Brahman is the determinate Lord or Īśvara related to the empirical world and the individual souls. The Absolute related to the spatio-temporal world is God. The cosmic Brahman is the omnipresent, omniscient and omnipotent creator, preserver and destroyer of the world, the inner controller of the universe and the individual souls, the Lord of the Law of Karma, the moral governor, and the harmonizer of all worlds. He is possessed of good qualities, and devoid of bad qualities. He is pure, sinless, untainted and holy.

All created beings spring from Him, live by Him, and are absorbed in Him.[2] He is the material cause and the efficient cause of the world. He is omniscient and all-knowing. He created formed and formless, temporal and non-temporal, contingent and necessary, conscious and unconscious beings, and the real and the unreal. Brahman is the creator of names and forms or diverse objects of experience.[3]

The world is said to be created by God. It is also said to emanate from Him, even as sparks emanate from a burning fire. It is the manifestation of His glory. It is covered with Him and clothed in His glory.[4] All created beings have their roots in Being; they exist in Being, and grounded in Being. Being is Brahman. The world is real. It is a manifestation

[1] Kena Up., i, 2, 3 & 5-8; i, 4; Kath. Up., i, 2, 8-9, 12 & 24; Br. Up., ii, 4, 14.

[2] Chānd. Up., iii, 14, 1.

[3] Chānd. Up., viii, 14, 1; Muṇḍ. Up., i, 1, 6 & 9; ii, 1, 3-9; Tait. Up., iii, 1-6; ii, 6.

[4] Muṇḍ. Up., i, 1, 9; ii, 1, 1; ii, 2, 7; Īśa Up., 1.

of Brahman. There are two kinds of manifestations, gross and subtle, formed and formless. All gross and subtle things are manifestations of Brahman. The world is an expression of God, as if it were His cloth tinged with yellow colour. 'Brahman is the creator of the world, the maker of all. The world is his ; it is, indeed, Brahman.'[1] The world is real and not an appearance. It has no existence apart from Brahman.

God is the ruler and governor of the world. The sun, the moon, the earth and the sky are kept in their places by His command. The wind blows, the sun rises, fire burns, the cloud thunders, and death overtakes all created beings at His command. He is the harmonizer of the different worlds. They are kept together by His unifying will. His will maintains, supports and harmonizes them. He is the bridge, the support and the unifyer of all worlds.[2]

God is the inner controller of the whole world with all its objects, and of the individual souls. 'He who resides in earth, water, fire, air, ether, heaven, space, the sun, the moon, stars, darkness, life, speech, eye, ear, manas, skin, and intellect, yet who is different from them, whose body they are, whom they do not know, who controls them from within, is thy immortal Ātman and inner controller.' 'He who resides in all creatures, who is different from them, whom they do not know, whose body they are, who controls them from within, is thy immortal Ātman and inner controller.'[3] 'He who resides in the self, who is different from it, whom it does not know, whose body it is, whom he controls from within, is thy immortal Ātman and inner controller'.'[4] Brahman is the world-soul and the inner controller of the entire universe. He is the inner controller of each finite object, and of each finite self. He is immanent in the universe and finite selves.

---

[1] Chānd. Up., vi, 8, 4 ; iii, 14, 1 ; vii, 25, 2 ; Bṛ. Up., ii, 3, 6.

[2] Bṛ. Up., iv, 4, 13 ; iii, 8, 9 ; v, 6, 1 ; Tait. Up., ii, 8, 1 ; Kaṭh. Up., ii, 3, 2-3 ; Chānd. Up., viii, 4, 1.

[3] Bṛ. Up., iii, 7, 3-21.

[4] Bṛ. Up., iii, 7, 22.

God is everywhere, upward and downward, before and behind, northward and southward. The east, the west, the north, the south, up and below are filled with Him. Heaven is His head ; the sun and the moon are His eyes ; the directions are His ears ; air is His life ; the world is His heart ; the earth is His foot. He is the inner soul of all creatures. 'The universe is God Himself.' 'All these, present, past and future, are God Himself.'[1] He is immanent in the entire universe.

But God is not immanent only. He also transcends the world. He is infinite and eternal, and so transcends the spatial and temporal world. 'Brahman has four quarters. The universe is one quarter. His three quarters are immortal in heaven. The universe is the manifestation of His glory. He is greater than His expression.' 'Heaven, the earth, the sky, the vital forces, and the internal organs exist in Him.' 'He is the Lord of the past and the future.' The past, the present, and the future are Brahman. What is beyond the three times is Brahman. Names and forms or diverse determinate objects exist in Brahman. He exists within all and outside all. All worlds are founded in Him ; none can transcend Him.[2] He transcends avyakta or prakṛti, which is the root of the universe. He is immanent in it. All gods are subordinate to Him ; none can transcend Him. He exists in all creatures. They exist in Him. He transcends the known and the unknown.[3]

He is the eternal ground of the temporal world. He is the self-caused cause of the world governed by causality. He is the necessary ground of the contingent world. He illumines the universe which abides in Him. He is the knower of the world. But He is not known by any knower. God, as the knower, transcends the known universe. Brahman is the infinite and eternal consciousness. All are governed by

---

[1] Chānd. Up., vii, 25, 1 ; Muṇḍ. Up., ii, 2, 12 ; ii, 1, 4 & 10.

[2] Chānd. Up., iii, 12, 6 ; viii, 14, 1 ; Muṇḍ. Up., ii, 2, 5 ; Kaṭh. Up., ii, 1, 5 ; ii, 2, 8 ; i, 3, 11 ; Māṇḍ. Up., i, 1 ; Subāla Up, 7.

[3] Kaṭh Up., ii, 1, 9 ; Iśa UP., 6, 7 ; Kena Up., i, 4.

this consciousness. Eternal consciousness is the ground of all.[1]

God is the Lord of all creatures and the universe. He is the ruler of all, the master of all, the Lord of all. He is their inner guide. All gods are subordinate to Him, who execute His commands. All creatures, all worlds, all vital forces, and all finite souls are subordinate to Him. He is the cause of the universe, but He has no cause. He is the Lord of the universe, but He has no Lord. He is the abode of all creatures. He is the inner Soul of all finite souls. He enters into them, and rules over them.[2] He is immanent in them, and transcends them.

God is the Lord of the Law of Karma. He accords fruits to all creatures in accordance with their merits and demerits. He fulfils their desires according to their moral deserts. He is the giver of the fruits of actions. He rewards virtues and punishes sins. He is the moral judge and moral governor. He is the supreme Person.[3]

God manifests Himself in various ways. He creates the world by māyā or various powers. One God is the omnipotent magician. He governs all worlds with His infinite powers. His supreme powers are of various kinds. They constitute māyā or prakṛti. God is endowed with the power of māyā and creates the world with its aid. One God conceals his nature with the guṇas of prakṛti, even as a spider conceals itself in its cobweb. He is devoid of sattva, rajas and tamas, which are His inessential powers. His intrinsić nature is hidden by them. He creates the world with His powers. They constitute māyā or prakṛti. Māyā is not an appearance. It is not the root of phenomenal appearances.[4]

---

1 Muṇḍ. Up., ii, 2, 11 ; iii, 2, 1, ; Kaṭh, Up., ii, 2, 2 ; Śvet. Up., iii, 19 ; Chānd. Up, iv., 15, 4 ; Ait. Up., v, 3 ; Bṛ. Up., iv, 4, 22 ; ii, 5, 15.

2 Māṇḍ. Up. l, 6 ; Kaṭh. Up., ii, 1, 9 : Śvet. Up., iv, 9 : Kaiṣ. Up., iii. 8.

3 Śvet. Up., vi, 6 ; vi, 11 ; Kaṭh. Up., i, 3, 11 ; ii, 3, 8 ; ii, 2, 13 ; ii, 1, 5 ; Bṛ. UP., iv, 4, 24 ; Chānd. Up., iv, 15, 2-4.

4 Bṛ. Up., ii, 5, 19 ; Śvet. Up., iv, 10 ; vi, 10.

God is the infinite, eternal, imperishable, omnipresent, omniscient, and omnipotent creator, preserver and destroyer of the universe. He is the inner guide of the world and finite selves. He is their master, ruler, and moral governor. He is sinless, pure, moral, holy and perfect. He is the eternal embodiment of moral perfection. He does not become perfect by righteous actions. Nor does He become imperfect by unrighteous actions.[1]

God is the creator of the Vedas. He is the author of the moral laws. He is the protector of the moral order. He is the highest end to be realized.[2]

Brahman is both indeterminate and determinate. In His transcendental aspect Brahman is devoid of attributes. But in His relation to the world and the individual souls He is endowed with attributes.

THE INDIVIDUAL SOUL (JĪVĀTMAN)

The individual soul is different from the body, the sense-organs, manas and buddhi. The body is the chariot, which is guided by the self, which is the charioteer. The intellect (buddhi) is the driver. The mind (manas) is the bridle. The sense-organs are the horses. The objects apprehended by them are the field. The sense-organs are directed by the mind. The mind is directed by the intellect which is directed by the self. The mind is superior to the sense-organs. The intellect is superior to the mind. The self is superior to the intellect. The body is its material vehicle. The sense-organs, mind and intellect are its instruments of knowledge and action. It is their agent and master. It is a knower, enjoyer, and active agent. It experiences joys and sorrows, which are the fruits of its actions. It is eternal, conscious and many.

[1] Bṛ. Up., iv, 4, 22 ; Chānd. Up., iii, 24, 2 ; viii., 1, 5 ; viii, 7, 1 ; iii, 14, 2 ; Īśa Up., 8 ; Kaṭh. Up., i, 2, 13 ; ii, 3, 17 ; ii, 2, 8 ; Muṇḍ. Up., ii, 2, 7, 10 & 12 ; iii, 1, 5 ; i. 1, 6-9 ; i, 2, 11 & 13 ; ii, 1, 2 ; Maitrāyaṇī Up., ii, 4, 11.

[2] Kaṭh. Up., i, 3, 11 ; Muṇḍ. Up., ii, 1, 6-7 ; Bṛ. Up., ii, 4, 10 ; Muṇḍ. Up., ii, 2, 5 ; i, 1, 5 ; Kaṭh. Up., i, 3, 12 ; i, 2 , 12 & 24 ; Muṇḍ. Up., iii, 1, 5 ; ii, 2, 3.

It is unborn and devoid of infinite knowledge and sovereignty. It is imperishable and immortal. It does not perish when its body dies. It is a disembodied, unborn and eternal spirit. It has no birth and death. It is unborn, eternal, immutable and ancient. The ātman associated with the sense-organs and manas is the individual self, that enjoys the fruits of its actions.[1]

A finite self with an uncontrolled and impure mind and devoid of discrimination enters into bondage, and undergoes birth and death. But one with a controlled and pure mind and endowed with discrimination realizes Brahman, and is freed from bondage, birth and death. An individual self acquires merits and demerits by its righteous and unrighteous actions, and experiences happiness and misery. It becomes virtuous by right actions, and vicious by wrong actions. This implies that it has the freedom of the will. The self (jīva) has desire ; as it desires, so it wills ; as it wills, so it acts ; as it acts, so it becomes. Its character is built on its desire and will.[2] Virtue and vice are the results of free voluntary actions. They are the expressions of volitions which are prompted by desires chosen by the self. It acquires virtue and vice through its free moral and immoral actions.

After death it transmigrates to another body. It is associated with an appropriate body, human, superhuman or subhuman in accordance with its merits and demerits. Just as corns wither away and germinate again, so mortal beings die and are reborn according to their moral deserts. It washes off merits and demerits, and acquires identity with God, when it knows Him.[3]

The individual soul has four conditions. In the waking condition it is called the Viśva, which knows and enjoys gross external objects through the external sense-organs. In the condition of dream it is called the Taijasa, which knows and

---

[1] Kaṭh. Up., i, 3, 3-4, 9-10 ; ii, 2, 13 ; i, 2, 18 ; Muṇḍ. Up., iii, 1 1 & 2 ; Śvet. Up., i, 9-10 & 12.

[2] Kaṭh. Up., i, 3, 1, 7-9 ; Muṇḍ. Up., iii, 1, 1 & 2 ; Bṛ. Up., iii, 2, 13 ; iv, 4, 5.

[3] Kaṭh. Up., ii, 2, 7 ; Chānd. Up., v, 10, 7.

enjoys subtle internal objects or cognitions through the manas. In the condition of dreamless sleep it is called the Prājña, which is one homogeneous consciousness and bliss, which does not apprehend external objects and internal cognitions. In the fourth ecstatic condition it is called the Ātman, which knows neither external objects nor internal cognitions, which is neither consciousness nor non-consciousness. It is one, non-dual, transcendental consciousness. The Ātman is one universal super-consciousness. This Ātman is Brahman.[1]

The individual self is encased in five sheaths. The body and the sense-organs constitute its bodily sheath which is sustained by food. The self is first identified with its body and its senses. Within the bodily sheath there is the vital sheath. The vital forces, which animate the body, are its parts. The vital sheath is composed of the vital forces. It is sustained by them. The self is identified with the vital forces, which maintain the body. Within the vital sheath there is the mental sheath which depends on the mind (manas). Volitions directed to selfish ends constitute the mental sheath. The self is identified with the mind and its functions. Within the mental sheath there is the intellectual sheath which depends on the intellect and its functions. Discriminative knowledge, which depends upon the distinction of subject and object, constitutes the intellectual sheath. The self is identified with the intellect and its knowledge involving distinction of subject and object. Within the intellectual sheath there is the blissful sheath. Subject-objectless consciousness and bliss constitute the blissful sheath. Ānanda is absolute freedom. It is infinite and non-empirical. It is not pleasure or joy due to the intercourse of the sense-organs or the mind with empirical objects. Bliss does not constitute a sheath of the self, but it constitutes the very essence of the self. The self with its transcendental consciousness and bliss or freedom is the Ātman or Brahman. The Ātman, the inner core of the empirical self, is absolute freedom. It is identical with Brahman. The intellectual self

[1] Muṇḍ. Up., iii, 1, 3 ; Māṇḍ. Up., i, 2-4.

is the knower and doer. It guides the external sense-organs and the mind. It is founded in the supreme imperishable Ātman or Brahman. When it knows the supreme Ātman, it becomes omniscient. The non-dual blissful Ātman cannot be comprehended by the mind and described by speech. The word 'mind' is used here for 'manas', the internal organ.

Brahman or Ātman resides in the cavity of the heart. The Ātman is the transcendental Self, which is the inner Soul of the empirical self. It is the imperishable Brahman. It is super-moral, non-temporal, and non-causal. It is full of bliss. When the individual self knows it by meditative trance, it is filled with bliss. A mortal person lives not through life, but through the Ātaman in which it abides. There is God, the self-luminous Lord of the past and the future, within the individual self. When it purges off all its impurities and knows Brahman or Ātman within it, it becomes Ātman. The intellectual self becomes identical with the supreme infinite Self. The infinite Self, or Brahman within the individual self is to be realized[1]. There is a thin distinction between the individual self and the supreme self in the earlier Upaniṣads.

THE INDIVIDUAL SELF AND THE SUPREME SELF

'Two birds, friendly to each other, sit in the same tree. One eats the sweet fruit thereof, while the other merely looks on. The jīva deluded by lack of freedom and sovereignty sorrows. But when it sees the adorable Lord and His glory, it is freed from misery'. When it sees the luminous Lord, it is purged of merits and demerits, becomes taintless and pure, and attains identity with Him. The individual soul and the supreme soul both reside in the cavity of the heart of the same body as darkness and light. The former experiences the fruits of actions, and feels happiness and misery. The latter does not experience them, but merely looks on as an indifferent spectator. When the jīva, the enjoyer of fruits of actions, knows God

[1] Tait. Up., iii, 1, 2-6 ; Praś. Up., iv, 9 ; Tait. Up., ii, 9 ; Muṇḍ. Up., iii, 2, 7 ; iii, 1, 7 ; Kaṭh. Up., i, 2, 13, 14 & 16 ; ii, 1, 12-13 & 15 ; ii, 2, 5 ; ii, 3, 17.

within him, he sheds all fear. Brahman, or Ātman, the inner Soul and guide within the individual self, is not affected by its joys and sorrows, merits and demerits, attachment and aversion.[1]

Both are unborn and eternal. The supreme soul is omniscient and omnipotent. The individual soul is ignorant and impotent. Its sorrow and bondage are due to its ignorance and impotence. Sometimes freedom of the individual soul is admitted. It becomes virtuous by righteous actions. It becomes vicious by unrighteous actions. Sometimes its freedom of the will is denied, and immanence of God is over-emphasized. He is all-doer. He causes those jīvas to do right actions, whom he desires to elevate from these worlds. He causes those jīvas to do wrong actions, whom he desires to degrade from them.[2]

Some texts clearly show the identity of the individual soul with the supreme soul. 'I am the person who dwells within the sun'. 'This Ātman is Brahman.' 'That thou art'. 'One who knows Brahman becomes Brahman'. 'The jīva, who realizes Brahman, delights in the Self, becomes united with the Self, enjoys bliss in the self, and becomes sovereign of his self'. 'One who knows Brahman, delights in himself (ātmarati), and sports with himself'. 'One who purges off merits and demerits, attains perfect identity with Brahman,' 'The individual soul, that knows the Lord, is divested of its names and forms, and attains Him, even as rivers merge in the sea leaving their names and forms.' 'One who makes any distinction is haunted by fear. But one who realizes identity, becomes fearless.'[3] 'I am Brahman.'

'Akṣara Brahman is the unseen seer, the unheard hearer, the unthought thinker, the unknown knower. There is no other seer, no other hearer, no other thinker, no other knower than this. This is thy Self, the immortal inner controller.' 'There

[1] Muṇḍ. Up., iii, 1, 1-3 ; Śvet. Up., iv, 6, 7 ; Kaṭh. Up., i, 3, 1 ; ii, 1, 5, 12, 13 ; ii. 2, 11-13.

[2] Śvet. Up., i, 9 ; Muṇḍ. Up., iii, 1, 2 ; Kaiṣ. Up., iii, 8 ; Bṛ. Up., iii, 2, 13 ; iv, 4, 5 ; Chānd. Up., ii, 4, 2, 4.

[3] Iśa Up., 16 ; Bṛ. Up., ii, 5, 14 ; lv, 4, 25 ; Chānd. Up., vii, 25, 2 ; Muṇḍ. Up., iii, 1, 3 & 4 or 3-4 ; iii, 2, 6-8.

is no plurality here. One who sees plurality, as it were, here, meets death after death.' 'So long as knowledge of duality persists, the individual self sees another thing, smells another thing, hears another thing, speaks another thing, knows another thing, as it were. But when it realizes one Ātman in all things, the distinction between it and the Ātman vanishes, and one Ātman shines as the knower'. 'When one self realizes its identity with Brahman or Ātman, it does not see, hear, smell, taste, touch, think, and know anything distinct from itself.' 'The individual soul becomes identified with the universal self'. 'Where there is duality, as it were, one sees, smells, tastes, hears, speaks, touches, thinks and knows another entity distinct from oneself. But where all become one Ātman, who will see, smell, taste, hear, speak, touch, think and know what ? Who can know that through which one knows all ?'[1] These texts treat duality of subject and object, distinction of the individual soul and the supreme soul, and plurality and difference of things and selves as appearances.

But there are some texts, which clearly show the difference of the individual self and the universal self. 'Brahman who exists in the self, yet who is different from it, whom it does not know, whose body it is, who guides it from within, is thy Ātman, immortal inner controller'. 'The individual self attains immortality by knowing the inner guide as different from it.' 'God is the Lord of the individual souls, who are the masters of the sense-organs'. 'God and the individual soul both are eternal. God is omniscient and omnipotent. The individual soul is ignorant and dependent.' 'God endowed with the power of māyā creates the world. The individual soul is bound by māyā.' 'God is the Lord of prakṛti and individual souls'. 'He is the eternal Lord among eternal souls. He is the supreme conscious Being among many conscious beings. He is the one Lord, who fulfils the desires of many souls.' 'The individual soul and Brahman reside in the same body. The one eats its

[1] Bṛ. Up., iii, 8, 11 ; iv, 6, 24-30 ; iii, 7, 23 ; iv, 4, 19, Kaṭh. Up., ii, 1, 11 ; Bṛ. Up., ii, 4, 14 ; iv, 3, 30, 31 ; iv, 4, 2 ; iv, 5, 15.

sweet fruits. The other does not eat, but only looks on'. 'God moves within the individual soul, which is His body, whom it does not know, and is the inner Self of all created beings, the one, sinless, luminous Nārāyaṇa'. These texts show the difference between the individual self and Brahman or God. 'The liberated soul enjoys all objects of desire with omniscient Brahman.'[1] It retains its integrity, and remains distinct from Brahman. It does not become indentical with the supreme Self.

BONDAGE AND LIBERATION : VIDYĀ AND AVIDYĀ

Ignorance (avidyā) is non-discrimination of the eternal and the non-eternal. Knowledge (vidyā) is discrimination between them. Ignorance is the knowledge of distinction, plurality, and individuality. It is intellectual knowledge involving distinction of subject and object. It is the knowledge of things limited by time and space, and determined by causality. True knowledge is the intuition of identity. It is above intellectual knowledge and not determined by time, space and causality. Ignorance is the sphere of actions, which spring from the knowledge of plurality. True knowledge is the sphere of higher knowledge of identity. Ignorance is the cause of bondage and transmigration. True knowledge is the cause of liberation from bondage.[2]

The individual soul's individuality is due to ignorance. It erroneously identifies itself with the body, the sense-organs, the mind and the intellect and is entangled in bondage. When it knows its identity with Brahman or Ātman, it realizes its innate freedom. Actions, which spring from ignorance cannot lead to liberation. Knowledge of the Ātman is liberation.

Works, concentration of mind, devotion and knowledge are the means to the attainment of liberation. But knowledge is

---

[1] Bṛ., Up., iii., 7, 22 ; Śvet. Up., i, 6 ; vi, 9 ; i, 9 , iv, 6 ; vi, 13 ; Subāla Up., vii, 1, Tait., ii, 1.

[2] Isa Up., 9-11 ; Bṛ. Up., iv, 4, 10 ; Kaṭh. Up., i. 1, 6 ; i, 2, 4-5.

the pre-eminent means. The duties should be performed with knowledge that God pervades the world. One who performs one's duties is not entangled in them. Prescribed duties should be performed throughout life. But actions and their fruits are non-eternal. Performance of duties leads to the attainment of heaven which is non-eternal. Eternal Brahman cannot be attained by the performance of duties. One who realizes the non-eternal nature of their fruits, acquires detachment, and seeks knowledge of the eternal Ātman. Prescribed duties are a shaky boat to cross the ocean of saṁsāra with. Actions spring from desires. Happiness springs from the fulfilment of desires. Earthly and heavenly happiness is agreeable. But the realization of the Ātman is the highest good which can be achieved by extinguishing desires. Freedom from desires gives true happiness. The mind is the cause of bondage and liberation. An impure mind is the cause of bondage. A pure mind is the cause of liberation. A mind tainted by desires for pleasure is impure. A mind free from the taint of desires for pleasure is pure. A mind attached to objects of enjoyment produces bondage. A mind detached from them produces liberation. Purity of mind destroys merits and demerits, which are the fruits of righteous and unrighteous actions. Egoism is the cause of bondage. Egolessness is the cause of liberation. Selfishness is bondage. Selflessness is liberation.[1] Immortality cannot be achieved by the performance of prescribed duties, gift of wealth, or procreation of children, but by renunciation only.[2] One who has renounced all desires, is free from desires and completely fulfilled. One whose desires for happiness

[1] Bṛ. Up., iv, 4, 23 ; i 4, 2 ; Chānd. Up., iii, 14, 4 ; iv, 14, 3 ; vii. 1, 3 ; viii, 4, 1 ; viii, 12, 1 ; Tait.Up., ii, 4 ; Muṇḍ. Up., iii, 2, 4, 8. HIP. Vol. II, pp. 436-39 ; Īśa Up., 2 ; Kaṭh. Up., i, 2, 10 ; Chānd. Up., viii, 1, 6 ; Muṇḍ Up., i, 2, 7, 12-13 ; Kath. Up., 1, 2, 2-20 ; Maitrāyanī Up., iv, 3, 4, 6 & 11 ; Brahmabindu Up., 1, 2 ; Maitreyī Up., i. 5, 6. Nirnaysagar Press, Bombay, 1925. Paiṅgala Up., iv, 19 ; Varāha Up., ii, 43. Bombay, 1925.

[2] Bṛ. Up., iv, 4, 6 ; Kaivalya Up., 3 ; Nārāyaṇa Up., xii, 3.

are worn out and directed to the Ātman, is completely fulfilled. Extinction of desire for sons, desire for wealth, and desire for power in this world is necessary for the realization of the Ātman.

Discipline of body and mind and practice of yoga purify the mind, and make it fit for acquiring knowledge of the Ātman. Penances generate purity of mind. Sense-control, mind-control, withdrawal of the senses from their objects, endurance of physical hardships, and trance due to meditation are pre-requisites for the intuitive realization of the Ātman within the individual self.[1]

Devotion to God also is a means of liberation. The Ātman cannot be realized by the teaching or the study of the Vedas or the power of retaining them. He can be realized by one, whom He chooses, and to whom He reveals His real nature. One who is devoid of attachment realizes the glory of the Ātman or the Lord through His grace, and becomes free from sorrow. God reveals Himself to those, who have supreme devotion to Him, and take refuge in Him. Knowledge of Brahman can never be attained without devotion.[2]

Knowledge is the supreme means of liberation. One who knows Brahman, attains the supreme goal. One who knows Brahman, becomes Brahman. Brahman is Ātman. The Ātman should be seen, heard, reflected and meditated on, because it is the dearest of all, and because by knowing it the whole world is known. We should meditate on the dear Ātman. We should pray to the Ātman. We should know the Ātman only, and give up all other talks. By knowing one Ātman in all creatures one becomes immortal. One who consciously lives in Brahman, attains immortality.[3]

---

[1] Bṛ. Up., iii, 5, 1 ; Subāla Up., 13 ; Maitreyī Up., i, 2 ; Kaivalya Up., 1, 4 ; Bṛ. Up., iv, 4, 23 ; Subāla Up., 9 ; Amṛtanāda Up., 6 ; 7-17, 19.

[2] Kaṭh. Up., 1, 2, 23 ; Muṇḍ. Up., iii, 2, 3 ; Kaṭh. Up., i, 2, 20 ; Śvet, Up. vi, 18, 23.

[3] Tait. Up., ii, 1 ; Muṇḍ. Up., iii, 2, 9 ; Bṛ. UP., ii, 4, 5 ; i, 4, 15 ; iv, 5, 6 ; Muṇḍ. Up., ii, 2, 5 & 6 ; Chānd. Up., ii, 23, 1.

The Ātman cannot be known by the senses. It cannot be known by reason. It is incomprehensible by discursive thought. It can be known by intuition which is above reason. It can be known by meditative trance. Intuition can be attained by non-commission of sins, control of the senses, concentration of mind, and abstention from sensual pleasures. The senses should be subordinated to the mind, the mind to the intellect, and the intellect to the Self. When the mind is completely concentrated on the Self, and absorbed in it, and identified with it, it can know it. The Self reveals itself to one whose mind becomes pure. It can be realized by pure knowledge. It can be realized by integral knowledge, when the mind is purged of all afflictions, attachment, aversion and the other emotions and passions, and freed from all desires. One who abstains from sensual pleasures, contentrates one's mind on Brahman, and is contented with supreme knowledge, enters into Brahman. Discrimination of happiness and the highest good, renunciation of enjoyments, extinction of desires, and purity of mind lead to the saving knowledge.[1]

Liberation (mokṣa) is freedom from bondage. Ignorance is bondage. True knowledge is liberation. It is knowledge of Brahman or Ātman in oneself and in all creatures. It is the intuitive realization of one infinite, eternal, universal Spirit. Knowledge of Brahman is becoming Brahman. Liberation is becoming Brahman. It is becoming all. It is the vision of one Self in all. It is the vision of the Self of the universe. It is life eternal. It is state of identity (sāmya, ekatva) of the individual self with the supreme self. It is free from love, hatred, delusion, joy, sorrow, and fear. It is free from merits and demerits. It is a state of supermoral transcendental purity. It is eternal peace, indefinable supreme bliss. It is a sense of perfect fulfilment. It is a state of delight in the Ātman, sport with it, and union with it. It is complete autonomy or freedom. It is a sense of oneness, devoid of duality and plurality. It is pure subject-objectless consciousness. It is a

[1] Iśa Up., 6; Kaṭh. Up., i, 2, 8-9, 12 & 24; ii, 3, 9 & 14; i, 3, 7-9; Muṇḍ. Up., i, 2, 13; ii, 2, 3; iii, 1, 5, 8 & 9; iii, 2, 2 & 6.

state of supreme wisdom, selfless will, and ineffable bliss. One who is free from all desires attains immortality on earth. One who lives, moves, and has his being in Brahman, becomes immortal. One who knows the Self hidden in one's heart enjoys all objects of desire with God.[1]

THE WORLD

The world is real. It is the expression of the glory of Brahman. It springs from Him, is sustained by Him, and absorbed in Him. All created beings abide in Him, originate in Him, and are founded in Him. Brahman is the cause of names and forms or determinate objects. It existed in an unmanifest condition in Brahman before creation. It was made manifest by Him. The world is pervaded by Brahman. The past, the present, and the future are Brahman. The south, the north, the east, the west, up and down are Brahman. The whole spatio-temporal order is Brahman. It has its root in Brahman, who transcends it. The uniformities of nature are controlled by His will. The world is permeated by the Divine Spirit.[2]

The origin of the world is traced to creation or emanation. All creatures come out from the Ātman or Brahman, as sparks come out from fire, as plants shoot forth on the earth, as hairs spring from a living body, or as threads come out from the body of a spider. The world emanates from the fulness of Brahman, and returns to it. This is the doctrine of emanation. The material elements—ether, air, light, water, and earth,—life, the sense-organs, and mind spring from Brahman. The rivers, seas, mountains, and plants spring from Him. Plants, vital forces, and corns spring from Him. Gods, men, beasts, and birds spring from Him. The Vedas, Ṛk, Sāma and Yajus

---

[1] Iśa Up., 6, 7 ; Kaṭh. Up., i, 2, 8-9, 12 & 24 ; ii, 3, 9 & 14 ; ii, 3, 7-9 ; Muṇḍ. Up., ii, 1, 10 ; iii, 1, 3 & 4; iii, 2, 7-9 ; Chānd, Up., vii, 25, 2 ; viii, 3, 4 ; Tait. Up., ii, 1,

[2] Bṛ. Up., i, 4, 7 ; Muṇḍ. Up., ii, 2, 7 ; Ait. Up., iii, 3 ; Chānd. Up., viii, 14, 1 ; vi, 8, 6 ; Iśa Up., 1 ; Muṇḍ. Up., ii, 1, 10 ; ii, 2, 5 & 7 ; Chānd. Up., iii, 14, 1 ; vii, 8, 4 & 6 ; viii, 14, 1 ; vi, 3, 2 ; Bṛ. Up., ii, 3, 6 ; Kaṭh. Up., ii, 3, 1-3 ; Tait. Up., ii, 8 ; Māṇḍ Up., i, 1.

spring from Him. The moral laws and duties spring from Him. Brahman is the source of the cosmic order and the moral order.[1]

Brahman ejects the world out of Himself, and withdraws it into Himself, even as a spider ejects threads out of its own body, and withdraws it. Brahman creates the world out of His own nature, and absorbs it in Himself. He does not create it out of any pre-existing material. There was one Ātman before creation. There was nothing else. He resolved: 'I shall create the worlds.' He created the worlds. He created the the formed and the formless, the subtle and the gross. Ether was created out of the Ātman; air was created out of ether; fire was created out of air; water was created out of fire; earth was created out of water; and plants were created out of earth. The world was in an unmanifest condition in Brahman. He made it manifest. He created names and forms or multiform objects. He manifested them. He differentiated them, which were in an undifferentiated condition.[2] Creation is transition from an undifferentiated to a differentiated state. 'Names and forms' do not mean appearances.

The *Śvetāśvatara*, a later Upaniṣad, advocates theism, and refers to the creation of the world by God out of māyā or prakṛti, which is constituted by his various powers. God is the Lord of prakṛti and individual souls. He is endowed with māyā or prakṛti. God, possessed of māyā, creates the world. His powers are supreme and various. These powers constitute māyā or prakṛti, which is real. One God creates diverse objects by means of His various powers. He conceals Himself with the products of prakṛti by nature, as a spider conceals itself with its own threads. God, the great magician, creates and rules over all worlds with His various governing powers. Prakṛti is one, unborn, composed of sattva, rajas, and tamas,

---

[1] Bṛ. Up., ii, 1, 20; Muṇḍ. Up., i, 1, 7; ii, 1, 1; Muṇḍ. Up., i, 1, 7 & 9; ii, 1, 1, 3-9.

[2] Muṇḍ. Up., i, 1, 7; Ait. Up., i, 1; Tait. Up., ii, 1, 6 & 7; Chānd. Up., viii, 14, 1; Bṛ. Up., i, 4, 7.

and mutable. It creates many similar products out of these constituents (guṇas).[1] Though God is devoid of sattva, rajas, and tamas, they are His powers by which He conceals His essential nature, and creates the world. He is the ruler of His powers.

Brahman is the infinite and eternal consciousness devoid of sattva, rajas, and tamas. Prakṛti, composed of them, is His own power. He creates the world out of His own power. Prakṛti is the conscious power of God, which can create the multiform world of various objects.

The *Subāla Upaniṣad* gives the following account of creation and dissolution of the world. 'There was neither being, nor non-being, nor being and non-being both. From this mass (tamas) was created. Primal matter was created out of mass. Ether was created out of primal matter. Air was created out of ether. Fire was created out of air. Water was created out of fire. Earth was created out of water.' 'All creatures are dissolved in earth. Earth is dissolved in water. Water is dissolved in fire. Fire is dissolved in air. Air is dissolved in ether. Ether is dissolved in the sense-organs. The sense-organs are dissolved in the subtle essences (tanmātra). The subtle essences are dissolved in primal matter. Primal matter is dissolved in mahat. Mahat is dissolved in avyakta. Avyakta is dissolved in akṣara. Akṣara is dissolved in mass. Mass merges in the supreme Lord. Beyond is neither being, nor non-being, nor being and non-being both.'[2] Avyakta is prakṛti. Akṣara is Brahmā or Ādi puruṣa. Para Brahma, Apara Brahma or Īśvara, tamas, Akṣara, avyakta, mahat or cosmic intellect, primal matter, the five tanmātras, and the five material elements constitute the order of creation.

The doctrines of triplication and quintuplication are suggested. The elements of fire, water and earth are combined in such a manner that one of them becomes the principal element while the other two become subordinate elements. In fire the

---

1 Svet. Up., iv, 10 ; iv, 9 ; vi, 8 ; iv, 1 ; vi, 10 ; iii, 1.
2 Subāla Up., 1, 2 ; Praś. Up., iv, 8 ; Maitrāyaṇī Up., iii, 2.

element of fire is the principal element, and earth and water are the subordinate elements. In water the element of water is the principal element, and earth and fire are the subordinate elements. In earth the element of earth is the principal element, and water and fire are the subordinate elements. This is called the doctrine of triplication of elements. The doctrine of quintuplication also is mentioned.[1]

[1] Chānd. Up., vi, 3, 3 & 4 : Paiṅgala Up., 1.

CHAPTER III

THE PHILOSOPHY OF THE BHAGAVADGĪTĀ

The *Bhagavadgītā* is a part of the *Mahābhārata* which is attributed to Vyāsa. It is regarded as one of the most sacred books of the Hindus. It is more a book on ethics than one on metaphysics. Even as a treatise on ethics it is not a compact philosophical work. It is an inspired poetical work with a philosophical theme. It is rightly called the *Song Divine*.

ONTOLOGY

The *Gītā* teaches theism, and regards God (Īśvara) as the supreme reality. He is higher than Brahman. God is the foundation of the immortal, infinite Absolute. He is holy and the ground of the eternal moral order. He is the fountain of eternal bliss.[1] He is the Supreme Reality. He is unequalled, unexcelled, infinite, eternal, and immutable. He is unborn, immortal, omnipresent, omniscient, and omnipotent. He knows the past, the present, and the future. He is ancient and without beginning, middle, and end. He is the First Cause and the ultimate ground of the universe. He is the creator, preserver, and destroyer of the universe. He is their Lord and Moral Governor. He is one in many. He is existent and non-existent. He is both transcendental existence and empirical existence. He is both immutable Being and mutation and becoming.[2] He is the Supreme Person. This is theism.

God is the Supreme Brahman (para brahma), which is unborn and eternal, neither existent nor non-existent. It is not existent as an empirical being, nor non-existent as a transcendental reality. It pervades the world, but it is not exhausted in it. It is immanent in it, and transcends it.[3] It is devoid of sattva, rajas, and tamas, and conscious of the

---

[1] BG., xiv, 27 ; xi, 43 ; iv, 6 ; x, 12 ; xi, 18 & 19, 38 ; xiii, 27 ; vii, 6 & 26 ; xiii, 13 ; xi, 40 & 43 ; iv, 31.

[2] BG., x, 8 ; xiii, 16 ; iv, 6 ; x, 15 & 33 ; xi, 43 & 44 : ix, 11, 15, 17-18.

[3] BG., vii, 19 ; xiii, 13.

empirical world composed of the guṇas. It is detached and sustains the relative world. It is devoid of all external and internal sense-organs, and yet it knows all sensible and intelligible objects. Brahman is moving and unmoving, remote and near, inside and outside the creatures. It is non-spatial, and yet extended in space. It is the immobile Spirit and the moving universe. It is transcendent and immanent. It is subtle and unknowable by the senses, mind, and intellect. It is the supreme light of lights and illumines all objects. It is the indwelling Spirit in the hearts of all beings. Brahman is the impersonal Absolute. It is an aspect of the Supreme Person or God. It is not equal to God, the ultimate Reality.[1]

The *Gītā* lays stress on the immanence of God in the universe in some verses. He is the indwelling Spirit in all creatures. He is their origin, middle, and end. He is the best of all things, beings, and qualities. He is the source of good and evil.[2]

But the *Gītā* does not teach pantheism. It teaches panentheism. God is not the world. The world is not God. But the world exists in God. All creatures exist in Him. He pervades them all as their inner guide. He is the eternal and imperishable essence abiding in perishing creatures. He is the immanent essence in all finite things and spirits as a thread running through beads. He is the seed and life of all creatures. All creatures exist in Him. But He is not identical with them. He pervades the universe by His unmanifest form. He is the invisible Spirit in the visible world. He is not affected by empirical objects and selves. He transcends the empirical objects and finite spirits entangled in them. He is the creator, sustainer, and destroyer of all creatures. They issue from Him, are maintained by Him, and reabsorbed in Him. He supports the entire universe by pervading it with His single fragment.[3] He is incorporeal, partless, undivided, infinite Spirit. The entire universe is a manifestation of a single fraction of Him.

---

[1] G., xiii, 13, 15, 17 & 33 ; xv, 6 & 12.

[2] BG., x, 20-40 ; xv, 13-15 ; x, 36 ; xi, 38.

[3] BG., viii, 20 & 22 ; vi, 31 ; ix, 4-7 & 18 ; vii, 7, 9 & 10 ; x, 42.

He transcends it to infinite beyond, and exists in immeasurable perfection. He is immanent in the universe and transcendent of it.[1] This is panentheism.

There are two puruṣas in the universe, the perishable (kṣara) Puruṣa and the imperishable (akṣara) Puruṣa. All created things and beings constitute the Kṣara Puruṣa. The immutable Puruṣa underlying them is the Akṣara Puruṣa.[2] The Akṣara Puruṣa is the eternal, inactive, immobile, and immutable self of all, yet unmoved and indifferent. It is timeless in time, spaceless in space, and non-causal in producing effects. The Kṣara Puruṣa is the dynamic, active, mutable, immanent, universal Soul of the world The Akṣara Puruṣa is the transcendent, inactive, immutable Self of all, from which proceeds mutation of things. The Kṣara Puruṣa corresponds to the Kṣara Brahman, and the Akṣara Puruṣa, to the Akṣara Brahman of the Upaniṣads.[3]

The Puruṣottama, Supreme Person, transcends the totality of mutable or empirical selves and the perishing material objects. He transcends the entire mutable universe and the immutable and imperishable Self of the world. He transcends the active, dynamic, universal Soul of nature, and its eternal, immutable, static, inactive, immobile Self, and integrates them together in His supreme unity. He is immobile in His mobility, inactive and indifferent in His activity, and immutable in His mutation and becoming. He inspires and informs the three worlds, and sustains and maintains them. He transcends the Kṣara Puruṣa and the Akṣara Puruṣa. He is the supreme, infinite Person. The Kṣara Puruṣa is the Soul immanent in the universe. The Akṣara Puruṣa is transcendent of it. It is indefinable, inconceivable, immutable, immobile, eternal, and unmanifest. This is the transcendent Self of the universe.[4] The Puruṣottama is superior to both the immanent Soul and the

---

1 BG., x. 20 ; xi, 38, 41 ; vii, 7 ; xv, 1, 2, 3, 13, 15.

2 BG., xv, 16.

3 Kaṭha Up., i, 2, 16.

4 BG., xv, 17 & 18 ; xii, 3 ; viii, 20 & 21.

transcendent Self, the mutable and the immutable. The Divine Person is higher than the Absolute. This is theism.

Prakṛti is the mother of the whole universe. God is the father, who fertilizes her, and produces the entire universe through her. Prakṛti is called māyā, which is not an appearance. It is the divine power inseparable from God. Prakṛti supervised by God produces all animate and inanimate creatures. They are re-absorbed in prakṛti in dissolution. Prakṛti is unmanifest. All manifest objects, inanimate and animate, spring from unmanifest prakṛti and dissolve in it.[1] God produces the world through His power, prakṛti or māyā. He is its efficient cause, and prakṛti is its material cause. The world produced by God through His power or prakṛti is real. It is mutable and perishable. The *Gītā* recognizes the reality of the world, which is informed by the Divine Spirit.

God has higher (parā) prakṛti and lower (aparā) prakṛti. The former constitutes the universe of animate and sentient creatures. It is conscious prakṛti, which sustains the world of conscious living beings. The latter is unconscious and composed of the five elements of earth, water, fire, air, and ether, and the three internal organs of manas, buddhi, and ahaṁkāra.

Sattva, rajas, and tamas are products of prakṛti. They delude the individual souls, and bind them to saṁsāra. They bind the incorporeal souls to their corporeal bodies. Sattva is pure, transparent, and free from pain ; it manifests objects. It produces knowledge and pleasure in the finite souls, and binds them to the world through them.[2] Rajas is of the nature of attachment. It produces action in the finite souls, and binds them to the world through it. It is the cause of desire and anger. Tamas springs from ignorance, deludes all finite souls, produces carelessness, laziness, and sleep in them, and binds them to the world. Sattva attaches them to pleasure ; rajas, to actions ; and tamas, to negligence. Sattva, rajas, and tamas

---

[1] BG., xiv, 3-4 ; vii, 14 : ix, 7 & 10 ; viii, 18-19 , ix, 8.

[2] BG., vii, 4-5. [3] BG., vii, 13 , xiv, 5-7.

are the primordial elements in the psychical nature. Sometimes sattva overcomes rajas and tamas, and becomes predominant. Sometimes rajas and tamas overcome the other two, and become predominant. Sattva is the cause of knowledge. Rajas is the cause of greed, desire for enjoyment, enterprise, action, and continuation of action. An action prompted by sattva produces pure pleasure ; that prompted by rajas produces pain ; that prompted by tamas produces ignorance. The guṇas constitute the internal organs—manas, buddhi, and ahaṁkāra. They move the individual selves to action.[1]

Prakṛti and the individual self (puruṣa) both are uncaused and eternal.[2] God is eternal. He is the creator, preserver, and destroyer of the universe through His twofold nature (prakṛti), subjective and objective. Prakṛti is the material cause of all physical and psychical phenomena. Puruṣa, the individual self, is the enjoyer of pleasure and pain, and the experiencer of all physical and psychical objects. It enjoys sattva, rajas, and tamas, the products of prakṛti, through the psychophysical organism. Its attachment to the guṇas binds it to saṁsāra, and makes it transmigrate from one body to another.[3] The Supreme Self, immanent in it, is the indifferent spectator, permitter, sustainer, and witness of all actions of the individual self. The *Gītā* agrees with the Kaṭha Upaniṣad that the individual self in the body is the enjoyer of fruits of actions, while the Supreme Self immanent in it is the witness of them. The former is the doer, while the latter is the spectator. Actions are done by the individual self made of the guṇas. The Supreme Self is not the doer. It is the eternal, infinite, trans-empirical self. It is not affected by the guṇas, because it transcends them. It is not moved by them. They are the cause of actions. The guṇas constitute the empirical nature of the individual self. The universal self immanent in it transcends them. It is the Supreme Self of all creatures. It is not active. It is not touched by actions of the individual self.[4] It neither acts nor apprehends

---

[1] BG., iii, 37 ; xiv, 8-17. [2] BG., xiii, 20. [3] BG., xiii, 21-22.
[4] BG., xiii, 23 & 30 , v, 7 ; Kaṭh. Up., i, 3, 7.

objects. The sense-organs act on their proper objects. The guṇas constitute the sensible objects and the sense-organs.[1] Egoism is made of the guṇas. The self determined by egoism wrongly thinks itself to be a free doer. God dwells in the hearts of all creatures. He moves them to action by his Māyā, and guides them as His instruments.[2] The individual self (jīva) is an eternal part of God. The soul in the body is unborn, eternal, permanent, ancient, indestructible and immortal. It is inexhaustible, omnipresent, stable, immobile, incorporeal, unproduced, indestructible, incorruptible and immutable. It is unthinkable, insensible, and unmanifest.[3] The self is rational and sentient. The rational self can control, regulate, and conquer the sentient self. The lower self should be delivered from saṁsāra by the higher self. This implies the freedom of the will. Every individual acts according to his psychical disposition made of sattva, rajas, and tamas. His actions spring from his inner nature, and conform to it. But he is not completely determined by his empirical nature. He has the power of counteracting his natural impulses and desires, and realizing his supra-organic, supra-mental, spiritual nature. The severe ethical discipline enjoined by the *Gītā* implies human freedom. It appears to recognize empirical necessity and spiritual freedom of the human soul.[4]

Both one and many are real. One is divided into many. The finite souls are real. They are unborn and eternal. They exist in God, and He exists in them. One exists in many. Many exist in one. One is not an aggregate of many. Many are not appearances of One. Both are inseparably related to each other.[5] God and the finite souls are co-eternal with each other. Affinity with God is the highest consummation of man.[6]

ETHICS AND RELIGION

The *Gītā* is not a book on metaphysics, but essentially one on ethics and religion. It lays down the different paths of

[1] BG., iii, 28. [2] BG., iii, 27 ; xviii, 61. [3] BG., xv, 7 ; ii,18, 20-21, 24-25.
[4] BG., vi, 5-6 ; iii, 33-34 ; vi, 7.
[5] BG., ix, 15, 4, 6 & 29 ; vi, 29-31. [6] BG., xiv, 2.

realization of God. It's teaching is universal and intended for all persons of different temperaments. Some are predominantly men of action. They ought to follow the path of action (karmayoga). Some are predominantly emotional. They ought to follow the path of devotion (bhaktiyoga). Some are predominantly intellectual. They ought to follow the path of knowledge (jñānayoga).[1] Action, devotion, and knowledge lead to union with God. God-realization is the highest good. It is the supreme end of human life. No relative good can satisfy the aspirations of a finite soul, which is informed by the Divine Spirit.

The *Gītā* uses the term *yoga* in the sense of union with God. It teaches the paths of union through works, knowledge, and devotion. Voluntary actions are due to five conditions, the active individual self, the organism, the sense-organs, various conscious efforts and bodily movements, and providence.[2] Man connot remain inactive for a single moment. He is compelled to do actions by sattva, rajas, and tamas, which are products of prakṛti. They are primordial psychical impulses. Even the maintenance of the organism depends upon actions. So action is certainly better than inaction. The *Gītā* does not teach inactivism. It regards the performance of duties as better than renunciation of actions, because the latter never leads to liberation. It inculcates selfless, disinterested actions (niṣkāma karma) dedicated to God. Works should not be actuated by attachment, aversion, and other emotions. They should not be motivated by egoistic desires. They should be devoid of the sense of 'I' and 'mine'. They should be free from prudential considerations of fruits or consequences. They ought to be performed without consideration of success or failure, victory or defeat, good or evil, pleasure or pain, which they will bring. Their fruits should be resigned to God. All works should be done as service to God. Disinterested works dedicated to God and enlightened by knowledge do not lead to bondage. The aspirant's will should be

[1] BG., iii, 3. [2] BG., xviii, 14.

surrendered to the Divine Will. He should be a perfect instrument of God, and consciously will the Divine Will.[1] He should aim at the good of the entire sentient creation. The doer of good of mankind never suffers here or hereafter.[2] The path of works is selfless pursuit of the moral good of mankind as service to God.

The *Gītā* does not enjoin the performance of ritualistic acts. Prudential duties are intended for the fulfilment of egoistic desires. They aim at enjoyment and prosperity. They lead to happiness in heaven. They lead to rebirth. They are not the means of liberation. The Vedas prescribe duties relating to sattva, rajas, and tamas. But mokṣa is a state of the soul, which transcends the guṇas. It cannot be attained by Vedic rituals. All egoistic desires should be extirpated. Transient pleasures spring from their fulfilment. But realization of the self yields supreme bliss, which is permanent.[3] Actions motived by desires for fruits lead to bondage. But if they are performed without such desires, they yield permanent peace. Vedic rituals are not necessary for liberation. The specific duties of an individual ought to be performed without any desire for fruits. When all desires are resigned to God, and duties are performed in a disinterested spirit by an aspirant, he is said to be a yogin. The *Gītā* inculcates the morality of altruism or selflessness. Egoism ought to be eradicated. It emphasizes the purity of inner life and condemns ritualistic morality. It stresses the performance of duties as service to God. It condemns renunciation of works, and enjoins on us an active life dedicated to God for the moral welfare of humanity. But it is emphatic on the eradication of egoistic desires and evil passions like attachment, aversion, fear, lust, anger, greed, egoism, hypocrisy, pride, self-conceit, sorrow, melancholy, and the like. It inculcates the cultivation of the virtues of fearlessness, purity of mind, concentration of the mind on knowledge of the self, charity, sense-control, sacrifice, study of the scriptures, penance,

[1] BG., ii, 38, 47-49, 51, 57 ; iii, 7, 9, 19-20, 25, 30 & 33 ; iv, 19-23, 41 ; v, 3, 10-13 ; vi, 2 & 4 ; ix, 27 ; xii, 10 & 13 ; xviii, 6, 9, 23, 26, 53, 57 ; xvii, 15.

[2] BG., v, 25 ; vi, 40.

[3] BG., ii, 43-45, 55, 70-71 ; iii, 13 & 42 ; v, 21-22 & 24.

straightforwardness, non-injury, truthfulness, conquest of anger, renunciation, tranquillity, absence of fault-finding, kindness to creatures, greedlessness, softness, modesty, firmness, courage, forgiveness, endurance, cleanliness, non-malevolence, non-conceit, steadfastness, and self-control. Temperance in eating, walking, efforts in activities, sleep, and waking leads to happiness. Equanimity or imperturbability in joy and sorrow, gain and loss, victory and defeat, success and failure, is called yoga. Love and hatred, lust and anger, fear and disgust, greed and delusion, pride and envy should be conquered. Enmity should be completely discarded. Good-will and amity for all should be cultivated.[1] Reverence for gods, Brāhmaṇas, preceptors, and wise men, cleanliness, straightness, celibacy, non-injury, truthfulness, study of the scriptures, tranquillity of mind, contentment, silence, self-control, and purity of heart should be cultivated.[2]

Self-control is the foundation of moral life. It means restraint of the external cognitive and motor sense-organs and the mind. All desires should be directed to the Ātman, which is unruffled by them, and thus sublimated and purified. Mere conformity to the moral law in external conduct is not morality. The mind should be purged of evil passions. If the mind meditates on improper sense-objects and enjoys them within, external conformity to the moral law is hypocrisy. The cognitive senses should be withdrawn from improper objects. The motor senses should not be allowed to indulge in improper activities. The external sense-organs should be controlled by the mind (manas). The mind is always restless and unsteady. It can be controlled by steadfast practice and detachment. The mind should be fixed on the Ātman and steadied like an unflickering flame of light. Then it is cleansed of all unrighteous desires.[3] Duties should be performed with a pure mind free from immoral desires and passions.

---

[1] BG., ii, 38, 48, 56-57, 62-64, 70-71 ; iii, 34 & 37 , iv, 19, 21-22, 30 ; v, 3, 12, 18, 23 & 26 ; vi 2, 4, 14, 17-18, 24 ; vii, 13 ; xii, 13 ; xvi, 1-4 ; xviii, 23 & 35. [2] BG., xvii, 14-16.

[3] BG., ii, 70 ; iii, 6 & 7 ; iv, 26-27 ; vi, 18-19, 24-26, 34.

Persons are divided into four castes according to their qualities. Their vocations are appropriate to their qualities. The members of the society are divided into four castes according to their qualities and functions.[1] The Brāhmaṇas, the Kṣatriyas, the Vaiśyas, and the Śūdras ought to perform their specific duties (svadharma) in conformity with their native endowments (svabhāva). Their duties are appropriate to their station in society. Their specific duties, which accord with their innate psychical dispositions constitute their svadharma. They are prescribed for them. They are their natural duties. An individual should never give up his natural and specific duties, and try to perform those of another person. They do not fit in with his natural aptitudes. So they may be pernicious to him. They are not his natural duties, and therefore they will fail to fulfil his mission, and attune him with God. One's own specific duties ill-done are always better than another's specific duties well done. An individual attains fulfilment of his being by performing his own specific duties. Dedication of them to God leads to his liberation. He should always do the duties prescribed for him. If he does not perform them, he commits sin.[2]

An aspirant should dedicate all his actions to God. Whatever he does, whatever he eats, whatever he offers in a sacrifice, whatever gifts he makes, and whatever penance he undergoes, he should dedicate to Him. They bring him in complete union with God. Divine energy flows into him, and actuates all his actions. He becomes an instrument of divine action.[3]

The *Gītā* teaches the path of knowledge (jñānayoga). The lowest knowledge is the knowledge of one single effect, for instance, an image as God, who is the complete reality. The higher knowledge is the knowledge of different objects as separate from and unconnected with one another. This is popular unscientific knowledge. The highest knowledge is the

---

[1] BG., iv, 13.

[2] BG., iv, 33 ; iii, 8 & 35 ; vi, 1 ; xviii, 23, 41, 45-47.

[3] BG., ix, 27 ; xviii, 65.

knowledge of one undivided infinite spirit in the divided existences. One God is immanent in all finite existences. This is the philosophical knowledge of One in many.[1] He who, established in oneness, worships God in all beings, abides in Him, in whatever condition he lives. God is never lost to him, and he is never lost to God.[2] The individual soul with integral knowledge of God in all beings is united with Him, and is not lost in Him. The aspirant who sees God in all beings, sees them all as equal to himself. He sees them all alike, and treats them all alike. Equality of treatment follows from the mystic vision of God in all beings.[3] The integral knowledge of God in all beings is expressed in universal benevolence to all without discrimination. It is expressed in love and respect for all human beings.

Jñāna is knowledge of God derived from the scriptures. It is indirect knowledge. Vijñāna is direct and immediate knowledge, mystic vision, or intuition of God. Jñāna is intellectual knowledge. Vijñāna is intuition. Faith is a precondition of knowledge. It can be acquired from the wise, who have a vision of Truth, through humility and reverence, investigation, and service. One devoid of faith and knowledge, and tossed in doubt perishes. Knowledge dispels doubt, and destroys ignorance and sins. Intuition due to yoga dispels non-discrimination, and fixes the mind on God.[4]

Self-control is the indispensable condition of acquisition of knowledge. Desire and anger are great enemies. They obscure knowledge as smoke covers fire. Knowledge is obscured by insatiable desire. Unrighteous desires, which spring from rajas, hinder knowledge. They spring from the external senses, manas, and buddhi. So they must be restrained in order to destroy unrighteous desires, which destroy knowledge and intuition. The senses should be controlled by the mind ; the mind should be controlled by the intellect ; the intellect should be controlled by the self. The lower sentient self should be

---

[1] BG., SBG., xviii, 20 ; BG., SBG., xviii, 20 ; BG., RBG., xviii, 20.

[2] BG., vi, 29-31. [3] BG., vi 32.

[4] BG., iv, 33, 34, 41-42 ; v, 16-17 ; ii, 52-53.

controlled by the higher rational self. Unrighteous desires can be extirpated by the self by complete sense-restraint and control of mind and intellect. Without absolute self-control knowledge and intuition cannot be acquired.[1]

Constancy in the knowledge of the self and God and insight into the goal of the knowledge of reality constitute true knowledge. The supreme Brahman is the object of true knowledge, which leads to immortality. There is nothing purer than integral knowledge of God in the universe and the finite beings. It purges all works of impurities and purifies them. It enlightens devotion to God, and unites the devotee with Him for ever. It leads to eternal peace. The knower of Brahman abides in Brahman.[2]

The *Gītā* teaches the path of devotion (bhaktiyoga). Devotion is undivided, single-minded, unswerving love of God. It completely unites the individual self with God. There are four kinds of devotees—distressed, inquisitive, selfish and wise. The distressed devotee prays to God for deliverance from distress. The inquisitive devotee prays to Him for wealth and other objects of pleasure. The wise devotee knows the nature of God, and prays to Him for His sake. He has single-minded devotion to Him, and is always united with Him. He is united with God, and realizes the supreme goal of life. Those who throw themselves at the mercy of God, completely surrender themselves to Him, and take shelter in Him, cross the ocean of mayā, made of sattva, rajas, and tamas. They can transcend the guṇas, conquer the natural impulses and desires, and acquire transcendental perfection. Those who are deluded by ignorance, are puffed up by egoism, and do not take refuge in God. Those who are attached to God, and take shelter in Him, know Him entirely. Those who take refuge in Him, and make incessant efforts for release from old age and death, know the supreme Brahman. The devotee dedicates all his works to God, takes refuge in Him, and realizes the infinite and eternal

---

1 BG., iii, 37-43.

2 BG., iv, 37-39 ; v, 17, 19-20 ; vii, 16-17 ; xiii, 11-12.

status through His grace. He fixes his mind on God, dedicates all his works to Him, makes Him the only end of his life, and overcomes all difficulties through His grace. Complete surrender to God and taking refuge in Him are essential to the cult of devotion. The grace of God is its cardinal doctrine. He cannot be attained through the study of the Vedas, performance of sacrifices, charity, rituals and severe austerities. He can be known in His real nature by undivided devotion. The devotee dedicates all his works to God, cleanses his mind of attachment and aversion, makes Him the only end of his life, and attains Him.[1]

The devotee of God is always contented. His senses are controlled. He is of firm resolution. He is unaffected by joy and sorrow, fear and anxiety. He does not cause pain to others. He is not affected by praise and dispraise. He can endure hardships. He is devoid of attachment and aversion. He is pure in body and mind. His mind is always fixed on God. He has undivided and unswerving devotion to Him. He conquers his natural desires, and attains affinity with God. He has compassion and good-will for all creatures. He posseses perfect tranquillity and equanimity. He is efficient in the performance of duties for the sake of God. He is detached from all egoistic works. He gives up works leading to good and evil. His life is dedicated to God. His mind and intellect are fixed on Him. His heart burns with the love of God. His will is completely surrendered to Him. He knows Him in His real nature. He is suffused with the Divine Spirit. There is complete union of the loving soul with the beloved Lord. They abide in each other. God abides in the loving soul, and it abides in Him after death.[2]

God accepts whatever the pure-hearted devotee offers Him with devotion. He is impartial to all creatures. None is dear to Him. None is hated by Him. But those who worship Him with devotion abide in Him, and He abides in them. Even if a

---

[1] BG., vii, 1, 14-15, 20-23 & 29 ; ix, 25 32-33 ; xviii, 47-48, 53-55, 56, 58. [2] BG., xii, 13-20 ; xiv, 25, 26.

very vicious person worships Him with undivided mind, he ought to be regarded as a saint. He is of holy determination. He quickly becomes a saint, and attains eternal peace. The devotee of God never perishes. The path of devotion is open to all, irrespective of caste or sex. God takes all his devotees into His bosom. His all-embracing love knows no distinction. Only He demands unconditional surrender to Him and undivided and unflinching devotion and love for Him. God looks after the welfare of His devotees, who worship Him with single minded devotion, and who are always united with Him. He destroys their ignorance due to tamas, and illumines their minds with knowledge. He gives them knowledge which leads to attainment of Him.[1]

The threefold paths of works, knowledge, and devotion imply one another. The aspirant who dedicates all his works to God without attachment and thought of consequences, free from egoism, knows Him and loves Him. He who knows God in all beings and all beings in God, dedicates all his works to Him, and is devoted to Him. He who loves God with single-minded devotion, performs all works for His sake, knows Him in His real nature. The three paths emphasize the different aspects of spiritual discipline in accordance with the temperaments of the aspirants. An enlightened intellect, a pure heart, and a holy will go together. A man does not live in compartments. His knowledge, emotion, and will are purified together. His whole being turns towards God, and is transmuted by His living presence in his soul. He has mystic vision and consuming love of God. His will pulsates with Divine Will, and works as a perfect instrument of God.[2]

Liberation (mokṣa) is the supreme goal. It is the supreme abode. It is the highest status beyond good and evil. It is the permanent status. It is the eternal and indestructible status. It is the seat free from all troubles.[3] It is free from

[1] BG., ix, 22, 26-27, 29-31 ; x, 10-11.

[2] BG., iii, 19-20 & 30 ; iv, 10 & 19 ; v, 17 ; ix, 34 ; x, 9-10 ; xi. 54.

[3] BG., vi, 45 ; viii. 21 & 28 ; ix, 28 & 34 ; xv, 6 ; xviii, 56 & 62.

birth and death.[1] It is absolutely free from pain. It is supreme perfection.[2] It is transcendental perfection of the individual self, which is not affected by the natural desires due to sattva, rajas, and tamas. First rajas and tamas are overcome by sattva which actuates the aspirant's mind. Then the sattva also is transcended by him. He becomes absolutely pure, and rises above virtue and vice, good and evil.[3] Mokṣa is abiding in Brahman.[4] It is extinction of egoism in Brahman. It is not dissolution of integrity. The individual soul is an eternal part of God, and its integrity can never be lost. Mokṣa consists in being Brahman.[5] Being Brahman does not mean identity with Brahman. It means attainment of qualitative similarity with Brahman or God.[6] Mokṣa is attainment of the nature of God.[7] Mokṣa is transcendental state of immortality.[8] It is life eternal. It is the highest goal.[9] It is the attainment of God. It is inseparable union with Him.[10] God abides in the individual souls devoted to Him. They abide in Him.[11] Mokṣa is not extinction of the individual soul in God. It is affinity with Him in essential nature.

Mokṣa is supreme quietude and the highest bliss[12] which spring from union with God.[13] It is delight in the self, contentment with the self, self-satisfaction, and self-fulfilment. It is free from moral obligation ; no duties are to be performed in this highest state.[14] It is a state of non-action. The liberated person neither acts nor causes others to act. He may work for the good of humanity without moral obligation. But he

---

1 BG., ii, 51.

2 BG., viii, 15 ; xii, 10 ; xiv, 1 ; iii, 4, 20.

3 BG., SBG, ii, 45, 48.

4 BG., ii, 72 ; v, 19, 20.

5 BG., v, 24, 25, 26 ; vi, 27 ; xi, 26 ; xviii, 53, 54.

6 BG., xiv, 2.

7 BG., iv, 10 ; xiv, 19.

8 BG., xiv, 20, 21, 25.

9 BG., vii, 18.

10 BG., viii, 7, 8, 10, 16 ; ix, 28, 34 ; x, 10 ; xi, 55 ; xviii, 55, 65, 68.

11 Mayi te teṣu cāpy aham. BG., ix, 29.

12 BG., xviii, 62 ; v, 19.

13 BG., vi, 27, 28.

14 BG., iii, 17.

has no duties to perform. Mokṣa is perfect tranquillity and desirelessness. It is total destruction of egoism. It is living in God.[1] It is transmutation of the individual soul by God. It is transformation of human life into divine life. It is indissoluble union with God.

[1] BG., ii, 71 ; iii, 20 & 25 ; v, 13 & 19 ; vi, 15 & 31 ; xv, 20 ; xviii, 49.

CHAPTER IV

THE CĀRVĀKA PHILOSOPHY

Bṛhaspati is said to be the founder of the Cārvāka philosophy. A few aphorisms and verses are attributed to him. A consistent and complete account of the Cārvāka system is not found in any work written by a Cārvāka thinker. It has to be reconstructed from the exposition of the doctrine by its Buddhist, Jaina, and Hindu critics. Accounts of the Cārvāka system are found in *Sarvadaśanasaṁgraha* and *Ṣaḍdarśanasamuccaya*.

The Cārvākas regard perception as the only means of valid knowledge, and reject the validity of inference. They are free thinkers. They reject the authority of the Vedas and the supremacy of the Brāhmaṇas. They are naturalists and accidentalists, and reject final causes and universality of causation. They are materialists, positivists, atheists and hedonists. They identify the soul with the body, and deny pre-existence, future life, Law of Karma, heaven and hell, bondage and release, and the existence of God. They admit the reality of gross matter. They advocate egoistic hedonism in ethics.

ACCIDENTALISM AND NATURALISM

The *Śvetāśvatara Upaniṣad* refers to accidentalism (yadṛcchāvāda). Śaṁkara explains it as the doctrine of accidental production of effects. They are due to chance. Śaṅkarāṇanda explains it as the doctrine of accidental conjunction of two events. Production of an effect is its sudden appearance. Accidentalism is also called the doctrine of sudden emergence (ākasmikatvavāda). Amalānanda explains it as the doctrine that effects are produced at any time without depending on definite causes. An effect does not depend on any cause, but suddenly comes into being. Accidentalism believes in spontaneous generation of an event. It had antecedent non-existence and has subsequent existence at any time.

A thing by its nature comes into existence at a particular time without any cause. Its appearance is uncaused. Gotama explains accidentalism as the doctrine that an effect is produced without any cause like sharpness of thorns and the like.[1] The Cārvākas are accidentalists.

The *Śvetāśvatara Upaniṣad* mentions nature (svabhāva) as the cause of the world. Śaṁkara explains it as the natural powers inherent in different things, *e.g.*, heat of fire. Śaṅkarānanda explains it as the power of producing a particular effect inherent in a particular thing. Fire has a natural power of burning. Water has a natural power of flowing downward.[2] The *Śvetāśvatara Upaniṣad* mentions accidentalism and naturalism separately. Vācaspati and Amalānanda also mention them separately. Amalānanda explains nature as that which exists so long as the thing exists. Breathing exists so long as the living body exists. So it is the nature of the living body. Aśvaghoṣa explains naturalism (svabhāvavāda) as the doctrine that all effects are produced by their very nature, and that they cannot be produced voluntarily. Sharpness of thorns, and various colours of beasts and birds are due to their very nature. They are not produced by anybody. Fire is hot, water is cool, and air has cool touch. Who has made them various? Their differences are due to their inherent natures. Some entities are eternal beings, others are eternal non-beings. Different things have different characteristics. Their peculiarties are due to their different natures inherent in them.[3] The Cārvākas are naturalists.

They do not believe in causality and its universality. Causality is an imaginary relation between antecedents and consequents, which are perceived together on many occasions. Only antecedence of one event and consequence of another event are

---

[1] Śvet. Up., 1, 2 ; SB., i, 2 ; Dīpikā, i, 2 ; Kalpataru on SBS., ii, 1, 33 ; Haridāsa's commentary on NKS., Benares, 1913, p. 9 ; Bodhinī on NKS, Allahabad, 1922, pp. 8-9, NS., iv, 1, 22.

[2] i, 2 ; SB, i, 2 ; Dīpikā, i, 2.

[3] Bhāmtī on SBS., ii, 1, 33 ; Kalpataru, ii, 1, 33 ; SDS., Ch. I ; NKSP., 1, 5, p. 19.

perceived. Invariable antecedence of one event and invariable consequence of another event are never perceived. Perception is confined to particular instances. It can never apprehend all instances in the present, past, and future. The sequence of two events perceived in the past on numerous occasions may fail in future under unforeseen circumstances. No necessary connection can be known to exist between an antecedent and a consequent. Repeated observation of one event being followed by another produces an expectation in the mind that the antecedent will be followed by the consequent in future on all occasions. Conjunction of two events on numerous occasions produces an expectation that they will always be conjoined.[1] The Cārvākas do not belive in the production of an effect by a definite cause and in necessary and invariable connection between them.

THE DENIAL OF INFERENCE

The Cārvākas recognize perception as the only means of valid knowledge. They reject inference and testimony as means of valid knowledge. Perception is either external or internal. External perception is due to the intercourse of the five sense-organs with their objects. Internal perception depends upon external perception. Manas, the internal organ, can work upon the material supplied by external perception. It is not independent of the external sense-organs. The perceptible world is the only reality. The things perceived by the five sense-organs only are real. The other things beyond the reach of perception are not real. Heaven and hell are not real, because they are not perceived. The tactual organ perceives softness, hardness, heat, cold, roughness, smoothness and the like. The gustatory organ perceives sweet, sour, pungent, astringent and other tastes. The olfactory organ perceives agreeable and disagreeable odours. The visual organ perceives walls, jars, posts, men, beasts, earth, mountains and the like. The auditory organ perceives various kinds of sounds. The

---

[1] NM., pp. 119 & 122. Cp., Hume.

perceptible world is real. It is an aggregate of perceptible things and qualities.[1] The Cārvākas advocate naive realism and empiricism. They regard perception as the only means of valid knowledge.

The Cārvākas reject inference as a means of valid knowledge. The Nyāya believes in a five-membered inference (parārthānumāna) for demonstration to others as shown below :

1. The hill is fiery ;
2. Because it is smoky ;
3. Whatever is smoky is fiery, like a kitchen ;
4. The hill is smoky ;

∴ 5. The hill is fiery.

The first three or the last three members of the inference are enough for inference for oneself. Inference depends upon the universal concomitance (vyāpti) between the middle term and the major term. The middle term (*e.g.*, smoke) is the sign (liṅga), which indicates the existence of the major term (*e.g.*, fire). It must be found to exist in the minor term (pakṣa) or the subject of inference (*e.g.*, the hill). The middle term must be invariably accompanied by the major term. The invariable concomitance of the middle term or probans (sādhana) with the major term or probandum (sādhya) is called vyāpti. It is the ground of inference. This universal relation must be unconditional. It must not be vitiated by any conditions (upādhi). The vyāpti does not cause inference by virtue of its existence, but by virtue of its being known. But how can vyāpti, the ground of inference, be known ? It cannot be known by perception, external or internal. External perception arises from the intercourse of the sense-organs with their proper objects. There can be no intercourse of the sense-organs with all individuals, past, remote, and future. Vyāpti is the invariable concomitance of all cases of the middle term with all cases of the major term. But all instances of the middle term and the major term cannot be perceived with the external sense-organs. Nor can vyāpti be known by internal perception.

[1] SDS., Ch. I ; SDSM., (Ch. S. S., 1905), LV., p. 72.

Manas is not independent of the sense-organs in apprehending external objects. It can elaborate the material supplied by external perception. Knowledge of vyāpti is not the knowledge of invariable concomitance between the genus of the probans (*e.g.*, the genus of smoke) and the genus of the probandum (*e.g.*, the genus of fire) because class-characters are not known by perception. Even if they are known by it, the invariahle concomitance between their class-characters does not establish the invariable concomitance between the particular instance of the probans and the particular instance of the probandum. Nor can vyāpti be known by inference, since it would lead to infinite regress. One vyāpti is known by inference, which is based on another vyāpti. This vyāpti is known by another inference, and so on to infinity. Nor can vyāpti be known by testimony, because it is included in inference. If testimony is not included in inference, it depends upon the words of a reliable person. The words are the signs of their meanings. They denote definite objects. Comprehension of the meanings of words depends upon the knowledge of universal concomitance of words with their meanings. So vyapti cannot be known by testimony, which also depends on the knowledge of another universal concomitance. It involves argument in a circle. We cannot believe in another person's statement that there is invariable concomitance between the probans (*e.g.*, smoke) and the probandum (*e.g.*, fire) any more than we can believe in a dogmatic assertion of Manu. If vyāpti is known by testimony only, there can be no inference for oneself, in which the vyāpti is not pointed out by any other person. Nor can vyāpti be known by comparison (upamāna), because it depends upon the universal relation between words and objects signified by them. Comparison is the knowledge of an object (*e.g.*, a wild cow) indicated by the statement of a forester that 'a wild cow is like a cow'. So it depends upon invariable concomitance between words and their meanings. Hence vyāpti cannot be known by comparison. It is not known by perception, inference, testimony and comparison. Inference is not possible, since vyapti, which is its ground, cannot be known.

Vyāpti is the invariable concomitance between the probans and the probandum free from all conditions (upādhi). A condition is that which does not invariably accompany the probans, but which invariably accompanies the probandum. The absence of all conditions, which vitiate the inference, can never be known. All conditions can never be perceived. The absence of all conditions can never be known by non-perception. If they are known by inference, testimony or comparison, the same difficulty will arise. Further, the knowledge of a condition must precede the knowledge of its absence. The knowledge of invariable concomitance between the middle term and the major term depends upon the knowledge of the absence of the conditions. The knowledge of the absence of the conditions depends upon the knowledge of the conditions. The knowledge of invariable concomitance, again, depends upon the knowledge of the conditions. Thus there is reasoning in a circle. Vyāpti, the ground of inference, can never be known. Therefore inference is not possible.[1]

Vyāpti is said to depend on uniform and uncontradicted perception. It is an enumerative induction based on simple enumeration. It is based on observation of concomitance of the probans (*e.g.*, smoke) with the probandum (*e.g.*, fire) on numerous occasions. But even if they have accompanied each other on numerous occasions in the past, they may not accompany each other in future. The invariable concomitance between them observed so far may have exceptions in future. No necessary connection has been established between them. The invariable concomitance between smoke and fire in all times, in all places, and under all circumstances, can never be known. If all instances of smoke and fire in all times and in all places in the whole world be not perceived, the doubt will persist that smoke may exist without being accompained by fire. Even if their agreement in presence be known by observation of numerous instances of their co-presence, their agreement in absence can never be known by observation of numerous instances. It is impossible to observe that all cases

[1] SDS., Ch. I

of the absence of fire are the cases of the absence of smoke. Non-fiery things are all things in the world other than fire. The non-existence of smoke in all non-fiery things can never be perceived. Thus the universal concomitance of the middle term with the major term can never be known, since their agreement in presence and agreement in absence in the whole world in the past, the present and the future can never be observed. Their invariable concomitance cannot be known through their class-characters because there are no class-characters or universals. So vyāpti, the ground of inference, can never be known. It cannot exist between all particular instances of the probans and the probandum with their infinite peculiarities due to different times, places, and circumstances. Vyāpti can neither exist nor be known. So inference is not possible.[1] It can never be valid.

The Cārvākas do not believe in causation and its universality. There is no necessary connection between cause and effect. There is only accidental conjunction of an antecedent and a consequent. The two events are found together on numerous occasions, and therefore produce an expectation in the mind that they will always go together.[2] But there is no certainty about their co-presence. This accidental conjunction of an antecedent and a consequent cannot ensure vyāpti, which is the ground of inference.

Perception is the only means of valid knowledge. The objects, which are perceived, exist. Imperceptible entities do not exist. If imperceptible objects were supposed to exist, then even imaginary things would exist, and the poor would remove their poverty with imaginary wealth, the servants would become masters by imagining themselves to be rich, and all would fulfil their desires with imaginary objects. The distinction between perceptible things and imaginary things would be abolished. There would, therefore, be total collapse of practical life, which depends upon the distinction between

[1] SDS., Ch. I, NM., pp. 119-20.

[2] NM., p. 122. Cp. Hume.

perceptible and imaginary things.[1] Therefore imperceptible things do not exist. The perceptible world as an aggregate of perceptible things and qualities exists.

THE DENIAL OF THE VALIDITY OF THE VEDAS

The Cārvākas reject the validity of the Vedas, because they are vitiated by falsehood, contradiction and tautology.[2] They are incapable of being the means of valid knowledge. They are false because they make statements which are false. They are contradictory because they make statements, which are incompatible with one another. They are tautologous because they repeat the same statement several times. A Vedic text declares 'one who desires a son should perform the *Putreṣṭi* sacrifice. Yet we find that a son is not born after the sacrifice has been performed. The text is false. Another Vedic text declares 'one who desires to go to heaven should perform the *Agnihotra* oblation'. If a text is false with regard to perceptible results, one with regard to imperceptible results must be false. In regard to the *Agnihotra* oblation there are the Vedic injunctions: (1) 'The oblation should be offered before sun-rise'; (2) 'The oblation should be offered after sun-rise'; (3) 'The oblation should be offered before sunrise after the stars have become invisible'. These injunctions are incompatible with one another. So at least some of them must be false. There is a Vedic text 'one should repeat the first verse thrice and the last verse thrice'. But a tautological assertion is made by a demented person. There is want of agreement among some Vedic texts. There is incompatibility among others. There is contradiction among others. So the Vedas have no validity as a source of knowledge. The three Vedas are inventions of cheats, knaves and demons. Their injunctions are meaningless jargon. The rites and ceremonies enjoined by the Vedas are the inventions of the Brahmanas, who cheat the other castes to earn their livelihood. They are devoid of intelligence and manliness,

[1] SDSM., LV., pp. 72-73.

[2] NS., ii, 1, 56.

and cannot earn their living by honest means. The Vedas are mere incoherent ramblings of knaves. The religious rites enjoined by them are intended to be the means of their subsistence.[1] Religion is priestcraft. If a beast killed in a sacrifice goes to heaven, why does not the person sacrifice his own father? If the food offered at the Srāddha ceremony appease the hunger of the departed souls, what is the need of supplying travellers with food for the journey? Their hunger may as well be appeased by the offering of food at home. If the departed souls are gratified with the food offered on earth, why are not persons on the first floor gratified with the food offered on the ground floor? If the soul, issuing out of its body, goes to the next world, why does it not return to this world out of affection for the dear ones? When the body is burnt to ashes, how can it come back again? The soul is identical with the body. The rites are the inventions of impostors for their livelihood.[2]

MATERIALISM : THE REALITY OF THE WORLD

The Cārvākas admit the existence of the world. It is composed of four elements, earth, water, fire and air, which are perceived. The existence of ether (ākāśa) is denied, because it is not perceived. The world is composed of the four gross elements. There are no atoms of earth, water, fire and air, because they are not perceived. Some Cārvākas admit the existence of ether, and regard the world as composed of the five gross elements.[3] The body is a mere aggregate of the material elements. Some Cārvākas believe in the existence of atoms. The sense-organs are produced by the atomic arrangement of the elements. Consciousness is produced by the material elements even as intoxicating liquor is produced by molasses when it undergoes fermentation.[4] When they are destroyed, consciousness is destroyed. Consciousness is found

[1] NBh., NV., ii, 1, 56; NM., p. 273; SDS., Ch. I; UNC xvii, 63-64 & 67.

[2] SDS., Ch. I, SDSm., 83.

[3] TRD., on SDSm, p. 300; Jaina Sūtras, (S.B.E.), Part II, 1895, i, 1, 7-8, p. 236.

[4] SDS., Ch. I, SDSm, 84.

in the modifications of the unconscious material elements of the body, even as red colour is found in the combination of betel, arica nut, and lime.[1] Some Cārvākas hold that consciousness is manifested by the material elements constituting the body. Consciousness is produced or manifested by the material ingredients of the body, even as intoxicating liquor is produced or manifested by its unintoxicating material ingredients. But it is objected that consciousness is always produced by the intercourse of the sense-organs with their objects in the form of sensations of colour, smell, taste, and the like. How can conciousness, then, be said to be produced by the material elements? The Cārvāka replies that the sense-organs and objects are mere aggregates of earth, water, fire and air, which are objects of direct perception. An aggregate is a mere collection of the constituent elements. It has no existence apart from that of the elements. When there is invariable concomitance between two things, they are causally connected with each other, one being the material cause of the other, which is its effect. Lamp and light are always found together. Therefore lamp is the material cause of light. There is invariable concomitance between a body and consciousness. So the body is the material cause of consciousness.[2]

NO SOUL

The soul is the body endued with consciousness. There is no proof for the existence of the soul apart from the body. Consciousness is an emergent quality of the body, because it is not a quality of its ingredients. Life, voluntary actions, consciousness, recollection and the like, are said to belong to the self. But they are always perceived inside the body, and never outside it. The body is said to be the substratum of the self. The qualities of the self which is contained in the body, cannot be identical with those of the body, which is the substratum. Cognitions, feelings, and volitions are said to be the qualities of

[1] Sarvasiddhāntasaṃgraha.

[2] Jaina Sūtras, (S.B.E.), Part II, p. 342n; TS., Vol. I, p. 520; TSP., 1886, pp. 525-26.

the self, but they are erroneously identified with those of the body. This is wrong. Curds are contained in a vessel. But the coldness of curds is never regarded as the quality of the vessel. So the body is not the substratum of the self, but it is identical with the self. Cognition is a quality of the body, because it is perceived as identical with it like its complexion. 'I see'. It means that the body has visual sensation. Pleasure and pain are attributes of the body, because they produce changes in it.[1] If they were attributes of the soul, they could not produce changes in the body. Actions to attain an object of desire and avoid an objeet of aversion are perceived in the body. They are expressions of desire and aversion, which therefore must belong to the body. Desire and aversion arise from cognitions of their objects. So cognitions also must belong to the body.[2]

The gross (dhūrta) Cārvākas identify the soul with the body endued with consciousness. There is no soul distinct from the body, whose consciousness may exist in it, and which may go to heaven or attain liberation. The body itself is conscious. It is the soul. What exists, when another entity exists, and what does not exist, when that entity does not exist, is a property of that entity. Heat and light exist, when fire exists. They do not exist, when it does not exist. So heat and light are properties of fire. Likewise, consciousness in its various forms exists, when the body exists, and it does not exist, when the body does not exist. Further, consciousness is experienced in the body, and it is never experienced outside it. So it is a property of the body. It is not a property of the soul distinct from the body.[3]

The soul's identity with the body is proved by such common experiences as 'I am fat', 'I am lean', 'I am fair', 'I am black', 'I am going' etc. Fatness, leanness, fairness, blackness, movement etc., are qualities of the body. Therefore the

---

[1] Jaiṇa Sūtras. Part II, i, 1, 12; SBS., iii, 3, 53; PP., p. 147; UNC., xvii, 52; UNCT, xvii, 52 & 54.

[2] NBh., iii, 2, 37.

[3] SSBG., xvi; 11; SBS., iii, 3, 53; TS., 1864; RA., ii, 108, 10.

soul is identical with the body endued with consciousness.[1] This is the view of the gross Cārvākas.

But the cultured (suśikṣita) Cārvākas maintain that there is a soul apart the body, which is the permanent knower, recollector and enjoyer of all experiences, but that it is destroyed along with the body.[2] It does not survive the death of the body, and transmigrate into some other body. If there were a transmigrating soul, it would recollect the experiences of the past births, even as a person recollects his past experiences of this life during childhood and youth. So the soul persists till the destruction of the body.

Some Cārvākas identify the soul with the body on the strength of such common experiences as 'I am fat', 'I am lean' etc. Some identify it with the external sense-organs on the strength of such common experiences as 'I am blind', 'I am deaf' etc. Some identify it with life on the strength of such common experiences as 'I am hungry', 'I am thirsty' etc. Others identify it with manas, the internal organ, on the strength of such common experiences as 'I am resolved,' 'I am in doubt' etc. Resolution and doubt are functions of manas.[3]

NO PRE-EXISTENCE AND FUTURE LIFE

The Cārvākas deny pre-existence. The body is the cause of consciousness. There was no pre-existent soul before the birth of the present body. The manas in the past body cannot produce the manas in the present body, because they reside in different bodies. Or the last cognition in the past body cannot produce the first cognition in the present body, because the two cognitions belong to two different series. There can be no causal connection between them. Therefore there is no pre-existence.[4]

The Cārvākas deny future existence. Consciousness is generated by the four material elements—earth, water, fire and

---

[1] SDS., Ch. I, UNCT., xvii, 54.

[2] NM., p. 467. [3] Vedāntasāra (Jacob's edition), p. 26 ; S.B.S., i, I, 1.

[4] TS., 1861 ; TSP., 1861-62.

air. Conseiousness emerges from them, when they are transformed into the body. It is destroyed, when it disintegrates into its constituent elements. It does not persist after disintegration of the body. The Buddhists hold that the dying consciousness of an Arhat does not produce another body. The Cārvākas argue that the last cognition of an ordinary person tainted with afflictions cannot produce another body, even as the last cognition of an Arhat free from afflictions does not produce another body. Therefore there is no future life.[1]

It may be urged that there is potency of consciousness in the foetus, which is produced by the dying consciousness in the past body. Therefore consciousness cannot be said to spring from the body itself only. The Cārvākas argue that there can be no consciousness in the foetus, which is devoid of the sense-organs. Consciousness is produced by the intercourse of the sense-organs with objects. But in the foetus there are neither sense-organs nor objects. So there can be no consciousness as their effect. Just as in a state of swoon there is no consciousness, so there can be no consciousness in the foetus. It cannot exist in a latent form also in it, because there is no substratum in which it can exist. There is no soul in which it can exist. There is no series of cognitions in which it can exist. The body only can be the substratum of consciousness. The past body ceased to exist. So the dying consciousness could not exist in the form of a potency. Therefore there is no future birth or transmigration.[2]

It may be argued that dying consciousness in the past body produces consciousness in an intermediate body, which is produced immediately after death, in which it exists. But the Cārvākas argue that the intermediate body is not perceived and therefore non-existent, and further that consciousness in different bodies cannot belong to the same chain. The consciousness in the dead body and the consciousness in the intermediate body exist in different bodies. Therefore they cannot belong to the same chain, even as the consciousness of an

---

[1] TS., 1863 ; TSP., 1858-59 ; RA., ii, 108, 17.

[2] TS., 1868 ; TSP., 1864-67.

elephant cannot exist in the body of a horse. The cognitions belonging to the same 'chain' of cognitions cannot exist in different bodies. So the consciousness produced by the dying consciousness cannot exist either in the permanent soul, which is non-existent or in an intermediate body. Therefore there is no rebirth.[1]

The Cārvākas deny the reality of souls, virtue (dharma) and vice (adharma), merit (puṇya) and demerit (pāpa), actions (karma) and their fruits (phala).[2] They deny pre-existence, future life, transmigration, Law of Karma, heaven, hell, and liberation. They are not perceived; therefore they are nonexistent. There are no duties relating to the castes and the stages of life, which can produce fruits in the form of happiness and misery. The material world is perceived, and therefore existent. The variety in the world is natural.[3]

Heaven is non-existent. Heavenly happiness is a figment of the imagination. No sacrifices (*e.g.*, *Agniṣṭoma*) involving expenditure of a large amount of money and intense bodily pain should be performed, because they do not produce happiness in heaven, which is non-existent. Sacrifices, charity and other acts of piety are performed for profit, fame, self-glorification and acquiring power over other people for success in battles. They are motivated by self-interest and prudence. No actions are altruistic and disinterested.

Hell is non-existent. There is no other hell than bodily pain produced by thorns and the like. Mundane pain is hell. It ought to be avoided. God is non-existent. The king, who rules over the people, is the supreme Lord. He is perceived by all. The extinction of the body is liberation.[4] There is no supra-mundane non-temporal good. Actions cannot have visible and invisible effects. They have not two series of

[1] TSP., 1869-70.

[2] Jaina Sūtras, Part II, i, 1, 12, p. 237; Rājaśekhara Sūri, Saḍdarśana-Samuccaya, Benares, 158-60.

[3] SSBG., xvi, 8; SDS., Ch. I; SDSm., 80.

[4] SDS., Ch. I.

consequences, mundane and supra-mundane. They have no deferred effects, which will appear in the next world or in a future birth.

HEDONISM

The Cārvākas reject virtue and liberation as the ends of life. They regard sensual pleasure as the supreme end. It is produced by the intercourse of the sense-organs with their objects. Pleasure arising from the embrace of a woman and other objects of enjoyment is the highest good.[1] Sensual pleasure does not cease to be good because it is mixed with pain. Pleasure only should be enjoyed. Pain that inevitably accompanies pleasure should be avoided as far as possible. Unavoidable pain that accompanies pleasure should be experienced for the sake of pleasure. A person should separate bones and scales from the fish to enjoy the pleasure of eating it. He should not discard it because it has scales and bones. He should take the trouble of separating the husk from the paddy to enjoy the pleasure of eating fine rice. He should not discard rice because he has to separate it from the husk. It is foolish not to sow seeds of corns because there are wild animals, which may devour the corns. It is foolish not to cook food because beggars may pester us for a share of food. It is improper to discard pleasure through fear of pain that inevitably accompanies it. One who rejects sentient pleasure, which is actually experienced, for fear of its accompanying pain, is as stupid as a beast. It is foolish to think that pleasure should be relinquished, which is produced by the intercourse of the senses with their objects, because it is attended with pain.[2] Hedonistic calculus has to be employed. The maximum of sensual pleasure with the minimum of pain is the highest good. There is no supra-mundane happiness. Injunctions and prohibitions should be discarded.

---

1 BG., xvi, 11; SBG., xvi, 11; RA., ii, 108, 13; SDS., Ch. I, UNC., xvii, 69; UNC., UNCT., xvii, 69.

2 SDS., Ch. I; UNC., UNCT., xvii, 83.

Wealth is a means to pleasure. It ought to be acquired for the sake of pleasure. Pleasure is an intrinsic value. Wealth is an instrumental value. Pleasure and wealth both constitute the human good. This is the view of the authors of Nītiśāstra and Kāmaśāstra. It is accepted by the Cārvākas, who deny the other-worldly good. Virtue consists in the enjoyment of sensual pleasure due to the gratification of desires. It is the highest virtue. Supreme happiness springs from the gratification of desires.[1]

Rightness consists in conduciveness to sensual pleasure. Wrongness consists in conduciveness to bodily pain. An action, which gives excess of pleasure over pain, is right. An action, which gives excess of pain over pleasure, is wrong. The Cārvākas advocate gross egoistic hedonism. The Brāhmaṇas, who are consummate in the art of fraudulence, and who composed the Vedas, delude foolish people to think that certain articles of food and drink are permitted while others are forbidden. They enjoin bodily austerities on the gullible people in the vain expectation of happiness in heaven, which is never perceived. They produce in the ignorant people foolish other-worldy madness of religion.[2]

'Eat, drink, and be merry.' The past is dead and gone. It never returns. Youth never returns, make the most of the present youth. Bodily pleasures of this world are perceptible and certain. The pleasures of heaven attainable through the mortification of the body are imperceptible, uncertain and illusory. Pursuit of distant, uncertain, and supersensible heavenly happiness at the cost of certain, immediate, perceptible earthly pleasures is foolish. Penances are deprivations of pleasure. Religious rites are childish play. Enjoy all kinds of pleasures attainable from earthly objects.[3] After death nothing remains.

The body is a fortuitous combination of the material elements. There is no pre-existence nor future life nor rebirth.

---

[1] SDS., Ch. I; BG., xvi, 12; TRD., SDSm., 86.
[2] LV., 81.
[3] SDSm., 82; LV., 85; TRD., pp. 302 & 305; UNCT., xvii, 69.

The body is not due to the merits and demerits acquired in the past birth. Pleasure and pain are not due to the maturation of the merits and demerits of the past birth. They are due to the intercourse of the sense-organs with their objects. The fortuitous conjunction of the material elements is liable to destruction at any moment. The present is certain ; the past is gone ; the future is uncertain. So enjoy pleasures of the present moment disregarding the past and the future. Enjoy the maximum of bodily pleasure with the minimum of pain disregarding the next world [1] Thus the Cārvākas advocate gross egoistic hedonism.

But Vātsyāyana, the author of *Kāma Sūtra*, makes a distinction between higher pleasures and lower pleasures, rational pleasures and sensual pleasures. He regards happiness (kāma), wealth (artha), and virtue (dharma) as the supreme ends of life. Wealth and happiness should be pursued in harmony with virtue. They should not be cultivated at the sacrifice of one another. Harmony of happiness, wealth and virtue is the highest good. One who pursues the triple ends (trivarga) enjoys supreme happiness on earth and in heaven after death. Wealth is superior to happiness. Happiness is superior to virtue. When there is a conflict among them, the former should be pursued at the sacrifice of the latter, but the latter should not be pursued at the sacrifice of the former, since the former are superior to the latter. If there is no incompatibility among the three ends, all should be pursued. This is the best course. If they are not realizable at the same time owing to their incompatibility, then two of them should be attained. This is the middle course. If even the two ends cannot be realized simultaneously owing to their incompatibility, only one of them should be achieved. This is the worst course. Excessive charity is conducive to virtue ; but it exhausts wealth, and thwarts happiness. Excessive penance sacrifices happiness, undermines health, and destroys the capacity for earning wealth. Excessive hoarding of wealth sacrifices happiness and virtue. Excessive indulgence

[1] LV., 82.

in sexual pleasure sacrifices wealth and virtue. So these should be avoided. When an action is conducive to one end and repugnant to the others, its comparative merits and demerits should be considered. Wealth, happiness and virtue should be pursued in harmony with one another ; they should not be pursued as destructive of one another. There are sixty-four fine arts (kalā) which yield refined pleasure. Both sensual pleasure and refined pleasure should be pursued. So Vātsyāyana is an advocate of refined egoistic hedonism. The *Bhāgavata Purāṇa* refers to persons who pursue the three ends of wealth, happiness and virtue (traivargika), and are averse to God. *Jayamangalā* interprets Vātsyāyana's doctrine as refined egoistic hedonism, which regards wealth and virtue as means to happiness. Vātsyāyana regards happiness as the only intrinsic value, and wealth and virtue as instrumental and extrinsic values.[1]

---

[1] Kāmasūtra, (K.S.S.), 1929, i. I ; ii, 47, 49-50 ; Jayamaṅgalā, ii, 51 ; Bhāgavata, Kapila Gītā, viii, 18.

CHAPTER V

EARLY BUDDHISM

Buddhism will be discussed in two chapters under the heads: Early Buddhism and the Schools of Buddhism. In this chapter the main teachings of the Buddha will be discussed. In the next chapter the four main philosophical schools of the Vaibhāṣika, the Sautrāntika, the Yogācāra, and the Mādhyamika will be discussed.

The Upaniṣads teach that the eternal Ātman or Brahman alone is real. It is the transcendental reality, consciousness and bliss. The Buddha teaches the opposite truth. Everything is impermanent ; there is no permanent self. The self is an impermanent mind-body-complex. There is no God as creator of the world. It is self-existent and without beginning or end. It is unsubstantial and soulless. There are no permanent substances, but only impermanent qualities or phenomena. They are subject to the inexorable law of becoming or dependent origination. They are produced by their causes and conditions. The law of causation is subservient to the Moral Law or the Law of Karma.

Life is full of suffering. Suffering is due to craving or will-to-live. Will-to-live is due to ignorance. Ignorance is false knowledge of the impermanent as the permanent. It is delusion of individuality which is the root of the cycle of birth and death. It cannot be killed by philosophical knowledge. The Buddha adopts anti-metaphysical attitude. There are ten indeterminable questions which are insoluble. Philosophical wrangling is unavailing, for it generates self-conceit and scepticism. The Buddha's teachings aim at the total extinction of suffering and attainment of nirvāṇa here on earth. Nirvāṇa is the cooling of passions, perfect peace and perfect enlightenment. The way to nirvāṇa is the eightfold path of right conduct, concentration, and insight. The delusion of individuality or egoism should be extirpated. When egoism is eradicated, will-to-live or craving is destroyed. When craving is destroyed the round of birth and death is ended, and nirvaṇa is attained. Non-injury (ahiṃsa) in thought, word, and deed, is the corner-stone of moral life. Religion of animal sacrifice, ritualism, and ceremonialism is condemned. The Buddha teaches neither Being nor Non-Being, but Becoming. He teaches neither self-indulgence nor self-mortification, but the middle path of moderation—right view, right speech, and right conduct. He teaches the religion of ahiṃsā and self-help.

THE FOUR NOBLE TRUTHS

The whole of the teachings of the Buddha is summed in the four noble truths : (1) there is suffering ; (2) it has a cause ; (3) it can be stopped ; (4) there is way to stop it.

Siddhārtha or Gautama (567 B.C.—487 B.C.) was overwhelmed with grief at the sight of disease, old age, and death. He was overpowered by abundant misery in the world. He renounced the world to find out the remedy for suffering. He discovered its cause and the way to stop it. He found the way to peace on earth, and preached it to the world. He became enlightened or Buddha.

The first noble truth is suffering. 'Birth is attended with pain ; decay is painful ; disease is painful ; death is painful. Union with the unpleasant is painful, painful is separation from the pleasant ; any craving that is unsatisfied, that too is painful. In brief, the five aggregates which spring from attachment are painful. The cause and conditions of individuality are painful. The whole world is on fire ; where is the scope for merry-making.' Sensual pleasure is transitory and followed by pain. 'Sorrow comes from merriment. Fear comes from merriment.' The loss of objects of sensual pleasure leads to sorrow. The world is completely unsubstantial, void of being and perpetual becoming. It is afflicted with death and decay, and full of suffering. Therefore the wise do not grieve, knowing the nature of the world. Mere grieving is unavailing. When a house is on fire it must be extinguished by water. A man, who is pierced by the arrow of grief, must draw it out.[1]

The second noble truth is concerning the origin of suffering. Craving which generates the cycle of birth and death is the cause of suffering. It is threefold : (1) craving for sensual pleasures, (2) craving for being, and (3) craving for wealth and power ! 'Verily, it is craving, causing the renewal of existence, accompanied by sensual delight, seeking satisfaction now here, now there—that is to say, the craving for the gratification of passions, or the craving for a future life, or the craving for success in this present life. This is the noble truth concerning the origin of suffering. Craving or will-to-live is the cause of suffering. All pain arises from individuality which is due to ignorance (avidyā). Ignorance is due to will-to-live which is the root cause of suffering.

The third noble truth is the extinction of suffering. It is complete destruction of craving or will-to-live. Delusion of individuality, desire for mind-body-complex, and egoism are the causes of suffering.[2] Destruction of egoism and will-to-live leads to extinction of attachment, aversion, delusion, and suffering. Nibbāna is the extinction of desire, doubt, and sensual pleasures based on the reflection on nothingness. It is total extinction of suffering, decay, and death. It is grasping at nothing, and possessing nothing. It is perfect calm and tranquillity undisturbed by desires and passions. It is complete desirelessness. All desires for this life and the next life are extinguished in it. Non-grasping is attained by the knowledge of impermanence and voidness.[3] Nibbāna is insuperable, unchangeable, matchless[4].

The fourth noble truth is the way to the extinction of

---

[1] Foundation of the Kingdom of Righteousness, 5 ; DP., 146 & 213 ; Visuddhimagga, xvii ; Sallasutta, 581, 584, 591, 592 ; DP., 278.

[2] MN., i, 5, 4 ; Foundation of the Kingdom of Righteousness, 6.

[3] MN., i, 140 ; Foundation of the Kingdom of Righteousness, 7 ; Attadaṇḍasutta, 944-54; Upasīvamāṇavapucchā, 1069; Kappamāṇava-pucchā, 1093 ; Tuvaṭakasutta, 920 ; Vāseṭṭhasutta, 634, 643.

[4] Pārāyanasutta, 1148.

6

suffering. It is the eightfold path: (1) Right Belief, (2) Right Resolve, (3) Right Speech, (4) Right Conduct, (5) Right Livelihood, (6) Right Effort, (7) Right Mindfulness, and (8) Right Concentration. When the four noble truths are grasped, and craving or will-to-live is extirpated, there is no more birth. The four noble truths are suffering, the origin of suffering, the destruction of suffering, and the eightfold way of destruction of suffering. The eightfold path consists of moral conduct, concentration, and insight. It leads every aspirant to the complete extinction of suffering.[1]

IMPERMANENCE (ANITYAVĀDA)

Existence is impermanent. All things, mental and physical, are transitory. Impermanence is the inexorable law of all existence. There are five things which are inevitable. What is subject to old age must grow old. What is subject to sickness must be sick. What is subject to death must die. What is subject to decay must decay. What is liable to pass away must pass away.[2] These cannot be over-ruled by supra-mundane God or by any mundane agency.

There is neither being nor non-being but becoming. Everything is becoming, change, flux. It is a phenomenon enduring for a moment and then passing away. It is produced by preceding phenomena, and produces succeeding phenomena. The world is a succession of transient phenomena.[3] All substances are mere aggregates of impermanent qualities. They are devoid of permanence and substantiality. The world of Becoming is governed by the Law of Causality (pratītyasamutpāda). It is without beginning or end.

All individuals are series of momentary states of consciousness. There is no permanent soul behind the series of momentary psychoses. There is only succession of momentary mental processes. A past mental process has lived, but it neither lives, nor will it live. A future mental process will

[1] MN., i, 140; MPS., ii, 2; DP., 191 & 273; DN., ii, 9, 5; MN., iii, 4, 11. [2] AN., ii. [3] SN., ii, 17; iii, 135.

live, but it neither lives nor has it lived. A present mental process lives, but it has neither lived, nor will it live.[1] The life of an individual lasts only while a mental process lasts. An individual is a child, a boy, a youth, a man, an old man. He is a succession of changes with no identity in his body and mind. His body continuallly changes from one state to another. His mind also continually changes from one mental process to another. There is continuity but no identity. The changes are causally connected with one another. Each component state is determined by its antecedent conditions.

All existences are essenceless and impermanent.[2] This is the universal law. The physical world and the psychical world are devoid of self or essence. They are unsubstantial, transient, and void. All component things are impermanent, unstable, and disintegrating. They are without substance and temporary. Form is impermanent. The eye is impermanent. Cognition is impermanent. Qualities are impermanent. All conscious and unconscious components are impermanent. They come together, take individual forms, and break up. All components and composite things are impermanent. Animals, gods, men, plants, and inorganic things are all impermanent.[3]

CAUSALITY : DEPENDENT ORIGINATION (PRATĪTYASAMUTPĀDA)

'Whatever exists arises from causes and conditions, and is in every respect impermanent'.[4] All existence is impermanent becoming. All becoming is subject to the Law of Causation. Causation is dependent origination. "I will teach you the Dhamma," says the Buddha, "that being present, this becomes ; from the arising of that, this arises. That being absent, this does not become ; from the cessation of that, this ceases."[5] Pratītyasamutpāda means arising (samutpāda) after getting (pratītya). It means the production of an effect out of a complement of cause and conditions. When the cause and conditions disappear, the effect appears. The effect emerges from

---

[1] Visuddhimagga, Ch. viii. [2] Uragasutta, 5. [3] MPS., ii, 10.
[4] MPS. [5] MN., ii, 32, i, 1, 9 ; i, 1, 2 ; i, 3, 8.

the destruction of its cause and conditions. It follows necessarily from the doctrine of impermanence. The cause and the effect both are impermanent. The cause vanishes ; then the effect emerges. The cause cannot continue in the effect. They cannot be synchronous. The cause must be prior to the effect. The effect arises from an aggregate of cause and conditions. A seed is the cause of a plant. But soil, water, light, and manure are its conditions. A distinction is made between a cause (hetu) and a condition (pratyaya). The former is the principal cause, and the latter is a concomitant condition. One cause cannot produce an effect. It must be aided by other concomitant conditions to produce it. An effect arises from a cause and a complement of co-operating conditions.

The law of causality or dependent origination applies to the past, the present, and the future. It is without beginning or end. It is applicable to all composite entities, mental and physical. It is not applicable to non-composite entities like space, since they are eternal. The cause transmits its causal energy to its effect. Causation is development or transformation. There is no immanent causality, in which a substance appears to be manifested as its qualities. Causation is dynamic, not static. Static view of causation is erroneous. The world-process is an active self-development.

The doctrine of dependent origination is opposed to accidentalism which denies the law of causality, and regards an event as an accidental happening. It is opposed to naturalism which ascribes an effect to its own inherent nature. It is opposed to fatalism which regards all things, good and bad, as pre-determined by Fate. It is opposed to supernaturalism. An event is not generated by the supernatural intervention of God. It is produced by an antecedent natural event. Accidentalism and naturalism were advocated by materialists. Supernaturalism was advocated by Brāhmanism. All existences, physical and psychical, according to Buddhism, are subject to the law of universal casuation. All that exist, are produced. Existence is becoming or production. Nothing is uncaused and eternal.

All are in the grip of causality.[1] There is no transcendental cause or first cause of the world.

THE WHEEL OF EXISTENCE (BHAVACAKRA)

The Buddha says, "He who knows dependent origination, knows dharma. He who knows dharma, knows dependent origination. The five aggregates of material form or body, feeling, perception, disposition, and self-consciousness originate from their causes and conditions".[1] An empirical individual is an aggregate of five groups of body, feeling, perception, disposition, and self-consciousness. The mind-body-complex is produced by ailments. 'Ailment is caused by craving. Craving is caused by feeling. Feeling is caused by contact. Contact is caused by five sense-organs and mind. They are caused by mind and body. They are caused by consciousness. Consciousness is caused by dispositions. Dispositions are caused by ignorance'[2] The twelve members in the chain of causation are stated thus : 'By reason of ignorance dispositions; by reason of dispositions consciousness ; by reason of consciousness mind-body-complex ; by reason of mind-body-complex contact ; by reason of contact feeling ; by reason of feeling craving ; by reason of craving grasping ; by reason of grasping becoming ; by reason of becoming birth ; by reason of birth old age and death and grief.'[3] By the destruction of ignorance, the dispositions are destroyed ; by the destruction of the dispositions, consciousness is destroyed ; by the destruction of consciousness, mind-body-complex is destroyed ; by the destruction of mind-body-complex, the six sense-organs are destroyed ; by the destruction of the six sense-organs, contact is destroyed ; by the destruction of contact, feeling is destroyed ; by the destruction of feeling, craving is destroyed ; by the destruction of craving grasping is destroyed ; by the destruction of grasping, becoming or will-to-be-born is destroyed ; by the destruction of becoming, birth is destroyed ; by the destruction of

[1] MN., i, 3, 8. [2] MN., i, 4, 8.
[3] DN., ii, 55ff. ; MN., i, 4, 8 ; AN., i, 177.

birth, old age and death and grief are destroyed. Thus (1) ignorance, (2) dispositions, (3) consciousness, (4) mind-body-complex, (5) six sense-organs, (6) contact, (7) feeling, (8) craving, (9) grasping, (10) becoming, (11) birth, and (12) old age and death are the twelve links in the chain of causation.

Ignorance (avidyā) is the root cause of suffering. It gives rise to birth and death. It is the false sense of individuality. It is knowledge of the impermanent series of mental and bodily processes as the permanent self. It generates dispositions. The dispositions of ignorance in the past life produce an inital consciousness in the embryo. This consciousness generates the new mind-body-complex. If consciousness did not enter into the womb, mind-body-complex would not arise in the womb.[1] The mind-body-complex produces the five external sense-organs and the internal organ or mind. They produce sense-contact with sensible objects or qualities. The sense-contact produces feeling due to sense-experience. The feeling produces craving. Craving produces grasping or clinging to objects. Grasping produces becoming or will-to-be-born. The will-to-be-born in the present life produces rebirth in the future life. Rebirth produces old age and death. The cycle of birth and death moves in this manner. The twelve links in the chain of causation are: (1) ignorance, and (2) dispositions belonging to the past life; (3) initial consciousness, (4) mind-body-complex, (5) six sense-organs, (6) contact, (7) feeling, (8) craving, (9) grasping, and (10) will-to-be-born belonging to the present life; (11) rebirth (12) old age and death belonging to the future life. Thus the twelve links extend to three lives, the past, the present, and the future.[2]

THE DOCTRINE OF NO-SELF (ANĀTMAVĀDA, NAIRATMYAVĀDA)

"Look upon the world," says the Buddha, "as void, having destroyed the view of oneself as really existing, so one may

Mahānidānasutta, ii, 2; MPS., ii, 6.

AK., iii, 20; ADS., viii, 3.

overcome death ; the king of death will not see him who thus regards the world."[1] The doctrine of No-self means two things : (1) the self is an aggregate of impermanent mental and bodily processes ; (2) the world is unsubstantial and void ; it is an aggregate of impermanent qualities devoid of substances.

The self is impermanent. It is an aggregate. It is a series of successive mental and bodily processes which are impermanent. There is no permanent self. The self is a stream of cognitions (vijñānasantāna). There is a continuity of constantly changing mental processes in it. Sometimes they are intermittent. So the self is sometimes compared to sleep and dream. The course of organic life is compared to dreamless sleep, in which consciousness is evoked by external stimuli, which is compared to dream. Conscious processes break in upon the stream of the subconscious processes. The self is an aggregate of body and four kinds of mental processes, feeling, perception, disposition, and self-consciousness. The body is not permanent. It is an aggregate of vital organs and their functions. It is an aggregate of changing qualities.

The Buddha is emphatic on the denial of the permanent self in the following texts. 'The world is empty of a self, or of anything of the nature of a self. The five seats of the five senses, and the mind, and the feeling that is related to mind : all these are void of a self or of anything that is self-like.' "When one says 'I', he refers either to all the aggregates combined or any one of them and deludes himself that that was 'I'. One could not say that the body was 'I' or that the feeling was 'I' or any other aggregate was 'I'. There is nowhere to be found in the aggregates 'I am' ". 'Since neither self nor aught belonging to self can really and truely exist, the view that holds that this I who am world, who am self, shall hereafter live permanent, persisting, eternal, unchanging, abide eternally ; is not this utterly and entirely a foolish doctrine ?' 'This self of mine is the knower, the enjoyer of the fruits of my good and bad actions : it is eternal and

[1] Mogharājamāṇavapucchā, 1118.

immutable, it will continue for infinite time: this thought is very childish'. 'The body is not-self; feeling is not-self; perception is not-self; disposition is not-self; self-consciousness is not-self. All dharmas are not-self'.[1] The five aggregates are impermanent. They are not the so-called permanent self. Belief in permanent self is a wrong view of the self (satkāyadṛṣṭi).[2] The last text does not mean that the self is eternal and transcendental. It clearly means that the five aggregates constitute the not-self. There is no permanent self. The self is an empirical aggregate. There is no self beyond them.[3] This is the unique and original teaching of the Buddha.

Once the Buddha kept silent on the existence or non-existence of the self. The wandering monk Vacchagotta said, "Is there the ego?" Buddha was silent. Again he said, "Is there not the ego?" Still Buddha kept silent. When the monk departed, the Buddha said to Ānanda that the affirmative answer would lead to eternalism (śāśvatavāda), and that the negative answer would lead to annihilationism (ucchedavāda). But both are wrong views. The ego or self is not eternal; nor is the self non-existent. If the self is non-existent, there can be no transmigration and reaping of the fruits of actions. The truth lies in the middle of the two extreme views. The phenomenal or empirical self exists.

The doctrine of No-self means also that the world is unsubstantial and soulless. All external things are aggregates of changing qualities. There is no permanent substance apart from impermanent qualities. The permanent identical subs tance is a fiction of the imagination. All forms of existence, material and psychical, are impermanent and soulless. They are subject to the inexorable law of becoming.[4]

KARMA

Brāhmanism makes too much of the permanent self. Buddhism puts impermanent dharma in its place. It stresses

[1] SN., iv, 54 ; iii, 130 ; MN., Sutta Piṭaka, i, 138 ; i, 1, 2 ; i, 4, 5.
[2] MN., iii, 1, 9. [3] Cp. Hume.
[4] AN., i, 286 ; SN., ii, 25 ; DN., ii, 198.

energy, effort, endeavour. Will is the man. Will is the man in action. The Buddha says, "Very pure will we become in deed, word, thought. We will neither exalt the self nor despise the other man."[1] 'Rouse thyself by thyself, examine thyself by thyself; thus self-protected and attentive wilt thou live happily, O Bhikṣu!' 'For self is the lord of self, self is the refuge of self; therefore curb thyself as the merchant curbs a good horse.'[2] 'Self is the lord of self, who else could be the lord? With self well subdued, a man finds a lord such as few can find'.[3] Thus Buddhism emphasizes the freedom of the will. Is it consistent with the empirical conception of the self as the collection of the five aggregates? In the empirical self some part may be regarded as dominant and others as dominated by it. The will is the dominant element in the individual. Sometimes the intellect is compared to the guardian of a city, who, standing at the cross roads, controls the traffic.[4] Intellect is will. Intellect is the theoretical aspect of will. Will is the practical aspect of intellect.

Buddhism lays great stress on the freedom of the will, moral effort, energy, and activity. We are the masters of our own destiny. We make ourselves pure by our own free good volitions and actions. We make ourselves impure by our own free bad volitions and actions. Man is the architect of his own destiny. He can work out his own salvation by free moral actions. 'Work out your salvation with diligence.'[5] 'Beings are owners of their actions, heirs of their actions; their actions are their matrix; their actions are their lineage, and by their actions are they established.'[6] Man is what he has made himself. His past actions are the determinant of what he is, as his present actions of what he will be. Man is the builder of his own character and destiny. The past self is wrought up into the present self. The future self is a projection of the present self. The self never is, but is always

---

[1] Mahā-assapura-sutta. [2] DP., xxv, 379-80.
[3] DP., xii, 160. [4] MP., p. 62. [5] DP., xii, 165. [6] MN., iii, 203.

becoming, evolving, to experience the fruits of its free actions in future lives. The self is not static, but fluid.

Our happiness is the result of our past good deeds. Our misery is the result of our past evil deeds. Our past good and evil actions in this life or the past life have brought about our present weal or woe. They are not caused by capricious Deity, the decree of an inexorable Fate, or blind chance. They are the inevitable results of our past free actions.[1] 'Whatever a man does through his body, speech, or thought, are to be called his own for they follow him when he departs from his life like a shadow that leaves him not.'[2] Action (karma) is the connecting link between one life of an individual and another.

TRANSMIGRATION

Action (karma) leads to rebirth. There is no transmigration of a permanent soul from one body to another. There is mere continuity of the same series of mental processes. The last mental act ceases, and transmits its causal energy to the first mental act in a new embryonic germ-cell. The last conscious act dies away, another conscious act arises in a new organism. This is called rebirth. There is neither absolute identity nor absolute difference. The fruit arises in the same psychical series in which the act was done. The child is trained ; the youth reaps its fruits. The child and the youth are neither absolutely indentical with, nor absolutely different from, each other. In rebirth there is 'transmigration of character' in the words of Rhys Davids, from the last conscious act in one life to the first conscious act in the next life. Moral responsibility attaches to the same series.[3] The Buddha says, "To say 'one acts, another reaps the fruits of those acts', is not true. And to say 'one and the same both acts and is affected by the result' is not true. I teach a Midway between both extremes, to wit, the doctrine of Becoming by way of Cause."[4]

---

[1] AN. [2] SN.

[3] Visuddhimagga ; *The Hibbert Lectures*, 1881, pp. 91-92.

[4] SN., ii, 20.

The Buddha explains transmigration by the example of the flame of a lamp. A lamp burns throughout the night. But the flame of light does not remain the same throughout. There is a continuous change in the flame ; there is no identity in the flame but continuity in the different flames of light of the lamp. Similarly, the last flash of consciousness of a person in one life goes out, and it kindles the first flash of consciousness in the embryo in the next life. The psychical series continues uninterrupted, but its members continually change, appearing for a moment and then disappearing.

The Buddha explains transmigration by the example of the different modifications of milk. Milk is modified into curds ; curds are transformed into butter ; butter is converted into melted butter. The same series continues, but its members continue changing. There is unbroken continuity in the series but no permanent identity. Similarly, the psychic series continues in transmigration, but there is no identity of the permanent soul. The first conscious act in the new birth is produced by the last conscious act in the preceding birth, which is modified by the accumulated dispositions of all the psychoses of this birth. Thus there is transmigration of the impermanent psychical series, though there is no identity of the permanent soul.[1]

THE LAW OF KARMA (DHAMMA)

All phenomena, mental and material, are subject to the the law of dependent origination, which is subservient to the Law of Karma. The Buddha says, "By Karma the world exists, by Karma mankind exists ; beings are bound by Karma as the linch-pin of a chariot keeps the wheel on."[2] The variety in the world is due to Karma. The whole world with all its variety is the combined effect of the acts of all beings.[3] The Law of Karma governs all physical and mental phenomena. It is the supreme, impersonal law of moral causation to which physical causation is subservient.

---

[1] MP. [2] Kathāvatthu, E. T., p. 315.
[3] E.R.E., Vol. vii, p. 674.

Sometimes the Law of Karma is called 'Dhamma' which applies to the chain of causation, the wheel of existence, progress of an individnal to enlightenment, and whatever is righteous or good. Sometimes 'Dhamma' means cause or ground, truth or reality, Good immanent in the world, and Moral Law immanent in it.

ATHEISM

The whole universe of phenomena is subject to the law of dependent origination. Material and mental phenomena, plants, animals, men, and gods are subject to origin and destruction. They are determined by their causes and conditions. The Buddha ridicules the conception of God, who is said to be the eternal and immutable creator of the universe which is temporary, perishing and mutable. Brahmā, the first created being, may think owing to delusion that he is the omniscient and omnipotent Creator of the universe, past, present, and fnture. But, in fact, he is as subject to origin and destruction as any other effect.[1] None among the Brāhmaṇans versed in the three Vedas has actually seen Brahmā, the Creator, but everybody has heard it from others, who, in their turn, have heard it from others, and so on. Tradition is no argument for the existence of God. The blind are misled by the blind.[2]

The variety in the world is due to karma. All things are transformations. There is neither creation nor destruction. The world has neither beginning nor end. All phenomena in the world are caused by other phenomena, which, in their turn are caused by other phenomena. Nothing is self-caused and uncaused. Every phenomenon in the universe, physical, organic, or mental, is determined by a number of conditions. The whole universe is a chain of causally connected phenomena, which is not determined by anything beyond the series of phenomena. The contingent world is not determined by a nessessary Being which transcends the phenomena. There is no intervention of a supernatural Being or God in the phenomenal

[1] DN., Pāthikasutta. iii, 1. [2] Tevijja-sutta, DN., i, 12-15.

series of causes and effects. Phenomena are not determined by their nature; nor are they predetermined by Fate; nor are they produced by accident. All phenomena are determined by the totality of antecedent conditions on which they are dependent. Physical causation, organic causation, mental causation, and moral causation are parts of the Dhamma or the Law. There is no room for God. Without beginning and end is this world-process. There is no First Cause. We experience no absolute beginning and absolute end. Dependent origination is without beginning or end. It has no Lord presiding over it. It has no Soul to inspire it. The cosmological argument for the existence of God is invalid.

It may be urged that every law has a law-giver. The law of dependent origination must be supervised by God. But this is wrong. The causal order is there. It is not intended or designed by God. It is the observed causal sequence of phenomenea in the world. It is not caused or designed by God. There is no purpose in nature. There is no conscious agent who adapts the phenomena of the world with a purpose. The teleological argument for the existence of God is invalid.

NON-MATERIALISM

Though the Buddha denies the existence of the permanent self and God or the Creator of the world, he is not a materialist. He does not reduce the mental processes to the material elements. He does not identify the soul with the body. Nor does he regard it as quite distinct from the body. Is the soul identical with, or distinct from, the body? It is an indeterminable question. If it is quite distinct from the body and eternal and immutable, it cannot be purified by moral conduct, concentration, and insight. This conception is subversive of morality. If, on the other hand, it is identical with the body, it is dissolved with the body, and cannot reap the fruits of its actions.[1] The Buddha believes in the Law of Karma, future life, and transmigration. He believes in

[1] AN., iii.

the complete extinction of suffering and achievement of perfect peace here on earth. Thus he rejects materialism and accepts spiritualistic outlook on life. He refutes the materialism of Pāyāsi who holds that there is neither future life, nor reaping of fruits of good and bad actions, nor rebirth of souls.[1]

Early Buddhism admits the reality of four permanent elements—earth, water, fire, and air which undergo changes. It sometimes includes ether in the elements, and sometimes treats it as a derivative. The external stimuli interact upon the sense-organs and produce consciousness. Early Buddhism believes in naive realism and causal theory of knowledge.

ANTI-METAPHYSICAL ATTITUDE

The Buddha solves only one practical problem : how to exterminate suffering. Philosophical wrangling does not solve this problem. Idle theoretical speculation does not soothe the agony of suffering. It generates self-conceit, arrogance, and scepticism. It does not draw out the arrow of agony. So the Buddha discourages philosophizing and emphasizes self-control, thoughtfulness, energy, activity, moral conduct, purity of mind, good-will, love, compassion, and peace. He says, "The Tathāgata is free from all theories." He rules out ten questions relating to the world, the relation of the soul and the body, and the condition after the attainment of nirvāṇa. These are indeterminable. They are as follows : (1) Is the world eternal ? (2) Is it non-eternal ? (3) Is it finite ? (4) Is it infinite ? (5) Is the soul identical with the body ? (6) Is it distinct from the body ? (7) Does the Tathāgata exist after death ? (8) Does he not exist after death ? (9) Does he both exist and not exist after death ? (10) Does he neither exist nor not-exist after death ?[2] These questions are fruitless for moral life. They are not conducive to detachment, peace, enlightenment, and nirvāṇa. So these metaphysical puzzles are ruled out. Wrangling over philosophical views is useless. Self-command is the way to perfection. The whole world is

---

[1] DN., ii, 10.

[2] DN., i, 187 ; MN., ii, 2, 3.

on fire. Extinguish the fire. Do not waste a moment in useless disputes. Overcome the torrent of passions and attain perfect peace and calm. Philosophical views lead to disputes; they do not lead to purity, but in the realization of nirvāṇa there is no dispute.[1]

RATIONALISM

The Buddha teaches rationalism to his disciples and condemns faith in tradition and authority. He advises them to trust in their own reason and believe in what commends itself to their reason. Authority is no source of truth. Its validity must be tested by reason and personal experience. Tradition is like a number of blind men leading one another. The first man does not see; neither does the middle one see; nor does the last one see. Tradition is an exceedingly weak argument. The Buddha makes a distinction between the mere reception of truth and the knowledge of truth which involves rational conviction.[2] 'One must not accept my Dharma from reverence, but first test it as gold is tested by fire.' 'You must trust to yourselves. You can take nothing from me. You must be righteous through your own efforts. You must depend on yourselves for the extinction of all suffering.'[3] 'Three things shine before the world and cannot be hidden. They are the moon, the sun, and the truth proclaimed by the Tathāgata. There is no secrecy about them.' 'He who questions the validity of reason by arguments contradicts himself.[4]' Instruction should be understood by reason and confirmed by personal experience.

The intelligible parts of the Buddha's doctrine should be understood by reason. But its unintelligible depths which are understood by the Buddha only should be accepted on faith. The nature of the action of Karma is not comprehensible. It has to be accepted on faith; there is no discredit in it.[5] Faith

---

[1] Khaggavisāṇasutta, 21; Dhaniyasutta, 4; Mahāviyūhasutta, 895 & 910. [2] AN., Kālāmasutta. [3] MN., i, 265.

[4] Jātakamāla, the story of Mahābodhi.

[5] AN., iv, 82; ii; 80; DN., iii, 138.

is an indispensable preliminary to entrance upon the path. It is a prelude to right knowledge. Faith in the complete enlightenment of the Buddha and his word leads to correct knowledge and conviction. The teaching of the Buddha saves the faithful, but destroys the faithless.[1] Thus faith in the authority of the Buddha, independent reflection or individual reason, and individual insight and intuition have their place in the life of an aspirant. Intuition is the consummation of moral discipline.

ETHICS

The Buddha rejects both Being and Non-Being and believes in Becoming. He adopts the metaphysical mean. He rejects both self-indulgence and self-mortification, and enjoins the ethics of moderation. He preaches the doctrine of the ethical mean. He lays down the eightfold path.

(1) Right view or belief consists in right knowledge of the four noble truths, which leads to nirvāṇa. It is not theoretical speculation which does not lead to dispassion, self-control, and peace.

(2) Right resolve consists in the determination to uproot attachment to sensual pleasure, ill-will towards others, and desire to do harm to them. Mere right knowledge of right and wrong does not help the aspirant reach his goal. It must be expressed in right resolve to do what is right and desist from doing what is wrong. Right resolve is aspiration towards renunciation, benevolence, and compassion.

(3) Right speech is an outward expression of right resolve. It consists in abstention from lying, slander, abuse, harsh words and frivolous talk. One should speak what is right, not what is unrighteous. One should speak what is pleasing, not what is unpleasing. One should speak what is true, not what is false. One should speak well. One should speak what does not pain oneself nor hurt others. Truth should be

[1] AN., iii, 21 ; Sumaṅgalavilāsinī, p. 31

in harmony with right and good. The just stand firm in what is true, in what is good, and in what is right.[1]

(4) Right conduct consists in abstention from the destruction of life, theft, sex-indulgence, lying, drinking intoxicating liquor, eating between meals, attending social entertainments, the use of unguents and ornaments, the use of luxurious beds, and the handling of gold and silver, which are binding upon the monks.[2] The first five duties are binding on lay men. They should observe chastity in their married life. These sins should neither be committed, nor caused to be committed, nor approved. Lay men have specific duties. The duties of parents, children, teachers, pupils, husbands, wives, masters and servants are laid down. Liberality, courtesy, kindness, and unselfishness should be cultivated by all.[3]

(5) Right livelihood consists in earning living by honest means. Trades in arms, animals, flesh, liquor, and poison are forbidden. Earning livelihood by under-weights, fraudulence, bribery, ingratitude, crookedness, mutilation, persecution, confinement, robbery, and plunder is forbidden.[4]

(6) Right effort consists in constant vigilance, effort, and activity which are necessary for self-control, sense-restraint, arrest of evil thoughts, stimulation of good thoughts, and concentration of the mind on universal good-will. Restless mind is not conducive to good thoughts, good emotions, and good conduct. Right effort consists in suppressing evil states and stimulating good states.

(7) Right mindfulness consists in recollection of the impurity of the body, the nature of feeling, pleasure, pain, and neutral feeling, the nature of mind endowed with greed, hatred, and delusion, the nature of dharmas, five aggregates, sense-organs, sensible objects, means to enlightenment, and four noble truths. Right mindfulness is an indispensable prerequisite of right concentration.[5]

---

[1] Subhāsitasutta. [2] Dhammikasutta.

[3] Sigālovāda Sutta ; Tevijja Sutta, ii.

[4] AN., 5 ; DN., p. 269. [5] Mahasatipittana Sutta, ii, 9.

(8) Right concentration consists of four meditations. It is the crown of the eightfold path. The first Jhāna is a state of joy born of seclusion, accompanied by reflection and investigation, in which sensuality is destroyed. The second Jhāna is a state of joy born of deep tranquillity, without reflection or investigation, which are suppressed; in it thought is tranquilized, and intuition predominates. The third Jhāna is a state of neutral consciousness in which all passions are destroyed. The fourth Jhāna is a state of complete tranquillity and self-possession in which joy and sorrow are destroyed.[1] Buddhism stresses right conduct, right concentration and right insight. Right insight purges the mind of lust, becoming, and ignorance.[2]

Buddhism emphasizes purity of the inner life. Mere pure external conduct does not suffice. The mind must be purged of all impurities. Greed, hatred, delusion, anger, envy, and jealousy must be rooted out. All passions that ruffle the calm of the mind must be extirpated. The mind must be sanctified.[3]

The Buddhist morality is altruistic. Though nirvāṇa is the highest good of an individual, it is realized through universal good-will and love. We should pervade the whole world with love, pity, sympathy, and equanimity. Universal love, compassion for the distressed, joy for the virtuous, and indifference to the vicious are enjoined. Love generates compassion, joy, and indifference, and is consequently higher than these. So the Buddhist ethics is altruistic.

The ethics of non-injury (ahiṁsā) is the keynote of Buddhism. Hatred should be conquered by love; harm should be conquered by good. Evil recoils upon one who offends a harmless, pure, and innocent person. Hatred generates hatred. A harsh word excites a harsh word. A blow incites a blow. Patience is the highest virtue.[5] We should be tolerant with the intolerant, mild with fault-finders, free from passion among

---

[1] Mahāsudassana Sutta, ii. [2] Dhammacakkapavattana Sutta, 4.
[3] Āmagandha Sutta, 241, 248; Munisutta, 211; Hemavatasutta, 173.
[4] Mahāsudassana Sutta, ii 8-11.
[5] Dhammika Sutta, 393; DP., 223, 5, 197.

the passionate. We should not offend any one by body, word, or thought. A man is not just, if he carries a matter by violence ; he is just, if he leads others, not by violence, but by law and equity.[1] Non-injury, in thought, word, and deed, love, good-will, patience, endurance, and self-purification constitute the Buddhist morality.

Buddhist morality is the mean between self-indulgence and self-mortification. Gautama underwent severe penances and self-torture which proved fruitless. Self-torture emaciates the body and fills the mind with evil thoughts. If the fires of lust, hatred, and delusion are not quenched, self-mortification can lead us nowhere. Craving for pleasure springs from egoism. When egoism is rooted out, craving for worldly and heavenly pleasures is quenched. On the other hand, self-indulgence is enervating and degrading. But to satisfy hunger and thirst, to keep the body in good health, to protect it from heat and cold, to save it from fatigue, to cover it comfortably and decently are necessary to keep the mind strong and pure. This is the Middle Path that avoids both extremes. The Dharma spurns both pursuit of pleasures and self-mortification. It aims at purity of heart, purity of conduct, equanimity, peace, and enlightenment.

NIRVĀṆA

The third noble truth is the extinction of suffering. It is nirvāṇa which has been described as extinction, as a state of happiness, as an inconceivable state, or as a changeless state.[2] It is the highest good.

(1) Nirvāṇa literally means 'cooled' or 'extinguished'. Passions are compared to 'fires'. Passionlessness is the 'cooling' of the fires. Nirvāṇa is the extinction of greed, hate, anger, and delusion which are called 'fires' and of the impurities, sensuality, will-to-be-born, and ignorance. It is the extinction of becoming or rebirth. It is the complete extinction of passions and consequent suffering. It is not extinction of

[1] DP., 405, 406, 391, 256-57. [2] E. R. E., Vol. IX, pp. 376-79.

existence or annihilation. It is deliverance from the sense of individuality. It is not inaction. It is compatible with active intellectual and social life. It is not renunciation of actions, but the purging of all actions of attachment, aversion, and delusion. It is renunciation of all the bases of rebirth, destruction of craving, will-to-live, and becoming.[1] In it the physical form remains, but the will-to-live is completely destroyed.

Nirvāṇa is a state of enlightenment which removes all ignorance. It is a state of perfect equanimity which removes attachment, aversion, and delusion. It is a state of stainless purity and good-will. It is a state of perfect self-possession and unconditioned freedom. It is a state of perfect peace. The liberated person has complete insight, complete passionlessness, unruffled calm, perfect self-control, tranquil mind, tranquil words, and tranquil deeds. He is devoid of egoism or the sense of individuatity, since his mental grasping, ignorance, and craving, which produce a new individual of five aggregates, are completely destroyed. There is extinction of individual existence.[2]

(2) In the Pāli texts nirvāṇa has sometimes been described as a state of bliss. The liberated person is free from evil desire ; he has a steadfast mind ; he has perfect knowledge of the noble truths ; he has obtained the fruit of the fourth path, and is immersed in ambrosia, and enjoys nirvāṇa.[3] The *Dhammapada* describes nirvāṇa as a state of bliss, crown of happiness, perfect peace, free from greed, hate, and delusion. The Arhats, meditative, persevering, ever energetic, attain to nirvāṇa, the highest bliss. Nirvāṇa is happiness or holiness which is distinct from pleasure. Pleasure is an empirical feeling which is transitory and therefore painful. Nirvāṇa is the blissful end.[4]

---

[1] Upasīvamāṇavapucchā, 1073-75, AN., iii, 359 ; ii, 118 ; MN., i, 304 ; ix ; SN., i, 134 ; iv, 251, 261 & 371 ; v, 8 ; DN., iii, 130.

[2] Sāmaññaphala-sutta, Dialogues, 1, p. 84 ; DP., 90, 94-96 ; Parinibbānasutta, J. R. A. S., Vol. viii, p. 238.

[3] Ratanasutta, vii, 14.

[4] DP., 202-03, 23 ; AN., v, 414.

(3) Nirvāṇa is deep, immeasurable, unfathomable as the ocean. It is inconceivable. It is an existence that is beyond reason and conception.[1] It is a non-empirical, ineffable state.

(4) The Buddha says, "There is something that is not born, not produced, not created, not compounded. Were there not something not born, there would be no possible exit for what is born'[2] Nirvāṇa is neiher annihilation nor eternal existence. It is an ineffable state of perfect wisdom, perfect peace, and perfect self-command.

Two kinds of nirvāṇa are described: (1) Sa-upādi-śeṣa-nirvāṇa and (2) Anupādi-śeṣa-nirvāṇa. The former means nirvāṇa with residual vital conditions or with the remainder of mental grasping, the cause of rebirth. The latter means nirvāna without residual vital conditions or without remainder of mental grasping. Parinirvāṇa literally means 'completely gone out.' One who is perfectly disciplined and calmed is said to be parinibbuta or perfected.[3]

RELIGION

Buddhism is a religion without God. It believes in transmigration and future life, though it does not believe in the permanent self. It emphasizes the Law of Karma or moral causation. It aims at the extinction of suffering by extinguishing craving or will-to-live. It aims at the purity of the heart, and the purity of external conduct. It rejects rites, ceremonies, sacrifices, and penances. It stresses the ethics of ahimsa, non-injury in thought, word, and deed. It enjoins extinction of egoism and ignorance. It aims at nirvāna on earth. Nirvāṇa is insight, peace, and selfless will. Buddhism is a religion of self-help. Libertion does not depend on the grace of God. It has to be wrought by one's own moral efforts.

Buddhism admits the reality of Brahmā, Indra, and other gods. But it regards them as subject to ignorance and passions

---

[1] SN., iv. 374; iii, 109; Alaguddūpamāsutta.

[2] Udāna, viii, 3; Itivuttaka, 43.

[3] Mrs. Rhys Davids, *Buddhism*, pp. 191-92.

birth and death. The Buddha is greater than gods. Buddhism believes in heaven and hell. Righteous actions lead to heaven. Vicious actions lead to hell. But nirvāṇa can be attained by complete extinction of desires for earthly or heavenly happiness. It is above heaven. The Buddha emphasizes the Law (Dhamma). He turns the wheel of the Law (Dhammacakka) which is irresistible. He lays the foundation of the kingdom of righteousness.[1]

Buddhism is catholic. It is open to all nations, races, castes, and creeds. The Buddha says, "Know, Vasettha, that (from time to time) a Tathāgata is born in the world, a fully Enlightened One, blessed and worthy, abounding in wisdom and goodness, happy, with knowledge of the world, unsurpassed as a guide to erring mortals, a teacher of gods and men, a Blessed Buddha. The truth does he proclaim both in its letter and spirit, lovely in its origin, lovely in its progress, lovely in its consummation: the higher life doth he make known, in all its purity and in all its perfectness."[2] "Subdue thy doubt about me, have faith in me, O Brāhmaṇa, difficult to obtain is the sight of the Buddha repeatedly."[3] Faith and reason both lead to salvation. Rational conviction, self-control and moral purity are essential to it. The Buddha does not grant liberation to men, but he teaches them the way to achieve liberation.

Buddhism is a rational religion. There is no secret in it. The Buddha does not make any distinction between esoteric and exoteric doctrines. He denounces all secret doctrines. Secrecy belongs to false doctrines and occult priestcraft. The religion of the Buddha shines by its light.[4] Buddhism is a religion of individual freedom and endeavour. The Buddha says, "O Ānanda, be ye lamps unto yourselves. Be ye refuges to yourselves. Hold fast to the Dhamma as a lamp. Hold fast as a refuge to the Dhamma. Look not for refuge to any one beside yourselves."

---

[1] Selasūtta, 554; Dhammacakkapavattanasutta.

[2] Tevijja Sutta; Buddhist Suttas, SBE., xi, pp. 186-87

[3] Selasutta, 559.

[4] AN; MPS.

Buddhism is a missionary religion. The gift of the Dhamma is the greatest of all gifts. "Go ye, O Bhikṣus, for the benefit of the many, for the welfare of mankind, out of compassion for the world. Preach the doctrine which is glorious in the beginning, glorious in the middle, and glorious in the end, in the spirit as well as in the letter. Proclaim to them a life of holiness. They will understand the doctrine and accept it." These words of the Master inspired his followers to spread the religion far and wide.[1]

In course of time a schism took place between the Hīnayāna and the Mahāyāna which differ in many respects. First, the Hīnayāna is conservative, whereas the Mahāyāna is catholic and progressive. Secondly, the former regards the Buddha as a historical person, while the latter regards the Buddha as the transcendental, eternal, Absolute, who saves all beings through his triple body. Dharmakāya, Law-body, or the Absolute, is immanent in all beings ; Sambhogakāya or Bliss-body, is God; Nirmāṇakāya or Transformation-body is a Divine Incarnation, the historical Buddha. Thirdly, the former believes in one Buddha, while the latter believes in an infinite number of Bodhisattvas who take a vow to attain perfection and liberate all sentient creatures. Fourthly, the former aims at the attainment of Arhathood or individual liberation, while the latter aims at the attainment of Bodhisattvahood to liberate all. The former aims at individual liberation, while the latter aims at universal liberation. Fifthly, the former believes that one person attained Buddhahood, while the latter believes that all may attain it because they have the Buddha-nature as their essence. Sixthly, the former opposes nirvaṇa to saṁsāra, while the latter believes that nirvāṇa is achieved through saṁsāra. The former emphasizes the monk's life of renunciation, while latter emphasizes the life of a house-holder. Seventhly, the former regards nirvāṇa as cessation of transmigration, while the latter regards it as transcendental experience of Sūnyatā. Eighthly, the former is realistic, whereas the latter is idealistic.

[1] *The Essence of Buddhism*, Ch. II.

The former believes in the reality of the external world and individual minds or streams of consciousness, while the latter believes in One Mind, Ālayavijñāna, which constructs the individual minds and the imaginary world. Lastly, the former believes in the impermanence of all phenomena, physical and mental, while the latter believes in the Sūnyatā or Emptiness, which is the noumenon behind the impermanent phenomena. Phenomena are the manifestations of the noumenon.[1] Hīnayāna Buddhism is called Southern Buddhism, because it flourished in Ceylon and Burma. Mahāyāna Buddhism is called Northern Buddhism, because it prevailed in Tibet, China and Japan.

The Hīnayāna and the Mahāyāna resemble each other in the following respects. First, enlightenment is the goal which is achieved by the removal of ignorance. Secondly, the world is without beginning or end, and all phenomena are subject to the law of causation. Thirdly, all is impermanent becoming devoid of being. Fourthly, there is no permanent self, but only an impermanent stream of consciousness. Fifthly, the Law of Karma governs moral phenomena. Sixthly, transmigration is due to karma; actions in empirical life produce karma. Seventhly, ignorance is the root cause of suffering and transmigration. Lastly, the Eightfold Noble Path destroys ignorance.[2]

The Hīnayāna is called Theravāda or Sthaviravāda, or the doctrine of the Elders. It is the small vehicle which can carry a few to salvation. The Mahāyāna is the great vehicle which is large enough to carry all to salvation. Universal salvation is the kernel of the Mahāyāna religion. Idealistic monism is its philosophical foundation.

---

[1] B.L. Suzukī, *Mahayana Buddhism*, 1948, pp. 14-15.

[2] Ibid, pp. 17-18.

CHAPTER VI

THE SCHOOLS OF BUDDHISM

The Hīnayāna Buddhism gave rise to two main schools, the Vaibhāṣikas and the Sautrāntikas. The Mahāyāna Buddhism gave rise to two main schools, the Yogācārs and the Mādhyamikas. The Vaibhāṣikas and the Sautrāntikas sprang out of the Sarvāstivādins. The Sarvāstivādins hold that everything exists. The elements, mental and physical, are real. The Vaibhāṣikas hold that external objects are real and perceptible. The Sautrāntikas hold that external objects are real and inferable. The Yogācāras hold that external objects are non-existent, and are mere cognitions. The Mādhyamikas deny the absolute reality of external objects and subjective cognitions, and regard them as essenceless, but they affirm the reality of the Śūnya. The Śūnya is not void or nothing, but predicateless Absolute. The Vaibhāṣikas and the Sautrāntikas are realists. The Yogācāras are idealists (vijñāvādins). The Mādhyamikas are Śūnyavādins. They are not Nihilists but phenomenalists and Absolutists.

THE VAIBHĀṢIKA

The Vaibhāṣikas recognize the reality of mind and matter. Mind is composed of elements. Matter is composed of elements. There is no permanent soul. Existence is either transient or eternal. Space and Nirvāṇa are eternal. The elements of matter, mind, and forces are transient and phenomenal. The elements of phenomenal reality are past, present, and future. The past and the future elements are as real as the present ones. There are only four elements—earth, water, fire, and air. Earth is hard ; water is cool ; fire is warm ; and air is mobile. Ether is not recognized as an element. External objects are aggregates of atoms. An atom has six sides. It is invisible, inaudible, intangible, untastable, and indivisible. Atoms cannot penetrate one another. The perceptible atom is an aggregate of imperceptible atoms.[1]

[1] AKV., ii, 22 ; Introduction, p. xx.

The Vaibhāṣikas criticize the Sautrāntika doctrine of inferability of external objects from their cognitions as contradictory language. If all external objects are inferred from their cognitions, then there are no objects of perception. There is therefore no observation of invariable concomitance (vyāpti) of the middle term with the major term, which is the ground of inference. Hence inference is not possible. This contradicts all actual experience. The Sautrāntika position is not tenable. There are two kinds of objects. Some are apprehended by indeterminate perception, and others are apprehended by determinate perception. Indeterminate perception is free from conceptual construction. Determinate perception is perception wrought up by conceptual construction, which is therefore not valid. The validity of inference can be tested by fruitful action. The Vaibhāṣikas recognize the reality of external objects, and regard them as objects of perception.[1] They advocate direct realism.

THE SAUTRĀNTIKA

The Sautrāntikas are representationists. They advocate indirect realism. They recognize the reality of external objects. But they regard them as objects of inference on the following grounds. (1) External objects produce their cognitions, and imprint their forms on them. The forms of cognitions are similar to those of external objects. When cognitions come into being, their objects have ceased to be. Present cognitions cannot perceive past objects. Therefore external objects are inferred from their cognitions. The forms of objects are inferred from those of their cognitions. Cognitions are copies or representations of their objects, which are their archetypes. (2) Cognitions are formless and homogeneous. They are diversified by their objects. Different external objects produce different cognitions, and impress their forms on them, which are perceived. The internal forms of cognitions are representtations of the external forms of objects. We infer external objects from their cognitions. If there were no objects, there

[1] SDS., ii, 55-56.

would be no diversity of cognitions. (3) The object-cognitions appear at certain times only, while the subject-cognitions are uniformly present. The Ālayavijñāna is of the nature of subject-cognitions. But the object-cognitions are of the nature of 'this'. The stream of subject-cognitions is uniformly present. But the object-cognitions appear and disappear at certain times. Therefore they must be produced by external objects. (4) External objects exist and produce perceptions of colours, sounds, tastes, odours, temperatures, pressures, pleasure and pain. Perceptions are produced by external objects, which are their basic condition.[1]

The Sautrāntika criticizes the Yogācāra Vijñānavāda in the following manner. The Yogācāra denies the reality of external objects, and reduces them to cognitions. This position is not tenable. (1) The Yogācāra argues that an external object (*e.g.*, blue) and its cognition (*e.g.*, cognition of blue) are invariably perceived at the same time. The external object can never be perceived apart from its cognition. So the object is identical with its cognition. But this argument is wrong. A cognition and its object are necessarily experienced together. The cognition is the experience of its object. But this does not prove that cognition is identical with its object.[2] (2) An object is different from its cognition. The cognition is internal or subjective, while the object is external or objective. The object is independent of its cognition. They cannot always be referred to the same time and the same space. Therefore they are different from each other. (3) If an object were a mere cognition, it would be apprehended as 'I', and not as 'this', But a blue object is never perceived as '*I* am blue', but as '*this* is blue'. It is 'given' or not-self. It is not a mode of the self. (4) The Yogācāra argues that an internal cognition appears to be an external object owing to illusion, though it does not exist. The distinction of cognition and object is illusory. Cognition alone is real. The Sautrāntika urges that if external objects are absolutely non-existent, an internal cognition cannot

[1] SDS., ii, 45-47. [2] J. N. Sinha, *Indian Realism*, p. 30.

appear to be an external object. It would be as absurd as to say 'Vasubandhu looks like the son of a barren mother.' The illusion of externality presupposes valid knowledge of externality somewhere. The sense of externality can never be produced by mere subjective cognitions. (5) The Yogācāra argues that an object is identical with its cognition because the appearance of distinction between them is illusory. Again, the distinction between cognition and its object is illusory because they are, in reality, identical with each other. The argument involves vicious circle. (6) External objects are actually perceived by us. We undoubtedly perceive them, and react to them. We pass over the cognitions of external objects. So it is wrong to argue that internal cognitions appear to be external objects. (7) The Yogācāra argues that a variety of object-cognitions is due to the variety subconscious impressions (vāsanā) within the stream of cognitions. The instinctive roots of ignorance imbedded in the subject-cognitions from beginningless time generate a variety of perceptions of sense-data. The beginningless uninterrupted stream of impressions of difference is the cause of the variety of perceptions of difference.[1] But subconscious impressions can produce recollections only. They cannot produce perceptions of external objects. The series of subject-cognitions in an individual is always present with impressions deposited in it. The subject-cognitions with the impressions being always present, the perceptions of objects would be always present. But in fact, object-cognitions appear at certain times and disappear at other times. Therefore they cannot be generated by impressions.[2]

THE DOCTRINE OF MOMENTARINESS

The Sautrāntika developed the doctrine of impermanence into the ontological doctrine of momentariness. All schools of later Buddhism believed in the doctrine of momentariness. The Vaibhāṣikas believed in the reality of the eternal elements and their momentary mainfestations. The Sautrāntikas rejected

[1] SDS., ii, 39. [2] SDS., ii, 48.

the eternal elements and advanced the following arguments to prove the momentariness of all existence. Whatever is existent is momentary like a mass of clouds. Existence consists in causal efficiency or production of effects. Causes produce their effects either simultaneously or successively. Only momentary causes can produce their effects either simultaneously or successively. Permament entities are not capable of simultaneous or successive production of effects, since the alternatives cannot be proved. When a permanent entity produces its effects at the present time, it has capacity of producing its effects in the past and the future. If it has the capacity, it must produce past and future effects in the present moment, since what is capable of producing an effect at a particular time must produce it at that time. If it has not the capacity, it can never produce past and future effects, for what does not produce an effect at a particular time is not capable of producing it at that time. A piece of stone can never produce a sprout. A permanent entity does not produce past and future effects at the present moment. So it is not capable of producing them at present. Capacity of production and production of effects must go together. Causal efficiency cannot exist without production.

If a permanent entity is said to produce its effects in succession with the help of concomitant conditions, the latter render an aid to the permanent entity or not. If they do not, they are unnecessary, and can be dispensed with. If they do, the aid is different or non-different from the permanent entity. If the aid is different from it, then the adventitious aid should be regarded as the cause, and not the permanent entity, because wherever the adventitious aid is present the effect is present and wherever it is absent the effect is absent. If it is urged that a permanent entity by its very nature produces its effect only when the concomitant conditions co-operate with it, then it can never be separated from the concomitant conditions in order to produce its effect because it can never be divested of its nature. Further, the aid (atiśaya) produced by the concomitant conditions produces another aid or not. If it produces another aid, it will require other concomitant conditions, and so on, and lead to infinite regress. If the aid does not produce another aid, then the permanent entity in co-operation with the concomitant conditions acquires an aid and produces an effect. If the permanent entity does not require the help of concomitant conditions, then the aid will always be present, and will always produce the effect. But it is contradicted by experience. Then the aid, though it depends on the permanent entity for the production of the effect, produces the effect independently of the permanent cause (*e.g.*, a seed) or as dependent on it. On the first alternative, the seed would not be the cause of a sprout. On the second alternative, there will be infinite regress. The aid will produce another aid in the permanent cause, and so on to infinity. If the aid is non-different from the permanent cause, then the so-called permanent cause ceases to be permanent, since it was devoid of aid before and it now acquires aid. A permanent cause is incapable of causal efficiency.

A permanent entity cannot produce its effect simultaneously. If it produces its effect simultaneously, it persists after production of its effect or does not. If it persists in future, then it will continue to produce the effect which it has already produced. But the effect which has already been produced need not be produced again. If the permanent cause does not persist after production of its effect, then it cannot be said to be permanent. Those entities are different from each other, which are endued with contradictory attributes like heat and cold.

It cannot be argued that a permanent entity has capacity to produce its effect at one time, and has no capacity to produce it at another time, since what produces an effect at a particular time possesses the capacity to produce it at that time, and what is incapable of producing an effect at a particular time does not produce it at that time. A stone can never produce a sprout at any time. Thus a permanent entity cannot produce its effect simultaneously or in succession. Only momentary entities are capable of causal efficiency. All existence is momentary, and consists in causal efficiency, which exists in momentary entities only. Permanent entities are incapable of causal efficiency.[1]

We attribute identity to a continuous series of similar momentary things. Identity is an illusion produced by similarity and continuity of a series of momentary entities. There is no identity or permanence of an external thing. The flame of a lamp appears to be the same, though it changes from moment to moment. The stream of water appears to be the same, though it changes every moment. All objects of the world are undergowing destruction every moment. But they appear to persist owing to illusion.[2]

The Sautrāntikas laid stress on the conception of the self as a series of momentary cognitions. There is no permanent self behind the continuous series of momentary cognitions. The preceding cognition leaves an impression which modifies the succeeding cognition. There is transference of impression from one cognition to another, which accounts for memory. Memory does not require a permanent self which is the substratum of impressions, and which recollects an object perceived in the past. A future member of the same series of cognitions remembers a past momentary object perceived by a past member of the same series. Recognition is a collection of perception and recollection. It does not presuppose a permanent self; nor does it apprehend a permanent object such as '*this* is *that* Devadatta'. The stream of momentary cognitions can account for memory and recognition both. Thus neither the self nor an external object is permanent and identical. Both are series of momentary entities.

THE YOGĀCĀRA VIJÑĀNAVĀDA

The Yogācāras do not recognize the reality of external objects. They reduce them to cognitions. Therefore they are called Vijñānavādins. The *Laṅkāvatārasūtra* regards external objects as unreal and false like dreams, day-dreams, illusions, and hallucinations. It regards them as transformations of the

[1] SDS., ii, 12-23 [2] Cf. Hume.

Ālayavijñāna, the cosmic mind, which is stirred up into the waves of mental modes. Object-cognitions are the modes of the cosmic mind. There are no objects apart from cognitions. When they are examined by the intellect, they are found to be indefinable and essenceless. Object-cognitions arise from the Ālayavijñāna or receptacle consciousness.[1]

Vasubandhu (500 A.D.) recognizes the reality of consciousness (vijñapti) only, which manifests non-existent objects like the illusory hair and double moon. Objects are self-creations of thought. The cosmic mind transforms itself, on the one hand, into different subjects, and into different objects, on the other. All dharmas, subjective and objective, are fruitions of the seeds or dispositions conserved in the Ālayavijñāna. One pure consciousness (vijñaptimātra) is the ground of the all-conserving mind. There are no external objects. They are transformations of the Ālayavijñāna into the form of knowable objects.[2]

Dharmakīrti reduces the so-called external objects to sense-data which are nothing but sensations. When we perceive an object, we perceive only its colour, length, breadth, thickness, weight, smoothness and the like sensible qualities. We can never perceive or infer the object apart from the sense-data. We never perceive it as an external object. We perceive only colours, sounds, tastes, smells, temperatures and pressures through the sense-organs. These sense-cognitions are elaborated by the mind (manas) which reflects upon them. Neither the mind nor the sense-organs perceive the external objects. They are nothing but cognitions. When we examine them thoroughly, they disappear into nothingness ; only their cognitions are left behind. Feelings of pleasure and pain are felt by the mind as subjective mental modes. Even the so-called external objects are forms of cognitions. The apprehending cognition and the apperehended object, subject and object, are the forms of cognition which is one and self-identical. The distinction of

[1] LS., pp. 44, 46-47, 95-96, 116.

[2] Viṁśikā, Triṁśikā ; Sthirāmati's Bhāṣya.

subject and object falls within cognition. The object is not outside cognition. Subject does not exist without object. Object does not exist without subject. They are inseparable from each other. They are forms or aspects of the same cognition. Cognition is the only reality. It is in its essential nature formless. But it assumes the forms of subject and object, cognitional forms and object-forms. Object-cognitions are due to the revival of the subconscious impressions deposited in the mind. They are not excited by external objects. Vijñāna is the only reality. The inner and the outer are its forms. The distinction of subject and object is illusory. We stick to it for the practical purposes of our life. The distinction is not real.[1]

Śāntarakṣita gives the following arguments for the non-existence of external objects. (1) A cognition is self-aware. Its essential nature consists in self-awareness. It reveals itself and does not apprehend an external object. It is not apprehended by the permanent self, since it is non-existent. There is neither a permanent self nor an external object. There is only a series of self-aware cognitions. Cognitions manifest themselves as cognitions of blue, yellow, and the like, though there are no external objects. (2) An object is said to be unconscious and material, while a cognition is conscious and mental. There is no relation of identity or causation between them. A cognition is not identical with an object. It cannot generate an object; nor can an object generate a cognition. Hence a cognition can never apprehend an external object. (3) Illusory cognitions arise owing to ignorance (avidyā), which reveal unreal forms, though there are no external objects corresponding to them. (4) The Sautrāntika holds that an external object imprints its form on the cognition produced by it so that there is similarity between the form of the cognition and the form of the object. If there is complete similarity between them, the cognition is unconscious like its object. If there is partial similarity between them, the part of the

[1] Pramāṇavārtika, iii, 202, 209, 212, 213, 215, 217, 219, 253-55; *Indian Realism*, pp. 17-18.

cognition which is not similar to its object apprehends it. Therefore every cognition can apprehend every object. Further, a uniform cognition apprehends a multiform object. An unextended cognition apprehends an extended object. Therefore there is no correspondence between a cognition and its object. Even a cognition with a form cannot apprehend an external object. (5) A cognition with a different form cannot apprehend an external object. If a cognition with one form apprehended an object with another form, then every cognition would apprehend every object, and a particular cognition would not be necessary to apprehend a particular object. Therefore a cognition can never apprehend an external object either with or without its form or with another form. So the cognition alone is the only reality. (6) The cognized object ('blue') and the cognition (of 'blue') are invariably apprehended together. Therefore they are identical with each other. (7) There is no evidence for the existence of an external object. It cannot be perceived by a formless cognition or by a cognition with a form. A formless cognition cannot come into relation with an object. A cognition invested with the form of an object perceives its own form. It does not perceive the form of its object. So an external object cannot be perceived. Nor can it be inferred from the harmony between it and the cognition. Harmony means either the capacity for leading to the attainment of the object or the capacity for fruitful actions. The external object can never be attained because it is non-existent. Cognitions can lead to fruitful actions. Therefore an external object cannot be inferred. (8) Even if an external object exists, it must be perceived either as an aggregate of atoms or as a complex whole made of atoms or as a gross object not composed of atoms. The first alternative is not tenable. Atoms are imperceptible. Only gross objects are perceived. Atoms connot produce the cognition of a gross object. The second alternative cannot be maintained. The external object cannot be a complex whole made of atoms. The relation between the whole and the parts cannot be explained. The hird alternative also is untenable. The external object cannot be a gross object not composed of atoms. Its nature cannot be defined. So it does not exist. It is an unreal appearance. Hence cognition is the only reality.'

All the arguments mentioned above tend to show that the Yogācāra Vijñānavāda was subjective idealism. But some Vijñānavādins believed in Tathatā, Śūnyatā, or the Absolute, and the Ālayavijñāna. The Ālayavijñāna is the cosmic mind, which is expressed in individual minds also. Cognitions and objects are transformations of the cosmic mind, Ālayavijñāna. Vasuvandhu recognized the reality of one eternal pure consciousness (vijñaptimātratā). The Ālayavijñāna is superimposed on it. Subjective cognitions and objective phenomena are its transformations. Vasubandhu's Vijñānavāda is absolute idealism.

Asaṅga (500 A.D.) believed in Suchness (Tathatā). It is the eternal reality, and exists in the past, the present, and the future. It is neither born nor modified. It is unchangeable, immutable, and eternal. It is the supreme reality, the essence of all beings. It is uncaused, unconditioned, necessary, and absolute. It is the essence of the whole universe, its noumenon. It is inseparable from the empirical world of phenomena which are its manifestations. Phenomena cannot exist apart from their noumenon or Suchness. It is grasped by absolute knowledge which is supernormal.[2] The Yogācāra Vijñānavādin believed in the existence of the absolute reality, Tathatā, and advocated absolutistic monism.

THE MĀDHYAMIKA ŚŪNYAVĀDA

The Mādhyamikas regard external objects and subjective cognitions to be equally essenceless with the Śūnya as their eternal basis. The Yogācāras recognize the existence of Tathatā, and identify it with Śūnyatā. They stress the subjectivity of the external world. Therefore they are called Vijñānavādins. The Mādhyamikas regard subjects and objects

---

[1] Tattvasaṁgraha and Tattvasaṁgrahapañjikā, Vol. I, pp. 559-75, 552-53, [2] Madhyāntavibhāga, p. 41.

as relative and conditional, and therefore essenceless. They posit the reality of the Śūnya which is the eternal and absolute reality. It is predicateless and not void or nothingness.

Nāgārjuna (200 A.D.) was one of the greatest philosophers in ancient India. He was a great dialectician, and showed by his dialectics that all categories of thought were self-discrepant and therefore relative, essenceless, or ultimately unreal. Subject and object, substance and quality, whole and part, cause and effect, time, space, relation, compounded and uncompounded dharmas, change, motion, rest, self-nature, other-nature, knowledge, self, God, saṁsāra, and nirvāṇa are self-discrepant and therefore relative or ultimately unreal. The nature of substance, relation and self is considered here.

Substance does not exist apart from qualities. Qualites do not exist apart from substance. Substance is a mere aggregate of qualities. Substance and qualities are correlative to each other. Colour, sound, taste, smell, heat and cold are mere sensations which depend upon the eyes, the ears, the tongue, the nose, and the skin. They are meaningless apart from the sense-organs. They are mere sense experiences. We do not know the real nature of a substance. Substance is a mere relation that harmonizes its qualities with one another. All relations are transient and unreal. Substance and quality are relative to each other, and therefore unreal. Substance is regarded as a mere collection of qualities from the conventional point of view. It is not an ontological reality.

The world is said to be a net-work of relations. But relations are unintelligible. Relation can exist between two distinct things. But they are not distinct from each other. A thing which is produced by another thing, cannot exist apart from it. A sprout cannot exist apart from a seed. The sprout is not therefore distinct from the seed. They are not distinct from each other. So they cannot be related to each other. No two things are ultimately distinct from each other. Therefore they cannot be related to each other. If, again, two things are distinct from each other, they cannot be related to each other. Two self-existent and unrelated things cannot be related to each other. If the distinctness of A is independent of B, then the distinctness of B also is independent of A. A and B are independent of each other. If two things are identical with each other, they cannot be related to each other. Identity and relation cannot exist together. Therefore there are no relations and relata. Relations are unintelligible and phenomenal. They are not ultimately real.[1]

Is the self indentical with, or different from, the five aggregates ? If the self is identical with the five aggregates, then it is subject to origin and destruction. If it is different from them, then it cannot be characterized by the five aggregates. The self and the aggregates are related to each other as subject and object, and therefore cannot be identical with each other. Subject and object must be distinct from each other. If the self does not exist, the mental aggregates cannot be said to belong to it. The aggregates are due to egoism which is not absolutely real. Egoism is destroyed when the aggregates are known to be unreal. When egoism is destroyed, the aggregates are no longer generated. The consciousness is not the self; the self is not endued with consciousness; there is no self in consciousness; there is no consciousness in the self. Body, perception, feeling, disposition, and consciousness cannot exist in the self; nor can the self exist in them. The aggregates are soulless. The self is soulless. They have no core of reality in them. The Buddha has taught neither the existence nor the non-existence of the self or ego.[2]

The Mādhyamika rejects the plurality of external objects and internal cognitions because of their relativity, and posits the existence of the unique, indefinable Essence of Being, the One-without-a-second. All the elements have relative and contingent reality. The Śūnya only has absolute reality. Nāgārjuna's doctrine is the middle path between existence and non-existence, between essencelessness and essence of being. Śūnyatā is not produced by other causes; it is absolute calm; it is one and apprehended by supra-intellectual

[1] MK., xvi, 3, 5-8. [2] MK., MKV., xviii, 1-6.

intuition. All dharmas are essenceless, relative and contingent. They are in their essence inexpressible. They are manifested as calm and pure in the state of enlightenment. The reality has been called Śūnya in order to refute all other views. But those who cling to the view of Śūnyatā are incurable. Nāgārjuna uses the word *Śūnyatā* in two senses the relative and the Absolute. All dharmas are relative (śūnya) but they are grounded in the Absolute (śūnya). Relativism is not the absolute truth. The relative is the way to the Absolute, which cannot be attained without the help of the relative. Nirvāṇa cannot be attained without knowing the Absolute.[1] Though the relative has been branded as unreal like an illusion, yet it has some reality. It has contingent and empirical reality which can serve the practical purposes of our life. It is unreal in relation to the Absolute. The Absolute is inexpressible. It can be described by imputed characters only. All relative and contingent phenomena become extinct in the Absolute. It cannot be called śūnya or aśūnya, or both, or neither ; but it is called śūnya in order to indicate its nature. The Absolute is neither existent, nor non-existent, nor both, nor neither. It is beyond these four empirical categories.[2] It is the transcendent, unconditioned, absolute ground of the empirical world of phenomena. Nāgārjuna is not a mere relativist, phenomenalist, or sceptic. He is an Absolutist, monist, mystic and intuitionist. Intellect gives an empirical world of relativity and plurality. Intuition gives the noumenon or the Absolute One which is the ultimate truth of all phenomena. Nāgārjuna is not a negativist or a nihilist. Only he does not in any way characterize the Absolute.

---

1 MKV,, pp. 445, 491, 500, 539 ; MK, xiii, 8 ; xxiv, 10.

2 MKV., pp. 41, 173, 177, 264, 334, 347, 457, 528 ; MK., i, 7 ; xviii, 5 ; SDS., ii, 31.

CHAPTER VII

THE JAINA PHILOSOPHY

According to the Jaina tradition Ṛsabha was the founder of Jainism. It was taught by twenty four Tīrthaṅkaras who attained liberation. Ṛsabha was the first, and Vardhamāna was the last Tīrthaṅkara. Vardhamāna, the last prophet, was a contemporary of the Buddha. He was born in 599 B.C. and died in 527 B.C. The Jaina scriptures are founded on his teachings. He was called the Jina, spiritual conqueror, Mahāvīra, great hero. He was not the founder of Jainism. He reformed the creed of Pārśvanātha, the twenty third Tīrthaṅkara, who is said to have died 250 years before Vardhamāna. Pārśvanātha was probably a historical person. The other Tīrthaṅkaras are legendary. The orthodox Jainas believe that the Jaina religion is eternal, and that it has been revealed by Tīrthaṅkaras in every one of the endless epochs of the world. Vardhamāna organized his disciples into a regular order with lay and monastic members of both sexes.

The Jaina philosophy is dualism of the soul (jīva) and the non-soul (ajīva). There are innumerable souls, earth-souls, water-souls, fire-souls, air-souls, plant-souls, animal-souls, human-souls, and god-souls. The soul is an eternal spiritual substance. It is an immaterial principle. It transmigrates from one body to another. The ajīva is matter, the principle of motion, the principle of rest, space, and time. Matter is either an atom or an aggregate of atoms. All atoms are homogeneous. Karma is a kind of subtle matter which enters into the soul, and causes its bondage. Matter cannot be derived from the soul. The soul and matter are entirely heterogeneous. There is no God. The world is self-existent and eternal. All objects of the world are multiform and endued with infinite qualities and relations. The reality can be considered from different points of view. The different systems of philosophy are only partial views of the reality. Jainism is the complete view of the reality. It embodies the absolute truth. All judgments are relative and probable. No judgments are absolute. There are seven ways of predication. The Jaina ethics is ethics of ahiṃsā and asceticism. The Jaina religion is the worship of the Tīrthaṅkaras and the attainment of liberation by sheer self-exertion. It is the religion of self-help. Divinity is innate in the human soul. It shines forth in its innate glory when it completely extirpates the veil of karma-matter that covers the soul and obscures its infinite knowledge, infinite perception, infinite bliss, and infinite power.

VALID KNOWLEDGE (PRAMĀṆA)

Vādi Deva Sūri defines valid knowledge as determinate cognition which apprehends itself and an object, and which is capable of prompting activity which attains a desirable object or rejects an undesirable object. Siddhasena defines valid knowledge as cognition, which apprehends itself and an object, and which is not contradicted. These definitions do not exclude recollection from valid knowledge. Harmony of knowledge with its object, practical efficiency, and non-contradiction are the marks of truth. Correspondence, pragmatic utility or capability of leading to the attainment of the intended object, and uncontradictedness characterize truth.[1]

The result of valid knowledge is cessation of ignorance, avoidance of evil, selection of good, and indifference. It is partly distinct and partly non-distinct from valid knowledge. The person who has valid knowledge removes his ignorance, avoids evil, selects good, and becomes indifferent on account of the knowledge of truth.

A cognition in itself is valid, since it cannot contradict itself. It is valid or invalid in relation to its object. If it is in harmony with its object, it is valid. If it is not in harmony with its object, it is invalid.[2] The validity (prāmāṇya) of knowledge consists in its agreement with its object, and the invalidity (aprāmāṇya) of knowledge consists in its disagreement

[1] PNT., i, 2, 3 ; Pramāṇaparīkṣā, p. 52 ; Nyāyāvatāra, i, 1.
[2] PMS., v, 1-3 ; RK., i, 19.

with its object. Both validity and invalidity of knowledge arise from extraneous circumstances, *viz.*, the proficiency or the deficiency respectively in their causes. But they are known by themselves in habitual cognitions, and they are known from extraneous circumstances, *viz.*, the knowledge of harmony or disharmony, and the presence or absence of contradicting experience in unhabitual cognitions.[1]

Invalid knowledge is the determinate knowledge of an object in what it does not exist. Its invalidity consists in its disharmony with the real nature of its object. It is of three kinds, illusion, doubt, and indefinite cognition. Illusion is determinate knowledge of one object as a different object. The perception 'this is silver' in a shell is an illusion. The Jaina advocates the doctrine of Anyathākhyāti. Doubt is the knowledge of an object as either this or that *e.g.*, 'Is this a post or a man ?' Indefinite knowledge is bare knowledge of 'something' devoid of specific qualities.[2] Invalidity of knowledge consists in its disagreement with the real nature of its object. Knowledge is invalid with regard to its object. It is not invalid in itself. It does not disagree with itself.

Valid knowledge is of two kinds, immediate knowledge or perception (pratyakṣa) and mediate or indirect knowledge (parokṣa).

PERCEPTION (PRATYAKṢA)

Perception is distinct (spaṣṭa) knowledge.[3] Distinctness consists in the apprehension of an object with its specific qualities without the mediation of any other knowledge. It is independent of other pramāṇas, and apprehends an object as 'this'. Knowledge of 'thisness' and particular qualities constitute distinctness of perception. It apprehends more than what is apprehended by inference and testimony. It is stronger than indirect knowledge as a kind of valid knowledge.[4]

---

1 PNT., RK., i, 20.   2 PNT., i, 7-12.   3 PNT., ii, 1-2.

4 PMS., ii, 4 ; PNT., ii, 3.

There are two kinds of perception, empirical and transcendental. Empirical perception is practical. It is uncontradicted perception which prompts successful action in the form of attainment of a desired object or rejection of an undesired object. It depends on the sense-organs and other conditions. Our ordinary perception is empirical. Transcendental perception depends upon mere proximity to the self, and not upon the sense-organs and other conditions. It is revelation of knowledge of all objects due to the extirpation of the karma-matter that enters into the soul. Empirical perception is sensuous or non-sensuous. Sensuous perception is due to the external sense-organs stimulated by external objects, which apprehends external objects with sensible qualities. Non-sensuous perception is mental perception, which apprehends pleasure, pain, cognition, and volition through the manas which is not a sense-organ. Both sensuous perception and mental perception apprehend a part of an object distinctly, but they cannot apprehend an object with all its infinite qualities and relations.[1] Knowledge is a revelation from within the self due to the removal of the crust of karma-matter covering it.

The Jaina does not recognize the existence and validity of indeterminate perception, because it cannot determine the nature of its object with its specific qualities, and because it cannot lead to attainment of good and avoidance of evil.[2] Valid knowledge is determinate cognition which apprehends itself and an object. Indeterminate perception is not determinate cognition. It neither apprehends itself nor apprehends an object definitely. So it is not valid. It is not vivid or distinct cognition. So it is not perception.

Sense-perception has four stages, avagraha, īhā, avāya, and dhāraṇā. (1) Avagraha is the first impression of an object endued with inferior generic characters arising from the formless cognition of mere beinghood just after the intercourse of a sense-organ with an object. The stimulation of the peripheral organs by the objects generates a formless

---

[1] PNT., ii, 4-5 ; PMS., ii, 5.

[2] RK., i, 2.

cognition which apprehends mere beinghood. It gives rise to the first impression of the object endued with the generic characters inferior to mere beinghood, *e.g.*, the generic character of man, and the like. For example, an object is perceived as a man, and not as mere being. (2) Īhā is the enquiry to know the particular features of the object apprehended by the first impression. For example, is the man perceived as an inhabitant of Karnāṭa, Lāṭa, or any other region? (3) Avāya is the right determination of the particular features of the object, which the self desires to know. For example, the man perceived is definitely known to be an inhabitant of Karṇāṭa. (4) Dhāraṇā is the firm retention of the perception of the object, which is the cause of its recollection in future. Retention is the cause of recollection. Perception produces a disposition, a particular power of the self, which generates its recollection in future. An object perceived in the sky as white is avagraha. Is the white object a row of herons or a flag? The desire to know it is īhā. The white object is definitely known to be a row of herons through its particular features such as flying upward and downward and movements of the wings. This is avāya. The firm retention of the perception is dhāraṇā. It is the cause of the recollection. 'This is that row of herons which I perceived in the morning'. This is the order of the different stages of perception.[1]

Transcendental perception depends upon the self alone. It is independent of the sense-organs and the manas. The self directly perceives objects on account of the subsidence or destruction of the karma-matter covering it, independently of the sense-organs and other conditions. It is either incomplete or complete. Incomplete transcendental perception is of two kinds: avadhi and manaḥparyāya. (1) Avadhi is the perception of sensible objects independently of the sense-organs and the manas due to the subsidence or destruction of the crust of karma-matter obscuring the knowledge. It is caused by right intuition, right faith, and right conduct. It is clairvoyance, clairaudience, and the like. (2) Manaḥpar-

[1] PNT., ii, 8-10; SS., i, 15, 17-18,

yāyajñāna is telepathic knowledge of the processes of other minds. It is direct or immediate knowledge caused by the destruction of a particular kind of karma-matter obscuring the knowledge, which is due to the purity of restraint or right conduct. (3) Complete transcendental perception is the omniscient's immediate knowledge of all substances and their modes in their infinite aspects. It arises from the annihilation of the entire crust of karma-matter due to right intuition, right faith, and right conduct.[1]

MEDIATE KNOWLEDGE (PAROKṢA)

Mediate knowledge is indistinct and devoid of perceptual vividness. It is of five kinds: recollection, recognition, induction (tarka), deduction (anumāna), and testimony.[2]

(1) Recollection is the knowledge of an object perceived in the past as 'that' due to revival of its disposition. Recollection is the effect of the revival of the disposition of the previous perception of an object. Valid knowledge determines the nature of an object as it really is. Recollection determines the real nature of an object perceived in the past. So it is valid knowledge.[3]

(2) Recognition is the composite cognition produced by perception and recollection. It apprehends an object in the forms: 'this is that', 'this is like that', 'this is different from that', 'this is correlated to that', and the like. 'This is that Devadatta'. 'A wild cow is like a cow'. 'A buffalo is different from a cow'. 'This is remote from that'. 'This is called a tree'. 'This individual is a cow'. These are recognition. Recognition apprehends identity, similarity, difference, correlation, relation of sign and signate, and the like.

Recognition is a distinct kind of valid knowledge. It knows a present perceived object as known in the past, *e. g.*, 'this is that Devadatta'. Perception knows 'this'. Recollection knows 'that'. But recognition knows 'this is that'. It knows an object as it really is, and is in harmony with its real nature.

---

[1] PNT., RK., ii, 18-23

[2] Ibid., iii, 1-2. [3] Ibid, iii, 3-4.

It is a distinct kind of valid knowledge.[1] Comparison (upamāna) is included in recognition. It is not treated as a distinct kind of valid knowledge.

(3) Induction (tarka) is knowledge of the invariable concomitance (vyāpti) of the middle term with the major term in the past, the present, and the future, arising from the observation of their co-presence and co-absence. Vyāpti is of two kinds : anvayavyāpti and vyatirekavyāpti. Wherever there is smoke, there is fire. This is anvayavyāpti. Wherever there is no fire, there is no smoke. This is vyatirekavāpti.[2]

(4) Deduction or inference (anumāna) is the knowledge of the major term derived from the knowledge of the middle term. Fire is inferred from smoke. 'Smoke' is the middle term. 'Fire' is the major term. Inference is based on universal concomitance of the middle term with the major term. It is based on vyāpṭi derived from induction (tarka).[3]

There are two kinds of inference, inference for oneself and inference for others. In inference for oneself a person perceives the reason or middle term, remembers the inseparable connection between the reason and the inferable object or the major term determined by induction, and at once knows the major term. Inference for others consists in the statement of the middle term, the major term, and the minor term. It consists of two propositions. (1) 'The hill is fiery ; (2) because it is smoky'. The example (dṛṣṭānta) is not present here.[4] This is intended for intelligent persons. For less intelligent persons the inference includes the example and consists of three propositions : (1) 'The hill is *fiery* ; (2) because it is *smoky* ; (3) whatever is smoky is fiery, as the *kitchen*.' The example is the object in which the middle term is perceived to be accompanied by the major term. The example (dṛṣṭānta), the application (upanaya), and the conclusion (nigamana) are necessary to convince persons of dull intellect of the truth of an inference. The application is reassertion of the presence of the middle

[1] PNT., iii, 5-6 ; PKM., pp. 97-98.
[2] PNT., RK., iii, 7-8 [3] PMS., iii, 9.
[4] PNT., iii, 9-10, 23 & 28.

term in the minor term in which the presence of the major term is to be proved. The conclusion is reassertion of the presence of the major term in the minor term. Inference for dull persons consists of five propositions : (1) 'The hill is fiery (pakṣavacana) ; (2) because the hill is smoky (hetuvacana) ; (3) whatever is smoky is fiery, as the kitchen (dṛṣṭānta) ; (4) the hill is smoky (upanaya) ; (5) therefore, the hill is fiery (nigamana)'.[1]

(5) Testimony is the knowledge of objects derived from the words of relible persons. For example, 'the north pole exists.' A reliable person is one who knows objects as they really are, and expresses his ideas correctly. His words are in harmony with their objects. They do not contradict the nature of their objects. Testimony is of two kinds, secular and non-secular. Testimony of Janaka and others is secular. Testimony of Tīrthaṅkaras is non-secular. The Jainas do not believe in the authority of the Vedas. They recognize the authority of the Tīrthaṅkaras only who attained perfection and became omniscient. Testimony is a proposition or a sentence. A sentence is a collection of interdependent words. A word denotes an object by virtue of its natural denotative power and convention. Just as a lamp illumines an object, so a word manifests an object by its natural power. But it differs from a lamp in that it depends upon convention to produce knowledge of an object. But its truth or falsehood depends upon excellence or imperfection of the speaker.[2]

ANEKĀNTAVĀDA

The Jainas hold that a real thing is endued with an infinite number of qualities and modes, which is comprehended by valid knowledge (pramāṇa).[3] All objects of knowledge are manifold or multiform (anekānta). They have infinite qualities and relations which distinguish them from the other objects. For example, a gold jar exists as a specific substance with its specific qualities in a particular place at a particular time. It does not exist as other substances in other places at other

[1] PNT., 49, 51 & 53. [2] PNT., iv, 1, 4-12. [3] SDSm., 55.

times. When it is considered as a substance, it exists as an aggregate of atoms ; it does not exist as a substance in the sense of space, the principle of motion, the principle of rest and the other substances. It exists as a collection of earth atoms. It does not exist as a collection of water atoms, fire atoms, and air atoms. It exists as a collection of earth atoms in the sense that it is made of a metal which is a modification of earth ; it does not exist as a lump of clay, and the like. It exists as a collection of gold atoms, and not of silver atoms or atoms of other kinds of metal. It exists as a collection of gold atoms in the sense that it is made of melted and pure gold moulded by Devadatta into the shape of a jar, and not of a jug, a pitcher, and the like. It exists as moulded into the shape of this jar, and not any other jar. As a substance its own qualities are not many. But the qualities of the other substances are infinite. It is distinguished from them by their infinite qualities. It exists in its own place, and not in other places. The qualities of the other things in time are infinite. The gold jar is distinguished from them by infinite qualities. It exists as endued with a particular degree of yellow colour. It exists as endued with a particular degree of taste. It exists as endued with a particular degree of smell. It exists as endued with roughness or smoothness, heat or cold, lightness or heaviness, in particular degrees. In magnitude it exists either as minute or large, short or long, and the like in relation to other substances. It can be distinguished from other substances by infinite magnitudes. It exists as comprehended by perception or inference by an infinite number of souls. The comprehended object must differ according as its comprehending modes of knowledge differ. So the gold jar must be endued with infinite natures according as it is comprehended by infinite cognitions of infinite souls. It exists as endued with innumerable qualities which differentiate it from the other similar and dissimilar substances. It exists in infinite relations to the other substances in infinite time. Thus all things possess infinite qualities and infinite relations.[1] The world is a system

[1] TRD.. PP, 212-18.

of interrelated objects possessing infinite qualities and infinite relations. This is the Jaina doctrine of relative pluralism (anekāntavāda).

THE DOCTRINE OF NAYA

This doctrine is a peculiar feature of the Jaina epistemology. Pramāṇa and naya are the different ways of knowing the reality. They enrich our knowledge of real things. Pramāṇa is the valid knowledge of a multiform object endued with many qualities. Naya is the valid knowledge of one part, aspect, quality, or mode of a multiform object. Naya is a part of pramāṇa. It is partial valid knowledge. A naya apprehends a part or aspect of a real thing comprehended by valid knowledge, and ignores its other parts or aspects. It is the standpoint of the knowing person embodying a particular purpose to understand a particular aspect of a thing to the exclusion of other aspects. He becomes indifferent to the other aspects of the thing for the time being. Nayas are the points of view from which things are considered. They are partial views of reality and inadequate to the whole reality. When the partial views are taken as the complete view, they become invalid. They are invalid because they deny the truth of the other aspects of things not relevant to the knower's purpose.[1]

Nayas are mainly of two kinds, dravyanaya and paryāyanaya. Dravyanaya considers a thing as a substance in which qualities and modes are unified. It emphasizes the substantial aspect of a thing, and ignores its qualitative and modal aspects. Paryāyanaya considers a thing as a conglomeration of qualities and modes, and ignores its substantial aspect. Dravyanayas are of three kinds, naigamanaya, saṁgrahanaya, and vyavahāranaya. They are also called arthanayas. They refer to objects or meanings. Paryāyanayas are of four kinds, ṛjusūtra, śabda, samabhirūḍha, and evambhūta.[2] They are also called śabdanayas, for they refer to words.

---

[1] AMV., 106; PNT., vii, 1—2; SS., i, 33; [2] PNT., vii, 5—6, 27; SVM., p. 203; SS., TSV., i, 33.

(1) Naigamanaya is interpreted in two ways. First, Pūjyapāda takes it as the standpoint which emphasizes the purpose of a series of actions, which is not yet completely accomplished. A person going with an axe, being asked for what purpose he is going, answers, 'I am going to bring a a wooden measure'. He is going to to cut a bamboo and make a measure out of it. The measure is the purpose to be realized in the action. Secondly, Candraprabha Sūri and Hemacandra Sūri interpret naigamanaya in another manner. It is the common-sense point of view which considers things as possessing both generic and specific qualities which are not distinguished from each other.[1] The Advaita Vedānta denies the specific qualities. Buddhism denies the generic qualities. The Jaina holds that a thing is an organic unity of both generic and specific qualities, which are equally real. This is the concrete view of the Jaina. The naigamanaya is the standpoint of the Nyāya and the Vaiśeṣika systems according to the Jaina. They hold that a thing is the complex of the universal and the particular, which are equally real and primary and different from each other. So far they agree with the Jaina. But they consider the distinction between the universal and the particular to be absolute, while the Jaina considers it to be relative. They consider them to be absolutely different from each other, while the Jaina considers them to be partially different from each other. The naigamanaya becomes naigamābhāsa at the hands of the Naiyāyikas and the Vaiśeṣikas.[2]

(2) Saṁgrahanaya is the class point of view. It refers to mere generality devoid of all specific qualities. It considers things from the general point of view, ignores the special features, and treats them as mere 'being'. The saṁgrahanaya is of two kinds, parasaṁgraha and aparasaṁgraha. Parasaṁgraha is the highest class view. All individual things in the world may be considered from the most general point of view as mere 'being' irrespective of their particular

---

1 SS., i, 33 ; TRV., i, 5, 33 ; PKM., p.204 ; NAV., 29, p.47 ; SVM., VRS., p.202. 2 PI., pp. liv-lv.

features. The Advaita Vedānta considers the world as mere one 'being', and denies the plurality of things. Its standpoint, according to the Jaina, is parasaṁgrahanayābhāsa. Aparasaṁgrahanaya is the inferior class view. It refers to the inferior classes as distinct from the highest class 'Being'. This standpoint considers dharma, adharma, space, time, soul and non-soul as identical with one another, since they have substantiality. It considers all earth vessels as earth irrespective of their particular features. This is the inferior class view. When the intermediate generalities alone are regarded as real, and the individuals are regarded as unreal, the standpoint becomes aparasaṁgrahanayābhāsa.[1] The Sāṁkhya commits this error, since it considers all material things, the living bodies, the sense-organs, manas, buddhi, and ahaṁkāra as modes of prakṛti irrespective of their essential differences.

(3) Vyavahāranaya is the practical point of view based on sense-perception. We do not react upon classes, but upon particular things perceived by us. Vyavahāranaya is the practical standpoint which considers the particular individuals alone, without taking cognizance of their generic qualities and specific qualities. When distinctions of real things are denied, and those of imaginary things are recognized, the standpoint is called vyavahāranayābhāsa. The Cārvākas recognize the reality of the elements of earth, water, fire, and air which are objects of practical use, and reject the reality of the soul. Their materialism is vyavahāranayābhāsa.[2]

(4) Ṛjusūtranaya is literally the straight standpoint which considers only the transitory modes of a thing at the present moment apart from the permanent substance. It does not consider the past modes which have vanished, and the future modes which have not yet come into existence. For example, 'pleasure exists at the present moment.' Here the transient mode of pleasure at the present moment is considered, and its substrate, the soul, is ignored. It is the extreme opposite of saṃgrahanaya. The former denies all continuity and identity,

[1] PNT., vii, 15-21; SVM., VRS., p. 202; SS., i, 33.
[2] SVM., VRS., p. 202; PNT., vii, 25-26.

while the latter denies all changes and differences. Ṛjusūtranaya is narrower than vyavahāranaya which considers individual things with a certain duration. When only the transitory modes of the present moment are considered to be real, and the substance in which they abide is denied, the standpoint becomes ṛjusūtranayābhāsa. The Buddhist standpoint, according to the Jaina, is ṛjusūtranayābhāsa, for it considers the transitory modes of the present moment to be real, and denies the reality of the substance, which is their abode, which exists in the past, present, and future.[1]

(5) Śabdanaya is the standpoint which refers to words and their meanings. A word implies a particular object, an attribute, a relation, or an action. Each word has its own meaning. Different words also may refer to the same object. The relation between words and their meanings is relative, and not absolute. Words differing in gender, number, person, case, and the like may refer to the same object. *Puṣya* (masculine), *Tārā* (feminine), and *Nakṣatra* (neuter) mean the same object,—star. *Dārāh* (plural) and *Kalatra* (singular) mean the same object,—wife. 'The potter makes a pot.' 'A pot is made by the potter.' The word 'pot' is used in the objective case in the first sentence, and in the nominative case in the second sentence. But they refer to the same object. 'The north pole was, is and will be.' Here śabdanaya considers the differences in the north pole corresponding to the verbs in the past, the present, and the future tenses, and ignores its identity in the past, the present, and the future.[2] When we consider the relation of words to their meanings to be absolute, we commit an error. The Grammarians commit śabdanayābhāsa, since they consider the relation of words to their meanings to be absolute.[3]

(6) Samabhirūḍhanaya refers to the different meanings of words according to their roots. *Indra* literally means 'all prosperous'. *Śakra* literally means 'all powerful'. *Purandara*

---

[1] PNT., vii, 28-31; SS., i, 33; SVM., VRS., p. 202; PKM., p. 205; PI., p. lviii.

[2] SS., i, 33; PNT., vii, 33. [3] NAV., 29, p. 47; PNT., vii, 34.

literally means 'destroyer of the enemies.' Samabhirūḍhanay emphasizes the literal meanings of the words, and ignore their identical derivative meaning. The three words have th same derivative or conventional meaning. They refer to th king of gods in heaven. Samabhirūḍhanaya is a specia application of śabdanaya. It distinguishes the synonyms fron one another, and applies each word appropriately to a specifi object according to its etymological meaning. If it ignores th identity of the derivative meaning of the synonyms, it become samabhirūḍhanayābhāsa. The Grammarians commit this error.

(7) Evambhūtanaya is a special application of samabhirūḍ hanaya. It restricts a word to one particular meaning whic emphasizes one particular aspect of an object suggested by it root. The word '*gau*' literally means a moving animal. moving cow is a *gau*. When it is at rest, it should not b called a '*gau*'. It should be designated by a different word This is the standpoint of evambhūtanaya. It uses a word i its strict etymological sense, and applies it to an object possess ing practical efficiency at the present moment. It applies th word '*Śakra*' to a man who is actually strong, implied by th word. If we ignore the nature of the object which is no strictly implied by the etymological meaning of the word, w commit an error. The Grammarians, according to the Jaina commit evambhūtanayābhāsa.[2] The last three are śabdanayas

A substance has infinite powers, and can be known fron various points of view.[3] The nayas are partial views which ar not adequate to the complete reality. They give relative truths and not absolute truths. All affirmations and negations ar relative to time, place, and circumstances. They are no unconditional and absolute. So the doctrine of nayas is relate to Anekāntavāda and Syādvāda.

SYĀDVĀDA : SAPTABHAṄGĪNYĀYA

Absolute judgments are possible in one-sided (ekānta systems. But they are not possible in the Anekānta philosoph

[1] PNT., vii, 36-38; PKM., p. 205; SVM., VRS., p. 202; SS., i, 33

[2] SS., i, 33; SVM., VRS., p. 202; PNT., vii, 40-43; PKM., p. 206

[3] SS., i, 33.

of the Jaina. All objects are multiform according to him. From their many-sided nature it follows that all judgments are relative. They are true under certain conditions. No judgments are absolutely true. The word 'perhaps' should be added to all judgments to indicate their conditional character. This is Syādvāda or the doctrine of relativity of judgments. There are seven different ways of making judgments about a substance or an attribute as follows: (1) 'Perhaps S is'; (2) 'Perhaps S is not'; (3) 'Perhaps S is, is not'; (4) 'Perhaps S is indescribable'; (5) 'Perhaps S is and indescribable'; (6) 'Perhaps S is not and indescribable'; (7) 'Perhaps S is, is not, and indescribable'. The first is an affirmative judgment. The second is a negative judgment. The third is an affirmative judgment and a negative judgment in succession. The fourth is simultaneons affirmative judgment and negative judgment. The fifth is an affirmative judgment combined with simultaneous affirmative judgment and negative judgment. The sixth is a negative judgment combined with simultaneous affirmative judgment and negative judgment. The seventh is successive affirmative judgment and negative judgment combined with simultaneous affirmative and negative judgment.[1]

1. 'Perhaps S is'. From the point of view of its own substance, place, time, and nature, a thing exists. The jar exists as an earthen substance possessing dark colour in winter at Pataliputra.

2. 'Perhaps S is not'. From the point of view of substance, place, time, and nature, a thing does not exist as other things. The jar does not exist as a watery substance possessing red colour in spring at Kanyakubja.

3. 'Perhaps S is and is not.' The jar exists as its own substance in its own place at a particular time with its own nature. It does not exist as another substance in another place at another time with another quality.

4. 'Perhaps S is indescribable'. The presence of its own

[1] SVM., VRS., pp. 276-77.

nature and the absence of its contradictory nature both are in a thing together. But it cannot be expressed. But it cannot be absolutely indescribable. What is absolutely indescribable like Māyā of the Advaita Vedānta is unintelligle and meaningless. It means that we cannot find an idea which includes both the thesis and the antithesis at the same time.

5. 'Perhaps S is and indescribable'. When a predicate is affirmed of a thing with reference to its own substance, place, time, and nature, and a predicate is affirmed of it as described above and denied of other things as different substances in other places and times and with different natures simultaneously, we have affirmation and indescribability.

6. 'Perhaps S is not and indescribable'. When a predicate is denied of other substances in other places at other times and with different natures, and a predicate is simultaneously affirmed of the thing and denied of other things, we have negation and indescribability.

7. 'Perhaps S is, is not, and indescribable'. When a predicate is affirmed of a thing as its own substance in its own place at its own time and with its own nature, and it is denied of other substances in other places at other times and with other natures, and affirmation and denial are made simultaneously, we have affirmation, negation, and indescribability. The Jainas admit only the sevenfold judgments (saptabhaṅgīnyāya).[1] Of these the affirmative judgment that a thing is in its own substance, its own place, its own time, and with its own nature, and the negative judgment that a thing is not in other substances, other places, other times, and with other natures are the main. The five other judgments are combinations of them. Affirmation implies negation. Negation implies affirmation. A thing is existent with its own nature, and non-existent with other natures. A positive thing is distinguished from other things. A thing devoid of all distinctions is inconceivable. The Jainas advocate relative pluralism. Syādvāda or relativity

---

TDTV., 14.

of judgments and Saptabhaṅginyāya or sevenfold judgments are logical corrollaries of it.

SUBSTANCE, ATTRIBUTE, AND MODE

A substance (dravya) has the characteristic of existence. It possesses generation, destruction, and permanence. Some new qualities are generated, some old qualities are destroyed, and some qualities remain permanent in it. Permanence means indestructibility and continuity of the essence of the substance. Recognition apprehends permanence of a substance in the form 'this is that'. When prominence is given to the indestructible essence of a thing, and its changing qualities are subordinated to its essence, it is called a substance. It is permanent in regard to its essential qualities, and impermanent in regard to its changing qualities.[1] A substance is possessed of attributes (guṇa) and modes (paryāya). Attributes coexist with one another in the substance. Modes succeed one another in it. Modes are changes in the attributes of a substance. They are partly different from their substance, for their substance persists even when they are destroyed. They are partly identical with their substance, because they cannot exist apart from their substance, and because they are nothing but its modifications.[2]

From the standpoint of substance, a substance is neither created nor destroyed, but has only existence. But from the standpoint of modes, a substance has creation, destruction, and permanence. A substance is both permanent and changing. It is permanent as a substance, and changing as modes. A substance is permanent through its changing modes.

A substance cannot exist without modes, which also cannot exist without it. They are partially different from, and partially identical with, each other. The relation of a substance to its mode is that of matter to its form. There can be neither matter without form nor form without matter.

A substance cannot exist without attributes, which also cannot exist without it. They are partly different from, and partly non-different from, each other in their nature.

---

[1] TS., v, 30 ; SS., v, 31-32. [2] TS., v, 38 & 42 ; SS., v, 41.

If a substance is entirely distinct from its attributes, then it may be transformed into infinite other substances. If the attributes are entirely distinct from a substance and can exist apart from it, there is no necessity for a substance. Both the alternatives are untenable. Hence a substance and its attributes are not entirely distinct from each other.[1]

The Jaina recognizes six substances (1) soul (jīva); (2) the principle of motion (dharma); (3) the principle of rest (adharma); (4) space (ākāśa); (5) matter (pudgala); and (6) time (kāla). The last five substances are called non-soul (ajīva). The first five substances are extensive like body (kāya), and occupy more than one unit of space. So they are called astikāyas. Soul, matter, dharma, adharma, and space are extensive substances. Time is unextended and composed of innumerable moments which are not coextensive with one another. So time is a substance devoid of extension.

THE SOUL (JĪVA)

The soul (jīva) is an eternal spiritual substance. It is incorporeal, immaterial, and different from the body or the sense-organs. But it is coextensive with the body it occupies, even as the light of a lamp is coextensive with the room in which it exists.[2] Cognition, feeling, and conation are its qualities. It is the knower, enjoyer, and active agent. It possesses knowledge and perception. Consciousness is not its accidental quality, but it constitutes its essence. The soul is not indifferent or inactive. It is the enjoyer of the fruits of its actions in the form of pleasure and pain. It is active and free. It can freely do right actions or wrong actions, and acquire merit or demerit. It is the master of its own destiny. It freely enters into bondage, and freely liberates itself from bondage. It is united with particles of karma-matter in the state of bondage, and separated from karma-matter in the state of liberation. The liberated soul moves upward to the summit of mundane space.

---

[1] P., 11-13, 50; TDTV., 11-12.

[2] TS., v, 16; DS., 2; P., 27 & 132.

From the practical standpoint, that is called the soul which is possessed of the five sense-organs, and vital forces, strength, duration of life, and inspiration and expiration. But from the ontological standpoint, that is called the soul which has consciousness. The soul is absolutely different from the non-soul. What is devoid of pleasure and pain and desire of doing good and avoiding evil is non-soul. The soul knows and perceives objects, desires pleasure, fears pain, does good and evil, and enjoys the fruits of its actions. The five sense-organs and the body are its accidental adjuncts, which are not conscious. But the soul is the principle of consciousness which manifests itself and other objects.[1]

The jīva is active because of its association with karma-matter. In the perfect state it is absolutely free from karmas, and becomes inactive. It transcends the causal series in the state of liberation. In the state of bondage it is the agent of its own actions, and the enjoyer of their fruits. It is blinded by ignorance on account of its bondage to karma-matter created by itself, and roams about in the world of birth and death. The faithful soul liberates itself from bondage by adopting the path of right faith, right knowledge, and right conduct. But the unfaithful soul roams about in the world of saṃsāra for ever. But both kinds of souls are the masters of their own career. The destiny of each jīva is entirely self-determined.[2]

Knowledge is not an adventitious quality of the self, but its intrinsic essence. The self is the knower by its very nature. It does not become the knower by union with the adventitious quality of knowledge.[3] Infinite knowledge, infinite perception, infinite bliss, and infinite power for right action are innate in the soul. But they are obscured by karma-matter in the state of bondage. When the shackle of karma-matter is completely broken, the soul realizes omniscience, eternal bliss, and infinite power.

The soul is a spiritual substance, and consequently unextend-

[1] DS., 3 ; P., 3, 128-29 & 132.

[2] P., 75 & 105.

[3] P., TDTV., 54-55

ed. But it is considered to be an extensive substance because it illumines the whole body with its consciousness. Just as a piece of red ruby placed in a cup of milk imparts its lustre to the milk, so the soul residing in a body imparts its consciousness to the whole body.[1] It is distinct from the body, though it appears to be identical with it when it functions in it.

The souls are of the essence of consciousness. Perception and knowledge are their essential characteristics. The souls are of two kinds, bound and liberated. The former are limited by adjuncts and have either gross body or subtle body. The latter are free from bodily adjuncts. They have neither gross body nor subtle body. The former are impure, while the latter are pure. The former have finite knowledge and finite perception owing to karmic matter which limits them, while the latter have infinite knowledge and infinite perception owing to the destruction of karmic matter. The former have false knowledge and perception, emotions and passions, while the latter have omniscience, infinite bliss, and infinite power. The perfect souls retain their identity and individuality.[2]

The omniscient soul pervades the whole universe by its consciousness. Even the bound soul occupies innumerable space-points. Though it occupies innumerable space-points, it can occupy the space of a small body or a large body by the contraction and expansion of the space-points, like a lamp. It is like a lamp which illumines a small room or a large room. Mundane souls cannot live apart from one another. The perfect souls are absolutely unconditioned. They have no causal relation to the cycle of saṃsāra. They are absolutely incorporeal and perfectly spiritual. They are entirely free from karma-matter. But the imperfect souls are united with karma-matter. Though in themselves incorporeal, they are embodied and associated with particles of karma.[3]

The jīvas are either embodied or disembodied. The former are bound, while the latter are perfect. The bound souls are either faithful or unfaithful. The former attain liberation,

---

[1] TS., v, 16; P., 33-34.

[2] P., TDTV., 31-32, 117.

[3] TS., v, 8, 15-16, 21.

while the latter never attain liberation but roam in the world for ever. The embodied souls are either non-moving or moving. Earth, water, fire, and air are endowed with souls. Earth-souls, water-souls, fire-souls, and air-souls have one sense-organ, *viz.*, touch associated with intense stupor. These are elemental souls. They live in elementary bodies. They live and die, and are reborn in the same or another elementary body. They are are either gross or subtle. The subtle elementary lives are invisible. Plants also are endowed with souls. They have the sense of touch only. All the five kinds of non-moving souls have four kinds of life-principles, strength of body, respiration, duration of life, and the sense of touch. They are microscopic organisms endowed with souls. The non-moving souls have no mental modes. But they are not unconscious. They are subconscious like a fœtus in an egg, or an embryo in a womb, or a man in a swoon. They have dormant consciousness. They have life and potency of consciousness.[1] Plants are jīvas with the sense of touch. Some ensouled organisms have two sense-organs. Sea snail, cowrie shell, conch shell, mother o' pearl, and earth-worm have two senses, touch and taste. They are moving souls. The louse, the bug, the ant, the scorpion, and other insects have three senses, touch, taste, and smell. The gad-fly, the mosquito, the fly, the bee, the black bee, the moth, and the like have four senses, touch, taste, smell, and sight. Higher animals living on land and in water, and birds have five senses, touch, taste, smell, sight, and hearing. Some souls have a mind or reason. They can distinguish between right and wrong. Others have no mind or reason. They cannot distinguish between right and wrong. Human souls are rational. Animal souls, plant-souls, and elemental souls are irrational. The embodied souls are of these five kinds.[2]

THE THEORY OF KARMA

Karmas are infra-atomic particles of matter which are produced by passions and actions of mind, body, and speech moved by desire, aversion, and delusion. There are four

---

[1] TS., ii, 12-13; P., 118-20, 127.

[2] TS., ii, 11, 14-15, 24; GTS., JK., 660-61; P., 121-24.

destructive (ghātīya) karmas and four non-destructive (aghātīya) karmas. The former are (1) knowledge-obscuring (jñānavaraṇīya), (2) perception-obscuring (darśanāvaraṇīya), (3) obstructive (antarāya), and (4) deluding (mohanīya). The latter are (5) age-determining (āyuṣ), (6) character-determining (nāma), (7) family-determining (gotra), and (8) feeling-determining (vedanīya).[1] (1) The knowledge-obscuring karmas obscure five-fold right knowledge, sense-knowledge, testimony, clairvoyance, telepathic knowledge of other minds, and omniscience[2]. (2) The perception-obscuring karmas obscure right visual perception, non-visual perception, perception of distant objects, perfect perception, sleep, deep sleep, restless sleep, very restless sleep, and somnumbulism.[3] (3) The obstructive karmas obstruct the inborn energy of the soul and prevent it from doing good actions in spite of the desire to do them. They obstruct charity, gain, enjoyment, the means to enjoyment, and power.[4] (4) The deluding karmas are mainly of two kinds, according as they delude right belief and right conduct. The former obscure right belief, wrong belief, and right belief mixed with wrong belief. The latter affect passions, *viz.*, anger, pride, deceit and greed, and slight passions, *viz.*, laughter, attachment, aversion, sorrow, fear, disgust, female sex-feeling, male sex-feeling, and an eunuch's sex-feeling. (5) The age-determining karmas determine the duration of hellish life, animal life, human life, and celestial life. (6) The character-determining karmas determine the transmigration of the soul to hellish, animal, human, and celestial life. (7) The family-determining karmas determine the birth in a high family or a low family. (8) The feeling-obscuring karmas are of two kinds according as they produce pleasure and pain. They obscure the innate blissful nature of the soul.[5]

MATTER, DHARMA, ADHARMA, SPACE AND TIME

The non-soul extensive substances (ajīvāstikāya) are: (1) dharma or the principle of motion, (2) adharma or the

[1] TS., viii. 4. [2] TS., viii. 6. [3] TS., viii. 7.
[4] TS., viii. 13. [5] TS., viii, 8-12.

principle of rest, (3) space, and (4) matter.[1] They are extensive and occupy more than one space-unit. Time is not an extensive substance because indivisible particles of time exist in space-points without mixing with one another.

Matter is a non-soul substance which has touch, taste, smell, and colour. Material substances have form or shape. Matter exists in the form of an atom or an aggregate. Atoms are indivisible units of matter. Aggregates are composed of atoms. Atoms arise from the division of aggregates. They are the furthest limit of division. They cannot arise from combination or from combination with division. An atom is one, indivisible, indestructible, and corporeal unit of matter. It is the maker and breaker of aggregates. It is a constituent unit of an aggregate which is broken into atoms. It is spatial, yet non-spatial. It occupies only one unit of space. It is the determinant of time and number.[2] It is without beginning, middle, and end. It is capable of modifications. Atoms are combined into aggregates. The aggregates are minute or large, and have touch, taste, smell, colour, and sound. But atoms each have one taste, one smell, one colour, and two tactile qualities. They are the causes of sounds, but devoid of sounds.[3] There are five kinds of colour, blue, yellow, white, black, and red. There are eight kinds of touch, softness, hardness, heaviness, lightness, cold, heat, smoothness, and roughness. Atoms have non-manifest or imperceptible qualities. They become manifest in their aggregates. Of the eight kinds of tactile qualities an atom has temperature, *i.e.*, heat or cold and degrees of roughness or smoothness. It has neither heaviness nor lightness. It is deviod of sound. But it is the cause of sound. Sound is generated by aggregates. An aggregate is composed of molecules or compounds of atoms. Sound is generated by the striking of aggregates against one another. It is the quality of an aggregate which occupies many space-points. An atom occupies only one space-point, and so cannot have sound.[4] Sound is not the quality of

---

[1] TS., v, 1. [2] TS., v, 5, 11, 23 & 25; TS., SS., v, 27; P., 84-85, 87.
[3] P., 85, 88; TDTV., 85. [4] SS., v, 23; TDTV., 85.

ether, it would be heard in a vacuum in which ether is present.[1] Atoms are homogeneous and deviod of qualitative differences. They are subtle and imperceptible to us. But they can be perceived by the omniscient only. An atom occupies one space-point. The same space-point is occupied by its qualities, touch, taste, smell, and colour. If the atom were divested of its qualities, it would be annihilated. The homogeneous atoms produce the four elements of earth, water, fire and air.[2]

One moment is the time taken by an atom to move from one space-point to the next space-point.[3] The change of position of an atom is the measure of time. An atom is also the measure of number or quantity. It is a unit of an aggregate. So the number of atoms determine the quantity of the aggregate. One atom occupies one space-time. Many atoms occupy many space-points. So they also indirectly cause quantitative differences of their aggregates.

One atom of matter and one particle of time exist in one unit of space. Matter, time, and space are three inseparable units of the physical world. They cannot be separated from one another, though they are different in their nature. Matter-space-time-units are the elementary substances of the dynamic world. Karma-particles are infra-atomic matter. They are finer than atoms.

Atoms are combined into aggregates. Aggregates are formed by integration. Large aggregates are divided into small aggregates. So aggregates are formed by disintegration. Some aggregates are formed by integration and disintegration.[4] When two primary atoms are combined, a binary aggregate occupying two space-points is formed. When a binary aggregate is combined with a primary atom, a tertiary aggregate occupying three space-points is formed. In this way aggregates of varying quantities are formed.[5]

Aggregates have manifest qualities of touch, taste, smell, colour, and sound. They have hardness, softness, heaviness,

---

[1] P., 85-86.
[2] YBh., iii, 52
[3] TDTV., 85, 88 ; P., 85.
[4] TS., v., 26.
[5] P., TDTV., 87 ; E. T., p. 85-86.

lightness, heat, cold, roughness and smoothness. They have atomic linking, dimension, figure, divisibility, opacity, and radiant heat-light.

Dharma is the imperceptible medium of motion of matter and souls. It is the principle of motion. It is supersensible and devoid of sensible qualities, taste, colour, smell, sound, touch, lightness, and heaviness. It is perceptible to the omniscient soul only. It is incorporeal, inactive, and eternal. It is coextensive with mundane space. It is continuous because its units of space are inseperable. Though it is coextensive with mundane space, it is regarded as occupying innumerable units of space from the practical point of view. It is without any gaps and motionless. It cannot impel matter and souls to move. When they begin to move, it assists their movement. Dharma is the neutral, external, auxiliary cause of motion of matter and living beings which move on account of their own material causes. It pervades mundane space. So it is called dharmāstikāya. It is a real substance which persists in the midst of changing modes.

Adharma is the principle of rest. Adharma is one, eternal, formless, inactive substance which is coextensive with mundane space. So it is called adharmāstikāya. It is an extensive substance. It is non-atomic and non-discrete in structure. It is simple, incorporeal, and formless. Its structure is not constituted by space-points. It is devoid of sensible qualities of material things. It is imperceptible to us, but perceptible to the omniscient soul. It is an external, neutral, auxiliary cause of rest of moving and stationary living beings and material things. It is not the principal cause of rest of living beings and non-living things. It does not generate their rest; nor does it impel them to rest. But it merely assists the rest of stationary or moving things. Adharma merely helps the rest of stationary and moving things, without which they would not be able to rest. It is the support of rest.[1]

The Jainas regard ākāśa as space. Space is one, eternal,

---

[1] DS., 17-18 ; DṢV., 17-18 ; TS., iii, 33-34 ; P., 93 ; SS., v, 8 & 17 ; TDTV., 90-92, 95-96.

pervasive, formless, and giving accommodation to living beings, matter, dharma, adharma, and time. It contains infinite space-points. Interpenetrability is the function of space.[1] Space is of two kinds, mundane space and supramundane space. Mundane space accommodates all souls, material things, dharma, adharma, and time. They are not distinct from the world. They together constitute it. But space is both identical with and distinct from the world. It is infinite, and contains the world. So mundane space is distinct from the world, and yet identical with it because it is conterminous with it. Beyond the world there is supramundane, pure space. It is infinite, eternal, formless, inactive, devoid of substances, and perceived by the omniscient souls only.[2] There is no dharma, adharma, matter, souls or time in it. Dharma, adharma, and mundane space are inseparable and co-extensive. They interpenetrate one another, and constitute one inseparable unity. Hence they are one in locality. But they are different in their functions. Motion is the function of dharma. Rest is the function of adharma. Accommodation or interpenetration is the function of space. They are three distinct incorporeal principles in the world.[3] They are eternal, uncreated, and of immense magnitudes. Mundane space contains souls, matter, dharma, adharma, and time.

Space is imperceptible. It is inferred from the fact that extended substances can exist in some place only. Space is what accommodates them. It is the necessary condition of their existence. Space does not make things extended. They are extended by their very nature. But they require a locus in which they can exist. Space is the locus of extension. It is not the same as extension. Space is occupied by substances.

The Jainas distinguish between absolute or real time and relative or empirical time. Absolute time is the auxiliary cause of continuance of substances. Relative time is the auxiliary cause of changes or modifications of substances. Continuance, modification, motion, temporal remoteness, and

---

[1] P., 97-98 ; DS., 19 ; TSār., iii, 38 ; TS., v, 9 & 18.

[2] DS., 19-20 ; P., 98.

[3] P., TDTV., 103.

temporal proximity, or oldness and newness of substances are the functions of time. Continuance is the function of real time. Modifications, activities, oldness, and newness are the functions of empirical time.[1] Substances continue in time. Their modifications are changes in time. Their movements occur in time. Their oldness and newness depend upon the passage of time.

Time has no extension. So it is not an extended substance. Extension is of two kinds, monodimensional and multi-dimensional extension. The moments of time exist in a mono-dimensional series, and have only linear extension. The other substances, living beings, matter, space, dharma, and adharma exist in a two-dimensional series, and have surface extension. The moments of time do not coexist with one another.[2]

Real time is one, eternal, formless, without beginning or end, and devoid of varieties. Empirical time has a beginning and an end, and consists of varieties, seconds, minutes, hours, and the like. Moments are momentary, but hours, days, weeks, and the like have long duration. Real time is an eternal substance. Empirical time is momentary or temporary because it is a mode of real time. Real time, when limited, produces empirical time. It is the material cause of empirical time. One time is modified into infinite moments.[3]

Time is confined to mundane space. It does not exist in supramundane space. It exists in mundane space in all its space-points. Innumerable particles of time existing in innumerable space-points are confined to mundane space. They do not step beyond it to pure supramundane space. Each particle of time exists in its own capacity in each space-point of mundane space, and is devoid of activity. Different particles of time exist in different space-points. They never mix with one another. This characteristic distinguishes time from all other substances. Time is the auxiliary cause of its own modifications and those of the other substances.[4] Infinite particles

---

[1] TS., v, 39 ; DS., 21 ; SS., v, 22 ; TSār., iii, 45-48. [2] P., 109.

[3] P,, TDTV., 108 ; DSV., 21 ; TS., v, 39 & 40.

[4] TSV., v. 40, p. 440 ; DS., 22 ; Tsāra., iii. 40 ; VP., xvi. 35.

of time are the modifications of one real time. Time is not a subjective cognition. It is a real substance. It has qualities and modifications. It is the substratum of conjunction and disjunction of substances.[1] Matter, space, and time are inseparable from one another.

THE NINE CATEGORIES (PADĀRTHA)

The Jainas recognize the reality of nine verities, *viz.*, (1) soul (jīva), (2) non-soul (ajīva), (3) merit (puṇya), (4) demerit (pāpa), (5) inflow (āsrava), (6) bondage (bandha), (7) stoppage (saṃvara), (8) shedding of karma (nirjarā), and (9) liberation (mokṣa). Jīva is a living being or soul. Ajīva is a non-living being or non-soul. Matter, dharma, adharma, space, and time constitute non-soul (ajīva). Puṇya is virtue or merit. Pāpa is vice or demerit. Āsrava is the inflow of karma-matter into the soul. Bandha is bondage, or investment of the soul by karma-matter. Saṃvara is the arrest of the inflow of karma-matter into the soul. Nirjarā is partial destruction of the accumulated karma-matter. Mokṣa is complete destruction of the accumulatied karma-matter and liberation of the soul from bondage. Of these nine categories jīva and ajīva are the primary existences. Merit, demerit, āsrava, bandha, saṃvara, nirjarā, and mokṣa are the conditions of the soul, which arise from its different relations to karma-matter.[2]

Pure thought or good will is an auspicious modification of the soul, which is subjective righteousness, virtue or merit. It produces an auspicious modification of karma-matter, which is called objective virtue. Subjective virtue produces objective virtue. Impure thought or bad will is an inauspicious modification of the soul, which is subjective unrighteousness, vice, or demerit. It produces an inauspicious modification of karma-matter, which is called objective vice. Virtue produces pleasure. Vice produces pain.[3] Subjective virtue produces auspicious karmas such as pleasure-bearing, good-

[1] DS., E.T., p. 63 ; DSV., 22 ; TSV., v, 39, 1 ; TS., v, 40.

[2] P., TDTV., 116.

[3] Ibid, 139 ; DSV., 38.

life-determining, good-character-determining, and good-family-determining karmas. Subjective vice produces inauspicious karmas such as pain-bearing, bad-life-determining, bad-character-determining, bad-family-determining karmas. Consciousness, bliss, and innate purity constitute the essential nature of the soul. So it cannot be said to have virtue, vice, bondage, and liberation. But it acquires virtue and vice according as it has auspicious and inauspicious thought-activities which produce auspicious and inauspicious karma-particles.[1]

Āsrava is the influx of karma-matter. There are two kinds of influx (āsrava) : (1) subjective influx (bhāvāśrava), and (2) objective influx (dravyāsrava). The modification of the soul which generates the influx of karma-matter into the soul is subjective influx. The physical influx of karma-matter into the soul is objective influx. Subjective influx is the modification of the soul through the five senses, and consists in thought-activities. It causes the physical influx of karma-matter into the soul. Influx is the effect of bodily, verbal, and mental actions, and the cause of the soul's bondage. It is said to be the channel through which karma-matter enters into the soul. It is the cause of virtue or vice. Subjective influxes are of two kinds, virtuous and vicious. Purity of mind, attachment to excellences of saints, and activities of body, speech, and mind prompted by compassion are virtuous subjective influxes. They generate the influx of pure karma-matter into the soul. They are the causes of virtue. They produce pure karma-matter.[2] Anger, pride, deceit, and greed agitate the mind, and produce impurity in it. Inordinate attachment to worldly things, impure emotions, indulgence in sensual pleasures, causing anguish to others, slandering others, and impure thoughts and emotions are the springs of vice. They are vicious subjective influxes, which produce impure karma-matter.[3]

---

1 TS., viii, 25-26 ; DSV., 38.

2 TS., v, 1-2 ; T Sār., iv, 3 ; P., TDTV., 142 ; DS., 29.

3 P., 143-44, 146-47.

Subjective influxes are of five kinds: (1) false belief, (2) want of control, (3) inadvertence, (4) bodily, verbal, and mental activities, and (5) passions. Objective or physical influxes are actual influxes of eight kinds of karma-matter into the soul, *viz.*, knowledge-obscuring, perception-obscuring, feeling-obscuring, deluding, age-determining, character-determining, family-determining, and obstructing karmas. The karma-matter which flows into the soul is very subtle and consequently imperceptible.[1]

The conscious state which causes the investment of the soul by karma-matter is called subjective bondage (bhāvabandha). The actual investment of the soul by karma-matter is objective bondage (dravyabandha). It is actual interpenetration of karma-particles with the soul. Subjective bondage is the alliance of the soul with conscious states generated by attachment and aversion. Objective bondage is the actual union of the soul with karmic matter. The soul, being defiled with passions, assimilates matter fit to form karma-particles. Bondage is this assimilation of karmic matter into the soul. Subjective bondage is the auspicious or inauspicious modifications of the soul tinged with attachment, aversion, and delusion. Objective bondage is the actual interpenetration of the soul with auspicious or inauspicious modifications of karma-particles. The union of karma-matter with the soul is due to the actions of mind, body, and speech which directly bring it about. Bondage is due to emotions of the soul tinged with desire, attachment, aversion, and delusion. These states are brought about by deluding karma which causes delusion. The actions of mind, body and speech are the external cause of bondage, since they directly bring about the union of karma-matter with the soul. The emotions of the soul are the internal cause of bondage.[2]

Objective bondage is of two kinds, bondage of the soul to good karmas, and its bondage to bad karmas. It is of four kinds according to the nature of karma, duration of

---

[1] DS., 30-31; DSV., 30.

[2] DS., 32; TS., viii, 1-2; P., TDTV., 154-55.

bondage, intensity and number of karma-particles interpenetrating the soul. Different kinds of karmas determine the nature of bondage. The karma-matter is combined with the soul for a longer or shorter duration. It may be mild or strong so that its fruition is mild or strong, immediate or delayed. The particles of karma-matter may be few or many, and interpenetrate the soul to a small or great extent. These are the four kinds of actual bondage. The nature and extent of bondage are due to the activities of mind, speech, and body. The duration and intensity of bondage are due to emotions and passions. Passions are the internal cause of bondage. Activities of mind, speech, and body are the external cause of bondage.[1]

First, there is a psychical disposition which generates the influx of karmic matter into the soul. This is subjective influx. Second, the subjective influx, generates the physical influx of karma-matter into the soul. This is physical influx. Third, there are emotional states due to desire, attachment, aversion and delusion. They produce subjective bondage. Fourth, subjective bondage produces physical bondage or union of the soul with karma-particles.[2]

Inhibition (samvara) is the opposite of influx (āsrava). Influx is the ingress of karma-matter into the soul. Inhibition is the stoppage of the influx of karma-matter into the soul. As there are two kinds of influxes, subjective and objective, so there are two kinds of inhibition, subjective and objective. The modification of consciousness which is the cause of stopping the influx of karma-matter into the soul is called subjective inhibition. The actual stoppage of the influx of karma-matter into the soul is called objective inhibition. The voluntary suppression of attachment, aversion, and delusion is subjective inhibition. The arrest of beneficial and harmful modifications of karmas caused by the suppression of the emotions is objective inhibition. Virtue and vice both should be avoided, for both produce karma-matter. Virtue produces pleasure. Vice produces pain. The moral aspirant should be

---

1 TS., viii, 3; DS., 33; DSV., 33; P., 155; SS., viii, 3.

2 VP., xvi, 43—44.

indifferent to pleasure and pain. The states of consciousness are pleasant, unpleasant, and pure. Only pure states of consciousness should be cultivated. The actual stoppage of all karma-matter through the great vows and meditation is the objective inhibition.[1]

Destruction of karmas is called shedding (nirjarā). It is of two kinds, subjective shedding (bhāvanirjarā) and objective shedding (dravyanirjarā). The pure thought activities which cause the destruction of karmas through penances after their fruits are enjoyed constitute subjective shedding. The destruction of karmas is objective shedding. Subjective shedding is the pure modification of the soul which facilitates the separation of karmas from the soul. Objective shedding is their actual separation from the soul. A person should practise inhibition to stop all further influx of karmas, and destroy the karmas, which have interpenetrated the soul, by means of penances.

Shedding of karmas leads to liberation (mokṣa). The modification of the soul, which is the cause of destruction of all karmas, is called subjective liberation (bhāvamokṣa). The actual separation of all karmas from the soul is called objective liberation.[2] Subjective liberation is freedom from the four destructive karmas and objective liberation is freedom from the four non-destructive karmas. In the state of liberation the soul realizes infinite knowledge, infinite perception, infinite bliss, and infinite power.

The liberated soul is absolutely self-determined, since it is firmly established in its instrinsic nature, and free from relations to other souls and objects.[3] But the conduct of a bound soul is self-determined as well as other-determined. It is self-determined when it is determined by its essentsal qualities. It is other-determined when it is determined by its accidental qualities. When the soul is moved by attachment and aversion to other things, and experiences pleasure and pain, it is other-

---

[1] TS., ix, 1-2; TDTV., 149; p., 149-150; DS., 34-35.
[2] DS., 37. 2 p. TDTV., 158.
[3] P., 165-66.

determined. When it is self-determined or determined by its essential nature, it is liberated from the bondage of karma-matter. The self determined by pleasant mental states yielding virtue, and painful mental states yielding vice which produce good karmas and bad karmas, is other-determined.[1] The liberated soul transcends virtue and vice and attains absolute purity. It shines forth in its innate glory. So the soul itself is the cause of its liberation.

ETHICAL DISCIPLINE

The subjective inhibition (bhāvasaṃvara) is brought about by (1) vows (vrata), (2) careful attitudes (samiti), (3) restraints (gupti), (4) observances (dharma), (5) meditations (anuprekṣā), (6) victory over troubles (pariṣahajaya), and (7) right conduct (cāritra).[2]

(1) The vows are of five kinds, *viz.*, non-injury, truthfulness, non-stealing, sex-restraint, and non-acceptance of unnecessary gifts. They consist in abstention from injury, falsehood, stealing, sex-indulgence, and acceptance of unnecessary gifts. They are called small vows, when there is limited abstention from them. They are called great vows when there is total abstention from them. The sins corresponding to the duties of non-injury, truthfulness, non-stealing, sex-restraint, and non-acceptance of unnecessary gifts are injury, falsehood, stealing, sex-gratification, and worldly attachment. Injury consists in hurting the life of a creature by actions of mind, body, and speech moved by passions. Falsehood consists in speaking untruth which gives pain to living beings through bodily and mental actions due to passions. Theft is misappropriation of others' property not given by them through vibrations of passions. Even covetousness is stealing. Incontinence consists in all acts of sex-indulgence due to passionate attachment of man and woman for each other. It nourishes injury, falsehood, and theft. Covetousness consists in attachment to the living and non-living objects of

---

[1] P., 162-64.

[2] TS., SS., ix, 2.

enjoyment, and in acquisition, preservation, and improvement of them. It is due to egoism or the sense that the external objects of enjoyment are mine. Covetousness nourishes injury, falsehood, theft, and incontinence.[1]

Vowers should be free from deceit, wrong belief, and desire for enjoyment of wordly objects. They are of two classes, householders and monks. Householders should observe small vows. Monks should observe great vows. Small vows are partial abstention from sins. Great vows are total abstention from sins. Householders should not kill animals, tell agreeable lies under the influence of emotions even in times of danger, make use of others' property without permission, and commit adultery. They should put a voluntary limit upon their possessions in life. These are the five small vows. Monks should not kill or injure any kind of life, indulge in falsehood in thought, word, and deed, and covet others' possessions under any circumstances. They should completely extirpate their attachment to objects of enjoyment. They should totally abstain from indulgence in sex-thoughts, sex-words, and sex-acts. They should not possess any property, and accept any gifts except what is absoutely necessary for bare subsistence. They should observe the vows with the utmost rigcur and vigilance.[2] They should not commit sins, cause sins to be committed, and approve of sins.

The moral aspirants should meditate on good-will or friendship for all living beings, delight at the sight of virtuous persons, compassion for distressed creatures, and indifference to vicious persons. The aspirants should meditate on the transitoriness of the world and life and impurity, unsubstantiality, transitoriness, and painfulness of the body. Buddhism also enjoins meditations on them.[3]

(2) Careful attitudes are of five kinds, *viz.*, the use of the trodden path to avoid injury to insects, gentle and good talk, receiving alms properly, care in lifting and laying down things, and excreting in solitary places. These are the means to avoid

[1] TS., SS., vii, 13-17.

[2] TS., SS., vii, 2, 18-20.

[3] TS., SS., vii, 9-12.

injury to life.[1] They stop the inflow of karma-matter due to carelessness.

(3) Restraints are of three kinds, *viz.*, restraint of body, restraint of speech, and restraint of mind. Restraint means control of the natural functions. Restraints are conducive to purification of the self. They are not conducive to worldly enjoyments.

(4) Observances are of ten kinds, *viz.*, cultivating habits of excellent forgiveness, excellent humility, excellent straightforwardness, excellent cleanliness, excellent truthfulness, excellent restraint, excellent austerities, excellent indifference, excellent non-possession, and excellent celibacy. They stop the influx of karma-matter due to transgression of the observances.

(5) Meditations are of twelve kinds, *viz.*, meditation on the transitoriness of the world, meditation on our having no other refuge than truth, meditation on the cycles of empirical life, meditation on one's sole responsibility for his own good and bad actions, meditation on the distinctness of the soul from the non-soul, mind, body, friends, and relatives, meditation on the uncleanness of the body, meditation on the influx of karma-matter into the soul due to sense-pleasures and passions, meditation on the inhibition of the influx of karma-matter into the soul, meditation on the destruction of karma-matter which has entered into the soul, meditation on the nature of the world, meditation on the difficulty of acquiring right faith, right knowledge, and right conduct, and meditation on the right path to liberation.[2] They remove negligence in the performance of duties and produce intense efforts in their performance..

(6) Conquest of troubles is of various kinds, *viz.*, conquest of hunger, thirst, cold, heat, bite of mosquitoes, languor, fatigue of walking, continuous sitting, sleeping on hard ground, pain of disease, pride of wisdom, despair arising from failure to attain knowledge, and despair arising from failure to attain the desired fruits even after penances, etc.

---

[1] TS., SS., ix, 5.

[2] TS., SS., ix, 4, 6-7.

(7) Right conduct is of five kinds, equanimity due to non-injury, sex-restraint, non-stealing, and non-acceptance of gifts for a certain period, paying penalties for faults due to inadvertence and recovering equanimity, purity due to absolute non-injury to living beings, conduct in which only subtle greed is present, and perfect conduct purged of all passions.[1] These kinds of right conduct completely stop the influx of karma-matter into the soul.

THE MEANS TO LIBERATION (MOKṢA)

The nature of liberation has been discussed in connection with the doctrine of nine categories. Right faith, right knowledge, and right conduct constitute the path to liberation. They must be determined by the pure nature of the self. If they are determined by external things and moved by attachment and aversion, they cannot lead to liberation. Devotion to an Arhat, Siddha, or Saṅgha produces beneficial karma which yields celestial happiness. But it does not liberate the soul from karmic matter. Absolute freedom from attachment is necessary for liberation. Devotion is an affection which disturbs the tranquillity of mind. Nirvāṇa is attained through devotion to one's self, absolutely free from attachment to any other thing or person. Extirpation of emotions and passions is necessary for liberation. Knowledge of the reality, devotion to the Tīrthaṇkaras and the scriptures, self-control and penance lead to heavenly happiness, but not to liberation. Nirvāṇa is attained by realization of the true nature of the self. Right conduct is the main constituent element of the path.[2]

The self is the abode of the three jewels of right faith, right knowledge, and right conduct. They exist in the self only. So they, being centred in the self, are the cause of liberation. Or the self itself, possessing the three jewels, is the cause of liberation.[3] Right faith is sincere belief in the essential principles of Jainism, jīva, ajīva, āsrava, bandha, samvara, nirjarā, and mokṣa. Right knowledge is the knowledge of the self and the not-self, free from doubt, illusion, and uncertainty.

---

[1] TS., SS., ix. 9 & 18. [2] P., TDTV., 113, 171-79. [3] DS., 39-40.

In mundane souls knowledge is preceded by perception. But in the perfect soul knowledge and perception arise simultaneously. From the ordinary point of view, vows, careful attitudes, and restraints constitute right conduct. Doing beneficial actions and abstaining from harmful actions constitute right conduct. But, from the realistic point of view, the arrest of all actions, external and internal, constitutes right conduct. The external acts of body and speech and the internal acts of the mind moved by attachment and aversion produce beneficial karmas and harmful karmas which are attached to the soul and cause saṃsāra. So right conduct consists in checking all kinds of acts which cause saṃsāra. By this means a person becomes free from all influx of beneficial and harmful karmas, realizes the real nature of his self, and attains liberation. From the ordinary and realistic points of view, liberation can be attained by meditation. Freedom from attachment, aversion, and delusion is favourable to meditation. Repetition of mantras and meditation on them are enjoined. All acts of body, speech, and mind should be restrained, and all faculties should be turned inward, and thought should be concentrated on the pure self. This is excellent concentration. Penances, vows, and knowledge of the scriptures are indispensable aids to meditation.[1]

Liberation is the absolute separation of the soul from all karmic-matter which has entered into the soul. The destruction of all accumulated karmic matter leads to the self's realization of its intrinsic purity. When karmic matter is burnt by right faith, right knowledge, and right conduct, it does not cause birth and death, even as scorched seeds do not germinate.[2] First, deluding karmas, which are the causes of saṃsāra, are entirely destroyed by right faith, right knowledge, and right conduct, when the influx of a new karma-matter is stopped, and the accumulated karma-matter is worn out. Then obstructive, knowledge-obscuring, and

[1] DS., 42, 44-45, 49 & 57 ; DSV., 46-48 & 56.

[2] TSār., viii, 2, 4 & 7.

faith obscuring karmas are simultaneously destroyed. Lordship appears in the soul separated from the four kinds of karma-matter. The person is called the supreme Lord. He becomes pure, enlightened, free from bodily and mental diseases, and omniscient. He is called the Victor (jīna). He attains nirvāṇa when the other four kinds of karmas, feeling-obscuring, age-determining, character-determining, and family-determining, are completely destroyed. The liberated soul moves upward to the summit of mundane space.[1] It realizes infinite knowledge, infinite perception, infinite bliss, and infinite power.

ATHEISM

The Naiyāyika argues that the world, which is of the nature of an effect, must have an efficient cause, just as a pot is made by a potter. God is the efficient cause of the world. He has created the world out of pre-existing eternal atoms which are its material cause. The world is of intermediate magnitude, consists of parts, and so is of the nature of an effect. It is produced by God who has direct knowledge of the material cause or atoms, desire to create the world, and the volition to do so.

The Jaina criticizes the Nyāya argument. If God is the creator of the world, He creates it with a body or without a body. He cannot create it without a body, just as a jar is not created by a potter without a body. Creation involves movement which is not possible without a body. If God creates the world with a body, it is either perceptible or imperceptible. It is not perceptible, since grass, plants, rainbow, clouds, and the like are found to be spontaneously generated without its aid. If God's body is imperceptible, what is its cause? If a special greatness is its cause, there is no reason to prove it, and it involves mutual dependence. God's imperceptible body depends upon His special greatness, and His special greatness depends upon His imperceptible body. Our body is caused by our merits and demerits. But God's body cannot be caused by

[1] Ibid, viii, 20-22, 24-25 & 27.

His merit and demerit because He is devoid of merit and demerit. Our merits and demerits also cannot be the cause of His inperceptible body. Therefore God cannot have a perceptible or imperceptible body. He cannot create the world without a body also.[1]

Even if we grant that the world is an effect, it does not follow that it is produced by one independent creator without accessories. If it is produced by one God, all effects in the world such as human productions may be produced by Him, and particular causes of particular effects are not necessary. Further, the world may be produced by the co-operation of many gods, even as a palace is made by the co-operation of many masons or as a bee-hive is made by the co-operation of many bees. The Naiyāyika argument that many gods will conflict with one another, frustrate one another, and produce a chaos, is invalid. If a society of bees can construct a bee-hive, a society of gods can create the world.[2]

Does God create variety in the world with the aid of the merits and demerits of the creatures or without their aid ? If He depends on them, He ceases to be the independent Lord. If He does not depend upon them, why does He make some creatures happy and others unhappy ? Then He is kind to some, and unkind to others, and thus guilty of partiality. If merits and demerits of creatures make them happy and unhappy, they become the Lord, and God ceases to be the Lord. The Law of Karma can account for variety in the world. The variety of the moving beings is due to fruition of the beneficial and harmful karmas produced by them. The variety of inanimate things is eternally existing in order to be objects of enjoyment of the conscious, moving, and non-moving souls. The Jainas explain variety in the world by the Law of Karma, and dispense with God as the Lord of Karma.[3]

Even if God exists, He cannot be eternal, ubiquitous, and omniscient. If God is eternal, is He of the nature of creative act or not of the nature of creative act ? If He is of the nature

---

[1] SVM., pp. 26-27. [2] SVM., pp. 27-28.

[3] Ibid, pp. 24-25, 31 & 33.

of creative act which is eternal, He can never desist from creating the world. If He desists from the creative act, He cannot be of the nature of creative act. Until the creative act is completed, not a single effect can be produced. If He is not of the nature of creative act, He can never create the world, since He cannot acquire creativity. Moreover, if He is absolutely eternal, He can neither create the world nor destroy it, since creation and destruction imply change, and God is admitted to be unchangeable and immutable. Creation and destruction are two distinct acts. They cannot be made by an eternal God who is not liable to change. Does God destroy the world by the same nature by which He creates the world? Or does He do so by a different nature? If He does so by the same nature, then creation and destruction of the world will be simultaneous owing to His identity of nature. If He does so by a different nature, then He is liable to change, and is not eternal. Diversity of nature is the characteristic of a non-eternal thing. Even if God is eternal, why does He not always create? If He does not always create owing to His volitions, then His volitions which depend upon His mere existence should impel Him to create always. If His different volitions are the causes of His different creations, then He ceases to be eternal. Eternal God cannot create the world.[1]

If God is the creator of the world, what is the motive of His creation? An intelligent being exerts himself owing to self-interest or compassion for others. So God being intelligent must create the world to serve His self-interest or out of compassion for His creatures. But He is an eternally fulfilled being, and has no unfulfilled desires. He has no self-interest. So He cannot create the world to fulfil His selfish end. Nor can He be moved by compassion for creatures. Compassion is desire to remove the sufferings of others. But before creation there is no suffering which is felt by the self through the mind, body, and sense-organs in intercourse with objects, which are not yet created. If God feels compassion for sufferings of creatures before their creation, then creation will depend upon

[1] SVM., pp. 33-34.

compassion, and compassion will depend upon creation and sufferings consequent on it. Hence God has no motive for creation.[1] If God creates the world in sport, then His creative act is purposeless like the play of a child. If creation follows from His nature then all effects may spring from the nature of their causes, and the hypothesis of God is unwarranted.

The Jainas do not believe in the existence of God. They are avowed atheists. According to them, the world is eternal and self-existent. Particular things in the world are created out of their material causes and destroyed into them. There is no creation out of nothing. There is no destruction of something into nothing. The phenomena in the world are governed by the law of causality subservient to the moral Law of Karma.

But though the Jainas do not believe in God, they believe in the innate divinity of each soul. Every soul can realize its intrinsic divinity by self-effort. It can realize its infinite knowledge, infinite perception, infinite bliss, and infinite power. In this sense, Jainism is not atheism. The Jainas worship the Tīrthaṅkaras or Arhats with devotion. They worship also the Siddhas, Ācāryas, Upādhyāyas, and Sādhus. They are called five Parameṣṭhins. The Jainas are full of religious fervour in their worship of the idols of the great souls.[2] They believe in worship, prayer, faith, and devotion, and recite mantras. They lay stress on meditation, penances, and right conduct for the realization of innate divinity. But their practical religion consists in tenderness for animal life. They have developed instinctive horror of killing animals and insects. They are scrupulous vegetarians. Jainism forbids killing life, causing life to be killed, and approving of killing life. It is a religion of morality without God. It believes in the inexorable Law of Karma.[3]

[1] Ibid, pp. 34-35. [2] DS., 50-54. [3] HIP., Vol. II, Ch. III.

CHAPTER VIII

THE VAIŚEṢIKA PHILOSOPHY

The term *Vaiśeṣika* is derived from the term *viśeṣa.* The Vaiśeṣika system lays stress on particularity (viśeṣa) of the eternal substances. Ether, space, time, souls, internal organs, and the atoms of earth, water, fire and air are eternal. Each of them has a particularity which is its distinctive feature. The Vaiśeṣika emphasizes the plurality and distinctness of physical things and individual souls. Its special feature is the doctrine of atomism.

Kaṇāda (300 B.C.), the author of the *Vaiśeṣika Sutra,* is the founder of the Vaiśeṣika system. It specializes in the philosophy of nature. Kaṇāda speaks of the six categories : substance, quality, action or motion, community, particularity, and inherence. The later Vaiśeṣikas clearly recognize non-existence as the seventh category. Kaṇāda does not clearly mention God in the *Vaiśeṣika Sutra.* Praśastapāda (400 A.D.), Śrīdhara (1000 A.D.) and Udayana (1000A.D.) discuss the theistic proofs, the nature of God, and His creation of the world out of the atoms and dissolution of it into them. The Vaiśeṣika discusses the nature of the individual self, the proofs for its existence, the plurality of finite souls, and their bondage and liberation.

KINDS OF INVALID KNOWLEDGE

Knowledge is a quality of the self, which inheres in it. It is in the nature of manifestation. It manifests an object, physical or mental. The genus of knowledge inheres in it. There are innumerable cognitions apprehending an infinite number of objects. But knowledge is mainly of two kinds, valid knowledge and invalid knowledge. Valid knowledge is what apprehends an object in its real nature. Invalid knowledge is what apprehends an object as different from it.[1] It is of four kinds : (1) doubt, (2) illusion, (3) indefinite perception, and (4) dream.

[1] SP., pp. 47 & 59 ; VS., VSU., ix, 2, 11 & 12.

Doubt is indefinite knowledge. The perception of the common quality of two objects and the recollection of their peculiar qualities generate a doubt as to whether the object perceived is one or the other. The common quality of a post and a man *e.g.*, height, is perceived. Then their special qualities are remembered. The mind oscillates between the two memory images. This is doubtful perception of an external perceptible object, which is expressed in such a form : 'Is it a post or a man ?'[1]

(2) Illusion is the knowledge of one object as another different from it. It is a definite knowledge which does not apprehend the real nature of an object. A cow is misperceived as a horse. Illusion is wrong perception by a sense-organ vitiated by the bodily humours—flatulence, bile, or phlegm, a subconscious impression produced by the perception of an object which is not present, conjunction of the self with manas, and demerit.[2]

(3) Anadhyavasāya is indefinite knowledge in which both alternatives are unmanifest. Ūha is a doubtful perception in which only one alternative is manifest to consciousness. When a familiar or an unfamiliar object is perceived as 'something' owing to inattention or interest in a special thing, we have indefinite perception. A person unfamiliar with a jackfruit tree has an indefinite perception of it. He has definite knowledge of an entity endued with beinghood, genus of substance, genus of earth, genus of tree, colour, and the like. He also perceives the genus of jackfruit tree. But he does not know that its name is jackfruit tree. He has indefinite knowledge of its name. His indefinite perception of the jackfruit tree as 'something' is anadhyavasāya.[3]

Dream is mental perception of a person through the sense-organs, whose sense-organs have ceased to function, and whose manas is overpowered by sleep. It arises from a particular conjunction of the self with manas called sleep, subconscious impressions, and merit or demerit. It appears like perception

[1] SP., p. 59 ; PBh., pp. 174-75. [2] SP., p. 59 ; PBh., p. 177.
[3] SP., p. 69 ; PBh., p. 182.

of unreal objects through the sense-organs. It is of three kinds. It arises from the strength of subconscious impressions, or defects of bodily humours, or merits and demerits. A person dreams of his beloved woman owing to the intensity of the subconscious impression of her generated by repeated thoughts of her. One dreams of flight in the sky owing to flatulence. One dreams of entering into fire owing to excess of bile. One dreams of crossing a river owing to predominance of phlegm. These dreams are due to defects of bodily humours. The auspicious dreams which betoken good are due to merit. The inauspicious dreams which betoken evil are due to demerit. Dreams are cognitions produced by the internal organ overpowered by sleep.[1]

KINDS OF VALID KNOWLEDGE

Valid knowledge is of four kinds, perception, inference, recollection, and intuition due to austerities. (1) Perception is external or internal. Internal perception is due to conjunction of the self with the internal organ. Cognition, pleasure, pain, desire, aversion, and volition are apprehended by internal perception. External perception is of five kinds, olfactory, gustatory, visual, tactual, and auditory. Perception is either indeterminate or determinate. Earth, water, and fire are perceived owing to the conjunctions of the self with the manas, of the manas with the sense-organs, and of the sense-organs with the objects, when they have extension and manifest colour, and consist of many parts. The substances endued with qualities, actions and communities, and qualified by other substances are perceived.[2]

(2) Recollection is produced by a particular conjunction of the self with manas, a subconscious impression, and suggestive forces or cues. The self is the inherent cause, conjunction of the self with manas, the non-inherent cause, and a subconscious impression, the efficient cause of recollection. It apprehends a past object, seen, heard, or felt in the past owing to a

---

[1] PBh., pp. 183-84 ; SP., p. 68. [2] PBh., pp. 187-88.

particular conjunction of the self with manas and revival of its subconscious impression produced by intensity, frequency, or emotional appeal of a past experience.[1] Perception, recollection, or thought of a connected experience is the exciting cause of recollection. Attention, intention to recall, inhibition of contrary suggestive forces, perception of a similar object and the like are its exciting causes.[2] Recollection is a kind of valid knowledge. It apprehends the real nature of an object perceived in the past.

(3) Intuition due to austerities is the intuition of the sages, who are the authors of the scriptures. It is immediate apprehension of the real nature of the past, present and future objects, of the Moral Law and other supersensible objects owing to a particular conjunction of the self with manas and a peculiar merit born of austerities. It is akin to yogic perception. It is produced by a special kind of merit born of austerities, while yogic perception is due to intense meditation. It is produced by the internal organ, and not by the external sense-organs. It is a distinct and vivid perception through the internal organ called prātibhajñāna. The sages have this kind of intuition in abundance. But even the common people have momentary flashes of intuitive non-sensuous perception. A young girl says, 'My heart says: my brother will come to-morrow.' This is non-sensuous intuition.[3] It is a kind of valid knowledge.

Inference is the knowledge derived from the mark, from which the existence of the probandum is inferred as its effect, or cause, or conjunct, or antagonist, or inherent. From a rainfall in the source of a river (cause) a flood in the river (effect) is inferred. From smoke (effect) the existence of a fire (cause) is inferred. From a body (conjunct) the existence of the tactual organ (conjunct) conjoined with it is inferred. From an infuriated serpent the existence of a mongoose (antagonist) hidden behind a bush is inferred. From the heat of water the existence of a fire (inherent) is inferred. Heat inheres in fire, but not in water.

[1] VS., VSU., VSV., ix, 2, 6; PBh., p. 256.

[2] NS., iii, 2, 44.

[3] PBh., NK., p. 258.

The mark is the means of inference, which is based upon the relations of causality, conjunction, opposition and inherence. The causal relation between the probans and the probandum is shown by the members of an inference. A mark or probans preceded by the knowledge of a well-known and well-established general principle leads to the knowledge of the probandum.[1]

THE CATEGORIES (PADĀRTHA)

Padārtha literally means the meaning of a word. It is an object of knowledge, and capable of being named. It is knowable and nameable. It is an object of valid knowledge. Kaṇāda brings all objects of valid knowledge under six categories. They are substance (dravya), quality (guṇa), action or motion (karma), generality (sāmānya), particularity (viśeṣa), and inherence (samavāya).[2] Kaṇāda does not mention non-existence or negation. The later Vaiśeṣikas add the seventh category of non-existence. Śridhara, Udayana and Śivāditya recognize seven categories including non-existence.

Substance is the substratum of quality and action. A book is a substance. Its colour, extension, solidity, dimension and the like are its qualities. Its motion is its action. Its qualities and motion subsist in it. Quality cannot subsist in itself, but it subsists in a substance, which is its substratum. Quality is comparatively permanent and passive, but action or motion is temporary and dynamic. The genus of man subsists in many individual persons. It is a generality or community. An eternal substance has particularity which distinguishes it from other eternal substances. Space is one, eternal and ubiquitous substance. It has a particularity which distinguishes it from other eternal substances, time, ether and the like. Inherence is the inseparable relation between substance and quality, substance and action, a generality and an individual, an eternal substance and its particularity, and a composite substance and its component parts. When a jar is destroyed, there is negation

---

1 VS., ix, 2, 1-2 & 4 ; VSU., ix, 2, 1 ; VS., iii, 1, 14-15.

2 VS., i, 1, 4 ; SP., p. 9.

or non-existence of the jar. Substance is the main category. All other categories depend on it for their existence. Substance is the substratum of quality, action, community, particularity and inherence.[1]

The first six categories have existence, nameability and knowability. They are objects of the positive notion of being. They can be known without depending on their counter-entities, and expressed by names. They are capable of being known, though they exist independently of being known. The three categories of substance, quality and action are related to beinghood (sattā) which subsists in them. The three categories of generality, particularity and inherence are related to themselves and devoid of relation to beinghood. They are neither causes nor effects. They are eternal and incapable of being expressed by the word 'object'. They are non-spatial and timeless ontological entities. Substance, quality and action are causes capable of producing effects and liable to destruction. They exist in time and space.[2]

SUBSTANCE (DRAVYA)

Kaṇāda defines a substance as an entity which has qualities and actions, and which is the inherent or material cause of an effect.[3] A substance is the substrate of qualities and actions. It is not a mere collection of qualities and actions. It is not a mere aggregate of qualities as the Buddhist realist maintains. Nor is it a mere complex of ideas as the Buddhist idealist maintains. It has a real, objective existence. It differs from its qualities and actions because it is their substrate. If it were not different from them, it would not be their substrate. Qualities and actions are devoid of qualities and actions. They are not self-existent, but they exist in a substance. The relation between a substance and its qualities and actions is inherence.

A substance is the material or inherent cause of its effect.[4]

---

[1] PBh., p. 7. [2] PBh., pp. 16, 17 & 19. [3] VS., i, 1, 15; x, 2, 1. [4] VSU., i, 1, 15.

This characteristic distinguishes it from a quality and an action which are non-inherent causes. Threads are the inherent cause of a cloth. They are the material out of which it is produced. But the conjunction of threads, which is a quality, is its non-inherent cause. The whole is not a mere aggregate of parts as the Buddhist realist maintains. It has an existence over and above that of its parts. They are its material cause ; it inheres in them. The relation between a material cause and its product is inherence.

A substance has the genus of substance which inheres in it. Substances are eternal and non-etermal. Non-eternal substances consist of parts, and are produced by their combination, and destroyed by their separation. Composite substances are produced and destroyed by something different from themselves. They are non-eternal. They are not self-subsistent and independent, but they subsist in their component parts.[1] But simple and partless substances like the atoms of earth, water, fire and air are eternal. They are neither produced nor destroyed. They are self-existent, independent and endued with particularities. Space, time, ether and souls, which are incorporeal and ubiquitous, are eternal. Minds (manas) are atomic and eternal. They are neither produced nor destroyed.[2]

QUALITY (GUṆA)

Kaṇāda defines a quality as an entity inhering in a substance, and devoid of quality, which is not an unconditional cause of conjunction and disjunction. Praśastapāda adds one more characteristic of a quality. He defines it as an entity related to the genus of quality, abiding in a substance, and devoid of quality and action.[3]

A quality inheres in a substance, which is its substrate. It depends upon a substance for its subsistence. But it is not identical with a substance. If it were so, it would not be related to a substance as the content of a substrate. A

[1] PBh., pp. 16-18.

[2] VS., VSU., i, 1, 8, 10 & 12 ; SP., MB., pp. 37-38 ; BhP., i, 3 ; SM., pp. 60-70 ; TBh., pp. 20-23 ; TSG., pp. 5-10.

[3] VS., i, 1, 16 ; PBh., p. 94.

substance is the substrate of its quality, which is its content. Qualities inhere in a substance. But sometimes a substance also inheres in another substance. A composite substance inheres in its component parts. So a quality is defined as devoid of qualities. A composite substance is not devoid of qualities. But a quality is devoid of qualities. An action or movement also inheres in a substance, and is devoid of quality. It is an unconditional cause of conjunction and disjunction. But a quality is not an unconditional cause of conjunction and disjunction. Hence a quality is different from an action.[1]

A quality is devoid of action. A substance only has an action. A fan has motion; but its colour is devoid of motion. A quality has no motion, but it seems to be in motion because its substrate is in motion. A quality is devoid of quality. Number is the quality of a substance, but it is not a quality of its colours, odours, tastes and other qualities. A quality has a community,—the genus of quality.[2] A colour has the genus of colour. A quality differs from community, particularity and inherence, which are devoid of community. It differs from a substance because it is devoid of quatities, while the latter is endued with qualities. It differs from an action, which is devoid of qualities, but which is an unconditional cause of conjunction and disjunction.. A quality is not their unconditional cause. A quality exists through relation to beinghood. The genus of quality subsists in a quality. It may possess an inferior community also. A colour possesses the genus of colour also.[3]

ACTION OR MOTION (KARMA)

Kaṇāda defines an action as an entity, which inheres in one substance, which is devoid of a quality, and which is an unconditional cause of conjunction and disjunction.[4] Action is physical motion, and resides in a substance like a quality.

---

[1] VSU., i, 1, 16. [2] NK., pp. 94-95; SM., p. 400; TBh., p. 24.
[3] PBh., NK., p. 17; ṬR., pp. 139-40. [4] VS., i, 1, 17.

But an action is its dynamic and temporary feature, whereas a quality is its static and enduring feature. Conjunction, which is a quality, resides in many substances, which are conjoined with each other. But an action or motion abides in one substance only. It does not reside in many substances. Conjunction of a book with a table resides in the two substances. But the motion of a fan resides in it only. An action, like a quality, resides in a substance, and is devoid of a quality. But it is an unconditional cause of conjunction and disjunction, whereas a quality is not their cause. The motion of a carriage is the direct and immediate cause of its disjunction from one part of the ground and conjunction with another part of it. An action is a non-inherent cause of conjunction and disjunction. The carriage which is a substance, is the inherent or material cause of its disjunction from one part of the ground, and of its conjunction with another part of it. But its motion is their non-inherent cause. Its colour, which is its quality, is never their non-inherent cause.[1] Motion has the genus of motion which inheres in it.

Motion resides in a corporeal substance of limited dimension. It is non-eternal, and resides in a non-eternal substance. An incorporeal, ubiquitous substance, like ether, time, space, or a soul, is incapable of motion.[2] It cannot change its position. Motion is produced by heaviness, fluidity, effort and conjunction. It is destroyed by the destruction of its basic substance, or its conjunction with another substance.

Five kinds of action or motion are recognized, *viz.*, upward motion, downward motion, contraction, expansion, and locomotion. Upward motion brings a body into contact with a higher region, *e.g.*, throwing a stone upward. Downward motion brings a body into contact with a lower region, *e.g.*, throwing a stone downward from a tree to the ground. Contraction brings the parts of a body closer to one another, *e.g.*, the rolling of a cloth. Expansion makes the parts of a body farther from one another, *e.g.*, the unfolding of a cloth. All other kinds of motion are comprised in locomotion.

[1] VSU., i, 1, 17; TR., p. 156. [2] TBh., p. 28.

Walking, evacuation, flow flaming up, and slanting motion are different kinds of locomotion.[1]

COMMUNITY OR GENERALITY (SĀMĀNYA)

Kaṇāda says, 'Community and particularity depend upon the intellect to indicate their existence.' They are not conceptual constructs, but ontological entities. Community is the cause of assimilation. It is the objective basis of the notion of common characters among many individuals, which are quite different from one another.[2] It is the essential and common character of many individuals. It is natural and not accidental. It is one and eternal, and exists in many individuals.[3] There is one community in many individuals. There is the genus of cow in many cows, which is one, and not different in different individual cows. Community inheres in many individuals. It exists in many individuals entirely and simultaneously without differing in its essential nature. It produces an abstract universal concept of many individuals.

(1) Community inheres in all its proper individuals. The genus of cow exists in all individual cows. It does not exist in all individuals—cows, goats, sheep and the like. It is not perceived in all individuals. Though a community is not limited to a particular place, it exists in all its proper individuals, which are produced by their causes and collocations of conditions.[4] They only are its substrates. (2) Community exists in all its proper individuals with an identical nature. It does not differ in its nature in different individuals. (3) Community exists in many individuals. The genus of cow exists in all cows. It does not exist in one cow. Ether is one. So there is no genus of ether. (4) Community is the cause of the concept of common character in many individuals. It is the universal class-essence existing in many

---

[1] BhP., 7; TR., pp. 156-58; TBh., p. 28; TSG., p. 94; SP., MB., p.39; KNR., pp. 152-58; VS., v, 2, 21.

[2] VS., i, 2, 3; PBh., p. 11; NK., p. 11.

[3] KV., p, 22; SP., p. 39; MB., p. 40; PBh., pp. 311 & 314.

[4] PBh., p. 314.

similar individuals, and produces a concept which is an assimilative cognition. A concept is produced by a community which is its objective basis. (5) Community exists simultaneously in its identical nature in many individuals. It does not cease to exist in one individual, when it comes to exist in another new-born individual.[1] (6) Community is eternal. It is one in many individuals, and therefore eternal. If it were not eternal, one community could not subsist in many non-eternal individuals past, present, and future. (7) Community is different from the individuals, which are its substrates. If it were not different from its substrates, it would be produced and destroyed with them. But it is not produced, when they are produced, and it is not destroyed when they are destroyed. It is eternal, while they are temporary. Further, the individuals are different from one another, and produce discriminative cognitions, which apprehend their different specific characters. But community produces assimilative cognition, which apprehends their common character. So a community is different from its proper individuals.[2]

The genus of earth is inferior to the genus of substance. The genus of colour is inferior to the genus of quality. The genus of upward motion is inferior to the genus of motion. So there is a hierarchy of genera with Being as the highest genus and the lowest genera at the bottom. There is the highest genus (parā jāti). There are the lowest species (aparā jāti). There are the subaltern genera and species (parāparā jāti).

Being (sattā) is the highest generality. Substances, qualities, and actions exist through relation to Being. Being is common to them. But it is different from them. Substances, qualities and actions are different from one another. But Being is identical in them. So it is different from its substrates, and inheres in them. There is one Being in substances, qualities, and actions. It does not differ in its different substrates. We perceive them all as existing. Being is the one, identical,

[1] NK., p. 313,

[2] PBh., p. 314 ; NK., pp. 314-16.

common factor in them. It has no special distinguishing marks. So Being is one.[1]

PARTICULARITY (VIŚEṢA)

Kaṇāda defines particularity as the ultimate distinguishing feature of an eternal substance, which is known by its discrimination from the other eternal substances. It depends upon the intellect to indicate its existence.[2] Particularities are the final distinctive characters of eternal substances. They subsist in the eternal substances,—the atoms, ether, time, space, self and manas. One particularity inheres in each of them, which distinguishes it from the other eternal substances.[3]

Particularities do not require other particularities to distinguish them from one another, because it would lead to infinite regress. They not only distinguish their substrates from one another, but they also distinguish themselves from one another. They distinguish their substrates from one another without the aid of other attributes, because then they would lose their distinctive character. They are devoid of a community. If they had a community, that would distinguish their substrates from one another. They exist in single substances only. They do not exist through inherence of Being in them, which is a generality.

Eternal substances have particularities, which distinguish them from one another. But their qualities have no particularities. They also are distinguished from one another by the particularities of their substrates. Eternal substances are infinite in number, and their particularities also are innumerable.[4]

Composite non-eternal substances are distinguished from one another by their parts, qualities, actions, conjunction with other substances, and the like. A white cow is distinguished

---

[1] NK., p. 12 & 17 ; BhP., 8-10 ; PBh., pp. 311-12 ; VS., VSU., i, 2, 7-8 & 17.

[2] VS., 1, 2, 3 & 6.

[3] PBh., pp. 13 & 321.

[4] SM., pp. 80-83 ; KV., pp. 24-25 ; TR., p. 159 ; SP., p. 12 ; MB., p. 12.

by her quality. A cow moving fast is distinguished by her action. A cow with a large hump is distinguished by a part of her body. A cow with a large bell is distinguised by her conjunction with another substance. But the two atoms of earth, which have the same form, quality, and action are distinguished from each other by their particularities. Composite substances are distinguished from one another by their parts. They do not require particularities to distinguish them from one another. But the eternal substances, for example, atoms, which are partless, homogeneous, and endued with the same qualities and actions, are distinguished from one another by their particularities. Two liberated souls, whose special qualities are destroyed, are distinguished from each other by their particularities. If they had no particularities, they would be indistinguishable from each other. Particularities are necessary to ensure their existence as distinct entities.[1]

INHERENCE (SAMAVĀYA)

Kaṇāda defines inherence as the relation between a material cause and its effect, which is the cause of the notion 'this subsists in this abode.' Praśastapāda defines it as the relation which subsists between two inseparable entities related to each other as the substrate and the content, and which is the cause of the notion 'this subsists in this abode'. It is not the relation between two entities, which are capable of separate existence and subsistence in different substrates. Separable entities are capable of existing apart from each other and residing in different substrates. A cloth subsists in its constituent yarns. Though the yarns subsist in their parts, which are different from the cloth, yet both cannot subsist in different substrates apart from each other. The cloth subsists in the yarns, which compose it. Though they have an independent existence apart from the cloth, yet it has no independent existence apart from them. The yarns are the substrate, and the cloth is its content. They are its material

[1] NK., p. 323 ; KV., pp. 24-25 ; SM., pp. 78-83.

cause, and it subsists in them.[1] Inherence is a relation between a substance and a qualitiy, a substance and an action, a genus and an individual, an eternal substance and its particularity, a whole and its parts. A quality inheres in a substance. An action inheres in a substance. A genus inheres in an individual. A particularity inheres in an eternal substance. A composite whole inheres in its constituent parts. An effect inheres in its material cause.

Inherence is inseparable relation between two non-pervasive entities, which are restricted to particular places and which are known to be different from each other. Inseparable relation implies incapacity of its relata for independent existence.[2]

Inherence is inseparable relation between two entities, one of which is incapable of separate existence apart from the other. A composite whole cannot exist apart from its parts. But when it is destroyed, the parts can exist apart from it. But so long as the whole exists, it and its parts cannot exist apart from each other. A quality cannot exist apart from its substance. But the substance can exist apart from its quality at the moment of its production. It acquires its qualities at the next moment. But so long as a quality persists, a substance cannot exist apart from it. An action cannot exist apart from its substance. But the substance can exist without its action. An action is temporary, while its substance is enduring. But so long as an action lasts, a substance cannot exist apart from it. An individual cannot exist apart from its genus. But the genus exists before the individual is born and after it is destroyed. But so long as the individual lasts, the genus cannot exist apart from it. The genus and the individual are inseparably related to each other. The genus exists in the other individuals. But its existencce in them does not affect its inseparable relation to a particular individual.[3] A particularity cannot exist apart from an eternal substance. An eternal substance also cannot exist apart from its particularity. There is mutual dependence

---

1 VS., vii, 2, 26 ; PBh., p. 14 ; NK., pp. 14-15.

2 PBh., pp. 324-25 ; NK., p. 325 ; SM., pp. 83-84.

3 KVB., p. 47.

here. But in the other instances there is one-sided dependence. Therefore inherence is an intimate relation, but it is not an internal relation. It is an external relation.

Inherence is one, because it has the same distinguishing feature. There is no evidence of its distinctions. One inherence can account for all notions 'this subsists in this abode'. So it is useless to assume many inherences. One inherence is enough to relate all its relata,—substances and their qualities, substances and their actions, wholes and parts, genera and individuals, eternal substances and their particularities.[1]

Inherence is eternal, though its relata are transient. It is not produced by any cause, and does not pertain to relations in time. It is different from conjunction, which is a temporary relation. Just as one Being inheres in many existing entities, so one inherence subsists between innumerable pairs of relata. Just as Being is eternal, so inherence is eternal. Inherence is different from conjunction, which is a temporary relation.[2] An effect is mainly produced by a material cause. It is produced by a non-material cause and an efficient cause with the aid of a material cause. If it had a material cause, it would be related to its cause either by itself or by another inherence. It cannot be related to its cause by itself, because then it would be substrate of itself. But no entity can be both a substrate and its content, and can subsist in itself. Nor can inherence be related to its cause by another inherence, for it would lead to infinite regress. Therefore inherence is uncaused and eternal.[3]

Inherence is not conjunction, since the latter is a relation between two substances, while the former is a relation between a substance and another substance or non-substance. Conjunction is a separable relation, while inherence is an inseparable relation. In conjunction the relata exist as unrelated to each other before they are conjoined. But in inherence the relata are always related to each other, when they

---

[1] PBh., p. 326; SM., pp. 85-86.

[2] PBh., p. 328; SP., p. 40; MB., p. 40.

[3] VSU., vii, 2, 26.

are related as a substrate and its content.[1] Inherence is eternal, while conjunction is temporary. Conjunction is produced, but inherence is uncaused. Conjunction is destroyed by disjunction of its relata, but inherence is indestructible. Conjunction is a relation between two independent substances, but inherence is a relation between a substrate and its content. Inherence is a natural and inseparable relation, while conjunction is an adventitious and separable relation. Inherence is a separate category, while conjunction is a quality. Inherence is one, while conjunctions are many. Inherence is imperceptible, while conjunction is perceptible.

Inherence is different from substance, quality, action, community, and particularity, because it is a relation between a substance and the other categories.[2] It is different from non-existence. So it is a distinct category.

NON-EXISTENCE (ABHĀVA)

Udayana divides the categories into existence and non-existence. He divides the former into substance, quality, action community, and particularity, and the latter into prior non-existence, posterior non-existence, absolute non-existence, and mutual non-existence.[3]

Prior non-existence is the non-existence of an effect in its material cause before its production. A jar is produced from clay. There is prior non-existence of the jar in clay. It is without a beginning, but has an end. It is destroyed by the production of the effect. When the jar is produced, its prior non-existence is destroyed. Thus prior non-existence is not produced but destroyed. It is beginningless but non-eternal. If it is not destroyed, the effect cannot be produced.

Posterior non-existence is the non-existence of an effect by its destruction. When an effect is destroyed, and loses its

[1] PBh., p. 326 ; MB., p. 40.

[2] VSU., vii, 2, 26 ; PBh., 326 ; NK., p. 326.

[3] Lakṣaṇāvalī, Benares, 1897, pp. 1 & 13 ; SP., p. 13 ; NK., p. 230.

specific nature, it has posterior non-existence. It has a beginning, but no end. Posterior non-existence is produced by the destruction of an effect, but it can never be destroyed. When a jar is destroyed by the stroke of a club, it has posterior non-existence in its fragments, which is produced by an efficient cause.[1]

The non-existence of a cow in a horse and the non-existence of a horse in a cow are mutual non-existence. It is one and eternal, but it is related to different objects when they are produced. The knowledge of non-existence of a cloth in a jar depends on the knowledge of the jar as well as the cloth, which is its counter-entity. Mutual non-existence has for its counter-entity identity between two things. Negation other than mutual negation is negation of relation.[2]

Absolute negation is non-existence in all times. There is absolute negation of colour in air. There is absolute negation of the genus of earth in water, and of the genus of water in earth. Absolute negation does not refer to production or destruction. It does not refer to the past or the future. It is neither prior negation nor posterior negation. It is negation in all times. It is neither produced nor destroyed, but eternal by nature. Absolute negation is different from mutual negation. Mutual negation is denial of identity between two things, which have specific natures. But absolute negation is denial of an absolutely non-existent entity in all times and in all places.[3]

The category of negation or non-existence is absolutely necessary for the Vaiśeṣika philosophy of realistic pluralism. If there were no prior non-existence, an effect would not be produced. If there were no posterior non-existence, there would be no destruction of an effect. If there were no mutual non-existence, there would not be different things with specific natures. If there were no absolute non-existence, all things

---

[1] NK., p. 230; TBh., p. 20.

[2] NK., p. 230; SM., pp. 89-92; TBh., p. 29.

[3] TBh., p. 29; TSG., p. 96; VSU., ix, 1, 9-10; NK., p. 230.

would exist always and everywhere. If there were no non-existence, all things would be eternal.[1]

EARTH, WATER, FIRE AND AIR

Earth has the genus of earth. It has colour, taste, smell, touch, number, magnitude, conjunction, disjunction, remoteness, proximity, weight, acquired fluidity, and velocity.[2] It has many kinds of colour, whiteness and the like. It has six kinds of taste, sweet, sour, salt, bitter, pungent, and astringent. It has two kinds of smell, agreeable and disagreeable. Its touch is neither hot nor cold, but due to heating.

Earth is eternal and non-eternal. The atoms of earth are eternal. Composite earthen substances, which are produced, are non-eternal. They are stable, composed of parts arranged in a particular order, manifold and possessed of lower genera. They serve many useful purposes of selves. Bodies, sense-organs and objects are the three kinds of effects of earth. Colour taste, smell, and touch of eternal and non-eternal earth are non-eternal and due to heating. Heating is contact with fire.[3]

The genus of water inheres in water. It has colour, taste, touch, natural fluidity, viscidity, number, magnitude, distinctness, conjunction, disjunction, remoteness, proximity, weight and velocity. It has white colour, sweet taste, and cold touch. Viscidity is the quality of water only.

Water is eternal and non-eternal. The atoms of water are eternal, and composite watery substances are non-eternal. The qualities of the eternal atoms of water are eternal, and those of non-eternal watery substances are non-eternal. The products of water are bodies, sense-organs, and objects. The gustatory organ is composed of water and can perceive taste.[4]

The genus of fire inheres in fire which has colour, touch, number, magnitude, distinctness, conjunction, disjunction, remoteness, proximity, acquired fluidity, and velocity. Fire has bright, white colour, hot touch, and adventitious fluidity.

Fire is eternal and non-eternal. The atoms of fire are

---

[1] NK., 230. [2] PBh., p. 27; BhP., i, 32; TBh., p. 20. [3] TBh., p. 20.
[4] PBh., pp. 35-36; BhP., i, 31, 39-40; TSC., p. 16; SP., p. 14.

eternal. The composite fiery substances are non-eternal. The products of fire are bodies, sense-organs, and objects. The visual organ is composed of light and perceives colour. Fire is of four kinds, fire having manifested or perceptible colour and touch, fire having unmanifested or imperceptible colour and touch, fire having unmanifested colour and manifested touch, and fire having manifested colour and unmanifested touch. Blazing fire and rays of the sun have manifest colour and touch, which are perceptible. The light of the visual organ has unmanifested colour and touch, which are not perceptible. Fire in hot water has unmanifested colour, which is not visible. But it has manifested touch, which is tangible. The light of a lamp has manifested colour, which is visible. But it has unmanifested touch, which is not tangible.[1]

The genus of air inheres in air, which has touch, number, magnitude, distinctness, conjunction, disjunction, remoteness, proximity, and velocity. Its touch is neither hot nor cold nor due to heating. It is devoid of colour and endued with touch.

Air is eternal and non-eternal. The atoms of air are eternal, and composite aerial substances are non-eternal. The products of air are bodies, sense-organs, and objects. The tactual organ, which pervades the body, is composed of air and perceives touch. Aerial objects are possessed of touch. There is one vital force in the body. But it is said to be manifold according to its functions. Life sustains the vital functions, and directs chyle, humours, and other ingredients of the body. It is a kind of air.[2]

There are atoms of earth, water, fire and air, which are eternal. They are neither created nor destroyed. They are combined into composite substances, which are produced and destroyed. The qualities of atoms are eternal, but those of composite products are non-eternal.

THE VAIŚEṢIKA THEORY OF ATOMISM

The Vaiśeṣika advocates the theory of atomism. Earth, water, fire and air are eternal as atoms, and non-eternal as

[1] PBh., pp. 38-39 ; TBh., p. 20-21 ; TSG., p. 17 ; SP., pp. 14-15.

[2] PBh., p. 44 ; TBh., p, 21 ; TSG., p. 19 ; SP., p. 15 ; BhP., i, 42-44.

composite products. There are atoms of earth, water, fire and air. They are the minutest and indivisible units of physical substances. They are globular, though they are partless. They cannot interpenetrate one another, for there is no intra-atomic space. They are inactive or motionless in themselves. Their motion is due to an external agent. The later Vaiśeṣikas maintain that God produces motion in the atoms, combines them into composite products with the aid of merits and demerits of the individual souls for their enjoyments and sufferings. The physical order is subservient to the moral order. The world is not a fortuitous combination of atoms governed by the mechanical law of causality. It is governed by the law of causality subordinated to the Law of Karma.

The Vaiśeṣika maintains that a dyad (dvyaṇuka) is produced by the conjunction of two atoms, which are active or moving. The motion of the atoms is produced by God. The two atoms are its inherent cause ; their conjunction is their non-inherent cause ; the unseen agencies, merits and demerits of individual souls, are its efficient cause. When there is an activity among three dyads, they come into conjunction with one another, and produce a triad (tryaṇuka). A quartrad (caturaṇuka) is produced by the conjunction of four triads, which are active. The quartrads are combined into larger and larger composite substances. The qualities of the composite products are produced by those of the component atoms, which are their inherent causes.[1]

An atom is eternal, because it is a substance, which is partless, like ether. The cause of destruction is either destruction of its substrate or disjunction of its parts.[2] A dyad is non-eternal, since its component atoms are disjoined from each other. It consists of parts, but atoms are partless. If they are said to be composed of parts since they are corporeal or of limited magnitude, then there will be infinite regress. If atoms have parts, they also have parts, and so on to infinity. So atoms are partless and eternal. They are not non-spatial,

[1] TBh., p. 21.

[2] NK., pp. 31-32.

but they have the minutest magnitude. They are spherical and supersensible. But they can be perceived by yogins and God. They have atomic magnitude. The magnitude of a dyad also is minute, but it is greater than that of an atom. Dyads also are imperceptible to us, but perceptible to the yogins and God. The magnitude of a dyad is due to the number of its constituent atoms. The magnitude of a product is due to the number, magnitude, and arrangement of its constituent parts. A triad is composed of three dyads, which is gross and perceptible. Its gross magnitude is due to the number, magnitude and arrangement of its constituent parts. The smallest visible particle is the mote in a sun-beam, which is a triad (trasareṇu). The large magnitude of triads, quartrads, and larger composite substances is due to the magnitude of their material causes or component parts as well as their arrangement.[1]

The following arguments are advanced by the Vaiśeṣika for the existence of atoms. First, there are different degrees of magnitudes, which have the highest limit in the largest magnitude of ether, and which have the lowest limit in the minutest magnitude of an atom. There are larger and larger magnitudes, which culminate in the largest magnitude of ether. There are smaller and smaller magnitudes, which end in the minutest magnitude of an atom. An atom is the minutest part, which is indivisible.[2] Secondly, if atoms had parts, then they also would have parts, and so on to infinity. Then there would be no difference in the dimensions of things. If all substances were endlessly divisible into an infinite number of parts, then there would be no difference in the magnitude of things, and a mountain and a mustard seed would be of equal dimension. So we must admit that atoms are the minutest parts of composite substances, which are partless and indivisible. Thirdly, composite products are transient, changeable, divisible, produced and destroyed. Therefore they are composed of atoms, which are eternal, unchangeable, indivisible, unproduced and indestructible. Fourthly, if there

[1] NK., pp. 31-32, SP., p. 51; MB., p. 52; KNR., p. 9.

[2] NK., p. 31; SM., p. 152.

were no indivisible atoms, there would be no dissolution. Dissolution is the disjunction of the component atoms of composite substances. Their destruction is due to disjunction of their parts.[1]

ETHER (ĀKĀŚA)

Ether is one, ubiquitous, eternal, imperceptible substance which has the special quality of sound. Kaṇāda proves the existence of ākāsa as the substrate of sound. The special qualities of the products of earth, water, fire and air are produced by the qualities of their material causes. Colour, taste, odour and temperature are special qualities of this kind. But sound is a special quality; it is not produced by the quality of its material cause. It is a special quality, because it has the genus of sound, and because it is perceived through one external sense-organ (*e.g.*, ear) only. It is not a special quality of earth, water, fire and air, which are tangible substances, because different degrees of colour, taste, smell or touch are not perceived in the same tangible substance. It is not a special quality of air, because it is destroyed even when air persists, while touch, a special quality of air, is destroyed when air disappears. It is not a special quality of a soul, for it is perceived through an external sense-organ. It is not a special quality of manas, since manas being atomic its qualities are imperceptible. Nor is it a quality of space and time, because their qualities are imperceptible, while sound is perceptible. Hence sound is a special quality of ether. It subsists in a substance, because it is a quality which is perceptible through a single external sense-organ, like colour.[2]

Ether is one individual, and has no genus. It has a particularity which distinguishes it from other eternal substances. It is one, since sound has no difference in kind. It has different degrees of loudness only. There are no different kinds of sound,

---

[1] KV., pp. 51-52; NK., p. 31; SM., pp. 148, 150-51; VV., p. 224; VSU., iv, 1, 2; TBh., p. 22; MB., p. 14.

[2] VS., VSU., ii, 1, 24-27; VSB., ii, 1, 25; VSV., ii, 1, 26.

which prove that there are no differences in ether. Sound subsisting in one substrate may differ in loudness owing to different causes. So ether, its substrate, is one. Though it is one, it appears to be many owing to its limiting adjuncts. Ether limited by a jar is not different from that limited by a house. Ether is one, simple, inactive, continuous substance. It is the medium through which atoms combine with one another.[1]

Ether is ubiquitous, because it is the substrate of sounds produced everywhere, and because it comes into contact with all corporeal substances of limited magnitude. It is pervasive since it is impenetrable and unresisting.[2]

Ether is eternal, because it is ubiquitous. It is neither produced nor destroyed. It is not the cause of all effects, though it is their invariable antecedent, because it is an accidental antecedent. It is the necessary, invariable antecedent of sound, and its material cause. Though ether is ubiquitous and eternal, it is the substrate and material cause of sound.

Ether has the qualities of sound, number, magnitude, distinctness, conjunction and disjunction.[3] Sound is its special quality. Ether fills all space, but it is not itself space. Sound is not a special quality of space (dik) in which all corporeal things exist.

SPACE (DIK)

Space is one, ubiquitous, eternal, partless substance. It is an individual, which has no genus of space. It has a particularity which distinguishes it from ether, time, souls, minds (manas), and atoms of earth, water, fire and air. All material things exist in space, and maintain their relative positions in it. If there were no space, they would interpenetrate one another. It has no special quality. But it has number, magnitude, distinctness, conjunction, and disjunction.[4]

The existence of space is proved thus : first, space is

---

1 VS., VSU., ii, 1, 30 ; PBh., p. 58 ; NK., pp. 61-62.
2 NS., NSV., NBh,, NV., iv, 2, 21-22 ; TBh., p. 23 ; TSG. p. 15.
3 TBh., pp. 22-23. 4 TBh., p. 23.

inferred from the cognitions of different directions.[1] Taking a corporeal substance of limited magnitude as a limit, we perceive other corporeal substances as to the east, west, north, south, upward and downward. Space is the efficient cause of these cognitions of directions, because they cannot be produced by any other cause. Corporeal substances of limited magnitude are mutually external to one another, and occupy different positions at different times. Their mutual externality is due to space. Therefore space is the efficient cause of the cognitions of mutual externality of corporeal substances, which are not their causes. If they were so, they would produce these cognitions, even if they were situated in some other order and occupied other positions. The qualities and actions of the corporeal substances also are not the causes of these cognitions. If they were so, the substances endued with the same qualities and actions would not be known as situated in particular directions from each other. Hence space is the cause of these cognitions of directions. Spatial relations of corporeal substances presuppose the existence of space. If space were non-existent, their spatial relations would not be possible. So space exists as an objective entity.[2] Secondly, space is inferred as the locus of the non-inherent cause of remoteness and proximity of corporeal substances. Space is not the locus of remoteness and proximity. Remoteness and proximity are due to conjunction of corporeal substances with space, which is their non-inherent cause. The conjunction subsists in space, which is its locus. But space is not the locus of remoteness and proximity, which reside in corporeal substances with specific positions in relation to one another. But corporeal substances are in conjunction with space. So space is the locus of conjunction with corporeal substances.[3] Remoteness involves conjunction of a body with a large number of space-points. Proximity involves its conjunction with a small number of space-points.

---

[1] PBh., p. 66.
[2] NK., pp. 67-68; KV., pp. 122-23; TBh., p. 23; TSG., p. 23.
[3] VSU., ii, 2, 10; SP., p. 42.

Space has no specific quality. It has the general qualities of number, magnitude, distinctness, conjunction, and disjunction. It is one and therefore distinct. It is ubiquitous and therefore eternal. It has conjunction with corporeal substances, which determines their spatial positions, and disjunction from them. It is a substance in which these qualities inhere. It is imperceptible. It is inferred from the conjunctions of directions produced by it.[1]

Space is different from ether. Ether has a specific quality. But space has no specific quality. Ether is the inherent cause of sound, but not the general cause of all effects. But space is the general cause of all effects, but not the inherent cause of sound.[2] It is the instrumental cause of spatial remoteness and proximity. Space resembles ether in being one, ubiquitous, eternal substance. Space is objective.

TIME (KĀLA)

Time is one, ubiquitous, eternal substance. It is an individual, and has no genus. It has a particularity which distinguishes it from ether, space, souls, minds (manas), and atoms of earth, water, light and air. It is a real and objective substance.

The following arguments are advanced for the existence of time. First, time is inferred from temporal remoteness or oldness and temporal proximity or newness, which subsist in old and new created substances. Temporal remoteness or oldness is produced in an old substance after the lapse of a large number of motions of the sun from its production. Its non-inherent cause is conjunction of the old substance determined by the motions of the sun with a ubiquitous substance, *viz.*, time. Time is the locus of the conjunction. Temporal remoteness and proximity, or oldness and newness, reside in an individual substance, and not in time. So time is not their locus. A substance itself is the inherent cause of its temporal

---

[1] VS., VSU., ii, 2, 12; SM., p. 208.

[2] TSP., p. 133.

remoteness or proximity. Its conjunction with time is their non-inherent cause. Time is their efficient cause.[1]

Secondly, time is inferred from the cognitions of simultaneity, succession, slowness, quickness, oldness and youth, which are its marks. The self is the inherent cause of these cognitions. Time is inferred as the efficient cause of the cognitions of these temporal marks, which differ from the cognitions of substances, qualities and the like.[2]

Thirdly, time is the cause of production, persistence and destruction of all effects. We speak of the time of production, the time of persistence, and the time of destruction. All effects are produced at a particular moment, persist for a certain duration, and are destroyed at a particular moment. Time is the efficient cause of production, persistence and destruction of all effects. Production is coming into existence. Persistence is relation to serial time. Destruction is cessation of existence. They would not be possible without the instrumentality of time.[3]

Slowness, quickness, simultaneity, succession and the like are absent from ether and other eternal substances. They are present in non-eternal substances. So time is the efficient cause of the production of all non-eternal effects. In the presence of time there is their production. In the absence of time there is no production of them. So time is the efficient cause of production of all effects. It is also the efficient cause of their persistence and destruction. Time is the abode of all effects or events, which cannot be related to each other as the abode and its content, since they occur at different moments in succession.[4]

Time is threefold, past, present and future. The future is indicated by the production of an effect; the present, by its persistence; and the past, by its destruction. When an effect is not yet produced, it is future. When it persists, it is present. When it is destroyed, it is past. When an action has not yet

---

1 KV., p. 114; SP., MB., p. 42; SM., p. 197; VSU., ii, 2, 6.

2 KV., p. 116.

3 K V., p. 118.

4 VSU., ii, 2, 9; BhP., 45; TSG., Nīlakaṇṭhī, pp. 22-23.

begun, it is future. When an action continues in a substance, it is present. When an action has ceased to exist, it is past. When an action is going on, it is perceived as present ; when it is not yet produced, it is perceived as future ; when it is no more, it is perceived as past.[1]

Fourthly, time is the cause of moments, hours, days, months, years and the like. Day, night, fortnight, month, season, year and the like are the artificial divisions of time. Time is the cause of the notions of these different divisions of time.[2]

Time is one, since its marks of priority, posteriority, simultaneity, succession, slowness and quickness are the same everywhere. There are no distinctive marks of different times. There is one time owing to the absence of different marks. One time appears to be many owing to its limitations by the motions of the sun.[3]

Time is distinct because it is one. It is ubiquitous, because it has conjunction with all corporeal substances of limited magnitude, which depends on its ubiquity. It has conjunction, since conjunction of a corporeal substance with time is the non-inherent cause of its oldness or newness. It has disjunction, because it destroys the conjunction. It is uncaused and eternal.[4]

Time has number, magnitude, distinctness, conjunction and disjunction. It is partless, since its parts are not perceived. It is an undivided whole. It is eternal, since it cannot be destroyed by the division of its parts.[5] It is the ground of the temporal order.

MANAS

Manas is the internal organ. It is one in each body. It is an immaterial, corporeal, partless,atomic, unconscious, eternal,

---

[1] NM., p. 139 ; NBh., ii, 1, 38.

[2] PBh., p. 63 ; NM., pp, 139-40.

[3] PBh., p. 63 ; NK., p. 66 ; NM., pp. 139 & 141 ; SM., p. 197.

[4] KVP., p. 143 ; PBh., p. 63-64 ; NK., p. 66.

[5] PhB., p. 63 ; NK., p. 66 ; VS., ii, 2, 7.

substance, which is capable of action or movement. Its existence is proved by the following arguments. First, though the self, the sense-organs, and the objects are present, perceptions of external objects are not present. Therefore the existence of manas is inferred from non-production and production of perceptions at particular times. The manas controls the external sense-organs.[1] When there is the intercourse of the self with the sense-organs, and of the sense-organs with the objects, there is perception on condition that there is conjunction of manas with the self and the sense-organs. When the manas is present, there is perception. When it is absent, there is no perception. The conjunctions of the self with manas, of the manas with the sense-organs, and of the sense-organs with the objects are necessary conditions of perception. The internal organ is necessary for perception of external objects. It is controlled by the self, and it controls the sense-organs. It is directed by the self to be disjoined from one sense-organ and conjoined with another sense-organ. The self has perception of external objects through the external sense-organs controlled by the internal organ. Secondly, cognition, pleasure, pain, desire, aversion and volition are perceived. Cognitions of these qualities of the self are perceptions. So they must have an organ. The external senses are not their organs. So the manas is their organ. Thirdly, recollections of colours, sounds tastes, smells and touch are produced, even when the external sense-organs do not function. Therefore they must be produced by the internal organ. The manas is the internal organ, through which the self recollects, infers, doubts and dreams. Fourthly, cognitions, volitions and the other perceptible qualities of the self are always successive. They are never simultaneous. Their non-simultaneity proves the existence of one manas in each body. If there were many internal organs, they would come into conjunction with the different sense-organs, and produce different kinds of perceptions simultaneously. But colours odours, tastes, sounds, and temperatures are never perceived simultaneously. So there is a single manas in each body.

[1] VS., ii, 2, 1 ; PBh., p. 89 ; NK., p. 90.

Sometimes they appear to be perceived simultaneously. But the appearance of simultaneous perceptions of them is due to their rapid succession due to quick movement of the atomic manas and its conjunctions with the different sense-organs in quick succession. The appearance is illusory.[1]

The internal organ is atomic. If it were of large magnitude it would come into conjunction with all sense-organs at the same time, and produce perceptions of colours, smells, tastes, sounds and temperatures simultaneously. But they are not perceived simultaneously. They are perceived in succession because the atomic manas comes into conjunction with them successively. Non-simultaneity of perceptions proves the atomic magnitude of manas. If it be ubiquitous like the self, then it cannot come into contact with the self. If there is no conjunction of the self with the manas, then cognitions, pleasures and other qualities of the self cannot be produced, because their non-inherent cause is absent. Manas is not of intermediate magnitude. If it were so, it would be composed of parts, and be non-eternal. It is an atomic internal organ, which is capable of conjunction with the self. One self has one manas, with which it transmigrates from one body to another.[2]

Manas is capable of movement. If it were inactive and motionless, it could not supervise the external sense-organs. It is corporeal (mūrta) because it is capable of movement. An incorporeal entity is incapable of movement. Though it is corporeal, it is eternal because it is partless and self-subsistent. Corporeality is not the cause of non-eternity. Manas has velocity or power of quick movement without which it cannot come into contact with the sense-organs in quick succession. It can come into contact with them because it is a substance. It is an unconscious organ of the self, which is its conscious agent. It is of limited magnitude. It is devoid of any specific

[1] VSU., iii, 2, 1-3 ; BhP., 85 ; SM., p. 397 ; VSU., iii, 2, 2 ; PBh., p. 89 ; NK., p. 90 ; KV., pp. 152-53 ; TBh., p, 23 ; TSG., p. 25.

[2] VSU., iii, 2, 1 & 3 ; SM., p. 398 ; TSD., p. 26 ; TBh., p. 23 ; SP., p. 19.

quality. It has the generic qualities of number, magnitude, distinctness, conjunction, disjunction, remoteness, proximity, and velocity. It is intangible. But it can move for it has limited magnitude. Each manas has a particularity which distinguishes it from other eternal substances. The genus of manas resides in it.[1]

THE INDIVIDUAL SELF (ĀTMAN)

The self is too subtle to be perceived. It cannot be perceived through the external sense-organs. It is an object of inference. First, the individual self is inferred from the perception of sound and other sensible qualities as its substratum. Perception is knowledge. It is produced by the intercourse of the external sense-organs with certain external objects. Sound is perceived through the auditory organ. Colour is perceived through the visual organ. Different sensible qualities are perceived through the different sense-organs, which are the instruments of knowledge. Knowledge as an effect must have a material cause. The self is its material cause in which it inheres[2]. Secondly, the activity of the sense-organs requires an agent who uses them in order to know objects, even as an instrument requires an agent to use it. The body, the sense-organs, and the manas cannot be the agent, since they are unconscious. They themselves are the instruments of experience. They require the individual self as the agent who uses them as organs of experience.[3] Thirdly, pleasure, pain, desire, aversion and volition are qualities. They are not qualities of the body or the sense-organs. They are not perceived by the external sense-organs. They persist even when the external senses are destroyed. They are always appropriated by the self. They are experienced as belonging to the ego: 'I feel pleasure'; 'I feel pain'; 'I feel desire'; 'I feel aversion'; 'I will to act'. So they cannot be the qualities of the body and the sense-organs. Ego-consciousness refers to

---

[1] PBh, p. 89; KV., pp. 156-57.

[2] VS., VSU., iii, 1, 2. [3] PBh., p. 69.

the self, and not to the body and its senses. The same self has apprehension, recollection, pleasure, pain, desire, aversion and volition, which cannot belong to the body or its sense-organs. Further, pleasure and pain are felt in connection with different parts of the body : 'I feel pleasure in the foot'; 'I feel pain in the head.' So pleasure and pain are not special qualities of the body and the sense-organs. Special qualities of a substance pervade the entire body of it. Colour subsists in a substance entirely. Pleasure and pain do not subsist in the entire body. So they cannot be its special quality. Pleasure and pain are not always experienced while the body lasts. So they are not its special qualities. They are not perceived through the external sense-organs like colour and temperature of the body. They are not imperceptible like its gravity. They are perceived through the manas. So they are not special qualities of the body. They are the qualities of the finite self. Fourthly, recollection and recognition prove the existence of the self. An object is perceived. The perception produces an impression, which produces a recollection of it. The perception, the impression and the recollection must inhere in the same substratum. The self is the substratum of all these qualities. The same self remembers an object, which it perceived in the past, and retained it in the form of an impression. Recollection proves the unity and identity of an individual self. Recognition also proves the permanence and identity of the self. 'This is that Devadatta.' The self perceived Devadatta in the past, and recognizes him at present. It is the same self that perceived him and recognizes him. There is unity and identity of the self. If the self were a series of momentary cognitions as the Buddhist holds, recollection and recognition would not be possible. An object perceived by a momentary past cognition cannot be remembered by a momentary future cognition. If it were possible, then an object perceived by Caitra would be remembered by Maitra. A series of momentary cognitions cannot account for recollection and recognition, which presuppose a permanent entity. Cognitions are qualities. They cannot be the qualities of cognitions. The substrate of qualities must be different from them. Momentary cognitions are the qualities of the permanent self.[1] Fifthly, the vital acts of inspiration and expiration, the opening and the closing of the eyes, the growth of the body, self-recuperation of wounds, the movement of the manas, and the impulsion of the sense-organs prove the existence of the self. These vital acts are not due to the vital forces only, but to the voluntary direction of the self. Life and its acts, growth of the body, inhalation and exhalation in deep sleep, self-reparation of injuries and the like, depend upon a kind of vital effort of the self. It is the self that directs the manas to apprehend its qualities, and to come into conjunction with the sense-organs to apprehend their objects successively. The self impels the sense-organs to function towards their proper objects. It is the agent that makes use of the manas and the external senses to perceive its qualities and those of external objects. Lastly, apperception proves the existence of the self. Colours, sounds, tastes, odours and temperatures of an object are perceived through the different sense-organs. Some of its qualities are remembered. They are combined into a single experience and referred to an external object by the self by its synthetic act of apperception.[2] These are the arguments for the existence of one's own self.

The following argument is given for the existence of another self. The voluntary actions of a body, which realize good and avoid evil, prove the existence of another self which directs the body, even as the movements of a chariot are guided by a charioteer. A self has knowledge of good and evil. It consciously and voluntarily directs its body to execute the movements, which are conducive to the realization of the good and the avoidance of evil. The voluntary movements for the achievement of a good and the avoidance of an evil are the outward expressions of the volitions of a self. Thus we

---

[1] PBh., p. 70; KV., pp. 129, 136-48; NK., pp. 94-95; VSU., iii, 1, 18.

[2] VS., VSU., iii, 2, 4; PBh., pp. 132-35 (B.S.S.); KV., pp. 132-36; NK., pp. 82-83.

infer the existence of other individual souls after the analogy of our own souls.[1]

The Vaiśeṣika recognizes the plurality of individual souls, which is inferred from the variety of experiences and conditions of different souls. Some are happy while others are miserable. Some are bound while others are liberated. These differences in the status of individuals prove the existence of many souls. The plurality of individual souls is confirmed by the Vedas also. The Upaniṣads speak of two beautiful birds residing in the same tree, one enjoying the sweet fruit thereof and the other merely looking on. They speak of the individual soul and the supreme soul residing in the same body, the former being subject to happiness and misery, and the latter, the inner controller, being a mere spectator without experiencing its happiness and misery. They advocate difference between the individual souls and the supreme soul.[2] The Upaniṣadic texts emphasizing the identity of the individual soul with the supreme soul is intended to convey similarity but not identity between them. If there were only one soul, the bondage of one would lead to the bondage of others, and the liberation of one would lead to the liberation of others. Each soul reaps the consequences of its own actions. It continues its identity in the midst of all its experiences. It transmigrates from one body to another to exhaust its own merits and demerits. Even in the state of liberation the finite soul retains its integrity, and is not merged in God. Each soul has its particularity by virtue of which it is distinguished from the other souls and God. Each soul is eternal, and its particularity is eternal.

Knowledge, pleasure, pain, desire, aversion, volition, merit, demerit, and disposition or impression are the special qualities of the individual self. Number, magnitude, distinctness, conjunction and disjunction are its generic qualities. It is ubiquitous. Its ubiquity consists in its relation to all corporeal substances. It is invested with pleasure, pain and the

[1] VS., VSU., iii, 1, 19 ; PBh., p. 69.

[2] VS., VSU., iii, 2, 20-21.

other special qualities owing to its conjunction with manas. It is divested of them owing to its disjunction from manas. So the self has conjunction and disjunction. Consciousness is not an essential quality of the self. It is its adventitious quality acquired from its conjunction with manas.[1]

THE MORAL ENDS : HAPPINESS AND LIBERATION

The end is what induces the self to act. The attainment of pleasure and the avoidance of pain are the natural ends of voluntary actions. Wealth, happiness, virtue and liberation are the four moral ends. Kaṇāda says : "Dharma is what accomplishes happiness and liberation".[2] Happiness is worldly happiness and happiness in heaven. Kaṇāda regards happiness as the end of positive actions (pravṛtti), and liberation as the end of negative actions (nivṛtti). The gratification of desires regulated by reason in conformity with the divine commandments is the end of positive actions. The extinction of desires, merits and demerits and the absolute negation of pain are the ends of negative actions. Both ought to be pursued by every person for a harmonious and perfect life. Liberation is attained when merits due to the performance of duties are destroyed. Only true knowledge of reality can lead to release. But it is aided by the purity of mind brought about by the performance of duties. Spiritual insight is the direct cause of liberation.[3]

Liberation is absolute negation of pain. It is prior negation of pain, which ends in complete destruction of all specific qualities of the self, cognition, pleasure, pain, desire, aversion, volition, impression, merit and demerit. When they are destroyed, there is no destruction of the self which is eternal. It exists in its essential nature in release.[4]

THE MEANS OF LIBERATION

Śrīdhara maintains that knowledge of reality and the performance of duties both are necessary for liberation.

[1] PBh., p. 70 ; NK., p. 88.

[2] VS., i, 1, 2. [3] VSU., i, 1, 2-4 ; vi, 2, 14; VSV., VSB., i, I,2.

[4] VSU., i, 1, 4 ; NK., pp. 6 & 286.

Liberation is not due to knowledge alone, but to the combination of knowledge with duties. The prudential duties should be discarded. But the compulsory daily and occasional duties must be performed. The non-performance of them produces sins of omission. The performance of them purifies the mind. Knowledge determines the nature of the self. Repeated practice of knowledge and obligatory duties lead to release.[1] Udayana also maintains that the performance of obligatory duties and the knowledge of the self are the prerequisites of release. But he does not regard them as equal in importance, and consequently does not speak of the combination of knowledge and works as the means of release. The works are auxiliary to knowledge. They bring about purity of mind, which is necessary for true insight into the nature of the self. Hence the knowledge of the reality itself is the direct means of release.[2] The performance of obligatory and occasional duties without any desire for fruits purifies the mind and destroys demerits. The destruction of demerits leads to right knowledge of reality. It destroys false knowledge. The right knowledge of reality is the immediate antecedent of release.

GOD

Kaṇāda does not refer to God or the supreme Soul in the *Vaiśeṣika Sūtra*. The famous aphorism which is repeated twice by him does not distinctly refer to God. 'The authority of the Vedas is due to the utterance of him or them.' It may mean that the authority of the Vedas is due to the utterence of God or the seers. Kaṇāda most probably traces their authority to the seers who perceive supersensible objects like merit, demerit, heaven, hell and the like. He believes in supernormal perception of the sages born of merit due to austerities and meditation. He does not regard God as the efficient cause of the world. God is not the cause of the first motion in the atoms. He does not combine them into dyads, and dyads into triads. Merits and demerits (adṛṣṭa) of the individual souls are the cause of the first motion in the atoms, which combine them

[1] NK., pp. 283-86. [2] KV., pp. 12-13.

into dyads, triads and gross objects of the world for the experiences of the finite souls. The early Vaiśeṣika system was atheistic. It was made theistic by the later Vaiśeṣika thinkers. Praśastapāda traces the authority of the Vedas to that of the speaker. He speaks of the sages as the authors of the Vedas, who have supernormal intuition of the past, the present, the future, and of supersensible entities like merit and demerit. He faithfully represents Kaṇāda's view in regard to the authority of the Vedas. But he is a theist, and ascribes periodic creation and destruction of the world to the creative and destructive will of God.[1] Knowledge of the six categories is the cause of liberation. It depends on virtue which is enjoined by God. Duality and plurality are produced by discriminative intellect. Large magnitude and length are produced in triads by plurality of dyads, which is due to the discriminative intellect of God. Minuteness and shortness in a dyad are produced by duality, which is due to God's discriminative intellect. Praśastapāda regards God as the efficient cause of the world and atoms as its material cause.[2] God is not the creator of the atoms, the individual souls, time, space, manas and ether, which are external to Him. He creates the world out of the atoms according to the Law of Karma, and adapts it to the merits and demerits of the individual souls.

The cosmological argument is advanced for the existence of God. The atoms of earth, water, fire and air are the material cause of the world. Their conjunction is its non-material cause. Merits and demerits of the individual souls are its auxiliary cause. God is its efficient cause. He creates the first motion in the atoms by which He combines the atoms into dyads, the dyads into triads and other gross objects for the diverse experiences of the individual souls in accordance with their merits and demerits. His discriminative intellect produces duality in two atoms, which produces minuteness and shortness in a dyad. It produces plurality in three dyads, which produces large magnitude and length in a triad. God produces gross

[1] VS., i, 1, 13 ; x, ii, 9 ; ix, 2, 13 ; v, 2, 13 ; PBh., pp. 213 & 258, 48—49

[2] PBh., pp. 7 & 131.

objects out of the atoms of earth, water, fire and air with the aid of the individual souls' merits and demerits. He has immediate knowledge of the atoms, the material cause of the world, and desire and volition to create it. His knowledge apprehends the atoms and merits and demerits of the individual souls. His detachment moves Him to create the world of diverse objects inpartially according to the Law of Karma. His sovereignty makes the souls' merits and demerits bear fruits when they mature. His motive for creation is compassion for creatures. He creates the world for their benefit. He creates variety in it according to the Law of Karma.[1] Though He is moved by compassion, He creates the diverse world of happiness and misery to suit the souls' merits and demerits. He creates misery as the proper retribution for demerits, which has an educative value, since it produces detachment in the suffering creatures by chastening their spirit, and leads them to the highest good. Creation of misery does not conflict with God's compassion for creatures. He accords right punishment through His even-handed justice. His omnipotence and independence are not compromised by His acting according to merits and demerits of the individual souls. God does not cease to be the omnipotent Lord, who respects the moral Law of Karma and awards proper rewards and punishments to His creatures in strict accordance with their moral deserts.[2]

The Vaiśeṣika gives another argument for the existence of God. He is the author of the Vedas. Their authority is due to their being the utterances of God. The validity of scriptural testimony is due to the authority of God, who is free from error, inadvertence, deficiency of the sense-organs, fraudulence and the like. He is eternal, omniscient and faultless. The Vedas are not impersonal as the Mīmāṁsaka maintains, because they are sentences like those spoken by us. They are not spoken by human beings because they are not omniscient, faultless and aware of the supersensible entities like merits,

[1] VV., p. 298 ; Setu, pp. 285-86, 288 ; Sūkti, pp. 280-82 ; NK., p. 53 ; KV., pp. 95 & 97.

[2] NK., pp. 53-54.

demerits, heaven, hell and the like. The validity of knowledge is produced by efficiency in its cause. The validity of testimony is produced by the right knowledge of its speaker about the objects spoken of. The validity of the Vedas is produced by the right knowledge of the supersensible entities in God who is their speaker. They are utterances of an omniscient and truthful person or God, because they are accepted as valid by great saints.

God is the promulgator of the Moral Law. Whatever is enjoined by Him is right; whatever is prohibited by Him is wrong. The command of God is the standard of right and wrong. The Divine Law is the moral standard.[1] This argument may be regarded as the moral argument for the existence of God. His injunctions and prohibitions are known from the Vedas, which are His utterances revealed to the sages.

The cosmological argument proves the existence of one God. If there were many gods, they would be non-omniscient like us, and so incapable of producing the world out of the atoms of which they were ignorant. If they were omniscient, one of them would be competent to produce the world and the others would become useless. If they were equal to one another, or if some were superior while others were subordinate, they would have no unity of purpose, and sometimes there would be no effect owing to the conflict of their wills. If they had the same purpose, one of them would be the sovereign Lord and the others would not be Lords. Hence the one sovereign Lord is God and others are not Lords. God is one.

He is omniscient. He knows all things with their distinctive characters. He is devoid of false knowledge which is due to non-apprehension of distinctive characters. False knowledge springs from attachment and aversion. They produce voluntary actions which are righteous or unrighteous. Righteous actions produce merits, and unrighteous actions produce demerits. Merits are the predisposing causes of pleasure, and demerits are the predisposing causes of pain. God is devoid of attachment

[1] KV., pp. 315-16; VSU., VSV., i, 1, 3; x, 2, 8 & 9; PBh., NK., pp. 7-8.

and aversion, volitions and actions actuated by them, merits and demerits, pleasure and pain. His knowledge is perceptual but not due to the sense-object-intercourse. He is devoid of impressions and recollection. He has knowledge, desire, volition, number, magnitude, conjunction and disjunction. This is the view of some Vaiśeṣikas. Others deny desire and volition to God. They maintain that His knowledge itself is the unobstructed power of action, and that His action is not preceded by desire and volition. He is devoid of afflictions, or attachment, aversion, egoism and ignorance, which are the causes of bondage. He is neither bound nor liberated. He is not liberated, because He was never bound. He is eternally liberated. Jayanārāyaṇa ascribes knowledge, desire and volition to God, which are eternal and relate to all objects. He is omniscient and omnipotent. His desire is one but becomes manifold owing to limiting conditions. His desire to create, desire to destroy and the like are due to conditions.[1] His will to create is subject to the Law of Karma.

THE DIFFERENT KINDS OF QUALITIES

Kaṇāda mentions seventeen qualities, *viz.*, colour, taste, smell, touch, number, magnitude, distinctness, conjunction, disjunction, remoteness, nearness, cognition, pleasure, pain, desire, aversion and volition. Praśastapāda adds seven more qualities, *viz.*, heaviness, fluidity, viscidity, faculty, merit, demerit and sound.[2] Some add lightness, hardness and softness. Some add laziness. But these four are not separate qualities. Lightness is the contradictory of heaviness. Laziness is the contradictory of volition. Softness and hardness are different degrees of conjunction. Thus there are only twenty four qualities. Demerit is not mere absence of merit. Pain is not mere absence of pleasure. Nearness is not mere absence of remoteness. Disjunction is not mere absence of conjunction. These are positive qualities and should be distinctly mentioned.[3]

---

[1] KV., p. 91 ; Śāstrārthasaṁgraha, Bombay, 1913, p. 368.
[2] VS., i, 1, 6 ; PBh., p. 95.
[3] TSP., pp.83-84.

Qualities are divided into general and special. (1) General qualities are those which abide in two or more substances jointly. Number, magnitude, distinctness, conjunction, disjunction, remoteness, nearness, derived fluidity, gravity and velocity are general qualities. (2) Special qualities are those which abide in one substance only at the same time, and not in two or more substances jointly. Colour, taste, smell, touch, viscidity, natural fluidity, cognition, pleasure, pain, desire, aversion, volition, merit, demerit, faculty, and sound are special qualities.

Qualities are further divided into (1) those which are perceptible through one external sense-organ, *e.g.*, sound, touch, colour, taste, and odour ; (2) those which are perceptible through two external sense-organs (*viz.*, eyes and the skin), *e.g.*, number, magnitude, distinctness, conjunction, disjunction, remoteness, nearness, fluidity, viscidity, and velocity ; and (3) those which are imperceptible through the external sense-organs, *e.g.*, gravity, merit, demerit, and faculty (bhāvanā). Cognition, pleasure, pain, desire, aversion, and volition are perceptible through the manas.

Qualities are divided into eternal and non-eternal. The qualities of eternal substance are eternal. The qualities of non-eternal substances are non-eternal. Colour, taste, odour, touch, remoteness, nearness, gravity, fluidity, viscidity, and velocity are qualities of corporeal substances. Cognition, pleasure, pain, desire, aversion, volition, impression, merit, demerit, and sound are qualities of incorporeal substances. Number, magnitude, distinctness, conjunction and disjunction are qualities of both corporeal and incorporeal substances.[1]

Conjunction, disjunction, duality and other numbers, and distinctness between two or more substances are qualities which reside in many substances. The remaining qualities, *e.g.*, colour, taste, odour, touch, sound, oneness, distinctness (of one substance), remoteness, nearness, cognition, pleasure, pain,

---

[1] PBh., pp. 95-97 ; BhP., pp. 401-04 ,

desire, aversion, gravity, fluidity, viscidity, faculty, merit and demerit are qualities which reside in one substance.[1]

Colour is a special quality, which is perceived by the visual organ only. It resides in earth, water and fire. There are seven kinds of colour, *e.g.*, white, blue, yellow, red, green, brown, and motley. All these qualities reside in earth. Colour is produced in earthy substances by the application of heat. So their colour is transient. The colours of the atoms of water and fire are eternal. Those of composite aqueous and fiery substances are transient. The colour of water is white but not bright. The colour of fire is bright white, and not due to the application of heat. The colours of all produced substances are produced by those of their material causes. They are destroyed when their substrates are destroyed. Taste is a special quality, which is perceived by the gustatory organ only. It resides in earth and water. There are six kinds of tastes, *viz.*, sweet, sour, saline, bitter, pungent, and astringent. The tastes of earthy substances are due to the application of heat. They are of six kinds. The taste of water is sweet, and not due to the application of heat. Tastes of the atoms of water are eternal. Those of composite aqueous substances are transient. Odour is a special quality, which is perceived by the olfactory organ only. It resides in earth only. All odours are transient. There are two kinds of odour, agreeable and disagreeable. The odours of produced substances are produced by the odours of their material causes. They are destroyed when their substrates are destroyed. The odours of the atoms of earth are produced by the application of heat. They are not eternal. Touch or temperature is a special quality, which is perceived by the tactual organ only. It resides in earth, water, fire and air. There are three kinds of touch, *viz.*, cold, hot, and neither cold nor hot. Water is cold. Fire is hot. Earth and air are neither hot nor cold. Hardness, softness and the like reside in earth only. Temperatures of the atoms of water, fire and air are eternal. Those of their composite products are

---

[1] PBh., p. 95; BhP., p. 402.

non-eternal. Sound is a special quality, which is perceived by the auditory organ only.[1]

Number is a generic quality. It is the cause of mathemetical enumeration. It is the cause of the use of one, two, three, etc. Of the numbers, unity is eternal in eternal substances, and non-eternal in transient substances. An atom is eternal, and its unity is eternal. A jar is transient, and its unity is non-eternal. Unity inheres in one substance. Duality and higher numbers inhere in many substances. Plurality is transient. When we perceive a jar, we perceive its unity. When we perceive another jar, we perceive its unity. Then by the relating activity of thought (apekṣābuddhi) we think together the two unities, and produce duality. Duality and other numbers are produced by discriminative intellect. The two jars are the material cause, their unities are the non-material cause, and the relating activity of thought is the efficient cause of duality. The knowledge of all numbers beyond duality is due to the relating activity of thought.[2]

Magnitude is the specific cause of measurement. There are four kinds of magnitude : minuteness, largeness, length and shortness. Magnitude is eternal in eternal substances and non-eternal in transient substances. The magnitude of ether, time, space, and souls is the largest. It is eternal, since they are eternal substances. The magnitude of an atom and manas is the minutest. It is eternal, since these substances are eternal. A composite substance like a jar has medium largeness. The magnitudes of a dyad and a triad are non-eternal, since they are composite products. The non-eternal magnitude of composite products is determined by the number, magnitude, and arrangement of parts.[3]

Distinctness is the quality of a substance, which distinguishes it from other substances. It is the basis of distinction of things from one another. It inheres in one substance, or

[1] PBh., NK., pp. 104-06 ; BhP., SM., pp, 100-04.

[2] PBh., pp 111-13 ; NK., pp. 113-30 ; KV., pp. 192-210 ; VSU., vii, 2, 1.

[3] PBh., pp. 130-31 ; BhP., 111 ; SM., p. 429.

in many substances. It is eternal in eternal substances. It is non-eternal in transient substances. Distinctness of an atom is eternal, because it is eternal. Distinctness of a jar is non-eternal, because it is transient. Distinctness of a composite product is produced by its causes, and destroyed when its causes are destroyed. Distinctness inhering in two substances is produced by the relating activity of thought. It is destroyed when the relating activity of thought is destroyed. Sometimes it is destroyed when its substrates are destroyed. Distinctness is not mutual negation. 'A jar is distinct from a cloth.' 'A jar is not a cloth.' These two cognitions are different from each other. So their objects must be different from each other. Distinctness is a positive quality. It is different from negation. Distinctness is different from particularity. Distinctness of an eternal substance refers to its numerical difference from other substances. But particularity of an eternal substance refers to its qualitative uniqueness.[1]

Conjunction is a quality, which is the cause of the knowledge of conjoined substances. It is the union of two substances which existed separately. It subsists in two substances, and does not pervade its entire substrates. It subsists in parts of its substrates. It is of three kinds : (1) conjunction due to the movement of one of the substances conjoined, *e.g.*, the perching of a flying bird on a fixed pole ; (2) conjunction due to the movement of two substances conjoined, *e.g.*, the contact of two wrestlers fighting with each other ; and (3) conjunction due to another conjunction, *e.g.*, the contact of a body with a tree due to the contact of a hand with the tree. Conjunction is partial contact of two substances, and not total interpenetration. It affects only parts of the two substances conjoined. It is destroyed by separation or by the destruction of its substrates.

Disjunction is a quality, which is the cause of the knowledge of divided substances. It is separation of the two substances, which were conjoined. It subsists in the two substances which are disjoined. It is of three kinds : (1) disjunction due to the movement of one of the two substances disjoined, *e.g.*,

[1] PBh., p. 138 ; NK., pp. 138-39 ; KV., pp. 218-20 ; VSU., vii, 2, 2.

disjunction of a bird from a fixed pole, which flies away from it ; (2) disjunction due to the movement of the two substances disjoined, *e.g.*, disjunction of two wrestlers fighting with each other ; and (3) disjunction due to another disjunction, *e.g.*, disjunction of a body from a tree due to disjunction of a hand from the tree[1].

Remoteness and proximity are the causes of the notions of 'far' and 'near'. Each of them is of two kinds, spatial and temporal. Spatial remoteness is expressed as farness. Spatial proximity is expressed as nearness. Temporal remoteness is expressed as oldness. Temporal proximity is expressed as youngness. Spatial remoteness involves a large number of contacts with space-points between the distant object and the body of the person. Spatial proximity involves a small number of contacts with space-points between the proximate object and the body of the person. Similarly, temporal remoteness or oldness involves a large number of contacts with time-points between the old object and the body of the person. Temporal proximity or youngness involves a small number of contacts with time-points between the young object and the body of the person.[2] Remoteness and proximity are relative to each other. They depend upon the relating activity of thought.

Gravity is a quality of earth and water, by virtue of which they tend to fall to the ground. Falling is due to gravity when conjunction, velocity and effort are absent. It is eternal in atmos of earth and water. It is non-eternal in the composite earthy and watery substances.

Fluidity is the cause of flowing. It exists in three substances. It is of two kinds, natural and acquired. Natural fluidity is a quality of water. Acquired fluidity is the quality of earth and fire. Natural fluidity is eternal in atoms of water, and non-eternal in composite watery substances. Acquired

---

1 PBh., pp. 139-41 & 151 ; NK., pp. 141-51 ; KV., pp. 220-30 : VSU., vii, 2, 9 ; BhP., 115 ; SM., pp. 433-35.

2 PBh., pp. 164-67 ; NK., pp. 167-71 ; KV., pp. 249-57 ; BhP., 121-25 ; SM., pp, 438-39 ; VSU., vii, 2, 21.

fluidity of earth and fire is due to conjunction with heat. Gold and butter become fluid in contact with fire.

Viscidity is oiliness. It is a special quality of water, by virtue of which particles of a substance come together and form a lump. Powder of parched gram mixed with water forms a lump owing to oiliness of water.[1]

Faculty (saṁskāra) is of three kinds : (1) velocity, (2) impression, and (3) elasticity. Velocity is the cause of motion. It keeps a thing in motion. It exists in earth, water, light, air, and manas. Impression exists in the individual souls only. It is produced by apprehension. It is the cause of recollection. Elasticity exists in some tangible substances. It is the quality of a substance, which makes it revert to its original state even when disturbed. The bow reverts to its original state by virtue of its elasticity when an arrow is discharged from it. Elasticity is the quality of the substances which are subject to contraction and expansion. Elasticity is eternal in eternal substances and non-eternal in transient substances.[2]

Cognition, pleasure, pain, desire, aversion, volition, impression, merit and demerit are the special qualities of the individual souls.

---

[1] PBh., pp. 263-66.

[2] PBh., pp. 266-67 ; NK., 267-68 ; VSU., v, 1, 17 ; TBh., pp. 27-28.

CHAPTER IX

THE NYĀYA PHILOSOPHY

Gotama, Gautama or Akṣapāda was the founder of the Nyāya philosophy. It is primarily concerned with epistemology and logic, and secondarily with ontology. It deals with the sources of knowledge, *viz.*, perception, inference, comparison and testimony, and conditions of their validity, and the nature of the world, souls and God.

Gautama (200 B.C.) was the author of the *Nyāya sūtra.* Vātsyāyana (400 A.D.) closely followed Gautama in interpreting his aphorisms. Uddyotakara (600 A.D.) wrote *Nyāyavārtika* on *Nyāyabhāṣya.* Vācaspati (1000 A.D.) wrote an illuminating commentary named *Nyāyavārtikatātparyaṭikā* on *Nyāyavārtika.* Udayana (1050 A.D.) wrote *Nyāyavārtikatātparyapariśuddhi*, a learned commentary, on *Nyāyavārtikatātparyaṭikā.* Gaṅgeśa (1200 A.D.) was the founder of the modern Nyāya school known as Navya Nyāya.

VALID KNOWLEDGE (PRAMĀ) : INSTRUMENT OF VALID KNOWLEDGE (PRAMĀṆA) : EXTRINSIC VALIDITY (PARATAH PRĀMĀṆYA) : TESTS OF TRUTH (PRĀMĀṆYAGRAHA)

The Nyāya epistemology deals with the nature of valid knowledge, its instruments, extrinsic validity and invalidity of knowledge, and the tests of truth. The knower, the known object, the instrument of knowledge, and valid knowledge constitute the reality. The self is the knower, which knows objects through pramāṇas, acts upon them, and experiences fruits of its actions. It desires to attain pleasant objects and avoid painful objects known through pramāṇas, acts for their attainment or rejection, and gets fruits of its efforts. Prameya is the object that is known. Pramāṇa is the instrument by means of which the self knows an object. Pramā is the valid knowledge of an object. Pramāṇa is the collocation of conditions, which is the immediate antecedent of the production of valid knowledge.. There are four pramāṇas, *viz.*, perception, inference, comparison and testimony, which generate different kinds of valid knowledge. The self and an object are the common causes of all cognitions of objects. In their absence there is no valid knowledge, which is produced when they are present. But even when they are present, it is not produced in the absence of a pramaṇa, which is its special cause. The self and an object are presupposed by a pramāṇa which is an instrument of the self by which it knows an object. It is a special cause of valid knowledge because it has not yet realized its end. An instrument depends upon an agent, but the latter does not depend upon the former. Knowledge cannot be specified by the self or an object. The self is the common inherent cause of knowledge which inheres in it. The conjunction of the self with manas is the common non-inherent cause of it. Pramāṇa is the complement of conditions other than the self and an object, which immediately produce valid knowledge.[1]

Valid knowledge is the knowledge that represents the real character of its object, or apprehends what exists in it. Error is the knowledge that does not represent the real character of its object, or apprehends what does not exist in it. So the knowledge which corresponds with the real nature of its object is valid, and the knowledge which does not correspond with its real character is invalid. Vācaspati excludes recollection from valid knowledge, and defines it as the certain knowledge of an object, which is in agreement with its real character, independent of previous perception and different from recollection. Viśvanātha defines valid knowledge as the knowledge of the generic character of an object as abiding in it, or as the apprehension of a mode (prakāra) corresponding to its object (viśeṣya). A jar is the object of the knowledge of a jar, which is its substantive. The generic character of a jar, which is manifested in consciousness is its cognized mode. The cognized mode corresponds to its object in valid knowledge. But in error the cognized mode does not correspond to the object or substantive of knowledge. When a nacre is misperceived as

[1] NBh., i, 1, 1; NVTT. i, 1, 1, pp. 16-17; NM., p. 12.

silver, silver is the cognized mode that is manifested in consciousness, which does not correspond with the nacre. The misapprehension of a nacre as silver is illusory because silver does not exist in it.[1]

The Nyāya definitions of knowledge are realistic. Truth is correspondence of an apprehension with its object. Valid knowledge implies a knowing self, an object of knowlege, apprehension of it, and its harmony with its real character. Correspondence is the content of truth.

Knowledge is the manifestation or apprehension of objects. Valid knowledge is the apprehension of the real character of an object. Invalid knowledge is the apprehension of an object as it is not in its real character. Truth is correspondence of knowledge with reality. Error is disagreement of knowledge with reality. Correspondence is truth, and non-correspondence is error. Knowledge generated by its cause is the bare apprehension of an object, which is neither valid nor invalid in itself. Its validity is produced by some positive excellence in the generating conditions of knowledge ; and its invalidity, by some positive defects in them. Validity and invalidity of knowledge are extrinsic, and depend upon extraneous conditions. Validity is neither produced by the general conditions of knowledge nor by the mere absence of defects, but by some proficiency in its cause. Invalidity is neither produced by the general conditions of knowledge nor by the mere absence of proficiency, but by some deficiency in its cause. Knowledge is not intrinsically valid or invalid, but it acquires validity or invalidity from extraneous conditions. For example, the intercourse of a sense-organ with an object is the positive excellence which generates the validity of perception. Distance or minuteness of an object, defect of a sense-organ or manas, and the like are the positive defects which generate the invalidity of perception. A specific effect has a specific cause. Validity and invalidity are the specific characters of apprehensions, which are due to different specific characters of the general conditions of knowledge, which either promote or

[1] NBh., i, 1, 4, NVTT., i. 1, 3, p. 63 ; BhP., 129 & 127 ; SM., p. 440.

vitiate them. They are extrinsic or adventitious characters of knowledge due to extraneous conditions.[1]

Validity and invalidity of knowledge are not known by valid knowledge itself or by invalid knowledge itself. Validity of knowledge is inferred from its capacity to produce successful activity, and invalidity of knowledge, from its incapacity to produce successful activity. Truth leads to successful action, and error, to unsuccessful action. Practical efficiency and practical inefficiency are the tests of truth and error by which they are known. Correspondence is the content of truth, but workability is its criterion. Non-correspondence is the content of error, but unworkability is its criterion.[2]

What is successful activity which determines the validity of knowledge? Vātsyāyana explains it as the fulfilment of activity prompted by the knowledge of an object. The validity of the knowledge of an object, which was not frequently known before, is known by a fruitful action. But the validity of an object, which was frequently known before, is known from a similar mark even before it produces a successful action. Action depends upon the knowledge of an object, but not upon the knowledge of its validity. Even doubt about an object gives rise to action. Valid knowledge is in harmony with the real character of its object, and capable of producing a successful action. Invalid knowledge is in disharmony with the real nature of its object and incapable of prompting a successful action.[3]

PERCEPTION : ERROR OR ILLUSION

Gautama defines perception as the knowledge which is produced by the intercourse of an object with a sense-organ, undefinable, determinate, and in harmony with its object.[4] It is produced by the intercourse of a present object with the

---

[1] BhP., 131 ; SM., pp. 443-44 ; NKS., ii, pp. 1-2, 5-6 ; NKSP., ii, pp. 2-5 ; NM., p. 171. [2] NM., p. 174.

[3] NBh., i, 1, 1 ; NVTT., i, 1, 1, pp. 8 & 18 ; NNP., i, 1, 1, p. 156 ; NM., p. 172. [4] NS., i, 1, 4.

external sense-organs, their conjuction with manas, and its conjunction with the self. The sense-organs are directed by manas, which is directed by the self. Conjunction of the sense-organs with manas and conjunction of manas with the self are the general causes of perception. The intercourse of a sense-organ with an object is a special cause of perception. Perception is generated by it, and not revealed. It is the immediate knowledge of a present object through a sense-organ. Valid perception apprenhends the real character of an object. Illusion does not apprehend the real nature of its object. Perception is different from inference, comparison and testimony, which are not produced by the sense-object-intercourse. Visual perception of a jar is produced by its conjunction with the visual organ, which is in the nature of light. Auditory perception of sound is produced by its inherence in the auditory organ or ether enclosed in the ear-hole. Visual perception of the colour of a jar is produced by the conjunction of the visual organ with the jar in which colour inheres. It is due to united-inherence. The manas is an internal organ. Perception of pleasure, pain, desire, aversion, volition and cognition is produced by the manas in conjunction with the self.

There are two kinds of perception, *viz.*, indeterminate and determinate. The former is undefinable and nameless. The latter is determinate and associated with a name. The ancient Nyāya regards the former as the apprehension of an object as qualified by a substance, quality, action and genus, but devoid of a name, and the latter as the apprehension of it as qualified by these qualifications but associated with a name. But the modern Nyāya regards the former as immediate, simple, non-relational apprehension of an object and its generic nature as unrelated to each other, and the latter as mediate, relational, synthetic apprehension of an object and its generic nature as related to each other.[1] Indeterminate perception is the immediate apprehension of an object and its qualifications unrelated to each other. It is devoid of subject-predicate-relation. It is

[1] NM., p. 99 ; TC., Vol. I, p. 809 ; SM., pp. 253-54.

14

not a perceptual judgment. The Nyāya regards it as a logical stage of perception. It is inferred from determinate perception as its prior stage.

Gautama's definition of perception does not apply to yogic perception which is non-sensuous. So Viśvanātha defines perception as immediate knowledge which is not derived through the medium of any other knowledge. This definition embraces all kinds of human perception and excludes inference, comparison and testimony. Inference is produced by the knowledge of vyāpti; comparison, by the knowledge of similarity; and testimony, by the knowledge of words.[1]

Recognition is a kind of perception qualified by past perception. 'This is that Devadatta'. Perception is produced by the intercourse of an object with a sense-organ. Memory is produced by a subconscious impression. Recognition is produced by both together. It is a single unitary cognition, and not a synthesis of perception and recollection as the Buddhists maintain. It is perception because the sense-object-intercourse is its principal cause while a subconscious impression is its auxiliary cause.[2]

Gaṅgeśa recognizes three kinds of extraordinary intercourse *viz.*, sāmānyalakṣaṇa, jñānalakṣaṇa and yogaja. We perceive a smoke, through ordinary intercourse. But when we perceive a smoke, we perceive all smokes through the perception of its generic character due to sāmānyalakṣaṇa-sannikarṣa. All individual smokes are not perceived through the sense-organs, but they are indirectly perceived through the knowledge of their generic character. Gaṅgeśa admits this kind of perception to ensure the knowledge of invariable concomitance between all smokes and all fires. Jñānalakṣaṇa-sannikarṣa is the extraordinary intercourse through the knowledge of an object revived from a past perception of it. Visual perception of a fragrant sandal is due to the intercourse of the visual organ with the sandal and the recollection of its fragrance perceived in the past through the olfactory organ owing to association. The idea of fragrance revived in memory brings

[1] SM., p. 237. [2] NM., pp. 448-49.

about the acquired visual perception of fragrant sandal. Yogic perception is produced by an extraordinary intercourse brought about by meditation. Intense meditation produces a peculiar merit in the self, by virtue of which it can perceive past, future, remote, hidden and subtle objects. This is intuition born of meditation. There are two kinds of yogic perception: yukta and yuñjāna. The former is the intuition of a yogin whose self has attained union with God, which is constant and effortles. The latter is the intuition of a yogin, who is endeavouring to attain union with God, and puts forth effort of will to perceive all objects. The perception of a generic character, a cognition, and a supernatural power born of meditation are the media of extraordinary intercourse.[1]

The ancient Nyāyā regards indeterminate perception and determinate perception both as valid, when they are in harmony with the real nature of their objects. Determinate perception is valid, because it apprehends an object as it really is with its qualifications which are real. Indeterminate perception is valid, because it is a means of valid determinate perception. But the modern Nyāya regards it as neither valid nor invalid, since it does not apprehend the relation between its object and its qualifications. Validity or invalidity of knowledge consists in relating the terms apprehended rightly and wrongly. Truth or falsehood is a predicate of the relational structure of knowledge, and not of non-relational immediate experience.[2]

The Nyāya advocates the Anyathākhyāti theory of error and regards it as the apprehension of an object as a different object or misperception of an object (*e.g.*, a nacre) as another object (*e.g.*, silver). This theory of error is also called Viparītakhyāti. When we perceive the qualities of silver in a nacre, we have an illusion, which is a single cognition of a perceptual character. 'This' is, in reality, a nacre endued with brightness which recalls the memory-image of 'silver' endued with its distinctive characters. A nacre in intercourse with the visual organ vitiated by a defect and aided by the recollection of silver is actually perceived as silver. The recollection of silver

[1] SM., pp. 274-85; BhP., 63-65. [2] NM., pp. 88 & 96; BhP. 135.

is due to the revival of its subconscious impression by the perception of similarity, *e.g.*, brightness. The modern Nyāya explains it by jñānalakṣaṇasannikarṣa. There is an extraordinary intercourse here through the medium of the idea of silver revived in memory. It is an acquired visual perception of silver through association. An illusion has an objective basis. It is not purely subjective. It is right so far as it apprehends the subject 'this', but it is wrong so far as it apprehends the predicate 'silver'.[1]

INFERENCE : KINDS OF INFERENCE : VYĀPTI : FALLACIES

Inference is mediate knowledge of an object (*e. g.*, a fire) derived through the medium of the knowledge of a mark (*e.g.*, a smoke) by virtue of the relation of invariable concomitance between them. It depends upon the perception of a mark and the recollection of invariable concomitance. First, there is the perception of a mark (liṅga), reason (hetu), or probans (sādhana) (*e.g.*, a smoke) in a subject (*e.g.*, a hill). Secondly, there is the recollection of invariable concomitance of the reason with a predicate, probandum (sādhya) or inferable object (*e.g.*, a fire). Thirdly, there is the inference of the existence of an unperceived object or predicate (*e.g.*, a fire) in the subject (pakṣa, *e.g.*, the hill). This is inference for oneself. This is the analysis of the psychological process of inference.

Inference is mediate knowledge, while perception is immediate knowledge. Perception apprehends present and near objects, while inference apprehends past, future and remote objects as well as present and near objects. Perception does not depend upon the knowledge of vyāpti. But inference is based upon it without which it is not possible. There is no scope for inference where we can have perception. Inference is called anumāna because it is a kind of knowledge (māna) which we get after (anu) some other knowledge or perception.[2]

Inference is of two kinds : (1) inference for oneself and

---

[1] NBh., i, 1, 4 ; BhP., 135 ; SM., pp. 451-52.

[2] NS., i, 1, 5 ; NBh., i, 1, 5 ; TSN., pp. 47 & 74.

(2) inference for others. The first kind of inference is a psychological process which does not require the formal statement of its different members. A person knows the invariable concomitance of smoke with fire by repeated observation. He perceives smoke in a hill, and doubts that a fire may exist there. Then he remembers the invariable concomitance of smoke with fire : 'whatever is smoky is fiery'. From this he infers that 'the hill has a fire'. This is the psychological analysis of inference for oneself.[1] The second kind of inference is intended for convincing others. It is a demonstrative inference which consists of the following five members (avayava) :

1. The hill is fiery (pratijñā) ;
2. Because it is smoky (hetu) ;
3. Whatever is smoky is fiery, for example, a kitchen (udaharaṇa) ;
4. The hill has smoke which is invariably accompanied by fire (upanaya) ;

∴ 5. The hill is fiery (nigamana).

The proposition is the thesis to be established, which makes a statement. The reason states the reason for the statement. The exemplification is the universal proposition which shows the invariable concomitance between the reason and the inferable predicate supported by an example. The upanaya is the application of the universal proposition to a particular instance. The nigamana is the conclusion drawn from the preceding members.

There are three terms in the demonstrative inference. The pakṣa is the subject in which the predicate or inferable object is doubted. The predicate is the object that is inferred in the subject. The hetu is the mark or sign which indicates the presence of the inferable object or predicate. The pakṣa, the sādhya and the hetu correspond to the minor term, the major term and the middle term of the Aristotelian syllogism. In the example given above 'the hill' is the subject or minor term

---

[1] TSG., p. 50.

(pakṣa), 'fire' is the major term (sādhya) and 'smoke' is the middle term (hetu) or the reason for establishing a relation between the subject and the predicate. They do not stand for terms but for real objects. The Nyāya is realist Logic as distinguished from nominalist and conceptualist Logic. The predicate is also called the pervader (vyāpaka) because it pervades the reason. The reason is also called the pervaded (vyāpya) because it is pervaded by the predicate. The middle term is pervaded by the major term. For example, smoke is pervaded by fire : wherever there is smoke, there is fire, but fire is not pervaded by smoke : wherever there is fire, there is no smoke. The reason is called the sign (liṅga) because it indicates the presence of the predicate. It is also called probans (sādhana) because it is the means of proving the existence of the predicate in the subject.[1]

There are five characteristics of the reason or mark : (1) existence in the subject, (2) existence in similar instances in which the predicate exists ; (3) non-existence in dissimilar instances in which the predicate does not exist ; (4) uncontradictedness ; and (5) uncounterbalancedness. It must be present in the subject ; *e.g.*, smoke must be present in the hill. It must be present in all homogeneous instances in which the predicate exists ; *e.g.*, smoke must be present in a kitchen in which fire exists. It must be absent from all heterogeneous instances in which the predicate does not exist ; *e.g.*, smoke must be absent from a lake in which fire does not exist. It must not be incompatible with the subject ; *e.g.*, it must not aim at proving the coolness of fire. It must not be counterbalanced by the absence of counteracting reasons leading to a contradictory conclusion. These are the five characteristics of a valid reason.[2] A reason with these characteristics is probative of the predicate.

The pakṣa is the subject in which the existence of a character or predicate is sought to be proved. A similar instance is one in which an inferable character or predicate is

---

[1] NS., NBh., i, 1, 32-39. [2] NM., p. 110.

certainly known to exist. A dissimilar instance is one from which a predicate is certainly known to be absent.[1]

There are five members (avayava) of a demonstrative inference. (1) The first member is the proposition which is the statement of the thesis to be proved. It is a judgment due to synthesis of a subject with a predicate. It is affirmation or denial of a predicate of a subject ; *e.g.*, 'sound is non-eternal.' What is inferred is of two kinds : (1) a predicate (P) as related to a subject (S) ; (2) a subject (S) as qualified by a predicate (P). A predicate is 'non-eternity of sound' or 'sound is non-eternal.' The proposition is different from the conclusion which states the existence of the predicate qualified by its distinctive character and known as such in the subject qualified by its distinctive character. The former is a statement to be proved while the latter is a statement proved by the inference. (2) The reason is the statement of the reason which is favourable to the inference of the predicate. It states similarity between the subject and an example in respect of a common character which is connected with the predicate, *e.g.*, 'because of producedness'. Or, it states dissimilarity between the subject and an example in respect of a character which is connected with the absence of the predicate. It is either affirmative or negative. The former is called sādharmyahetuvākhya while the latter is called vaidharmyahetuvākya. 'Sound is non-eternal, because it is produced, like a jar.' 'Sound is not eternal, because it is not unproduced, like a soul'.[2] (3) The exemplification is a general proposition which states the invariable concomitance of the reason with the predicate illustrated by an example in which they are perceived to exist. It is of two kinds. Either it states the invariable concomitance of the presence of the reason with the presence of the predicate. Or it states the invariable concomitance of the absence of the predicate with the absence of the reason. 'Whatever is produced is non-eternal, like a jar'. 'Whatever is unproduced is eternal, like a soul'. The statement of an example shows that

[1] NM., p. 110 ; TSG., p. 58.

[2] NS., NBh., i, 1, 33-36 ; NV., i, 1, 36 ; NSV., i, 1, 33.

the general proposition is the result of induction. Its material truth is guaranteed by induction. It embodies affirmative uniform relation or negative uniform relation between the reason and the predicate. Examples are of two kinds: homogeneous example which shows invariable concomitance of the presence of the reason with the presence of the predicate and heterogeneous example which shows invariable concomitance of the absence of the predicate with the absence of the reason. (4) The application states the existence of the reason in the subject, which is invariably concomitant with the predicate as stated in the exemplification. It is the application of a general principle to a particular instance. It conveys the knowledge of the presence of the reason pervaded by the predicate in the subject (parāmarśa), which leads to the conclusion. It removes all doubt as to the presence of the reason in the subject without which there can be no conclusion. The proposition, the reason, and the exemplification are not adequate to prove the conclusion. The application is a necessary member of a demonstrative inference. It is affirmative or negative. 'What is produced is found to be non-eternal, *e.g.*, a jar. Sound is so produced'. 'What is unproduced is found to be eternal, *e.g.*, a soul. Sound is not so unproduced'. There are two kinds of reason, two kinds of exemplification, and two kinds of application. The application shows that a demonstrative inference is deductive. So it is neither inductive nor deductive but inductive-deductive or formal-material. (5) The conclusion is the restatement of the proposition as established. The proposition states what is to be proved, but the conclusion states what is proved.[1] It synthesizes all members of a demonstrative inference, and proves the existence of the predicate in the subject. It is not a mere restatement of the proposition. It conveys the knowledge of the predicate as existing in the subject, which depends upon the prior knowledge of parāmarśa. The reason is without any basis without the proposition. It states the mark or sign or similarity with an example. The exemplification states the invariable concomitance of the mark

[1] NS., NBh., i, 1, 33-39; NM., pp. 570-85.

or reason with the predicate as shown in an example. The application removes doubt as to the existence of the reason in the subject by stating that the reason pervaded by the predicate exists in the subject. The conclusion proves the existence of the predicate in the subject after interrelating all the members of a demonstrative inference.[1] It cannot be called a syllogism, because it is an inductive-deductive inference. Many scholars have wrongly called it a syllogism.

The Nyāya demonstrative inference may be compared with the Aristotelian syllogism. First, the former consists of five members while the latter consists of three propositions. 'All men are mortal; Socrates is a man; therefore, Socrates is mortal'. The first proposition is the major premise; the second, the minor premise; and the last, the conclusion. The first three propositions of the Nyāya demonstrative inference correspond to the conclusion, the minor premise, and the major premise of the Aristotelian syllogism. The last three propositions of the former correspond to the major premise, the minor premise, and the conclusion of the latter. Secondly, the Nyāya inference is inductive-deductive and concerned with material truth, while the Aristotelian syllogism is deductive and concerned with formal truth. The universal major premise of the latter is not shown to be the conclusion of induction. But the exemplification or the universal major premise of the former is the conclusion of induction from known instances. It embodies a vyāpti or universal relation of the reason with the predicate which is established by the joint method of agreement in presence and agreement in absence. Induction (vyāpti) is the ground of deduction in the Nyāya inference. It applies an induction reached by generalisation from particular instances observed to a particular instance. Thirdly, the universal major premise of the Aristotelian syllogism is not illustrated by an example. Fourthly, the application contains the major term, the minor term, and the middle term interrelated to one another, while no premise of the Aristotelian syllogism contains the three terms. It states the existence of the reason pervaded by the

---

[1] NM., p. 585.

predicate in the subject, which makes the conclusion possible. Hence Gautama's five-membered inference is not borrowed from Aristotle's syllogism.

Gautama mentions three kinds of inference: (1) Pūrvavat; (2) Śeṣavat; and (3) Sāmānyatodṛṣṭa. Vātsyāyana gives two meanings of each of them. (1) A pūrvavat inference is the inference of an unperceived effect from a perceived cause. A future rainfall is inferred from dense clouds which are perceived. (2) A śeṣavat inference is the inference of an unperceived cause from a perceived effect. A past rainfall in the source of a river is inferred from its fulness, muddiness of water, and swiftness of current, which are perceived. These two kinds of inference are based on the causal relation. In the first, an effect is inferred from a cause. In the second, a cause is inferred from an effect. (3) A sāmānyatodṛṣṭa inference is the inference of an imperceptible object from a perceived mark, which is known to be uniformly related to it. The movement of the sun is inferred from its different positions in the sky, which are perceived, even as the movement of a person is inferred from his different positions on earth. Uddyotakara observes that sāmānyatodṛṣṭa inference is not based on the uniformity of causation but on the non-causal uniformity. The existence of water is inferred from a row of herons perceived in the sky. There is no causal relation between them.[1] Vātsyāyana gives other meanings also of these kinds of inference. (1) A pūrvavat inference is based on previous experience of invariable concomitance of two perceived objects. The existence of an unperceived fire is inferred from a perceived smoke on the ground of uniform relation between them perceived in the past. (2) A śeṣavat inference is inference by elimination. Sound is not a substance because it inheres in one substance, *viz.*, ether. It is not an action, since it is a cause of another sound. It is not a community, a particularity or inherence. So it is a quality. (3) A sāmānyatodṛṣṭa inference is the inference of an unperceived object from a mark which is perceived, though the relation between them in not perceived.

[1] NV., i, 1, 5.

We infer the existence of the soul from the qualities of cognition, pleasure, pain, desire, aversion and volition, which must inhere in a substance. The soul is inferred as the substance in which they inhere.[1]

Viśvanātha mentions three kinds of inference : (1) Kevalānvayi, (2) Kevalavyatireki, and (3) Anvayavyatireki. (1) In Kevalānvayi inference the reason has affirmative uniform relation with the presence of the predicate. It has an affirmative reason which exists in all similar instances, and has no dissimilar instances. 'The jar is nameable, because it is knowable'. The reason 'knowability' exists in all nameable objects. There are no knowable objects which are not nameable. The reason is not the counter-positive entity of the negation of the predicate. Here the major premise is a universal affirmative proposition ; it cannot be a universal negative proposition. The minor premise and the conclusian also are universal affirmative propositions. 'All knowable objects are nameable ; the jar is a knowable object : therefore, the jar is nameable'. The uniform affirmative relation between the reason 'knowability' and the predicate 'nameability' is established by the method of agreement in presence. (2)In Kevalavyatireki inference the reason has negative invariable concomitance with the absence of the predicate. Its reason exists in the subject only. It is devoid of similar instances in which the reason and the predicate may coexist. It depends upon a negative invariable concomitance or uniform relation between the absence of the reason with the absence of the predicate, which is established by the method of agreement in absence. For example : 'earth differs from the other elements, because it has odour'. Or, 'what is not different from the other elements has no odour ; earth has odour; therefore earth is different from the other elements'. In this inference the reason 'odour' is the uncommon attribute of the subject 'earth' ; it is coextensive with the subject ; there is no similar instance in which it may exist. In Kevalavyatireki inference the major premise is a universal negative proposition, the minor premise, a universal affirmative proposition, and the

[1] NBh., i, 1, 5.

conclusion, a universal affirmative proposition. (3) In Anvayavyatireki inference there is a universal affirmative relation of the reason with the predicate as well as a universal negative relation between them. The former is known by the method of agreement in presence, and the latter, by the method of agreement in absence. In this inference the reason is present in similar instances, and absent from dissimilar instances[1]. For example: (1) 'all smoky objects are fiery; the hill is smoky; therefore, the hill is fiery.' (2) 'no non-fiery objects are smoky; the hill is smoky; therefore, the hill is fiery.' Smoke exists in similar instances, *e.g.*, a kitchen, in which fire exists. It does not exist in dissimilar instances, *e.g.*, a lake, in which fire does not exist.

Inference is based upon vyāpti which is the invariable concomitance of the reason with the predicate. It depends upon two conditions. First, the reason must be known to be present in the subject. Secondly, it must be known to be invariably concomitant with the predicate. The universal relation of the reason with the predicate is the logical ground of inference.[2] Vyāpti is a uniform, unconditional, or natural relation between the reason and the predicate. There are two kinds of vyāpti, *viz.*, anvayavyāpti and vyatirekavyāpti, The former is invariable concomitance of the presence of the reason with the presence of the predicate. The latter is the invariable concomitance of the absence of the predicate with the absence of the reason. The vyāpti is known by the joint method of agreement in presence and agreement in absence based on repeated observation aided by favourable hypothetical reasoning. When conditions are not observed to vitiate the natural relation in spite of the best efforts to find them out, it is taken to be unconditional. According to Jayanta, first there is the perception of a mark; then there is the recollection of vyāpti; then there is the knowledge of the presence of the reason pervaded by the predicate in the subject (parāmarśa); then there is the inference of the predicate in the subject. The

[1] SM., p. 463; BhP., 143-44. [2] NS., iii, 2, 12, 69 & 71; ii, 2, 16; iv, 1, 5; i, 2, 46 & 59.

knowledge of parāmarśa is directly the cause of inference, while the perception of vyāpti is its cause through its recollection. The knowledge of vyāpti is the logical ground of inference, while that of parāmarśa is its psychological ground.[1]

Vyāpti is the unconditional uniform relation of the reason to the predicate. It is free from conditions (upādhi). Smoke has unconditional relation to fire ; it is pervaded by fire ; wherever there is smoke there is fire. But fire has no unconditional relation to smoke ; there is fire where there is no smoke ; for example, red hot iron ball is smokeless. The relation of fire to smoke is conditional ; it depends upon the presence of wet fuel as a condition. 'The hill is smoky, because it is fiery'. Wet fuel is a condition which pervades smoke, but does not pervade fire. Thus a condition pervades the predicate, but does not pervade the reason.[2]

There are no formal fallacies in the Nyāya, which is not concerned with formal truth. The fallacies are faulty reasons (hetvābhāsa). All fallacies of inference are due to the fallacies of the reason or middle term, which cannot prove the existence of the predicate in the subject. Fallacious reasons are not-reasons which are devoid of the characteristics of a valid reason, but which appear to be reasons owing to their similarity with it. They hinder the production of a valid inference of a real object, when they are known.

The Nyāya recognizes five kinds of fallacies of the reason ; (1) inconclusive (savyabhicāra), (2) contradictory (viruddha), (3) counterbalanced (prakaraṇasama), (4) unproved (sādhyasama), and (5) mistimed (atītakāla) or contradicted (bādhita).[3]

(1) Gautama defines an inconclusive reason (savyabhicāra or anaikāntika) as one which has variable concomitance with the predicate. A reason is conclusive, which has uniform relation to the predicate. It is inconclusive if it has concomitance with the predicate and its absence. Variable concomitance is the existence of a reason in the subject (pakṣa), similar instances (sapakṣa), and dissimilar instances (vipakṣa). 'Sound is eternal, because it is intangible'. Intangibility is concomitant

---

[1] NM., pp. 122-23, 125-26. [2] NKS., iii, p. 30. [3] NS., i, 2, 45.

with eternity and non-eternity. Intangible souls are eternal, but intangible cognitions are non-eternal. So the reason is inconclusive or irregular (anaikāntika).[1]

Viśvanātha divides inconclusive reasons into three kinds : (1) common ; (2) uncommon ; and (3) indefinite. (1) A common (sādhāraṇa) inconclusive reason is one which exists in the locus of the predicate and the locus of its absence. 'Sound is eternal, because it is intangible', (2) An uncommon (asādhāraṇa) inconclusive reason is one which exists in the subject only, and is excluded from similar and dissimilar instances. 'Sound is non-eternal, because it has the character of sound'. The character of sound exists in sound only ; it does not exist in other non-eternal objects (sapakṣa) and eternal objects (vipakṣa). (3) An indefinite (anupasaṁhāri) inconclusive reason is one which is not a counter-positive entity of the absence of the predicate, or which exists in all objects. 'All are eternal, because they are knowable', It hinders the knowledge of invariable concomitance of the reason with the predicate, because there is a doubt as to the existence of the predicate in all objects.[2]

(2) Gautama defines a contradictory (viruddha) reason as one which contradicts the predicate, though it is employed to prove its existence. It contradicts an admitted truth, and is contradicted by an admitted truth. It occurs when a proposition is contradicted by a reason or a reason is contradicted by a proposition. 'Sound is eternal, because it is produced'. Producedness of sound is known to be true by a means of valid knowledge. It contradicts the proposition 'Sound is eternal'. Producedness is pervaded by non-eternity, and so it cannot prove the existence of eternity. A contradictory reason is a counter-positive entity of the absence which pervades the predicate. It proves the non-existence of the predicate, though it is advanced to prove its existence.

Viśvanātha distinguishes a contradictory reason (viruddha) from a counterbalanced reason (satpratipakṣa). A contradictory

[1] NS., NBh., i, 2, 46. [2] SM., pp. 334-35.

reason in an inference proves the non-existence of the predicate. But a reason in one inference is counterbalanced by another reason in a different inference, which proves the non-existence of the predicate.[1]

(3) The reason which is counterbalanced by another reason, and cannot resolve the controversy as to the real character of an object, is counterbalanced (prakaraṇasama). Two reasons of equal strength, proving the presence and the absence of the predicate in two arguments are counterbalanced by each other. Two inferences cannot be of equal strength, one proving the existence of the predicate, and the other proving its non-existence. 'Sound is eternal, because it is audible, like the genus of sound'. 'Sound is non-eternal, because it is produced, like a jar.'[2]

Vācaspati distinguishes a counterbalanced reason (prakaraṇasama) from an inconclusive reason (anaikāntika). In the former no common character of eternal and non-eternal things, for example, admitted by both parties is taken as a reason, whereas in the latter a common character is taken as a reason, which generates a doubt. Jayanta distinguishes a counterbalanced reason from a contradictory reason. The former is not known to exist or not to exist in similar instances ; nor is it known to exist in dissimilar instances ; whereas the latter is known to exist in dissimilar instances.[3]

(4) Gautama defines an unproven reason (sādhyasama) as one that requires to be proved like the predicate. But it should not require any proof. Viśvanātha calls it unproven reason (asiddha) and mentions three kinds of unproven reasons (asiddha) : (1) svarūpāsiddha ; (2) āśrayāsiddha ; and (3) vyāpyatvāsiddha. (1) Svarūpāsiddhi is the absence of a reason invariably concomitant with the predicate from the subject. 'A lake is a substance, because it has smoke.' (2) Āśrayāsiddhi is the absence of a quality that determines the special character of the subject from it. 'A golden mountain is fiery, because it has smoke'. A mountain is not golden.

[1] NS., NBh., i, 2, 47 ; SM., p. 335.
[2] NS., NBh., i, 2, 48. [3] NVTT., p. 236 ; NM., pp. 602-03.

(3) Vyāpyatvāsiddhi is the absence of invariable coexistence of a reason and the predicate in the same locus. 'The hill has a fire, because it has golden smoke'. Goldenness does not exist in smoke. 'The hill has golden fire, because it has smoke'. Goldenness does not exist in a fire.[1]

(5) A contradicted reason (bādhita) is contradicted by perception, inference, and Vedic testimony. (1) 'Fire is cold, because it is a substance'. It is contradicted by perception which apprehends hotness of fire. (2) 'Atoms are made of parts, because they are corporeal'. It is contradicted by inference, which proves partlessness of atoms which have the minutest magnitude. (3) 'Sacrifices are not the means of attaining heaven'. It is contradicted by Vedic testimony.[2]

A cantradicted reason (bādhita) is different from a contradictory reason (viruddha). The former is contradicted by some other pramāṇa, perception, inference, comparison or testimony —which proves the contradictory of the predicate in the subject, while the latter proves the contradictory of the predicate in the same inference. A contradicted reason (bādhita) is different from a counterbalanced reason (satpratipakṣa). The former is contradicted by some other pramāṇa, which indubitably proves the contradictory of the predicate, while the latter is counterbalanced by another reason in another inference which seeks to prove the contradictory of the predicate, and thus produces an unsettled state of the mind as to the real character of an object. In the former there is certain knowledge of the absence of the predicate, while in the latter there is a doubt as to the existence or the non-existence of the predicate in the subject.[3]

COMPARISON (UPAMĀNA)

Comparison is the means of knowing an unknown object through its resemblance with another well-known object. A person familiar with a cow in a town learns from a reliable

---

1 NS., NBh., i, 2, 49 ; SM., pp. 338-39.

2 NKL., p. 15 ; TR., pp. 228-30 ; NSār., p. 11.

3 NSV., i, 2, 47 ; NSār., p. 7.

forester that a wild cow (gavaya) resembles a cow. He goes to a forest, perceives a strange animal resembling a cow, remembers that a wild cow resembles a cow, and knows the animal to be a wild cow through the knowledge of its resemblance with a well-known cow. His knowledge that the strange animal bears the name 'gavaya' is comparison.[1] Comparison contains the following factors : (1) the perception of an unfamiliar object which was not perceived before ; (2) the indirect knowledge of its resemblance with a familiar object, which is acquired from testimony of a reliable person who perceived them both and knew their similarity ; (3) the perception of resemblance of the unfamiliar object with the well-known object ; (4) the recollection of the varbal statement of the reliable person ; and (5) the knowledge of the relation between a name and the unfamiliar object which is perceived. The knowledge of resemblance involves testimony and perception. The knowledge acquired from the verbal statement 'a wild cow is like a cow' is testimony. The knowledge 'this animal has similarity with a cow' is perception. The perception of similarity of the strange animal with a well-known cow aided by the recollection of the verbal statement of the forester is the cause of the knowledge of the relation between it and the name 'gavaya'. A person who does not perceive the similarity of a wild cow with a cow, does not know on the strength of the mere verbal statement of a forester that the wild cow is called a 'gavaya'. Nor does he know it through the perception of similarity without the verbal statement of the forester. So comparison is different from testimony and perception. It is due to the knowledge of similarity aided by the recollection of the verbal statement. Recollection is due to the revival of the impression of the knowledge of the verbal statement. The perception of similarity aided by the recollection of the forester's statement produces the knowledge of the relation between a name and an unknown object. The knowledge of similarity is comparison. The knowledge of the relation of a name to an object is its result.

---

[1] NS., i, 1, 6 ; NBh., i, 1, 6.

Comparison is neither perception, nor inference, nor testimony. A wild cow and its similarity with a cow are perceived. But that it bears the name 'gavaya' is not perceived. Nor is comparison inference, since there is no knowledge of invariable concomitance between a name and an object in it. Nor is it testimony, since the knowledge of the verbal statement of the forester is testimony which cannot yield the knowledge 'this animal bears the name 'gavaya' before it is perceived. The perception of similarity with or without the knowledge of the verbal statement is not comparison. Nor is testimony without the perception of similarity comparison. It is an independent means of valid knowledge. It is not recollection, because it was never perceived in the past.[1]

It is objected that if there is perfect similarity (*e.g.*, 'a cow is like a cow'), there can be no comparison; that if there is great similarity (*e.g.*, 'a buffalo is like a cow'), no comparison is possible; and that if there is slight similarity (*e.g.*, 'mount Meru is like a mustard seed'), there can be no comparison. The Nyāya replies that these objections are beside the mark. Comparison does not depend upon the quantity of similarity, perfect, great, or slight. But it depends upon perceived similarity of an unknown object with a well-known object, which indicates the relation of an unknown object with a particular name. It apprehends something which is not apprehended by perception, inference, or testimony.[2]

Viśvanātha regards the perception of similarity as the instrument, the recollection of the verbal statement of a reliable person as the causal operation, and the knowledge 'a wild cow is called gavaya' as the result of comparison. The knowledge 'This is called gavaya' is not result of comparison, because then any other wild cow cannot be called gavaya.[3]

Comparison is different from analogy of Western Logic. Analogy takes the form: S and P resemble each other in

---

[1] NKS., iii, 10, pp. 49-50; NV., ii, 1, 45, p. 260; NVTT., i, 1, 6, p. 133.

[2] NS., NBh., ii, 1, 42 & 43; NVTT., pp. 284-85.

[3] BhP., 79 & 80; SM., pp. 355-59.

many respects ; S has another characteristic *x* ; therefore P also may have *x*. The earth and Mars resemble each other in many respects, *e.g.*, temperate climate, atmosphere, clouds, rain, etc. The earth has another characteristic that it is inhabited by living beings. Comparison is not analogy, though both are based on similarity. First, unlike analogy, comparison depends upon testimony. Secondly, unlike analogy, comparison yields the knowledge of the relation between a name and an object. Thirdly, unlike analogy, comparison sometimes depends upon dissimilarity. A person recognizes an animal as a horse, because it has, unlike cows, no cloven hoofs.[1]

The Vaiśeṣika regards comparison as testimony, which produces the knowledge of relation between a name and an object. The testimony of a reliable person is the essential element in comparison. So comparison is testimony. But Jayanta urges that in comparison a reliable person makes a statement 'a wild cow is like a cow', and indicates another means, *i.e.*, the perception of an unknown object similar to a cow in a forest through which an inhabitant of a town knows that it is a wild cow. He perceives an animal similar to a cow in a forest as instructed by a reliable forester. So his knowledge that it is a wild cow is not produced by testimony, but by comparison.[2]

It is objected that comparison is inference, since an unperceived relation of a name (gavaya) to an object is inferred from a perceived similarity of an unfamiliar animal with a cow. The Nyāya replies that, first, when a wild cow is perceived, it is known by comparison to bear the name 'gavaya'. It cannot be known by inference. Secondly, comparison is intended for another person. A person who has perceived a cow and a wild cow both makes a statement 'a wild cow is like a cow' for the benefit of another person, who has perceived a cow only, but not a wild cow. He knows through comparison that a wild cow bears the name 'gavaya'. Thirdly, comparison is based on the knowledge of similarity, while inference is based on the knowledge of vyāpti. In comparison there is the knowledge of

[1] NV., NVTT., i, 1, 6. [2] NM., pp. 141-42.

similarity 'a wild cow is like a cow'. But in inference there is no knowledge of similarity 'a fire is like a smoke'. So comparison is different from inference.[1]

TESTIMONY

Gautama defines testimony as the instruction of a trustworthy person, who has immediate knowledge of the Moral Law, and who is competent to guide others in the performance of their duties and abstention from sins for the attainment of good and the avoidance of evil. Trustworthy persons are those who perceive objects as they exist in their real nature, and communicate their right knowledge to others for their benefit out of compassion for them. They are free from attachment and aversion, and have immediate knowledge of eternal verities that exist in all times. Sages are the seers of truths. The assertions of those who know truths but speak falsehoods are not valid. The assertions of those who are ignorant of truths, but speak what they know are not valid. The assertions of trustworthy persons, which are not fit for guiding persons in the performance of right actions and the non-commision of sins are not testimony. Untrustworthy persons are tainted with delusion, mendacity and fraudulence. Testimony is an instruction which is expressed in a sentence or proposition. The knowledge of a proposition is testimony, and the knowledge of its meaning is the result. Testimony is due to the knowledge of a sentence or words, while perception is due to the sense-object-intercourse, inference, to the knowledge of vyāpti, and comparison, to the knowledge of similarity.[2]

Testimony is of two kinds, *viz.*, testimony about perceptible objects and testimony about imperceptible objects. The former objects are found in this world. The latter are found in the next world, such as heaven, hell, transmigration and the like. The modern Naiyāyikas divide testimony into two kinds, *viz.*,

---

[1] NS., NBh., ii, 1, 44-46.

[2] NS., NBh., i, 1, 7; NM., pp. 150-52; NVTT., pp. 135-36; SM., pp. 360-61.

secular testimony and scriptural testimony. The Vedas are not impersonal but personal compositions of God, the omniscient person, and are therefore valid. The secular testimony of trustworthy persons is valid, while that of untrustworthy persons is invalid.[1]

Testimony is expressed in a sentence, which is a combination of words conveying a meaning. Its comprehensibility depends upon certain conditions. First, a sentence consists of words which imply one another. Mutual implication is called expectancy. A word cannot by itself convey a full meaning. It must be related to other words in order to convey a complete meaning. The word 'bring' does not make full sense. It produces an expectancy in the mind for some other word or words. The sentence 'bring a horse' makes full sense. The words imply one another, and convey a complete meaning. Secondly, a sentence consists of words which have fitness for one another. Mutual fitness of words is another condition of the intelligibility of a sentence. The sentence 'quench your thirst with water' conveys a meaning, because its component words have mutual fitness or compatibility. But the sentence 'quench your thirst with fire' is unintelligible, since its constituent words are incompatible with one another. Thirdly, a sentence consists of words which are in close proximity to one another. The words constituting a sentence should be uttered in close succession without a long interval between one word and another. If the words 'bring', 'a', and 'horse' are uttered at long intervals, they do not convey any meaning. Proximity of words is a condition of the comprehension of a sentence. Sentences devoid of expectancy, compatibility, and proximity are not means of valid knowledge. Fourthly, the comprehension of the meaning of a sentence depends upon the knowledge of the intention of the speaker. The sentence 'saindhavam ānaya' means 'bring a horse', when the speaker gets ready for starting on a journey. It means 'bring salt' when the speaker is taking his meal. It has different meanings in different contexts according to the intentions of the speakers. Some

[1] NBh., NS., i, 1, 8; NVTT., p. 136; TSG., p. 79.

opine that the context, which determines the intention of the speaker, is a cause of understanding the meaning of a sentence. But it is wrong, since there is no common property in the contexts of different sentences. Some opine that the knowledge of the speaker's intention is a cause when some word in a sentence is equivocal. Hence a sentence, in order to be intelligible, must consist of words, which are interdependent on, compatible with, and juxtaposed to, one another, and convey a meaning in conformity with the speaker's intention. Compatibility implies formal consistency, while the knowledge of the speaker's intention implies material consistency.[1] This is the syntactical analysis of a sentence.

The Nyāya holds that a word denotes an individual bearing a genus and with a particular form or configuration. The word 'cow' denotes an individual cow bearing the genus of cow and with a particular configuration or arrangement of parts, *e.g.*, a hunch, horns and a dewlap. An individual is a perceptible substance endued with qualities and movements. It is a corporeal body composed of parts which are united with one another. A genus subsists in many individuals, produces a common concept of them, and brings many individuals under one class. A configuration is a definite arrangement of parts, which is the peculiar mark of a genus.[2]

THE WORLD

The Nyāya conception of the world is the same as the Vaiśeṣika view of it with slight variations. It is composed of the five physical elements, earth, water, fire, air and ether. There are the atoms of the first four elements. Ether, time and space are one each, ubiquitous and eternal. They are undivided, unique wholes. Atoms, ether, time and space are coeternal with souls and God. Atoms are the material cause of the world, while God is its efficient cause. Causation is real and objective. Effectuation is emergence of new effects from their causes, in which they did not pre-exist. Causation is

[1] NVTT., p. 139 ; NM., pp. 399-401 ; BhP., 82-84 ; SM., pp. 389-94.
NS., ii, 2, 68 ; NS., NBh., ii, 2, 69-71.

teleological and subservient to the moral Law of Karma. Atoms are combined with one another by God into gross material objects, living organisms, and the multiform world, and adapted to the enjoyments and sufferings of individual souls in accordance with their merits and demerits. Difference of objects is real and not illusory or apparent. All things are non-eternal and diverse. The atoms are eternal, while their composite products are non-eternal. The objects are real and not mere subjective ideas. The composite products are wholes which are not mere aggregates of parts. Substances are not mere conglomerations of qualities. Universals are real and eternal, and subsist in individuals. They are not unreal and imaginary. Qualities and actions are real. Particularity, inherence and negation are real. The Nyāya advocates realistic pluralism, dualism and Deism. It admits the reality of diverse objects externally related to one another, dualism of matter and souls, and the existence of God external to the world and individual souls.

The body is the seat of voluntary actions, sense-organs and objects. It is not a mere aggregate of parts, but a unique, undivided whole. The whole living organism is the vehicle of experience. The self, which is all-pervading, experiences pleasure and pain through it only. It is not the seat of vital acts only. If it were so, then plants also would have bodies. It is the seat of voluntary actions for the attainment of good and the avoidance of evil. Conjunction of the self endued with volition with the body is their non-inherent cause. The living organism is the seat of the sense-organs, which are affected by its health and disease in apprehending their objects. The imperceptible atoms which produce them are their receptacles in which they reside. Earth is the principal ingredient of the body, and odour is its special quality.

The sense-organs are the instruments of direct valid knowledge in contact with the organism only. They are direct causes of valid perception, but they produce illusions with the aid of subconscious impressions. They are composed of the physical elements. The auditory organ or ether limited by the ear-hole and manas are eternal and devoid of substrates. The olfactory organ, the gustatory organ, the visual organ, the tactual organ, and the auditory organ are composed of earth, water, light, air, and ether respectively, endued with odour, taste, colour, touch, and sound respectively, and consequently perceive these qualities respectively. They can perceive those qualities with which they are endued in excess.

CAUSALITY

The Nyāya gives an empirical definition of a cause. Udayana defines it as an invariable antecedent of an effect. He also regards it as its unconditional or necessary antecedent. If an unconditional antecedent, which is always present when an effect is present, and which is always absent when an effect is absent, were not regarded as its cause, then the effect would be uncaused. Gaṅgeśa also defines a cause as an unconditional or necessary, invariable antecedent of an effect. Vardhamāna defines a cause as an unconditional, invariable, immediate antecedent of an effect. Laugākṣi Bhāskara avers that a cause must exist in the same place at the immediately preceding moment.[1] Gaṅgeśa defines a cause also as a necessary invariable antecedent, which is synchronous and coexistent with it. This definition applies to the inherent cause, the non-inherent cause, and the efficient cause. A cause is an antecedent in relation to its effect. It is produced by the activity of a principal or material cause in co-operation with the auxiliary causes, and consequently exists immediately after the assemblage of the auxiliary causes. It exists at a time when it is produced by its cause and related to it. A cause coexists with the prior non-existence of its effect, and so it must be its antecedent. Though a cause is an immediate antecedent of its effect, it is also synchronous with it.

A cause is an antecedent of an effect, since it produces the effect. It is not a variable antecedent, but an invariable antecedent which is always followed by an effect. An ass is a variable

[1] NKS., i, p. 89 ; ATV., p. 66 ; TCIA., Ch. S.S., pp. 14, 56 ; BhP. 16 ; NKSM., i, p. 18 ; SMD., pp. 120-21 ; TK., p. 7. Cp. David Hume & J. S. Mill.

antecedent of all jars, and consequently not their cause. But some invariable antecedents of an effect are not necessary for its production. The colour or the generic character of a staff is an invariable antecedent of a jar, but it is not its cause. There are some invariable antecedents which are unnecessary, conditional and casual antecedents. A conditional (anyathā-siddha) antecedent depends upon other conditions in order to be followed by an effect, which is not necessary for its production. It is an unnecessary concomitant of an effect. A cause is not a remote antecedent of its effect, but its immediate antecedent. Immediacy follows from unconditionality. A is a cause of B. B is a cause of C. A is a remote antecedent of C. A is followed by C after being followed by B. A's antecedence of C depends upon its antecedence of B. So A is a conditional antecedent of C. But B is an unconditional, immediate antecedent of C, and hence its cause. A cause is an unconditional or necessary antecedent which produces an effect.

Gaṅgeśa mentions four kinds of unnecssary antecedents. (1) That which is antecedent to an effect by virtue of its relation to its inherent cause, is its unnecessary antecedent. The colour of a staff depends upon its inherent cause in order to be invariably followed by a jar. So it is its unnecessary antecedent. (2) That which is known to be antecedent to an effect after it is known to be antecedent to some other effect as its cause, is its unnecessary antecedent. Ether is already known to be an antecedent of sound as its inherent cause. So it is an unnecessary antecedent of a jar, though it is its invariable antecedent, since it is not necessary for its production. A cause is determined by its presence and absence both—not by its presence only. Eternal and ubiquitous substances, which cannot be eliminated, are unnecessary antecedents. (3) That antecedent, which is other than the invariable, necessary antecedent of an effect, is its unnecessary antecedent. The prior non-existence of colour is an unnecessary antecedent of smell due to heating, since the prior non-existence of smell is its invariable, necessary antecedent or cause. (4) That which cannot be known to be antecedent to an effect without knowing its antecedence to its cause is its unnecessary antecedent. The cause of a cause is not the cause of an effect, but its unnecessary antecedent. A potter is the efficient cause of a jar, and hence its invariable necessary antecedent. But the potter's father, who is a cause of the potter, is its unnecessary antecedent. A cause is not a remote antecedent, but an immediate antecedent of its effect. Vardhamāna adds another kind of unnecessary antecedent. (5) That which is antecedent to the effect, together with the cause, is its unnecessary antecedent. A staff is an auxiliary cause of a jar, whose presence is followed by its production, and whose absence is followed by its non-production. It is its necessary antecedent. But the generic character of a staff is not followed by the production of a jar independently of the staff. Hence it is its unnecessary antecedent. A cause is an unconditional, invariable, immediate antecedent of an effect, which is an unconditional, invariable, immediate consequent of a cause.[1]

The Nyāya admits three kinds of causes, *viz.*, the material cause, the non-inherent cause and the efficient cause. Causal activity is in the nature of physical motion, which requires the direction of a conscious agent, who exerts action upon an object. He produces an effect with the aid of an instrumental cause for the benefit of some conscious being out of a particular unconscious material cause, which is its locus. Sometimes he separates a part from a whole, *e.g.*, when he cuts a branch from a tree. Thus an effect is produced by a collocation of causes centring round a conscious energiser. The unconscious factors of a cause depend on a conscious agent without whose direction they are ineffective. An instrumental cause is an auxiliary cause, which by its activity immediately brings about an effect. In this sense, it is called a special cause or the most effective cause. Its activity being produced by it produces its effect. An axe is the instrumental cause of cutting. Its activity is its conjunction with a tree, which is

[1] NKS., i, p. 88 ; TCIA., p. 56 ; BhP., 19-22 ; SM., pp. 114-22 ; TBh., p. 3 ; TSG., p. 40.

produced by it, and produces its effect (*e.g.*, cutting). The ancient Nyāya regards an instrument as an instrumental cause. But the modern Nyāya regards its action as an instrumental cause. God, his knowledge, desire and volition, prior non-existence, time, space, and merits and demerits are the common causes of all effects. Hence by the causes of effects we mean their special causes or necessary, invariable, immediate antecedents.[1]

The Nyāya regards a cause as an aggregate of necessary, invariable, immediate antecedents, which are positive causal conditions, and the absence of counteracting causes or negative conditions of an effect. A cause is the aggregate of the principal or material cause and auxiliary causes which render an aid to it. When they are present, an effect is produced ; when they are absent, it is not produced. There is no causal power in addition to them. Straw, fire and blowing together are the cause of burning, each of which singly is not its cause. But they are its positive conditions only, which can produce its effect when its negative conditions are absent. A fire-extinguishing gem is its negative condition, which must be absent in order that burning may be produced. Just as the presence of the positive conditions is a cause, so the absence of the negative conditions is a cause. The absence of any member of the aggregate of causal conditions—the principal cause and the auxiliary causes—is the main counteracting cause.[2] The entire collocation of positive causal conditions must be present and the counteracting causes or negative conditions must be absent in order to produce an effect.

The Nyāya rejects plurality of causes. The causal relation is reciprocal. The same cause produces the same effect, and the same effect is produced by the same cause. But sometimes we find that the same effect is produced by a variety of causes, *e.g.*, burning is produced by straw, fire and blowing together, or by two pieces of fire-wood and intense friction together, or

[1] NM., p. 494 ; TK., p. 6 ; TSG., p. 38.

[2] NM., pp. 10, 18 & 47 ; NKS., i, p. 18 ; NKSP., i, pp. 90-91 ; TR., p. 164 ; TCIA., Ch. SS., p. 37. Cp. J.S. Mill & Bain.

by a fire-exciting gem and concentration of the rays of the sun on it. The Nyāya argues that the specific causes produce specific effects which appear to be the same, because they have special attendant consequences. If they are considered with their distinctive features, then specific effects have specific causes. If there is a specific difference in the causes, there must be a specific difference in the effects, even though they appear to be homogeneous. If specific effects are not due to specific causes, their specific characters will be uncaused. The specific differences in the effects are due to the specific differences in the auxiliary causes which produce different peculiarities in the same homogeneous cause and diversity in it. A specific cause has a specific effect. Diversity of effects requires diversity of causes. Where a generic effect is observed, a generic cause should be regarded as its cause. The generic character of fire is the effect of conjunction of a combustible substance with light endued with a particular degree of heat. Specific effects cannot be produced by a generic cause.[1]

An effect is a new creation. It is non-existent in its material cause, but it is produced anew out of its material cause owing to the rearrangement of its atoms. Curd is non-existent in milk, but it is produced from milk owing to the disintegration of its parts and a fresh collocation of its atoms.[2] The particles of milk endued with a particular colour and a particular taste produce curd with a particular taste due to the peculiarity produced by heating. Likewise a sprout is produced from a seed owing to the rearrangement of its atoms due to heat. They are qualified by a peculiarity due to heat, and produce a new effect. They produce a first peculiarity in the shape of the first swollen condition, then an intermediate swelling, and then the last peculiarity in the shape of germination. A peculiarity is an aid, excess or additament produced in the principal material cause by the auxiliary causes for the production of an effect, which is therefore not momentary. It is

[1] ATV., pp. 767-68 ; NKS., v, p. 37 ; i, 32 ; ATVP., p. 95 ; TCIA., pp. 47-48.

[2] NKS., i, p. 58.

an intermediate aid favourable to the production of an effect.[1] The Nyāya-Vaiśeṣika advocates Asatkāryavāda.

THE PROOFS FOR THE EXISTENCE OF THE INDIVIDUAL SELF (ĀTMAN)

The Nyāya arguments for the existence of the finite self are similar to the Vaiśeṣika arguments. The Nyāya admits the perception of the self, while the Vaiśeṣika denies it. According to the Nyāya, the self is an object of internal perception or 'I'-consciousness, inferred from marks, and known from the testimony of the Vedas. (1) The self is an object of 'I'-consciousness or mental perception. It is perceived by intuition owing to a particular kind of conjunction of it with manas due to meditative trance.[2] (2) The self is inferred from desire, aversion, volition, pleasure, pain, and cognition. Desire for an object depends upon the recollection of a similar object which was perceived in the past, and afforded pleasure. It proves the identity of the self which perceived a similar object in the past, remembers the pleasure yielded by it, and desires to attain a similar object. Similarly, aversion to an object depends upon the recollection of a similar object which was perceived in the past, and yielded pain. It proves the unity and permanence of the self, which perceived a similar object in the past, remembers the pain yielded by it, and avoids a similar object. Volition is actuated by desire and aversion. It is striving for the attainment of good which is an object of desire. Or it is striving for the rejection of evil which is an object of aversion. It proves the permanence and identity of the self, which is the agent of perception, recollection, desire, aversion, and volition. Pleasure arises from the perception of an object, because a similar object yielded pleasure in the past. It proves the unity and identity of the self which perceived a pleasant object in the past and remembers it now. Pain arises from the perception of an object because a similar object yielded pain in the past. It proves the permanent identity of the self, which perceived a

[1] NKS., i, pp. 53, 57; NKSB., pp, 28-29 & 31-32.

[2] NV., iii, 1, 1, p. 345; NBh., i, 1, 3.

painful object, in the past and remembers it now. Cognition also proves the existence of the self. It has a desire to know the real nature of an object. First, it has an uncertain and doubtful knowledge of it. Then it has a certain and undoubted knowledge of it. The same self has a desire for knowledge, indefinite knowledge, and definite knowledge. Thus desire, aversion, volition, pleasure, pain, and cognition prove the existence of the self. They are the qualities of the self in which they inhere.[1] They are not qualities of the body, the sense-organs, or manas. (3) The self is inferred from the synthesis of the sensations of colour, taste, smell and touch of an object into a unity of perception. The visual organ gives the sensation of colour only, the gustatory organ, the sensation of taste only, the olfactory organ, the sensation of smell only, and the tactual organ, the sensation of touch only. These sensations are combined into a unitary perception of an object by the self. Perception depends upon the synthetic activity of the self. The sense-organs which apprehend their own objects, the different qualities of an object, cannot combine them into a unity. They are unconscious organs of perception, through which the conscious self perceives an object endued with different qualities.[2] (4) There is recognition of an object perceived by the right eye, which was perceived by the left eye in the past. If the sense-organs were conscious, one sense-organ could not recognize an object perceived by another sense-organ. But there is such a recognition, which proves that the conscious self is distinct from the sense-organs, and is the agent of perception, recollection and recognition. If one sense-organ could remember the objects perceived by the other sense-organs, then the different senses would not be restricted to different kinds of objects. But one conscious self can perceive colour, taste, smell and touch through the visual organ, the gustatory organ, the olfactory organ, and the tactual organ respectively, synthesize them into a unitary percept, remember the different qualities perceived, and recognize the

---

[1] NS., NBh., i, 1, 10 ; iii, 2, 36 & 40.

[2] NBh., iii, 1, 1-3.

object through one sense-organ, which was perceived through another sense-organ. (5) I perceive the same object (*e.g.*, a jar) through the tactual organ which I perceived through the visual organ. I recognize the object through one sense-organ, which I perceived through another sense-organ. These two perceptions are recognized as belonging to the same self or knower. They are not known by the body or the sense-organs. One sense-organ cannot remember the apprehension of another object by another sense-organ, because they are restricted to their own objects. The conscious self perceives all objects and recognizes them.[1] (6) Recollection is a quality of the self. It perceived an object in the past, retained a subconscious impression, revives it, and remembers the object at present. Perception produces a subconscious impression, which abides in the self and produces recollection. The recollection of the object comprises the cognition of the object, the cognition of the past cognition, and the cognition of the cognizer, which are remembered. These three cognitions have only one knower; they are not without knowers, nor have they many knowers. There is one self in each body, which perceives all kinds of objects, remembers and recognizes them and its own cognitions. Perception and recollection of the same object are qualities of the same self or knower.[1] Devadatta cannot remember what was perceived by Yajñadatta. Recollection is an effect of a subconscious impression, which cannot be without a substrate. The self is its substrate as its material cause. Momentary cognitions related to each other as cause and effect cannot account for recollection, since the antecedent cognition is destroyed no sooner than it is produced, and cannot modify the succeeding cognition with its residuum. One permanent self only can account for it. (7) One perceives the colour of a mango, remembers its taste, and desires to taste it. His recollection of its taste produces saliva in his tongue. One sense-organ cannot directly produce a modification in another sense-organ. The self has visual perception of the colour of a mango,

[1] NS., iii, 1, 1 ; NBh., iii, 1, 1-3, 7, 14-15 ; NV., iii, 1, 1-3 ; NVTT., i, 1, 10.

and recollection of its taste which produces saliva. The intervening recollection accounts for salivation. Recollection is not a quality of the body, because what was perceived in childhood is remembered in old age, though the old person's body is different from the child's body. The sense-organs, which are unconscious, cannot be the substrate of recollection. Hence the conscious self is its substrate.[1]

THE NATURE AND KNOWLEDGE OF THE INDIVIDUAL SELF: PRE-EXISTENCE AND TRANSMIGRATION.

The Nyāya concept of the self is the same as that of the Vaiśeṣika. It is a substance, which has cognition, pleasure, pain, desire, aversion, volition, impression, merit and demerit. The first six qualities are transitory and the last three qualities are permanent. They subsist in the permanent self. Pleasure and pain are feelings which are apprehended by a cognition, which is different from them. Cognition is apprehension, while feelings are apprehended. Desire is produced by the recollection of an object which produced pleasure in the past, and aversion, by the recollection of an object which produced pain in the past. Volition is produced by desire and aversion; it is an effort of the self to attain a good or pleasant object, or to reject an evil or painful object. An impression is a permanent, imperceptible residuum produced by a past perception, which is a cause of recollection. Merit and demerit also are permanent, imperceptible qualities produced in the self by free right and wrong actions, and produce pleasure and pain. Merits and demerits of the previous birth determine the birth of the present body.

The self is a substance, because it is the inherent cause of cognitions. It is ubiquitous, because it is an eternal and incorporeal substance. It is incorporeal, because it is motionless. It is motionless, because it is eternal. If it were not a substance, it would be devoid of qualities. If it were endued with movement, it would be corporeal. If it were corporeal,

---

[1] NS., NBh., iii, 1, 12-14; NV., iii, 1, 14; NVTT., i, 1, 10; iii, 1, 13, p. 359.

it would not be the substratum of cognition, pleasure and other qualities which are perceived by us. If it were not ubiquitous, manas would not be proved to be atomic, since the succession of its actions is due to its conjunction with the self, which accounts for the succession of cognitions.

The self has relative freedom of the will. Its freedom is limited by the divine will. Its free extertions bear fruits only when they are favoured by God. They become ineffective when they are not favoured by God. The self cannot command success of its free actions without the aid of God. It earns merits by free righteous actions, and earns demerits by free unrighteous actions. But its freedom is limited by the merits and demerits acquired by free actions in the past births, though it can counteract them by free actions in future. Hence the freedom of the individual self is subject to the divine will and the Law of Karma.[1]

The self is an object of mental perception. It is an object of intuition born of meditation. This is the view of the Nyāya. 'I know' : this experience is undeniable. The self is the principal object of this experience. An object is its indirect object. The self is perceptible, because it is perceived by 'I'-consciousness or self-consciousness.[2]

The self is eternal and devoid of origin and end. It has pre-existence, and undergoes transmigration until it achieves liberation. It leaves a dead body, and assumes another body. Birth is association of the soul with a body, and death, its dissociation from a body. An organism is born and perishes, but a soul is unborn and immortal. If it perishes with the body, it cannot reap the fruits of its free right and wrong actions and the consequent merits and demerits, and it experiences joys and sorrows which are not earned by it, and thus the Law of Karma is nullified.[3]

---

1 NS., NBh., ii, 2, 64 & 69-72 ; iii, 2, 36 & 45 ; iv, 1, 9-21 ; ATV., pp. 809, 811-12. 2 NBh., i, 1, 3 ; NV., iii, 1, 1 ; NM., p. 430.

3 NS., NBh., i, 1, 19 ; iv, 1, 10.

A sperm and an ovum of the parents are the material cause of a body which is produced out of them. Merits and demerits of the soul which ensouls it are its instrumental cause, and God is its efficient cause, who associates it with the soul. The union of the parents only is not the cause of the birth of a body. When the peculiar merits and demerits of a soul are present, there is birth of a body, which is a fit vehicle for the experience of their fruits in the shape of enjoyments and sufferings, and when they are absent, there is no birth of it. So they are its instrumental cause. The different kinds of bodies are born owing to the different kinds of merits and demerits of different souls. When they are completely destroyed, there is no more birth. They are extirpated by true knowledge of the self. The same unseen agencies cannot be the cause of birth and death. Death is due to the maturation of some karmas and their fructification and destruction. Rebirth is due to the other potencies of actions which have not yet matured and borne fruits. If a body were generated by the physical elements independently of the unseen agencies, there would be no cause of death of a body. When delusion is completely destroyed by true knowledge of the self, a soul purged of attachment does not perform any bodily, verbal and mental actions which produce merits and demerits and consequent rebirth. Since there are no causes of rebirth, the soul is not associated with any other body.[1]

A new-born baby is attracted to his mother's breast, because he feels a desire to suck her milk. Desire is due to recollection of an object that produced pleasure in the past. So the baby's desire for milk must be due to recollection of objects which were frequently perceived in the past birth to appease hunger of his previous body. It is the same soul, which departed from its past body, assumed its present body, recollects the appeasement of hunger by certain objects repeatedly perceived in the past birth, and desires to suck the breast of his mother. The same soul continues in the past body and the present body. The baby's desire to suck his mother's breast depends upon the

[1] NS., NBh., iii, 2, 67-72 & 75-76.

recollection of its conduciveness to pleasure due to the revival of the impressions by his merits—produced by the knowledge of conduciveness of food to pleasure acquired in his past birth. It cannot be explained without the hypothesis of the past birth.[1]

LIBERATION AND ITS MEANS

Liberation is absolute cessation of pain and rebirth. The body, the sense-organs and manas are the causes of pain. Pleasure is invariably accompanied or followed by pain. All these are pain in a derivative sense. At the time of dissolution the soul becomes free from pain. Its merits and demerits remain dormant during dissolution at the will of God, and are activated again at the time of creation, when it assumes a body fit for their maturation and consequent enjoyments and sufferings. So during dissolution the soul has relative freedom from pain and possibility of its recurrence and rebirth. But liberation is the soul's absolute freedom from pain. The Nyāya view of liberation is the same as the Vaiśeṣika view. Liberation is the complete extinction of the special qualities of the soul, *viz.*, cognition, pleasure, pain, desire, aversion, volition, merit, demerit, and impression. The soul is free from cognition in the state of liberation. Cognition is produced by the intercourse of a sense-organ with an object, the conjunction of a sense-organ with manas, and the conjunction of manas with the soul. But the body, the sense-organs and manas are destroyed in liberation. So there can be no cognition in it. Pleasure, pain, desire, aversion and volition also are experienced in connection with the body. When it is destroyed, they cannot be experienced. In fact, they are accidental qualities of the soul, while ubiquity is its natural condition. Liberation consists in the soul's existence in its natural condition. It is the existence of the soul in its transcendental condition free from its empirical qualities. It has no natural consciousness, which is different

---

[1] NS., NBh., NV., iii, 1, 19-21.

from adventitious cognitions.[1] In liberation the soul is devoid of merits and demerits, and consequently free from pleasure and pain. There is no transcendental bliss beyond empirical pleasure and pain due to the sense-object-intercourse.

True knowledge of the self ultimately leads to liberation through the destruction of merits and demerits and the consequent cessation of rebirth. It destroys egoism or false identification of the self with the body. It dispels delusion and destroys attachment and aversion which arise from it. The soul can be known by listening to the scriptures, reflection and meditation. Eightfold yoga practices facilitate the attainment of true knowledge. Faith in the Vedas, mental tranquillity, endurance of physical pain, dispassion for worldly enjoyments, and concentration prepare the mind for the advent of true knowledge. Attachment is decreased by discerning the faults of the objects of enjoyment and removed by detachment. False knowledge is destroyed by true knowledge. Delusion, attachment and aversion are attenuated by meditation on the contrary excellences. When they are destroyed, actions are not conducive to bondage and rebirth. The performance of prudential duties for the fulfilment of desires leads to heaven. The commission of forbidden acts leads to hell. Both bring about bondage. The performance of daily obligatory duties and occasional duties saves an aspirant from sins of omission. Liberation cannot be achieved by the performance of duties, which can lead to heaven, which is non-eternal. The practice of yoga, austerities, the performance of duties, and abstention from sins are subsidiary to the acquisition of true knowledge. Release can be achieved by intuition of the self. It destroys false knowledge, and incapacitates merits and demerits from producing their effects like burnt seeds in the absence of passions. Persons in all stages of life including householders can attain release through true knowledge directly, and not through merit. There is no embodied release. True knowledge is not discursive knowledge

[1] NS., NBh., i, 1, 22; NVTT., p. 162; NM., pp. 507-08, 511-12.

but immediate intuition of the self, which can destroy false knowledge with its potencies and stop rebirth.[1]

THE NATURE OF GOD AND HIS RELATION TO THE WORLD AND INDIVIDUAL SOULS : THEORIES OF CREATION

Vātsyāyana regards God as a particular soul endued with merit, knowledge, intuition and sovereignty. He is devoid of demerit, false knowledge and inadvertence. He has eight kinds of supernatural powers due to His merit and intuition. His merit is the result of His volition, which directs the merits and demerits of the individual souls and the physical elements to produce their effects.

Uddyotakara invests God with eternal knowledge, number, magnitude, distinctness, conjunction and disjunction. His knowledge, desire and volition are untainted by afflictions and unrestricted in regard to their objects. He is devoid of demerit, and, consequently, of pain. He has no aversion and detachment, since He is devoid of pain. His lordship is eternal and independent of merit. His merit does not generate His sovereignty, but activates and directs the accumulated merits and demerits of the finite souls to produce their fruits. In fact, He is devoid of merit. His lordship is eternal. His knowledge is one, eternal and intuitive. He has perception of all past, present and future objects, which is not produced by the intercourse of the sense-organs with objects. His knowledge is not derived from inference and testimony. He is devoid of subconscious impressions and recollection. He has one eternal cognition which apprehends all objects.[2]

Jayanta Bhaṭṭa recognizes five qualities of God, *viz.*, knowledge, happiness, desire, volition, and merit, which are eternal, and regards Him as free from pain, aversion, demerit, impression, false knowledge, attachment, aversion, and delusion.

---

[1] NS., NBh., i, 1, 2 & 22; iv, 2, 38-47; NVTT., pp.470-71; NM., pp. 513-24; ATV., pp. 935-36.

[2] NS., NBh., NV., iv, 1, 21.

God transcends the atoms, time, space and ether which are coeternal with Him. He is the efficient cause of the world, but not its material cause. He creates the world out of the atoms in time and space by conjoining them with one another, and destroys it by disjoining them from one another. He creates it through His immediate knowledge of the atoms and the souls merits and demerits, desire to create, and volition without a body. He creates motion in them by a fiat of will and conjoins them, and produces dyads and gross physical objects. He preserves the world by His will, and destroys it by His will. Creation and destruction are periodical.

But God creates the world of manifold objects in accordance with the merits and demerits of the finite souls for their enjoyments and sufferings. He adjusts the world to their moral deserts, and makes it a proper sphere of their moral life. God's freedom is limited by the Law of Karma, which emanates from His moral will. So this limitation is self-limitation. The variety of the world is due to the variety of merits and demerits of the finite souls. If God created the world independently of the finite souls' merits and demerits, then He would be guilty of cruelty, the Moral Law would not be obligatory, and the finite souls would never be liberated. If He created miseries for the finite souls irrespective of their demerits, He would be cruel. If the virtuous were not rewarded with happiness, and the vicious were not punished with misery, the Moral Law would cease to be obligatory. If the finite souls did not exhaust their merits and demerits by appropriate enjoyments and sufferings, and eradicate the potencies of their actions by true knowledge, they would never be released.[1] God's freedom is not independent of the Law of Karma, but it consists in directing the merits and demerits of the individual souls. God cannot violate the destiny carved out by the individual souls by their own free actions, and so cannot but direct their demerits to bear their inevitable consequences. Though He is omnipotent, He cannot alter the nature of things.[2] His freedom

[1] NM., pp. 202-03.

[2] NV., iv, 1, 21, p. 465 ; NVTT., p. 419 ; NM., p. 203.

is limited in these two respects. God is not the creator of the individual souls. He transcends them in this sense. They have limited freedom to obey or infringe the Moral Law, perform righteous or unrighteous actions, earn merits or demerits, and experience proper retributions. They cannot escape from the operation of the Law of Karma.

God and the individual souls belong to the genus of soul. They are substances endued with qualities. Non-eternal knowledge, pleasure, pain, desire, aversion, volition, merit, demerit, and subconscious impression are the acquired qualities of the individual souls. Eternal knowledge, happiness, desire, volition, and merit are the qualities of God. Some deny happiness and merit to God. Both individual souls and the supreme soul possess the generic qualities of number, magnitude, distinctness, conjunction and disjunction. Both are ubiquitous and eternal substances. God is not the creator and destroyer of the individual souls. They are neither parts, nor qualities, nor modes of the divine substance. They are not unreal appearances of one impersonal Brahman. They are real and different from God.

But God is omniscient, omnipotent and morally perfect, while the individual souls have limited knowledge, limited powers, and moral imperfections. God is free from pain, false knowledge, attachment, aversion, delusion, inadvertence, demerit, and impression, while the individual souls possess them all. God has eternal supernatural powers, while the individual souls are ordinarily devoid of them, but can acquire them to a limited extent through meditation and austerities. God has eternal moral perfection, while the individual souls can acquire moral purity by severe moral discipline and true knowledge. God is neither bound nor liberated, while the individual souls are first bound by their own free actions, and then achieve release. God is never in bondage, and consequently cannot attain liberation.

God is like father to the individual souls and treats them as a father treats his children. He teaches them the Moral Law, rewards them for their virtues, and punishes them for their vices. God is the moral guide of the individual souls, and the dispenser of the fruits of their actions. He cannot override the Law of Karma. He lays down moral injunctions and prohibitions for the good of mankind, and favours their free actions with their fruits.[1] Without His favour free human actions are ineffective. The Nyāya advocates Deism.

Uddyotakara discusses some theories of creation. It is objected that an action is motivated by the idea of attaining a good or avoiding an evil. God has no unfulfilled desire or unrealized end. He is completely free from pain, and so cannot be actuated by the idea of avoiding an evil. He has no good to attain, and no evil to avoid. (1) Some maintain that God creates the world for sport. But this view is not right. A person feels discomfort, and plays to remove it and get pleasure. But God is absolutely free from pain, and so cannot indulge in creative sport for pleasure. God is endued with eternal bliss, Jayanta argues, and has no need for creative play for the sake of pleasure. (2) Some maintain that God creates the world to display His infinite powers and glory. But God is eternally perfect, Uddyotakara argues, and does not pass from imperfection to perfection. He does not gain anything by creation or lose anything by lack of it. (3) God creates the world by His nature. Creative activity follows from His nature. But if it follows from His nature, it may by objected, then it will never cease, and there will be no dissolution. His nature will produce all effects simultaneously, and there will be no order in creation. There will be no diversity of the world due to the uniform nature of God. Uddyotakara replies that the diversity of the world follows from the intelligent nature of God, who creates it with the aid of the finite souls' merits and demerits which mature at different times. (4) Jayanta maintains that God creates and destroys the world out of compassion for creatures. He creates the world, heaven and hell for the individual souls' enjoyments and sufferings in accordance with their virtues and vices. He destroys the world, and makes

[1] NBh., NSV., NV., iv, 1, 21.

their moral deserts dormant to give them respite from the round of births and deaths.[1]

THE PROOFS FOR THE EXISTENCE OF GOD

Uddyotakara gives the following arguments for the existence of god. (1) God is the efficient cause of the world, and directs the atoms, which are its material cause, and brings about their conjunction, which is its non-inherent cause. The movements of atoms are supervised by an intelligent agent or God, because they are unconscious, like an axe. This is the cosmological argument. (2) The physical elements, which are unconscious and perceptible, are supervised by an intelligent agent, in order to produce pleasure and pain, because they have colour and other qualities, like a shuttle. God adjusts the material world to pleasures and miseries of the individual souls. This is a blend of the cosmological argument with the moral argument. (3) Merits and demerits are supervised by an intelligent agent in order to produce pleasures and sufferings of the individual souls, because they are instruments, like an axe. They cannot be supervised by the individual souls, because they are unconscious of them. They have to be rewarded with happiness for their merits and punished with misery for their demerits. So they cannot be the arbiter of their own destiny. Their bodies are due to their merits and demerits. They are unconscious before the birth of their bodies, and so cannot guide their merits and demerits. So God who is conscious of their moral deserts conjoins them with adequate enjoyments and sufferings. This is the moral argument. (4) The unconscious atoms and merits and demerits are supervised by an intelligent agent or God, because they are unconscious. The atoms are self-existent and eternal. The merits and demerits of the individual souls are the effects of their free righteous and unrighteous actions. God creates the world of manifold objects in accordance with their merits and demerits for their enjoyments and chastisements. This is a blend of the cosmological argument with the moral argument.

---

[1] NV., iv, 1, 21, p. 467 ; NM., pp. 202-03.

(5) The activities of the different material elements are supervised by an intelligent agent or God, because they are unconscious, like an axe. All causes produce their effects under the guidance of God. He is the common cause of all effects. All physical causality is guided by the will-causality of God.[1]

(6) Jayanta gives the teleological argument. The arrangements of mountains, rivers and other material objects are produced by an intelligent agent, like cloths produced by human agents. Whatever objects are arranged in an order are produced by an intelligent agent. Just as the arrangement, order and unity in jars, cloths and the like are not accidental, but produced by human agents endued with knowledge, desire and volition, so the arrangements of mountains, trees and other natural objects are not accidental, but produced by God who is omniscient and omnipotent. The arrangement and order of the world are designed, willed and produced by God. It may be objected that the arrangements of parts in the natural objects differ from those of human productions. Therefore we cannot infer the existence of God as the creator from the specific arrangements of the natural objects. Jayanta replies that there is an invariable concomitance between arrangement in general and the existence of a creator, just as there is an invariable concomitance between smoke in general and fire in general. The smoke and the fire in a kitchen differ from those in a forest ; and yet we disregard their specific differences, and infer the existence of fire from the existence of smoke on the strength of the invariable concomitance between smoke in general and fire in general. Similarly, we infer the existence of God from the arrangement of the world as its creator on the strength of the invariable concomitance between arrangement in general and the existence of a creator.[2] This is the teleological argument.

Udayana gives the following arguments.

(7) God is the creator of motion which is the cause of conjunction of the atoms into dyads. A dyad is produced by

---

[1] NV., iv, 1, 21. [2] NM., pp. 194, 195-97.

two atoms, the material cause, their conjunction, the non-inherent cause, and the agency of God, the efficient cause. The atoms are unconscious and inactive in themselves. They can be set in motion and conjoined with each other only when they are guided by an intelligent agent, like an axe. The activity of unconscious entities is known to be due to the volition of an intelligent agent that supervises them. The individual souls which are unconscious of the atoms and incapable of acting upon them cannot create motion in them and conjoin them with each other into dyads. Their merits and demerits also cannot bring about the activity and conjunction of the atoms, because they are unconscious. God only who is omnisceint and omnipotent can know the atoms, create motion in them, and combine them into dyads, triads, quartrads and gross physical objects. Though bodily action is created by the human will, motion in the atoms cannot be created by it. A specific effect is produced by a specific cause. Bodily action is a specific effect ; a human volition is a specific cause. Therefore a volition is a generic cause of activity or motion, which is a generic effect. It is determined by the method of double agreement.[1]

(8) The whole universe directly or indirectly depends upon the volition of God to support it in its place and prevent it from falling. God supports it by His sustaining will. He maintains all objects by His volition which directs them. Without His directing and sustaining will they cannot be maintained in their positions. Their relation with the knowlodge, desire and volition of omniscient God is the cause of their maintenance. He rules over the world by a fiat of His will, which is unobstructed.

The whole universe including the dyads is destroyed by the will of God, because they are destructible. He creates motion by His destructive will, and disjoins the atoms of dyads and the like. He is the destroyer of the world. The atoms are unconscious, and cannot disjoin themselves from one another. The individual souls' unconscious merits and demerits also

[1] NKS., pp. 54-55.

cannot bring about their disjunction. Destruction of the universe is beyond the power of the individual souls with their limited knowledge and will.[1]

(9) God guarantees the validity of the knowledge of the Vedas, which is produced by the proficiency of its generating conditions, because it is valid knowledge, like perception and the like. Knowledge has no intrinsic validity, but it has extrinsic validity due to the excellence of its cause. The validity of testimony is due to the reliability of its speaker. The validity of the Vedas which are accepted as authoritative by great saints, is due to the reliability of God, who is their speaker. It is not due to the authority of non-omniscient seers who are ignorant of the supersensible entities mentioned therein. It is guaranteed by God, who is the omniscient creator of the moral injunctions and prohibitions.[2]

God is the creator of the Moral Law which is not an impersonal moral imperative. It is a command which impels a person to act upon it with a view to realizing his good. It is not a property of a person who is under moral obligation to obey it,—either his desire, or volition, or bodily action. It is the property of a reliable person who imposes the moral law upon persons. It conveys the intention of the Supreme Person of moral authority. It is a personal command of God, which impels them to perform righteous actions and abstain from unrighteous actions.[3] This is the moral argument for the existence of God.

(10) The Vedas are created by omniscient God, because they are the Vedas. What are not created by an omniscient Being are not the Vedas, like sentences uttered by human beings. The Vedas deal with supersensible entities of which persons are ignorant. They do not originate in human perception. They are not creations of crafty priests, tainted with error and motivated by fraudulence. They have not their origin in tradition, because they are destroyed at the time of dissolution.

---

[1] NKS., v, pp. 58-59.

[2] NKS., v, p. 62 ; NKSH., p. 69.

[3] NKS., v, 7 & 15 ; NKSP., v, pp. 75 & 82.

They are created by God, because they cannot have any other origin. They are valid, because they are accepted as valid by great saints who act upon them and realize the supersensible truths enshrined in them.

(11) The sentences in the Vedas are creations of a person, because they are sentences, like sentences composed by men. Just as the *Kumārasambhava* was composed by Kālidāsa, so the Vedas were composed by God. Just as threads cannot arrange themselves into a cloth, so the words of the Vedas are not arranged into sentences by themselves. Just as a weaver arranges threads into a cloth, so God arranges the words of the Vedas into sentences. Just as the arrangement of a mountain differs from that of a jar, so the arrangement of the Vedas differs from that of a human composition. Just as a jar is produced by a human being, while a mountain is produced by God, so an epic is composed by a human being, while the Vedas are composed by God. Just as the different parts of an epic are composed by one poet, so the different branches of the Vedas are composed by one God, because they have unity of purpose. Parsimony of hypotheses demands one author of the four Vedas. The sentences in them praising righteous actions and condemning unrighteous actions are composed by omniscient God who knows their moral values. They are composed by God independently of the sense-organs, manas, and the vocal organs.[1]

[1] NKS., v, 16, pp. 62-63 ; NKSH., p. 83 ; NM., pp. 236, 239 & 240 ; HIP., Vol. I, Ch. VIII.

CHAPTER X

THE SĀṀKHYA PHILOSOPHY

The Sāṃkhya system advocates the ontological dualism of prakṛti and individual souls (puruṣas). It believes in the evolution of the cosmos including matter, life, and mind out of the eternal and ubiquitous prakṛti to serve the ends of an infinite number of individual souls. The dualism of prakṛti and souls is the fundamental doctrine of the Sāṁkhya system. It recognizes unconscious finality in the evolution of prakṛti, vehemently criticizes the Nyāya theism, and strongly advocates atheism.

The Sāṁkhya system derives its name from the word *saṁkhyā*, meaning number, since it enumerates the metaphysical principles of reality. Or, the word *saṁkhyā* may mean perfect knowledge. The system is called Sāṁkhya, since it gives perfect knowledge of the self (puruṣa) as quite distinct from prakṛti and its evolutes, body, sense-organs, mind (manas), intellect (buddhi), and egoism (ahaṁkāra), which annihilates all kinds of suffering.

Tradition ascribes the origin of the Sāṁkhya system to Kapila. The Sāṁkhya works, *Sāṁkhyapravacanasūtra* and *Tattvasamāsa* are ascribed to him. But there is no evidence to prove it. *Sāṁkhyakārikā* of Īśvarakṛṣṇa (200 A.D.) is the earliest available work in the Sāṁkhya system. Īśvarakṛṣṇa describes himself as a disciple of Pañcaśikha, who was a disciple of Āsuri. Āsuri was a disciple of Kapila, the founder of the Sāṁkhya system.[1] Gauḍapāda (800 A.D.) wrote a commentary on *Sāṁkhya-Kārikā.* Vācaspati Miśra (1000 A.D.) the great scholiast, wrote a commentary on *Sāṁkhya-kārikā*, known as *Sāṁkhyatattvakaumudī* which is regarded as the most authoritative work on the Sāṁkhya system. The *Sāṁkhya-pravacanasūtra* was probably composed in the fourteenth century. Aniruddha (1500 A.D.) wrote a commentary on it known as *Sāṁkhyasūtravṛtti.* Vijñānabhikṣu (1600 A.D.) wrote

[1] SK., 70.

a commentary on it, named *Sāṁkhyapravacanabhāṣya* with a theistic bias.

THEORY OF CAUSATION—SATKĀRYAVĀDA OR PARIṆĀMAVĀDA

The Sāṁkhya theory of evolution of the cosmos out of prakṛti is based upon its theory of causation. According to the Sāṁkhya, the effect pre-exists in the cause in a potential condition ; the effect is a modification (pariṇāma), manifestation, development, or redistribution of the cause. The effect is not a new beginning as the Nyāya-Vaiśeṣika holds. It is not a new creation. It is not non-existent in the cause. It exists in the cause prior to its manifestation. So the Sāṁkhya advocates the doctrine of Satkāryavāda as distinguished from the Nyāya-Vaiśeṣika doctrine of Asatkāryavāda or Ārambhavādā. The effect and the cause are equally real, the former being a modification of the latter.

The Sāṁkhya offers the following arguments to prove the pre-existence of the effect in the cause. (1) If the effect is non-existent in the cause prior to its operation, none can bring it into existence out of the cause ; blue cannot be turned into yellow even by a thousand artists. The effect is related to its cause. If it is non-existent prior to the operation of its cause, it cannot be related to it. The causal relation exists between two entities which are existent. So the effect exists both before and after the operation of the cause. Effectuation is nothing but manifestation. All that is done by the cause is the manifestation of the pre-existent effect. Oil is pressed out of sesamum ; rice is threshed out of paddy. A non-entity is never found to be manifested or produced. So the effect pre-exists in the cause in a latent or unmanifest condition. (2) A particular effect can be produced out of a particular material cause. A jar can be produced out of clay only ; cloth can be produced out of threads only. There is a law that particular causes can produce particular effects. This proves that the effects are per-existent in their causes in a latent condition. The effects are pre-existent in their causes prior to their operation, since they are related to their material causes.

(3) If the effect unrelated to the cause could be produced, then every effect would arise from every cause. But every effect does not arise from every cause. So the effect is pre-existent in the cause, and the cause produces the effect when it is related to it. A non-existent effect unrelated to the cause cannot be produced by the cause unrelated to the effect ; only an existent effect related to the cause can be produced by an existent cause related to the effect. (4) The effect pre-exists in the cause, since it can be produced by a potent cause only. A potent cause has causal energy to produce a particular effect. The causal energy in the cause is inferred from the perception of the effect. This accounts for regularity in the production of particular effects by particular causes. The causal energy to produce a particular effect resides in a potent cause only. If it resides in all causes, then any effect will arise from any cause. If it resides in the potent cause only, the cause cannot be unrelated to the effect ; the causal energy unrelated to the effect cannot produce it. So the causal energy residing in the cause must be related to the effect, and the effect must be existent in the cause. If it is non-existent, the causal energy cannot be related to it. If the causal energy is unrelated to the effect, then any effect will arise from any cause. Hence the effect must be pre-existent in its potent cause only. (5) The effect pre-exists in the cause, since it is identical in nature with its cause. The effect is not different from the cause. The cause is existent ; therefore, the effect cannot be non-existent. There can be no identity between an entity and a non-entity.[1]

Production is manifestation ; destruction is disappearance, absorption into the cause or passing into a latent condition. Production is transition from an implicit to an explicit condition ; destruction is transition from an explicit to an implicit condition. Production is unfoldment ; destruction is enfoldment. Production is development ; destrution is envelopment. Production is evolution ; destruction is dissolution. Gold is transformed into ornaments ; ornaments are melted into gold. Clay is transformed into jars ; jars are powdered into clay.

[1] SK., STK., 9 ; SPS., i, 114-18.

There is neither creation of the non-existent nor destruction of the existent. So production is not creation of a non-existent entity, but manifestation of a pre-existeent latent effect.

The effect is identical with the cause in essence. The Sāṁkhya offers the following arguments to prove the identity of the cause and the effect. (1) The effect is not different from its material cause, since it is a property of the cause and inheres in it. A cloth is not different from the threads which constitute it, because it is a property of the threads and inheres in them. If an object is different from another in essence, it can never inhere in it. A cow is different from a horse, and so cannot inhere in the latter. But a cloth inheres in the threads, and so does not differ form them in essence. (2) There is the causal relation between the material cause and the effect constituted by it. So they are not different from each other in essence. The causal relation can never subsist between two objects which essentially differ from each other. There is no causal relation between a jar and a cloth, which are essentially different from each other. But there is the causal relation between a cloth and the threads. So they cannot differ from each other in essence. (3) If two objects are different form each other, they can be conjoined with each other, (e.g., a pool and a tree), and they can exist separately from each other, (e.g. the Himalayas and the Vindhyas). But there is neither conjunction nor separate existence of a cloth and the constituent threads. So they are not different from each other in essence. The material cause and the effect cannot be conjoined with each other ; nor are they capable of separate existence. Hence they are not different from each other in essence. (4) The material cause and the effect are identical with each other in essence, because there is quantitative equality between them. The threads and the cloth are equal to each other in weight. This fact conclusively proves the essential identity between the material cause and the effect.[1]

[1] STK., 9.

Cause and effect are different states of one and the same substance. So they are distinct from each other. Their distinction is based on our practical interests. A jar can hold water, but a lump of clay cannot. They are distinct from each other because they serve different purposes. But they are not different from each other in their essential nature.[1]

The Sāṁkhya recognizes two kinds of causes, material cause and efficient cause. The material cause enters into the constitution of the effect and contains the potentiality of being reproduced in the form of the effect. The efficient cause exerts an extraneous influence on the effect, co-operates with the causal power inherent in the material cause and liberates it. Gold is the material cause of an ornament, enters into its constitution, and continues to be operative as long as the ornament lasts, and after its destruction it relapses into the potential condition again. But the activity of the goldsmith is the efficient cause of the ornament, because it liberates the causal energy inherent in the material cause, and because it actualizes the potentiality of the effect; its causalitty ceases with the production of the ornament.[2]

PRAKṚTI

The Sāṁkhya infers the existence of prkṛiti from the complex and mànifold products in the universe. Īśvarakṛṣṇa argues for the existence of prakṛti on the following grounds. (1) Individual things manifest to our experience are caused, and depend upon other causes which contain them in a latent condition. The cause must contain at least as much reality as the effect contains. Every effect has a cause. Therefore the ultimate cause of the whole universe must be uncaused. Prakṛti is the uncaused cause of the whole world of effects which are its modifications. (2) Individual things are transient and dissolved into their material causes. Therefore the ultimate material cause of the whole universe is eternal. Prakṛti is the ultimate material cause into which the whole world is

[1] SK., SGB,. xv.

[2] N. L. Sinha, *The Sāṁkhya Philosophy*, Preface, p. ii.

dissolved, which is never dissolved into a more primal cause. While individual things are transient, prakṛti, the ultimate cause, is eternal. (3) Individual things are non-pervasive or limited in magnitude. An effect is pervaded by its cause, but a cause is not pervaded by its effect. A cause must contain more reality than its effect ; or, at least, it must contain as much reality as its effect does. Therefore the ultimate cause of the whole universe must be all-pervasive. Prakṛti is the ubiquitous cause of the finite effects. (4) Individual things are active, mobile, and subject to change and mutation. Therefore the ultimate cause of the universe is inactive and immobile. Prakṛti is subject to transformation, but devoid of motion. (5) Individual things are manifold, conditioned, determined, composed of parts, subordinate, and manifest. Therefore the ultimate cause of the universe is one, unconditioned, indeterminate, devoid of parts, independent, and unmanifest.[1]

Individual effects are manifold, while prakṛti is one. They subsist in their causes, while prakṛti does not subsist in any other cause. They are determinate, while prakṛti is indeterminate. They are composed of parts, while prakṛti is partless. They are differentiated and heterogeneous, while prakṛti is undifferentiated and homogeneous. They are subordinate to prakṛti, while prakṛti is self-subsistent and independent.[2] Prakṛti is the matrix of the whole psycho-physical universe—the first cause of matter, life, mind (manas), intellect (buddhi) and egoism (ahaṁkāra). The unintelligent world cannot be a transformation of an intelligent principle, since spirit cannot be transformed into matter.

Prakṛti is the state of equilibrium of sattva, rajas, and tamas which are substances, and constitute prakṛti. They are in a state of equipoise which is not inactivity but a kind of tension. Prakṛti is the triad of guṇas—sattva, rajas, and tamas, and not a different entity which is their substratum. They are not its attributes, but its very form. This is the definition of the original prakṛti (mūlā prakṛti), the root evolvent, which is not caused. It is the uncaused cause or

[1] SK., 10 ; SPS., i, 124. [2] STK., 10.

the First Cause. Prakṛti is imperceptible owing to its subtlety. Subtlety does not mean atomic nature, since prakṛti is all-pervasive. Subtlety means a general attribute which prevents the right cognition of it by perception. Prakṛti is called pradhāna, because all effects are founded on it. It is absolutely unmanifested, while its evolutes are manifested. So it is called avyakta. Prakṛti cannot be called primal matter, because it is the ground of all modifications, physical and psychical. All inorganic, organic, and mental products are modifications of prakṛti, which is the prius of all creation. Prakṛti is the unconscious matrix of all modifications, physical and psychical—the root cause of all objective existence.[1]

The Sāṁkhya advocates the dualism of prakṛti and individual souls (puruṣa). Prakṛti is unconscious, while souls are conscious. Prakṛti is known, while souls are the knowers. Prakṛti cannot give rise to a soul, which also cannot give rise to prakṛti. So the Sāṁkhya advocates neither materialism nor spiritualism. It holds that prakṛti evolves for the sake of the souls. The evolution of prakṛti is subservient to the ends of the souls' experience and liberation.[2] It is not mechanical but teleological, though there is unconscious finality in it.

GUṆAS : SATTVA, RAJAS AND TAMAS

Prakṛti is constituted by sattva, rajas, and tamas, which are called the guṇas. They are not qualities but substances, which are the ultimate elements of prakṛti. They are called guṇas because they are subordinate to the souls, realizing their ends ; or because they are the three strands in the constitution of prakṛti even as three strands in a string ; or because they fetter the souls to empirical life. They are substances because they are capable of conjunction and disjunction, and because they have qualities. They are not perceived, but inferred from their effects. They are of the nature of pleasure, pain and delusion ; they are feeling substances. Sattva manifests an

[1] SPS., i, 61, 67 & 126 ; SPB., i, 109, 125 & 136 ; SSV., i, 142 ; SSM., i, 61 ; SK., 21.

[2] SK., 21 ; SPS., iii, 58.

object to consciousness. Rajas is the principle of activity, and makes an object move and act. Tamas is inertia, resistance, or restraint. Sattva, rajas, and tamas have the functions of manifestation, activity and restraint respectively. They produce pleasure, pain, and delusion or indifference respectively. Pañcaśikha says that sattva is in the nature of pleasure in various forms such as transparence, lightness, love, joy, renunciation, contentment, and the like ; rajas is in the nature of pain in various forms such as grief and the like ; tamas is in the nature of delusion in various forms such as sleep and the like.[1] Sattva is light, illumining, buoyant and has the power of manifestation. Rajas, the principle of motion, urges sattva and tamas to act. Tamas is heavy and obstructs activity. Sattva and tamas, which are inactive in themselves, are incited to act by rajas which energizes them. Just as a lamp can burn when oil, light, and wick co-operate with one another, so the three guṇas function only in co-operation with one another. They overcome one another ; they support one another ; they produce their effects in co-operation with one another ; they intermingle with one another. Though they are antagonistic to one another, they never exist in isolation. Sometimes sattva preponderates over rajas and tamas, overcomes them, and produces its effect, pleasure or manifestation. Sometimes rajas preponderates over sattva and tamas, overcomes them, and produces its effect, pain or action. Sometimes tamas preponderates over sattva and rajas, overcomes them and produces its effect, delusion or restraint. Sattva is the essence to be realized or manifested ; tamas is the obstacle to its realization or manifestation ; rajas is the energy which overcomes the obstacle and realizes the essence. They coalesce with one another, and function in co-operation with one another. Sattva, rajas, and tamas though antagonistic to one another, co-operate with one another to produce their effects.[2]

Sattva, rajas, and tamas are infinite in number. An infinite

[1] SPS., i, 127 ; SPB., i, 61 & 127 ; SK., 12 ; SJM., 12 ; SGB., 13.
[2] SK., STK., SGB., 13 ; SSV., i, 127-28.

number of individual sattva, rajas, and tamas bring about diversity of effects by conflict and co-operation, by excess and diminution. If they were single and ubiquitous, they could not bring about diversity of effects, which is due to conflict of the guṇas. If they were single individuals, they could not bring about increase and diminution.[1] They cannot be created or destroyed. They cannot change into one another. All changes are due to the combination and separation of the guṇas, which are always integrating and disintegrating. All effects are due to particular arrangements and collocations of the guṇas which are indestructible and eternal. Prakṛti is eternal. It is the ultimate reality behind changing phenomena which are of the nature of manifestation and non-manifestation, evolution and envelopment of the guṇas. Prakṛti is eternal, but its modifications are always changing. Prakṛti is eternal, though mutable.[2]

EVOLUTION

Prakṛti is the substratum of the changing phenomena of the world. It is the equilibrium of sattva, rajas, and tamas. It is not a state of inactivity, but a kind of tension. The tendencies to manifestation and activity are held in check by the tendency to restraint and obstruct. Infinite number of sattva, rajas, and tamas counteract their activities and bring about a state of tension. They relieve the tension and break the equilibrium under the influence of the individual souls. The equilibrium of the guṇas is disturbed by some kind of influence of the individual souls. Prakṛti evolves to realize their ends—experience and liberation.[3]

When the equilibrium of the guṇas is disturbed, some guṇas overpower the other guṇas, and start the process of evolution. There is neither creation nor destruction of the guṇas. The total amount of sattva, rajas, and tamas can neither be created nor destroyed, increased nor decreased. But within the

---

[1] SPB., i, 127.
[2] SSV., vi, 16 ; YBh., TV,, iv, 13.
[3] SPS., i, 61 ; SPB., iii, 58 ; SK., 21.

universe some guṇas can overweight the others and produce heterogeneous effects. Production is manifestation or evolution; destruction is non-manifestation or envelopment. The Sāṁkhya clearly enunciated the doctrine of evolution. The manifold world is not created by God out of nothing, but it is evolved from prakṛti. The world is unconscious, and cannot be the transformation of a spirit which is unchangeable and immutable. It is the transformation of the unconscious prakṛti or of sattva, rajas, and tamas. Prakṛti and its evolutes (vikṛti) are subject to transformation. They can never be deprived of their essential nature of modifiability—evolution and dissolution. Evolution is the transformation of the homogeneous into the heterogeneous. Dissolution is the transformation of the heterogeneous into the homogeneous. The guṇas are always changing and can never remain without modification for a moment. Evolution is due to excess of some guṇas and diminution of others. Some guṇas are increased and others are decreased. The excessive guṇas overpower the other guṇas owing to disturbance of their equilibrium, and produce heterogeneous effects. Evolution is transition from the homogeneous to the heterogeneous—from the undifferentiated to the differentiated; it is due to the integration of the guṇas. Dissolution is the opposite process and due to disintegration of the guṇas. It is counter-evolution in which heterogeneous effects are disintegrated into the homogeneous reals. Sattva, rajas, and tamas are transformed into their similar modifications. Sattva is transformed into sattva; rajas, into rajas, and tamas, into tamas. In dissolution the heterogeneous is transformed into the homogeneous. Evolution is due to disequilibrium of sattva, rajas, and tamas, and their transformation into heterogeneous modifications. Dissolution is due to disintegration of these heterogeneous modes into the homogeneous guṇas.[1]

Evolution is transition from the potential to the actual, from the undifferentiated to the differentiated, from the indeterminate or non-specific to the determinate or specific,

[1] STK., ii, 15-16; SSV., vi, 42.

from the unmanifest to the manifest, and from the separable to the inseparable.[1] Evolution is transition from the homogeneous to the heterogeneous. The guṇas are transformed into all the evolutes.

Prakṛti is transformed into Mahat or cosmic intellect (buddhi). Mahat is transformed into Ahaṁkāra or cosmic egoism. Ahaṁkāra is transformed into the eleven sense-organs, and the five tanmātras or subtle essences of sound, touch, colour, taste, and smell. The five subtle essences are transformed into the five gross elements of ether, air, fire, water, and earth. These are the twenty four principles. In addition to these there are individual souls (puruṣas). These are the twenty five principles according to the Sāṁkhya.[2]

Vācaspati holds that Ahaṁkāra in its sāttvika aspect evolves into manas, the five organs of knowledge, and the five organs of action. Ahaṁkāra in its tāmasa aspect (bhūtādi) evolves into the five subtle essences. Ahaṁkāra in its rājasa aspect plays its part in both. The five subtle essences evolve into the five gross elements of earth, water, light, air, and ether by a preponderance of tamas.[3]

Vijñānabhikṣu gives a slightly different account of the evolution of the cosmos. Ahaṁkāra is modified into the eleven sense-organs, on the one hand, and the five subtle essences, on the other. The five subtle essences are modified into the five gross elements. Ahaṁkāra in its sāttvika aspect evolves into manas. Ahaṁkāra in its rājasa aspect evolves into the ten sense-organs, the five organs of knowledge and the five organs of action. Ahaṁkāra in its tāmasa aspect evolves into the five tanmātras.[4]

The subtle essence of sound has the quality of sound only. The subtle essence of touch has two qualities, sound and touch. The subtle essence of colour has three qualities, sound, touch, and colour. The subtle essence of taste has four qualities, sound, touch, colour, and taste. The subtle essence of smell

---

1 YS., ii, 19 ; YBh., ii, 19 ; iii, 44.

2 SK., 22 ; SPS., i, 61.

3 SPB., i, 61 ; ii, 18.

4 STK., 25.

has five qualities, sound, touch, colour, taste and smell. The subtle essences are called the fine elements. They are indeterminate or non-specific modes. The five gross elements, ether, air, light, water, and earth are the determinate or specific modes of the indeterminate or non-specific subtle essences.[1]

The atoms of the five elements are generated from the subtle essences. They are not the finest and indivisible parts of gross elements. They are evolutes of the subtle essences. The earth atom is generated from the five subtle essences of smell, taste, colour, touch and sound, of which that of smell is the chief. The water atom is generated from the four subtle essences of taste, colour, touch and sound, of which that of taste is the chief. The light atom is generated from the three subtle essences of colour, touch and sound, of which that of colour is the chief. The air atom is generated from the two subtle essences of touch and sound, of which that of touch is the chief. The ether atom is generated from the subtle essence of sound. The subtle essence of smell is the chief cause of the earth atom. The subtle essence of taste is the chief cause of the water atom. The subtle essence of colour is the chief cause of the light atom. The subtle essence of touch is the chief cause of the air atom. The subtle essence of sound is the cause of the ether atom. Each of these subtle essences is the chief constituent of the specific kind of atom generated by it, though other subtle essences are combined with it.[2]

The atoms are not partless and indivisible. They are effects, and so non-eternal, whereas prakṛti is the ultimate cause. The Sāṁkhya analyses the atoms into the subtle essences which are finer than the atoms, and traces the subtle essences finally to prakṛti.[3]

When the gross atoms combine with one another, their qualities are found in their products. The earth atom has solidity, the water atom, viscosity, the light atom, heat, the air

---

[1] YBh., ii, 19.

[2] TV., i, 44; YBh., YV., i, 45.

[3] SSV., SPM., v, 87.

atom, mobility and the ether atom, penetrability. The atoms combine with one another and form aggregates. An atom is an insparable aggregate of subtle essences, one of which is the predominant element. Its parts cannot be separated from one another without breaking its integrity.[1]

The gross body is composed of the five elements—earth, water, light, air, and ether. Some hold that it is composed of the first four elements. They do not regard ether as its constituent. Others consider earth to be the only constituent of the gross body. They consider the other elements as giving an impetus to the combination of the atoms of earth. Or there are different kinds of bodies composed of either earth, water, light, air, or ether. The human body is composed of earth.[2]

UNCONSCIOUS TELEOLOGY

The Sāṁkhya does not advocate mechanical evolution of prakṛti. It believes in unconscious teleology in its evolution. Prakṛti is the matrix of all things in the world, physical and mental. The physical order is subservient to the moral order : physical causation is governed by moral causation. Prakṛti evolves into the subtle essences, the atoms, the gross elements, and physical things, on the one hand, and into the sense-organs, mind, intellect, and egoism, or the psychical apparatus, on the other, for the enjoyment and suffering of the souls in bondage. The evolutes of prakṛti are adapted to their merits and demerits. Even as unconsious trees bear fruits according to the merits and demerits of different persons, so prakṛti evolves into various modes in accordance with the merits and demerits of the bound souls owing to the beginninglessness of their empirical life.[3] Prakṛti resolves its evolutes into their constituents, and relapses into its primeval, quiescent state for the liberation of the souls. Evolution is a means to the experience of the bound souls. Dissolution is a means to the liberation of the bound souls. Thus evolution and dissolution

[1] YBh., iii, 13 & 44.   [2] SPB., iii, 17-19.
[3] SK., 21 ; SPS., ii, 46 ; iii, 51 ; SSV., iii, 62.

are instrumental to their experience and liberation. Prakṛti unconsciously realizes their ends. Thus the Sāṁkhya believes in unconscious teleology in cosmic evolution. It believes in external teleology in the sense that prakṛti realizes the purposes of the puruṣas which are foreign to it.

The Sāṁkhya advocates periodic evolution and dissolution of the world. Dissolution is relapse of prakṛti into the original quiescent state. It is the period of complete rest of the bound souls whose merits and demerits are not entirely exhausted by enjoyments and sufferings. Evolution is the transformation of prakṛti into physical things and the psychical apparatus for the experience of the bound souls. Dissolution is the complete cessation of the creative function of prakṛti owing to a soul's discrimination between itself and prakṛti.[1]

PRAKṚTI AND ITS EVOLUTES

The Sāṁkhya recognizes twenty five principles of reality. Of these an individual soul is neither a cause nor an effect. Causation is transformation of the guṇas sattva, rajas, and tamas. The soul is not composed of them, and is therefore neither a cause nor an effect.

Prakṛti is the First Cause of the eggregate of all effects in the world. It is their ultimate cause, which is not the effect of any other cause. If it had any other cause, it would lead to infinite regress. Prakṛti is a cause but not an effect. It is not a modification of any other ultimate cause.

Cosmic intellect (Mahat, Buddhi), cosmic egoism (Ahaṁkāra), and the five subtle essences of sound, touch, colour, taste, and smell are both causes and effects. They are effects of some causes and causes of some other effects. Cosmic intellect is an effect of prakṛti and the cause of cosmic egoism. Cosmic egoism is the effect of cosmic intellect, and the cause of the five subtle essences. The subtle essences of sound, touch, colour, taste, and smell are the effects of cosmic egoism. They are the causes of the atoms of ether, air, light, water, and earth respectively. The essence of sound generates ether, the

[1] SK.; 21 : SPS., iii, 58 ; SSV., iii, 63.

essence of touch, air, the essence of colour, light, the essence of taste, water, and the essence of smell, earth. The essences of sound, touch, colour, taste, and smell are the chief constituents of ether, air, light, water, and earth respectively. So the seven principles of cosmic intellect, cosmic egoism, and the five essences of material elements are causes as well as effects.

The five sense-organs of knowledge, the five sense-organs of action, the internal organ (manas), and the five gross elements are only effects. They are not causes of any other principles. Though the gross elements of earth, water, light, air, and ether are transformed into various inorganic things, vegetable organisms, and animal organisms, they are not be considered as their material cause, since they do not give rise to other principles of reality, but simply generate new qualities owing to their different collocations and arrangements. The five elements and their aggregates in the form of inorganic things, plant and animal organisms ere equally apprehended by the external sense-organs, and are therefore to be considered as gross matter. The inorganic things and vegetable and animal organisms are not principles of reality different from the gross elements. Thus, the sixteen principles —the ten external sense-organs, the internal organ (manas), and the five gross elements are only effects, and not causes.[1]

Prakṛti is unmanifest, but all its evolutes, cosmic intellect, cosmic egoism, the internal organ, the external sense-organs, the subtle essences, and the gross elements are manifest. The unmanifest prakṛti is uncaused, eternal, ubiquitous, motionless, one, self-subsistent, irresolvable, partless and independent. But the manifest evolutes of prakṛti are caused, non-eternal, limited, mobile, manifold, subsisting in their material causes, resolvable into their elements, composed of parts, and dependent. All the evolutes of prakṛti, from cosmic intellect down to gross elements are effects produced by some causes. They are non-eternal because they spring from their causes. They are non-pervasive or limited, because the effects are pervaded by their causes. The cause contains more than the effect

[1] STK., 3 ; SGB., 3.

does, but the cause can never be less than its effect. Cosmic intellect and the other evolutes of prakṛti cannot pervade prakṛti, their material cause. So they are non-pervasive or limited. The evolutes of prakṛti are capable of motion. Prakṛti is active in the sense that it is transformed into its effects. But it is devoid of physical motion and so immobile.[1]

The evolutes of prakṛti are manifold. Intellects, egoisms and minds are different in different individuals. The subtle essences and the gross elements also are manifold. The modifications of the gross elements also are manifold. The evolutes of prakṛti subsist in their material cause. Though there is identity between cause and effect, there is the difference of substance and modification. The evolutes are related to their causes as modifications to their substances. Cosmic intellect subsists in its cause, prakṛti. Cosmic egoism subsists in its cause, cosmic inlellect. The internal organ (manas), the ten external sense-organs, and the five subtle essences subsist in their cause, cosmic egoism. The five gross elements subsist in their causes, the five subtle essences of sound, touch, colour, taste, and smell. The evolutes of prakṛti are resolved into their constituent elements. The five gross elements are resolved into the five subtle essences. The five subtle essences and the eleven sense-organs are resolved into cosmic egoism. Cosmic egoism is resolved into cosmic intellect. Cosmic intellect is resolved into prakṛti. The evolutes of prakṛti are endued with sound, touch, colour, taste, and smell, while prakṛti is devoid of these qualities. Or they involve intermingling or conjunction of constituents which can exist apart from one another. For instance, the elements of earth, water, and the like can come into conjunction with one another. The subtle essences can come into conjunction with one another. But prakṛti cannot come into conjunction with cosmic intellect, cosmic egoism, and the like, since they are identical with each other in their essential nature. Likewise, sattva, rajas, and tamas cannot come into conjunction with one another, since they can never

[1] SK., STK., 10.

exist apart from one another. The evolutes of prakṛti are dependent on other principles. Cosmic intellect depends upon prakṛti ; cosmic egoism depends upon cosmic intellect ; the subtle essences and the sense-organs depend upon cosmic egoism, and the five gross elements depend upon the subtle essences to produce their respective effects. The unmanifest prakṛti is uncaused, eternal, ubiquitous, motionless,—though not inactive,—one, self-subsistent, irresolvable, partless or devoid of conjunction or qualities, and independent. It is opposed to the manifest evolutes of prakṛti.[1] These are the dissimilarties between prakṛti and its effects.

The unmanifest prakrti and its manifest effects have the following similarities. They are composed of sattva, rajas, and tamas, inseparable, objects, common to many souls, non-intelligent, and productive. Prakṛti and its effects are composed of the three guṇas—sattva, rajas, and tamas. They are feeling-substances, pleasure, pain, and delusion, which are not the qualities of the self. Prakṛti and its effects are inseparable. Prakṛti cannot be separated from itself. Cosmic intellect, cosmic egoism, and the like also cannot be separated from prakṛti owing to their identity in nature. Or, the manifest effects of prakṛti can produce their effects only in co-operation with one another. None of them can produce its effects singly, but in co-operation with others. No effect can be produced by a cause singly. Prakṛti and its effects are objects of consciousness. So they are common to many selves apprehending them. If they were mere cognitions, they would not be the common objects of many persons' cognitions. They are known objects while the souls are the knowers. Prakṛti and its effects are unconscious, while the souls only are conscious. Intellect and its modes are unconscious. They appear to be conscious owing to the reflection of the intellect in souls. The mental modes are non-intelligent in themselves. But they appear to be intelligized by the souls. Prakṛti and its effects are always productive; they are either creative or destructive. They always undergo transformation ; they either pass from the homogeneous to the

[1] STK., SGB., 10.

heterogeneous ; or they pass from the heterogeneous to the homogeneous. They can never be deprived of similar or dissimilar transformation. They are subject to constant modification every moment.[1]

INDIVIDUAL SOULS (PURUṢA)

The Sāṁkhya advocates the dualism of prakṛti and souls. They are entirely different from each other, because they have opposite characteristics. Prakṛti is composed of sattva, rajas, and tamas, while souls are not composed of them. Prakṛti is non-discriminating, while souls are discriminating. Prakṛti is an aggregate, while souls are simple. Prakṛti is the object of knowledge, while souls are the subjects of knowledge. Prakṛti is common to many persons, while souls are different in different bodies. Prakṛti is unconscious, while souls are conscious. Prakṛti is productive and transformed into modifications, while souls are non-productive and not subject to modification. Souls are neither causes nor effects. They are unchangeable and immutable. All things change every moment except the conscious souls. Prakṛti is active, while souls are inactive. Prakṛti is constant in the midst of mutations, while souls are eternal and beyond all mutations. The essential difference between prakṛti and souls lies in that the former is the unconscious and known object, while the latter are the conscious knowers or subjects.[2]

The Sāṁkhya puts forward the following arguments to establish the existence of a soul. (1) Prakṛti, cosmic intellect, cosmic egoism and the like are aggregates of sattva, rajas, and tamas, and therefore means to the ends of other beings, like beds, chairs, and the like. They are unconscious and serve the ends of conscious souls. The body is an aggregate of the five gross elements and enjoyed by a soul even as a bed is enjoyed by it. The soul is not an aggregate. It is different from the body, mind, intellect, and egoism, which are aggregates of sattva, rajas, and tamas. (2) All knowable objects are

[1] SK., STK., 11; SPS., ii, 10.

[2] SK., 3 & 11 ; STK., 6 ; SSV., vi, 13.

non-intelligent, non-discriminating, objects of knowledge, and composed of sattva, rajas, and tamas. Therefore they presuppose an intelligent, discriminating subject of knowledge, devoid of sattva rajas and tamas. All knowable objects presuppose the knowing self. (3) All non-intelligent products of prakṛti, inorganic things, plant organisms, and animal organisms, must be controlled and directed by the intelligent souls even as non-intelligent chariots move when they are controlled and guided by charioteers. Matter is inert and cannot act by itself; it can act only when it is controlled by a soul. So all material objects of the world require guidance by intelligent souls. Prakṛti and its activities are guided by the souls which supervise them. (4) Prakṛti is composed of sattva, rajas, and tamas, which are held by some to be feeling-subtances—pleasure, pain and delusion. They are objects of experience, and presuppose the subjects of experience. The mind (buddhi) cannot be the experiencer, because it is unconscious. Pleasure and pain are mental modes. The mind cannot be self and not-self, subject and object at the same time, since it is self-contradictory. The self, which is different from the mind, is the experiencer of pleasure and pain, which are its modes. Each self feels its own pleasure and pain, which are modes of its mind. Experience belongs to the immutable self. It cannot belong to the body, or the mind, which is not-self, and cannot therefore, become the knowing self. (5) Some spiritual aspirants strive and struggle to achieve liberation. Liberation consists in absolute cessation of three kinds of pain. The mind and the like are themselves in the nature of pain. They are mental modes. So the mind can never be relieved from pain. It is only the self, which is distinct from the mind and the like which can be relieved from pain and achieve liberation.[1]

The Sāṁkhya recognizes the existence of many souls and puts forward arguments for their existence. (1) Birth, death and the sense-organs are different in different persons. If there were one soul only, the birth of one person would lead to the birth of all, the death of one would lead to the death of all

[1] SK., STK., SGB., 17; SPB., i, 140, 142-44.

and the defects in the sense-organs in one would lead to the same defects in the sense-organs in all. Deafness, dumbness, and lameness of one would make all others deaf, dumb, and lame. Madness of one would make all others mad. So there are many souls. There are different souls in different bodies. The soul is immutable and incapable of birth and death. Birth consists in the connection of a soul with a unique aggregate of body, sense-organs, mind, and mental modes. Death consists in the soul's severance of connection with the unique aggregate or mind-body-complex. The soul, which is unchangeable, is neither born nor dies. Different souls are connected or disconnected with different mind-body-complexes. (2) If there were one self in different bodies, the activity of one person would lead to the activity of all. But, in fact, different persons are engaged in different kinds of activity. Some are engaged in the pursuit of virtue. Some are engaged in the pursuit of vice. Some are engaged in cultivating detachment. Others are engaged in acquiring knowledge. Hence, there are different souls engaged in different kinds of activity. Activity is the expression of a volition, which is a mental mode. The soul is inactive. Activity is attributed to it owing to its connection with the mind, which is active. If there were one soul in all bodies, it would move them all at the same time. But, in fact, different bodies move at different times. So there are different souls in different bodies. (3) Different souls are equipped with different moral endowments. Gods are endowed with minds in which sattva predominates. Men are endowed with minds in which rajas predominates. Beasts are endowed with minds in which tamas predominates. Again, among men some are happy owing to the excess of sattva; some are unhappy owing to the excess of rajas; others are under delusion owing to the excess of tamas. So there are many souls, which are devoid of the guṇas, but are endowed with different mind-body-complexes with an excess of either sattva, rajas, or tamas.[1]

---

[1] SK., STK., SGB., 18; SPS., vi, 45; SPB., i, 149.

The Sāṁkhya recognizes the plurality of souls and the spiritual unity of each soul. The soul is distinct from its material vestment, the body, mind, intellect and egoism. It is distinct from prakṛti and its effects and devoid of sattva, rajas, and tamas. It is discriminating, simple, intelligent, non-productive, uncaused, eternal and immutable. It is beyond time, space, and causality. It is the conscious knower. It is not an object. It is the witness, the seer. A witness is one to whom objects are shown. Prakṛti shows its modifications to the self which is their witness. The self is the witness to which the mind shows its mental modes. It is inactive, while the mind is active, since it is composed of the guṇas. The self appears to be active owing to its connection with buddhi. But it is not really active. Buddhi is unconscious. But it appears to be conscious owing to its connection with the self. Thus, the self is conscious but inactive. It is ubiquitous and devoid of movement. It is said to have movement owing to its limiting adjunct, the body, which is capable of movement. It is indifferent and free. It is free from pleasure, pain, delusion, attachment, aversion, and desire, since it is devoid of sattva, rajas, and tamas. It is entirely free from entanglements in the meshes of prakṛti.[1]

Puruṣa is eternal, pure, conscious, and liberated. It is eternal in the sense that it is beyond the temporal order. It is devoid of merit and demerit which are mental modes. It is eternally conscious, and its essential nature of consciousness never ceases. Pain is a mental mode, which is wrongly appropriated by the self owing to non-discrimination. Bondage is phenomenal and due to confusion of the self with its mind. When the cofusion is dispelled by discrimination, the self realizes its intrinsic freedom.[2]

The self is the seer or knower. But it is not an inert substance, which acquires the attribute of consciousness in conjunction with the manas, as the Nyāya holds. Matter does

---

[1] SPS., i, 12-13, 49, 51, 139; SPB., ii, 12; i, 61; SK., 3, 11 & 20; STK., 19; YBh., iv, 33. [2] SPB., i, 19.

not manifest itself. If the self were an inert, material substance, it would require another conscious substance to manifest it. The parsimony of hypotheses demands that the self itself be of the essence of consciousness, which manifests all things in the world. Consciousness is not a mode of the self, since it is devoid of the guṇas, and therefore unmodifiable. The self is immutable and not liable to modification. So consciousness cannot be a mode of the self. Cognition is not its quality, since it is capable of conjunction with objects, and does not depend upon a substratum to support it. Cognition is, therefore, neither a mode, nor a quality of the self. It constitutes its essence, the self being essentially conscious.[1]

The self is distinct from matter, because it is the knower or seer, while matter is an object of knowledge. The self is of the essence of consciousness, and manifests or apprehends matter. Manifestation is not its mode, but it constitutes its essence. Matter is unconscious and manifested by the self. If the self also were a material substance, it would be manifested by some other entity. So it should be considered to be of the nature of manifestation. If it were material, it would not be the witness of dreamless sleep. But we have an experience, 'I slept soundly.' The self is the witness in three grades of empirical life, waking, dream, and dreamless sleep. The self is a witness in the sense that it is of the essence of consciousness only.[2]

The self is inactive, while the guṇas are active. It appears to be active in connection with them. Volition, which is expressed in action, is a mode of the mind. It is attributed to the self owing to its connection with the mind. Sometimes egoism is said to be active. Volition is a mode of egoism. The self, which is immutable, cannot have volition. Egoism is a mode of the mind, which is a mode of sattva, rajas, and tamas. So volition is said to be a mode of the guṇas, mind or

[1] SPS., i, 145-46 ; SPB., i, 146 ; SSV., i, 146 ; YV., ii, 20.

[2] YS., ii, 20 ; SSV., i, 145, 148, 160-61 ; vi, 50 ; SPS., iii, 26 ; Candrikā on SK., 19.

egoism. The self is inactive in the sense that it is devoid of desire, aversion and volition.[1]

The self is free from merit and demerit which are the modes of the mind or egoism. It is eternally pure, and does not acquire moral qualities. It is free from dispositions or impressions which are mental modes. The self which is devoid of the guṇas, cannot be the substratum of dispositions. The mind (buddhi) is the substratum of all dispositions. The self is devoid of pleasure, pain, desire, aversion, volition, merit, demerit, and disposition, which are mental modes.[2]

THE EMPIRICAL SELF (JĪVA)

The Sāṁkhya draws a distinction between the transcendental self and the empirical self, and calls the former puruṣa and the latter jīva. The transcendental self is an eternal, ubiquitous, immaterial, inactive, immobile, eternally pure, conscious, and free spirit. It is non-temporal, non-spatial, non-causal, and devoid of the guṇas. It is unchangeable, immutable, noumenal self. It has no empirical cognitions, feelings, and volitions. It is devoid of pleasure, pain, desire, aversion, volition, merit, demerit, and disposition, which are unconscious mental modes. It is of the nature of consciousness. It is a conscious subject, seer, or witness. It is not active, but it appears to be active in conjunction with the mind.

The transcendental self is not an agent and enjoyer, since it is immutable. But the empirical self (jīva) is an agent and enjoyer. The transcendental self as determined by the body and the sense-organs is the empirical self. It can act and enjoy in their absence. The self, in its intrinsic nature, is not an empirical self. If it were an active empirical self, it would cease to be immutable. The self appears to be active on account of its proximity to the mind in which it is reflected. Aniruddha defines the empirical self as the self determined by

[1] STK., 17-18 ; SK., 19-20 ; SSV., i, 52, 106 & 153 ; v, 66 ; vi, 54 SPS., SPB., v, 66 ; vi, 54 ; YS., ii, 7-8 ; SGB., 20.

[2] SPB., i, 19 , ii, 42 ; SSV., i, 52 ; ii, 43-44 ; vi, 62 ; SPS., v, 25.

the body, the external sense-organs, mind, intellect, and egoism. The self which is devoid of empirical cognition, merit, demerit, and other mental modes is transcendental (ātman).[1] The pure self is immutable, and free from attachment to the guṇas. So its activity is false. Activity implies change or modification. Attachment is the spring of action. So the self cannot be active. The empirical self becomes identical with the transcendental self when its material vestment is destroyed by intense meditation. When meditation matures, dispositions gradually diminish and the mind is destroyed. When the mind is destroyed, dispositions are destroyed. When dispositions are destroyed, the body is annihilated, and no other body can be produced. Then the empirical self is deprived of its limiting adjuncts, the mind-body-complex, and becomes identical with the ubiquitous pure self (ātman) and free from merit, demerit, and activity.

Vijñānabhikṣu defines the empirical self as the self limited by egoism. Vital acts belong to the empirical self; they do not belong to the transcendental self. The empirical self differs from the transcendental self in that the former is limited by the adjunct of the internal organ, while the latter is free from all determinations. Vijñānabhikṣu defines the empirical self also as the self reflected in the internal organ (buddhi), which is active, as distinguished from the pure self (puruṣa) which is immutable and of the nature of transcendental consciousness, and therefore inactive.[2] The empirical self is the self as limited and determined by its body, the senses, mind, intellect, and egoism. All empirical cognitions, feelings, emotions, volitions, actions, merits and demerits belong to the empirical self, while the transcendental self is free from all these mental modes. The empirical self is limited in time and space in its experience, while the transcendental self is eternal and ubiquitous. When the limiting adjunct of the psychophysical organism is completely destroyed, the empirical self becomes identical with the transcendental self, and realizes its intrinsic freedom. It is divested of all

[1] SPS., vi, 63; SSV., i, 96-97, 106; vi. 63.
[2] SPB., i, 97; vi, 63; SSV., i, 97; vi, 59 & 63.

empirical modes including merit, demerit, disposition, and activity. It is manifested as pure, transcendental consciousness entirely free from all entanglements in prakṛti.[1] So the empirical self is a mixture of matter and spirit, prakṛti and puruṣa. When it completely breaks the shackles of prakṛti, it becomes the transcendental self.

Every empirical self has a subtle body formed of the ten sense-organs, mind, intellect, and egoism, the five subtle essences, which is the basis of rebirth. The gross body is born of the parents, but the subtle body is not so born. The gross body is the effect of the subtle body. The enjoyment of the subtle body is real, while that of the gross body is apparent, which has no enjoyment in death. The subtle body is the medium of enjoyment. Merit and demerit are the individuating principles. The empirical selves differ from one another on account of their different moral deserts. Merit and demerit are modes of egoism, which is an evolute of intellect. So they are also modes of intellect. The bondage of the empirical self is due to the subtle body through which merit and demerit, which are mental modes are wrongly appropriated by the self. So long as the subtle body continues, merit and demerit are wrongly owned by the pure self. When it achieves discrimination, merit and demerit are destroyed, and therefore no longer appropriated by it, and it attains liberation. Discrimination destroys merit and demerit, dissolves the subtle body, annihilates empirical life, and leads to liberation.[2]

TRANSCENDENTAL SELF (PURUṢA) AND PRAKṚTI

The distinction between puruṣa and prakṛti has been discussed. The relation between them is a crux of the Sāṁkhya philosophy. Prakṛti is active but unconscious. The soul is inactive but conscious.[3] Prakṛti acts to realize the ends of the souls. It evolves the world for their experience, and dissolves it for their liberation. Prakṛti is the state of

---

[1] SSV., vi, 59.

[2] SPS., iii, 7-8 10 & 16 ; vi, 62, 67-70 ; SSV., iii, 8-9 ; vi, 62, 67-70.

[3] SK., 20.

equilibrium of sattva, rajas, and tamas, and the material cause of the world. The equilibrium of the guṇas is disturbed by the proximity of the souls. Just as a magnet attracts iron by its mere proximity, so the souls move prakṛti by their mere proximity. Just as the magnet is the unmoved mover of iron, so the souls are the unmoved movers of prakṛti. The union of a soul and prakṛti is the cause of evolution of the latter, even as the union of a lame man and a blind man is the cause of the movement of the latter. A lame man of good vision mounting on the shoulders of a blind man of sure foot guides the latter in his movements. Likewise, the inactive, conscious soul guides the evolution and dissolution of the unconscious active prakṛti. The soul is compared to a lame man. Prakṛti is compared to a blind man. Just as a lame man guides a blind man, so the souls guide prakṛti. Prakṛti is blind and unconscious and evolves the manifold world under the guidance of the souls to realize their ends. The evolution of prakṛti is not mechanical but teleological, and serves the ends of the souls. But its teleology is unconscious. Prakṛti unconsciously realizes the ends of the souls. There is unconscious teleology in the evolution of prakṛti. It is suggested by other analogies. The non-intelligent prakṛti acts to realize the ends of the souls, even as non-intelligent milk flows for the nourishment of the calf, or even as non-intelligent trees bear fruits under the influence of merits and demerits for the enjoyment of the souls. The diversity of effects is due to the variety of merits and demerits of the souls. Prakṛti is the material cause of the world. It can be transformed into a variety of effects owing to the variety of merits and demerits which are their efficient cause.[1] The activities of prakṛti are adapted to the moral deserts of the souls. Natural causation of prakṛti is subordinate to moral causation. The evolution of prakṛti is subservient to the souls' experience. Its dissolution is subservient to their liberation. Prakṛti is one. But the souls are

[1] SK., 21 & 57; SPS., i, 61, 96 & 144; ii, 1; iii, 51, 58-59; v, 20; vi, 41; SPB., i, 96; vi, 41; iii, 51; SSV., ii, 1; iii, 51 & 62; v, 20; vi, 41.

many. Some wrongly identify themselves with prakṛti and its evolutes, mind, intellect, and egoism, and enjoy the manifold objects of the world. Prakṛti evolves the manifold world for them. They are in bondage due to non-discrimination. Others attain discrimination between themselves and prakṛti and its evolutes, and realize their intrinsic freedom. They achieve liberation. Prakṛti ceases to evolve the world for them and dissolves it for their liberation. The evolution of prakṛti continues even after the liberation of some souls for the enjoyment of others, since there are innumerable souls. The evolution of the manifold universe continues till the souls attain discrimination between themselves and prakṛti. Prakṛti never loses its innate nature to evolve. Non-discrimination is the cause of evolution; discrimination is the cause of dissolution. Bondage is due to non-discrimination between the souls and prakṛti; liberation is due to discrimination between them. The souls are eternally liberated. Their bondage and liberation are only phenomenal. In reality, prakṛti has bondage and liberation. Bondage is activity of prakṛti for the souls devoid of discrimination. Liberation is the cessation of its activity for the souls which have attained discrimination. Prakṛti is never divested of its active nature. It retires from its creative activity after accomplishing discrimination of the souls, even as a dancing girl retires from dance after entertaining the spectators. It acts for the liberation of the souls, and ceases to act after achieving their liberation, even as a person in bondage strives for freedom from bondage, and becomes inactive after achieving freedom, since his desire has been fulfilled.[1]

The soul is the pure self. It is eternally pure, transparent, conscious, and free. Its bondage and liberation are merely phenomenal. It wrongly identifies itself with prakṛti and its evolutes, mind, intellect, and egoism owing to non-discrimination. It does not actually transfer itself to intellect, but wrongly identifies itself with it owing to

[1] SK., 21, 56-59; SPS., i, 144; ii, 1; SPS.,SSV., iii, 47, 63, 69, 71-72; vi, 43; ii, 4-5; SPB., ii, 4-5.

non-discrimination. There is no actual transference of the self to intellect. But there is the reflection of the self in intellect, which leads to a false sense of identity between them. There can be no transuent causation between them, since there can be no conjunction between them. The soul seems to be identical with intellect, even as a white crystal seems to be tinged with red colour in proximity to a red flower. The false sense of identity between the soul and prakṛti is due to non-discrimination.[1] The soul is absolutely different in nature from prakṛti. It comes to be indirectly related to prakṛti through its evolute, intellect, which is transparent owing to the excess of sattva, and catches its reflection. The soul is related to intellect, through its reflection in it, as Vācaspati holds. Or it is related to intellect through its reflection in intellect, which is reflected back in itself, as Vijñānabhikṣu holds. The Sāṁkhya finds it extremely difficult to account for the relation between the soul and prakṛti, since it starts with uncompromising dualism. The theory of reflection is a poor intellectual device to relate the two heterogeneous realities to each other.

THREE KINDS OF PAIN AND BONDAGE

As the science of medicine has four divisions, disease, removal of disease, the cause of disease, and treatment of disease, so metaphysical ethics has four divisions, pain, absolute destruction of pain, the cause of pain, and the means to the removal of pain. Three kinds of pain are to be avoided. Total destruction of three-fold pain is avoidance. The cause of the avoidable is non-discrimination due to conjunction of the self with prakṛti. The direct and immediate knowledge of the distinction between the self and prakṛti is the means to the total destruction of three-fold pain.

There are three kinds of suffering, ādhyātmika, ādhibhautika and ādhidaivika. The sufferings due to bodily disorders and mental agitation caused by emotions and passions are of the first kind; those caused by men, beasts, birds, reptiles, and the

[1] SPS., SSV., vi, 27-28.

like are of the second kind ; and those caused by supernatural agencies, planets, ghosts, demons, and the elements, *e.g.*, heat and cold, are of the third kind. The past pain is past and does not need destruction ; the present pain will be destroyed after the second moment ; the future pain only should be destroyed.[1]

The transcendental self (puruṣa) is eternally liberated, enlightened, and pure. It is devoid of association with the guṇas. But it has a false sense of bondage owing to non-discrimination between itself and prakṛti, or its product, the mind-body-complex. Is the self bound or liberated ? If it is bound by nature, it can never be divested of it, and achieve liberation. If it is liberated by nature, it need not strive for liberation, and be engaged in meditation and the like. It is not really bound ; nor is it really liberated from bondage. But it is naturally and eternally liberated. Bondage and liberation of the self are only phenomenal, and not real. They do not really belong to the self. Its apparent bondage is due to non-discrimination, and its apparent liberation is due to discrimination. Bondage and liberation really belong to prakṛti. The activity of prakrti for the undiscriminating self is bondage, and its inactivity for the discriminating self is liberation. The self has a mere feeling of bondage and liberation though it is not really bound or liberated. The self, which is free from association with guṇas, is not really tinged with the mental mode of pain, but it appears to be tinged with it and feels it to be its own experience owing to the superimposition of egoism on it.[2] Thus bondage of the self is not real, but phenomenal.

Bondage is accidental and due to the accident of a particular conjunction of the self with prakṛti.[3] It is phenomenal. Just as a white crystal appears to be red owing to its proximity to a red flower, so the eternally pure and liberated self appears to be in bondage owing to the reflection of pain, a

[1] STK., 1 ; SPS., SPB., SSV., i, 1.

[2] SPS., SSV., i, 19, 159-60 ; ii, 1 & 8 ; iii, 71 & 72 ; vi, 28 ; SPB., vi, 28.

[3] SPB., i, 19

mode of buddhi, in the self. The self itself is eternally free from pain ; but it appears to experience pain and be in bondage owing to its reflection in it and its non-discrimination of itself from the reflection. The self can never be bound without non-discrimination. But its bondage due to non-discrimination is a mere appearance.[1]

LIBERATION AND ITS MEANS

The self is eternally pure, enlightened, and liberated. It appears to be in bondage and to be liberated from bondage. Its apparent bondage is due to its non-discrimination between itself and prakṛti, and its apparent liberation is due to discrimination between them. Liberation consists in absolute cessation of pain, which is the highest good. Supreme happiness is not the highest good, since it is exhausted. There is no unalloyed happiness in our empirical life. Every body seeks to get rid of pain ; but every body does not seek pleasure. Pleasure is always attended with pain, and so regarded by the wise as pain. Liberation does not consist in happiness, but in total extinction and non-production of pain. Virtue, wealth and happiness are good to the self. But they are not the highest good, for they are exhausted and yield sensuous pleasure due to external objects. Liberation is the highest good, because it is eternal manifestation. Supreme happiness which is unmingled with pain, which is not eclipsed afterwards by pain, and which is attained as soon as it is desired, may be called heaven. But it is exhausted and followed by pain, and so it is not the highest good. Pleasure and pain are modes of buddhi, and not attributes of the self. Disembodied isolation of the self is the highest good. The disembodied self which has realized its distinction from prakṛti and its evolutes is beyond pleasure and pain.[2]

Liberation is the absolute negation of three-fold pain. The supreme release is total annihilation of three-fold pain without

---

[1] SSV., SPB., i, 19.

[2] SPS., i, 1-2 & 19 ; SPS., SSV., i, 1 ; vi, 5-6 & 8 ; iii, 71 ; SPB., i, 5 & 19.

leaving any trace of it. It is brought about by discrimination only, and not by any other means. Release partly resembles deep sleep and trance which are lacking in consciousness of external objects and feeling of pain. But it differs from them because they contain dispositions, while there is complete destruction of them in release. In deep sleep and trance there is temporary arrest of mental functions, while in release there is complete destruction of mental functions, or their complete re-absorption in prakṛti.[1] In the state of release there is complete isolation of the self from prakṛti and its evolutes, the mind-body-complex ; there is destruction of mental functions, and of all dispositions also. Release is either embodied or disembodied isolation of the self. In the former traces of dispositions persist, which preserve bodily life. In the latter even these traces are completely destroyed and the body is dissolved. In disembodied release there are no empirical cognitions of external objects, which are known through the medium of mind which is destroyed. There is neither experience of pain nor possibility of reappearance of pain nor germs of pain in the forms of merits, demerits, and dispositions. The self remains in its pristine purity, transparence, and freedom. It remains in its essential nature of transcendental consciusness, free from empirical cognitions, devoid of association with mind and its modes, attachment and aversion, pleasure and pain, merit and demerit.[2]

The self is in reality neither bound, nor released, nor transmigrates from one body to another. Prakṛti, in the form of mind, egoism, subtle essences, and the sense-organs, is bound, released, and transmgrates. The self has neither bondage nor release, but prakṛti binds and liberates itself. The subtle body with merit and demerit is entangled in bondage. Prakṛti binds itself with its seven-fold forms, virtue, dispassion, lordliness, vice, ignorance, attachment, and powerlessness and liberates itself by knowledge. Prakṛti acts for the release of the self. It shows its activities to the self and then desists

[1] SPS., i, 1 ; SPS., SSV., iii, 84 ; v, 116-18.

[2] SPS., i, 19 ; SPB., v, 116 ; SPM., iii, 79, 83 & 84 ; v, 116.

from them. When the self apprehends its distinction from prakṛti, it becomes completely fulfilled. So prakṛti withdraws its creative acts from it. When it withdraws its acts, the self abides in its intrinsic nature, realizes its innate purity, and remains as its indifferent seer. Liberation is the indifference of prakṛti and puruṣa to each other. The indifference of prakṛti consists in its inactivity towards the discriminating puruṣa. The indifference of the self consists in its lack of attachment to prakṛti.[1]

Virtue leads to transmigration to higher spheres of empirical life, and vice, to lower spheres of empirical life. They are the causes of future life. Error leads to bondage, and knowledge, to release. Excess of energy is the cause of attachment, which is the cause of bondage. Excess of purity or essence is the cause of dispassion, which is the cause of absorption in prakṛti or absorption of the soul in prakṛti, mind, egoism, and subtle essences. Ignorance persists in this condition. True knowledge is the cause of release. It is discrimination between the soul and prakṛti. It is not theoretical knowledge, but direct and immediate knowledge of the self, as distinct from mind, egoism and the like.[2]

Discrimination is release, while non-discrimination is bondage. Non-discrimination, bondage, and transmigration are identical with one another, since they are related to one another as cause and effect. Non-discrimination is the cause of bondage, and bondage, the cause of transmigration. Non-discrimination is destroyed by discrimination even as darkness is destroyed by light. Discrimination arises from listening to the instruction of an adept, reflection on it, and intellectual conviction. It is direct and immediate knowledge of the self as distinct from prakṛti and its evolutes. Suffering is due to ignorance, desire, merit, and demerit. Ignorance is error, and its disposition is the cause of desire. Destruction of

[1] SK., 58-59, 62-63, 65-66 ; SGB., 62-63 ; STK., 44 ; SPS., SSV., iii, 65 & 73.

[2] SK. SGB., STK., 44&45. [3] SPS., SSV., vi, 13-14, 16 & 18 ; SSV., v, 85 ; SPB., vi, 43.

suffering is total extinction of its cause, and non-production of suffering in future. It can be accomplished by the true knowledge of the self, which is its means. The true knowledge of the self destroys ignorance. Liberation can be achieved by the immediate knowledge of distinction between the self and the not-self.[1]

Action cannot bring about release. Performance of prudential duties for the fulfilment of desires leads to enjoyment. Performance of daily obligatory duties leads to knowledge. Performance of daily obligatory duties purifies the mind. Action is phenomenal like a dream. Knowledge is noumenal like waking experience. Combination of knowledge and action cannot bring about release, because action is not ultimately real in the sense that it cannot produce an absolute result, and because action is full of pain. If liberation were effected by action, it would be full of pain. Action is transitory, and so its result, liberation, would be transitory. Further, Vedic rites involve killing animals, and consequently entail suffering. Suffering produces suffering and cannot destroy non-discrimination. Vedic rites involve impurity and sin of killing, so their effects are transitory and relative. The Saṁkhya condemns animal sacrifice like Buddhism and Jainsm. Performance of duties without any desire for fruits brings about knowledge which brings on release. In this sense, duties for the sake of duties free from empirical motives indirectly lead to release.[2]

Knowledge is the direct means to release. It is discrimination of the self from prakṛti and its evolutes or direct knowledge of the self. It annihilates suffering. It is aided by the practice of eightfold yoga. Desire for objects is arrested in trance. The sense of identity of the self with egoism due to non-discrimination is arrested by meditation, dispassion, and total suspension of mental functions. Meditation is the destruction of attachment which is due to the excess of rajas.

[1] SSV., ii, 1 ; SK., 44 ; STK., 23.

[2] SPS., i, 84 ; SPB., i, 6 & 84 ; SSV., i, 85 ; iii, 25-27, 32 & 73 ; SPM., iii, 25-26.

Its prefection can be achieved by the arrest of mental functions, and performance of specific duties relating to one's caste and station in life. Mental functions can be arrested by dispassion and constant practice of meditation also. Discrimination gives rise to higher dispassion which arrests all mental functions and brings about release. Then prakṛti withdraws its activities and stops creation, when all sufferings of the bound soul are completely annihilated and it becomes completely fulfilled.[1]

TRANSMIGRATION

Non-discrimination is the cause of bondage which is the cause of transmigration. The transcendental self is eternally pure and free ; it is neither bound nor released ; it does not transmigrate. The empirical self (jīva), transmigrates with the help of the subtle body which is composed of intellect, egoism, mind, five subtle essences, and ten sense-organs. Virtue leads to heaven, and vice leads to hell. Virtue is the cause of exaltation and the highest good. Virtue arising from Vedic rites leads to happiness on earth and in heaven. Virtue arising from the practice of the eight-fold yoga leads to embodied release.[2] Virtue and vice are mental modes. The empirical self has virtue and vice. But they cannot touch the transcendental self which is eternally pure, and devoid of them. Virtue and vice are the causes of the relationship of the owner and the owned between puruṣa and prakṛti. Puruṣa is the owner, and prakṛti is owned. This relationship causes bondage. It is destroyed by discrimination which dawns when the unseen agencies of virtue and vice are destroyed, and the relationship of the owner and the owned between puruṣa and prakṛti is destroyed. This relationship continues so long as the subtle body transmigrates to a gross body. Liberation arises ftom the complete extinction of transmigration. Transmigration is destroyed by the destruction of the relationship of the owner and the owned between puruṣa and prakṛti. This relationship is destroyed

[1] STK., 2 & 23 ; SSV., iii, 32 ; vi, 57 ; SPB., ii, 3 ; iii, 63 & 84 ; SSV., iii, 30-32 ; vi, 26-29 ; SPS., iii, 30-32.

[2] SPM., vi, 16 ; SPS., SSV., iii, 9 ; SK., STK., 23 & 44.

by discrimination which arises from the extinction of the unseen agencies of virtue and vice.

Virtue and vice are the causes of empirical life. Virtue is the cause of transmigration to a higher sphere. Vice is the cause of transmigration to a lower sphere. Greater and greater moral excellences lead to births in higher and higher spheres of empirical existence. But transmigration ought to be avoided, because it is full of suffering. Total extinction of transmigration is release.

The empirical self is born as a god in the upper region of heaven owing to predominance of sattva. It is born in the nether region of hell owing to predominance of tamas. It is born in the middle region of the earth owing to predominance of rajas. In men rajas predominates over sattva and tamas and so their lives are full of suffering. Pain is a specific mode of rajas. Persons acquire virtue and vice by actions. Virtue brings them happiness and vice brings them misery.[1]

The self as determined by the subtle body undergoes transmigration. The subtle body is the seat of dispositions of actions performed in previous births, of virtue and vice, of pleasure and pain. The gross body enjoys and suffers through it. Conjunction of the subtle body with a gross body is birth, and its disjunction from the gross body is death.[2]

ATHEISM

The Sāṁkhya believes in future life, but it does not recognize the existence of God. According to it, God is not the creator of the world ; prakṛti is its material cause ; merits and demerits of the souls are its efficient cause. Prakṛti evolves into the manifold world in accordance with their moral deserts. Transcendental influence of the souls disturbs the equilibrium of prakṛti and starts its evolution. Prakṛti evolves for their experience and dissolves for their release.

[1] SK., STK., SGB., 54 ; SPS., iii, 48-50 ; SSV., iii., 52 ; v, 25 ; vi, 62, 67, 69-70 ; SPB., i, 19.

[2] STK., 62 ; SSV., iii, 8.

God is not the creator, preserver and destroyer of the world.

Vācaspati interprets the Sāṁkhya doctrine as atheism. From cosmic intellect down to gross elements, earth, water, light, air and ether, all things are produced by prakṛti. God is not their efficient cause or material cause. Intelligent spirits cannot be the material cause of the unintelligent world. Spirits are immutable, and cannot be modified into the world. Nor is it produced by prakṛti supervised by God. He is an inactive spirit, and therefore cannot supervise prakṛti, and help it produce the world. A carpenter is active, and therefore can manipulate his tools. But God cannot supervise prakṛti, because He is inactive.

It may be argued that prakṛti is unconscious and therefore cannot act by itself without the supervision of an intelligent spirit ; that individual souls, though intelligent, cannot supervise prakṛti, because they are ignorant of its nature ; and that therefore there must be an omniscient supervisor of prakṛti, or God. The Sāṁkhya gives the following reply. Prakṛti, though unintelligent, acts to realize the souls' ends, even as milk flows from the udder of a cow for the nourishment of her calf. Prakṛti is not conscious of the ends, even as milk is not conscious of nourishment. Even if God be supposed to be the supervisor of prakṛti, what is His motive of creation ? A wise person's action is actuated by self-interest or benevolence. But God can be moved by neither of them. God is said to be an eternally fulfilled Being, and cannot be moved by unfulfilled desires. Nor can He be moved by compassion for others' suffering. There is no suffering before creation, since the bodies, the senses, and the objects necessary for creatures' suffering are not yet existent. God cannot be said to be moved by compassion for suffering subsequent to creation, because this would involve mutual dependence : creation would depend upon compassion ; and compassion would depend upon creation. Further, if God created the world out of compassion, He would create only happy creatures. If the manifoldness of the world be said to be due to variety of the souls' merits and demerits, there is no need of postulating God as their supervisor. Prakṛti is unintelligent, and can be moved neither by self-interest nor by benevolence. It acts unconsciously to realize the souls' ends, evolves the world for their experience, and dissolves it for their liberation. The existence of God is a gratuitous hypothesis.[1]

Aniruddha also refutes the Nyāya argument for the existence of God. The Nyāya argues that the earth and the like are produced by an intelligent agent, God, out of the pre-existing atoms, even as a jar is produced by a potter out of pre-existing clay. Aniruddha contends that God, with or without body, cannot be the efficient cause of the world. Further, is He bound or liberated? If He is bound, He has merits and demerits, and therefore He cannot be the Lord. If He is free, He cannot be an active agent, for He is devoid of cognition, desire to act, and volition. He cannot be the Lord, if He is bound or free. Nor can He be like an individual soul which has attained embodied release, since such a soul is not possessed of lordship. Again, if God were the independent creator of the world, He could create it without the aid of the souls' merits and demerits. But the Nyāya holds that He creates the manifold world in accordance with their merits and demerits. Then merits and demerits may be regarded as the cause of the world, and there is no necessity for God to supervise them. If God depends on the souls' merits and demerits, He loses His independence. Again, God has no motive for creation. He is moved by neither self-interest nor benevolence. He is devoid of unfulfilled desires and so of self-interest. If He were moved by benevolence, He would create a happy world only. But it abounds in misery and so cannot be the creation of a benevolent creator. Further, even benevolent acts are done for some selfish ends; no acts are absolutely selfless. There is no need of God for the creation of the world. The souls' merits and demerits are enough to serve as the efficient cause of the world, while prakṛti is its meterial cause.[2]

---

[1] STK., 57. [2] SSV., i, 82, 92-93; v, 2.

The Nyāya argues that God is the author of the Vedas. But the Sāṁkhya contends that they are impersonal, since their personal author does not exist. The existence of God has been disproved. The Vedas are impersonal, and embodiments of eternal truths, which are revealed to the seers. God is neither perceived, nor inferred, nor proved by Vedic testimony. The Vedic texts 'He is the knower of all and the creator of all' and the like are really eulogies of the released souls, or the souls endowed with supernatural yogic powers, and do not refer to the Lord. There is no proof for the existence of God, as conceived by the Nyāya. Aniruddha gives an atheistic interpretation of the Sāṁkhya system.[1] Vācaspati and Aniruddha think that the Sāṁkhya denies the existence of God.

But Vijñānabhikṣu thinks that the Sāṁkhya is not avowedly atheistic. It holds that the existence of God cannot be proved. It does not deny the existence of God. The *Sāṁkhya Sūtra* says 'because there is no proof for the existence of God'.[2] It does not say 'because God does not exist'. This negation of God is a bold assertion of some thinkers who do not find any necessity for God in the Sāṁkhya system. The main objects of the system are the supreme good of the self and discrimination between the self and prakṛti, the means to its realization. The main object of the Vedānta, on the other hand, is the Lord. Theism lays stress on His lordliness, and enjoins the aspirants' vision of His perfect, eternal, and pure lordliness. But the Sāṁkhya exclusion of God is intended to enjoin dispassion for His lordliness which is an obstacle to the practice of discrimination. The Sāṁkhya does not condemn the theistic theory. The *Mahābhārata* describes the Sāṁkhya as the highest knowledge. Its superiority to all other systems is only in respect of discrimination between the self and the not-self, but not in respect of the exclusion of God. The Sāṁkhya exclusion of God is a concession to current views or a dogmatic assertion. Its atheism may be deliberately intended to hinder the

---

[1] SPS., v, 46; i, 95; SSV., v, 2, 41, 46; i, 82, 92-94, 128; iii, 57; SPM., vi, 65.

[2] SPS., i, 92.

knowledge of sinners. Thus there is no contradiction between the Vedānta and the Yoga, on the one hand, and the Sāṁkhya, on the other. The Sāṁkhya atheism is only for practical purposes.[1]

Vijñānabhikṣu admits the reality of a supreme soul. The original self (ādipuruṣa) turns prakṛti into cosmic intellect by mere conjunction, even as a magnet attracts a piece of iron by mere proximity. Though the supreme self is devoid of desire or volition, He is an agent by mere conjunction. He moves prakṛti to evolve into cosmic intellect by mere conjunction or proximity. The souls are absorbed in prakṛti by dispassion for cosmic intellect and the like. They are not released, but they again appear as emergent Lords. The soul absorbed in prakṛti in the previous creation becomes in the next creation the original self or the Lord (Īśvara) who is the knower of all and the doer of all. He is the created Lord. The existence of the eternal Lord is an object of controversy. The original self is supreme, universal, omniscient and omnipotent. He gives an impetus to prakṛti by His mere proximity like a magnet. Viṣṇu with the adjunct of cosmic intellect is the preserver. He is said to be the supreme Lord, Brahmā. In the Sāṁkhya system the causal Brahman is intended to be the genus of self free from the guṇas, since God is not admitted.[2] Vijñānabhikṣu tries to reconcile the Sāṁkhya dualism with the Vedānta monism.[3]

---

[1] SPB., Introduction.
[2] SPB., i, 96; iii, 54, 56, 57; vi, 66.
[3] HIP., Vol. II, Ch. I.

CHAPTER XI

THE YOGA PHILOSOPHY

The Yoga adopts the Sāṁkhya metaphysics and engrafts the concept of God upon it. It is called the theistic Sāṁkhya, while the Sāṁkhya system is called the atheistic Sāṁkhya.[1] The Yoga recognizes the reality of prakṛti and its evolutes, countless individual souls (puruṣa), and God. Prakṛti is the material cause of the world, and God is its efficient cause. He is not the creator of prakṛti ; nor is He the creator of souls. Prakṛti and souls are co-eternal with God. He disturbs the equilibrium of sattva, rajas, and tamas, and starts the evolution of prakṛti. He is the creator of the Vedas and reveals them for the enlightenment of souls at the end of each cycle. He associates and dissociates souls and prakṛti in accordance with their merits and demerits, and brings about evolution and dissolution of the world. He removes obstacles to the evolution of prakṛti, and to the achievement of liberation by souls.

The Sāṁkhya believes in the reality of twenty-five principles, prakṛti, mahat, ahaṁkāra, manas, ten external sense-organs, five tanmātras, five gross elements, and souls. The Yoga assumes the reality of these twenty-five principles and adds the principle of God to them. It recognizes the reality of twenty-six principles. It adopts the Sāṁkhya ontology with slight variations. It agrees with the Sāṁkhya in holding that bondage is due to non-discrimination between the self and prakṛti, and that liberation is due to discrimination between them. But it lays stress on the practice of yoga as an indispensable means to discriminative knowledge. This is the special feature of the Yoga system.

Patañjali was the author of the *Yoga Sūtra.* He systematized the Yoga conceptions in it. It is the first work in the system. Vyāsa's Commentary on the *Yoga Sūtra,* called *Yoga-Bhāṣya* (400 A. D.) is the most important and authoritative work in the system. Vācaspati (1000 A. D.), the great

---

[1] SDS., p. 266.

scholiast, wrote a glossary on it called *Tattvavaiśāradī*. Vijñānabhikṣu (1600 A. D.) also wrote a glossary on it called *Yoga Vārtika*. These three works are the standard expositions of the Yoga principles.

POWER AND CAUSATION—SATKĀRYAVĀDA

The Yoga advocates the theory of Satkāryavāda or Pariṇāmavāda. There is neither production of a non-existent thing nor destruction of an existent thing. A non-existent thing cannot be produced; but what was existent in an unmanifest condition appears in a manifest condition. Production is manifestation; destruction is envelopment. A present cause contains its effect in a latent condition. Milk is turned into curd which it contained in a potential condition. All effects are particular collocations of the guṇas—sattva, rajas, and tamas which are the ultimate constituents of all phenomena. They are the material cause of all effects. They undergo various modifications, but are neither generated nor destroyed. They appear to be generated and destroyed on account of their modes passing from the latent to the actual condition, and from the actual to the sublatent condition.[1] What is non-existent in the cause cannot be produced by it. What exists in a subtle condition in it can be produced by it. The causal power in the form of an unmanifest condition is turned into an effect. The effect passes from the present or actual to the past or sublatent condition. It is not completely destroyed. It is destroyed as a mode but continues to exist in a subtle condition in its material cause. It is not perceived owing to its subtlety.

The material cause possesses the power to produce a particular effect. Power exists in the causal substance to produce a specific effect. It is a quality that is inferred from the production of a particular effect. Earth can produce a jar. Threads can produce a cloth. These causal powers are not perceived, but inferred from the production of different effects. They are of the nature of qualities. So they are not different

[1] YBh., iv, 12-13; iii, 11; ii, 19; TV., ii, 18-19.

from the causal substances in which they reside. They are latent conditions of their effects prior to their production. The potent cause cannot be deprived of its causal power, since they are identical with each other.[1]

The causal energy or the latent condition of an effect is liberated by an efficient cause or a concomitant condition. It cannot generate a non-existent effect, but it can only manifest a pre-existent latent effect in the material cause. A slab of marble is the material cause of a statue which exists in a potential condition in it, which is liberated by chiselling, which is its efficient cause. Mustard is the material cause of oil which exists in a latent condition in it, which is liberated by pressing which is its efficient cause. Paddy is the material cause of rice which exists in an unmanifest condition in it, which is liberated by husking which is its efficient cause.[2] Potential energy is stored up in a collocation of the guṇas, the sum of material causes, which is liberated by the action of the efficient cause, which removes the barriers, liberates the causal energy, and produces the effect which is a fresh collocation of the guṇas. The efficient cause can only make the latent effect actual, but it cannot produce a non-existent effect.[3]

Prakṛti evolves manifold things for the enjoyment and suffering of the souls according to their merits and demerits. Sattva, rajas, and tamas are the ultimate material causes of all effects including merit and demerit, which are modifications of the mind (citta). Effects cannot move their causes to action. So merit and demerit cannot move the guṇas to action, and make them produce manifold effects. They can only break the barrier, remove the counteracting forces, and liberate the causal energy. When the counteracting forces are removed by merit and demerit, which are the efficient causes, the material causes themselves are modified into particular effects. Merit and demerit do not interfere with the material causes, but only liberate the potential causal energy in them, and manifest particular effects. Merit only overpowers demerit, and demerit

[1] YBh., ii, 19; iii, 13-14; TV., iii, 15; Ch. V., iii, 14.

[2] SPB., i, 129.

[3] YBh., iv, 12.

only overpowers merit. They do not move the material causes to act. Thus merits and demerits of the souls are the efficient causes of the production of various effects out of their material causes. God is the efficient cause of the world because He disturbs the equilibrium of sattva, rajas, and tamas, and removes the necessary barriers to the production of particular effects out of them. He also has a negative function. He removes obstacles to the evolution of prakṛti to adjust it to the merits and demerits of the souls. God and merits and demerits liberate the causal powers in the material causes. Physical agents, which are efficient causes, counteract the manifestation of other effects. Thus the efficient causes have a negative function of counteracting the opposing forces.

The Yoga holds that all effects exist potentially in all causes. Sattva, rajas, and tamas are the material causes of all effects, which are their particular arrangements. But they do not produce all effects simultaneously. Their causal efficiency is regulated by the law of place, time, form, and merit and demerit. Saffron grows in Kashmir, but not in Panchāl; its seeds germniate in a particular environment. This is the limitation of place. Different crops grow in different seasons. This is the limitation of time. A female deer cannot give birth to a human being. This is the limitation of form. A person endowed with demerit does not enjoy happiness; a person endowed with merit does not feel unhappiness. This is the limitation of merit and demerit. A sprout is not produced from a piece of stone, because a particular arrangement of parts prevents the production of it from the stone. But the will of God can remove all barriers and turn even a stone into a sprout, even poison into nectar. In fact, concomitant conditions only remove the counteracting forces which prevent the production of particular effects.[1]

THE PLACE OF GOD IN THE YOGA SYSTEM

Mādhavācārya describes Patañjali as the founder of the theistic Sāṁkhya.[2] He recognizes three realities—prakṛti,

[1] YBh., iii, 14; ix, 3; YV., TV., Ch.V., iv, 3; iii, 14.
[2] SDS., p. 266.

souls and God. But he does not regard God as an integral part of his system. Īśvarapraṇidhāna is one of the means to yoga or complete arrest of mental activities, which is the chief subject of his discussion. It means either devotion to God, or resignation of all actions or of their fruits to Him. God helps the aspirants achieve yoga by removing their obstacles to the attainment of it. He removes the barriers to the transformation of prakṛti into various effects, but He does not move it to action. Even as a peasant floods lower fields by removing the barriers from higher fields full of water, so God removes obstacles to the transformation of prakṛti into various modes without energizing it into activity. God is the inactive efficient cause of the evolution of prakṛti. Patañjali does not distinctly mention God as its efficient cause. Vyāsa regards the souls' merits and demerits as its efficient cause, since they overcome demerits and merits which obstruct prakṛti, and help it transform itself into various effects. But they do not move it to action. Vyāsa does not regard God as the efficient cause of the evolution of prakṛti. But Vācaspati clearly states that God is the efficient cause of the evolution of prakṛti into various effects, whose function consists in the removal of barriers for the fruition of merits and demerits, which are the effects of prakṛti.[2] Effects cannot move their cause to action. Therefore merits cannot move prakṛti to transform itself into various effects. They cannot be the efficient cause of its evolution. They can merely remove obstacles in the shape of opposite demerits. Demerits also can merely remove obstacles in the shape of opposite merits. Nor can the souls' ends move prakṛti to action. But God moves it to action for the realization of their ends by mere presence. Vijñānabhikṣu also agrees with Vācaspati. They hold that prakṛti is the material cause of the world, while God is its efficient cause in the sense that He disturbs the equilibrium of sattva, rajas, and tamas, removes all barriers to their redistribution into various modes, and guides their evolution for the souls' enjoyment and liberation. Prakṛti is the potential cause of all effects which are

[2] YS., i, 23; ii, 1; iv, 3; YBh., ii, 1; iv, 3; TV., YV., iv, 3.

mere redistribution of its constituents—sattva, rajas, and tamas. Though they can be transformed into all kinds of effects, yet they are transformed into particular effects owing to certain concomitant causes. Time, merits and demerits, and God liberate the causal powers of prakṛti to transform itself into particular modes. Merits and demerits remove barriers in the shape of opposite demerits and merits. Time awakens merits and demerits and ripens them for fruition. Other accessory causes remove other barriers to the modification of prakṛti into particular effects. God removes all barriers to the transformation of prakṛti into particular effects.[1] He starts the evolution of prakṛti and guides it for the realization of the souls' ends. The Yoga believes in external teleology. God consciously realizes the souls' ends through the evolution of prakṛti which He guides from without. He somehow adapts the heterogeneous and homogeneous transformation of prakṛti to the moral deserts of the souls for their enjoyment and liberation. But He is not organically related to prakṛti and souls. He is not their immanent Spirit.

PROOFS FOR THE EXISTENCE OF GOD

Patañjali gives an ontological argument[2], for the existence of God. The law of continuity points to His existence. God is the supreme Being who is the emobodiment of the highest degree of omniscience. Magnitude admits of degrees, higher and lower. Ether has the largest magnitude, and atoms have the smallest magnitude. Similarly, knowledge admits of degrees. Knowledge of the past, present, future, remote, and supersensible objects, individual and collective, is found in different degrees, small and great; it increases more and more, and reaches its culmination in God who is omniscient. He is the highest limit of omniscience. Vyāsa applies the law of continuity to power and lordship. There are different degrees of lordship, which point to the existence of the highest Lord. God is the repository of the greatest power, unequalled and unsurpassed. Power increases more and more and culminates

[1] TV., YV., Ch.V., iv, 3,

[2] Cp. Anselm.

in God, the supreme omnipotent Lord. If there were a more powerful Lord than God, He would be the highest Lord. If there were another equally powerful Lord, their wills would be thwarted by each other. So God is the Supreme Person whose lordship is unrivalled and unexcelled.

The Vedas refer to God. Therefore He must exist. The scriptures are authoritative and cannot deceive us. They are the creations of God. But is it not an argument in a circle? The Vedas are authoritative because they are the creations of God, the perfect person ; and God exists because the Vedas bear testimony to His existence ; the existence of the Vedas depends upon God, and the existence of God depends upon the Vedas. But Vyāsa urges that there is a beginningless relation between the Vedas and the pre-eminence of God.[1]

God is the Prime Mover of prakṛti, upsets its equilibrium and starts the evolution of the world. He cannot create, preserve or destroy prakṛti which is the material cause of the world. He is the inactive efficient cause of the world. He removes all barriers to the transformation of prakṛti into various effects and guides the evolution of the world for the enjoyment of some souls and liberation of others.[1] He adapts the modifications of prakṛti to the souls'moral deserts. He mechanically relates prakṛti to the souls from without. He is not immanent in them, and does not control them from within. The souls are unconscious of their merits and demerits, and cannot bring about their fruition in the shape of enjoyment and suffering. Prakṛti is unconscious and cannot unfold its evolutes to the souls for their enjoyment and suffering in accordance with their merits and demerits. But God is omniscient and omnipotent. He knows the souls' merits and demerits, prakṛti and its infinite potentialities, removes all barriers and starts and directs the evolution of prakṛti for the enjoyment and suffering of some individual selves, and dissolves it for the liberation of others. God is the unmoved Mover of prakṛti, the efficient cause of the world, and its Moral Governor.

Prakṛti and souls are independent realities. They can

---

[1] YS., i, 24-25 ; RM., i, 25.

neither associate themselves with each other nor dissociate themselves from each other. But their association is the cause of the evolution of prakṛti and the empirical life of the souls, and their dissociation is the cause of the dissolution of the world and the liberation of the souls. Their association and dissociaton cannot be accounted for without the will of God. He has no end of His own, because He is eternally fulfilled. But compassion for creatures is the end which moves Him to effect conjunction and disjunction between souls and prakṛti. His merciful resolution to liberate all souls through their moral education is the end of creation and dissolution which depend upon conjunction and disjunction of prakṛti and souls. God brings about their conjunction and disjunction.[1]

THE NATURE OF GOD

Patañjali describes God as a particular self untouched by afflictions, actions, fruits, and dispositions.[2] He is the perfect self free from all taint of imperfections. He is eternally free from afflictions, ignorance, egoism, attachment, aversion, and fear of death. He is eternally fulfilled, and does not perform actions—good, bad, and indifferent. He does not experience fruits of actions—enjoyment and suffering. He has no dispositions of past experiences. The bound souls are subject to all these afflictions, actions, fruits, and dispositions. But God is eternally free from them. He is not a liberated self which was subject to afflictions in the past. He is not a self absorbed in prakṛti during dissolution which will be subject to afflictions and consequent empirical life after creation. He had no relation to afflictions in the past; He has none at present; and He will have none in future. He is eternally liberated. He is the eternal Lord. He is omniscient: He knows the past, present, future, and supersensible objects individually and collectively. He has intuitive knowledge of the whole universe, which is supreme and perfect. He is the supreme omnipotent Lord. His lordship is unequalled and unexcelled. There is no other

[1] YBh., iv, 3; TV., YV., iv, 3; ii, 22; i, 26.

[2] RM., i, 25-26.

Lord equal to, or, superior to, Him. The Yoga system believes in monotheism. God is one. If there were two rival Lords, they would be of equal or unequal powers. If they had equal powers, they would thwart each other's will, and fail to realize their ends. If they had unequal powers, the superior Lord would be the true Lord, and the other would be inferior to Him. Though the Yoga system believes in one supreme God, it recognizes the existence of many gods who are entangled in empirical life owing to ignorance.[1] God has eternal knowledge, desire, and will, which do not lapse even during dissolution. He is immutable—free from the mutations of sattva, rajas, and tamas. But He assumes pure sattva untainted by rajas and tamas to create the scriptures. His excellence of sattva is expressed in them. They bear testimony to the pre-eminence of His sattva. God teaches true wisdom and morality to the individual souls through the scriptures. He cannot create them without supreme knowledge and capacity for action, which depend upon pre-eminence of sattva. So He assumes pre-eminent sattva to create the scriptures and enlighten mankind. He has supreme knowledge, perfect righteousness, complete detachment, and infinite power owing to His pre-eminent sattva. There is an eternal relation between words and their objects. God's convention merely manifests the relation, but he does not create it. So God manifests the eternal relation between the scriptures and His pre-eminence of sattva. God is the pure, blissful, free, and transcendental Self. He is immutable and eternal, uncaused and indestructible. He is free from afflctions, devoid of merits and demerits, and not subject to birth. He is not entangled in empirical life, enjoyment and suffering. He is beyond time and space. He is eternal and all-pervading.[2]

God is omniscient, omnipotent, contented, independent, and ubiquitous. He has eternal knowledge and eternally manifested powers. He has ten eternal qualities—konwledge, detachment, lordship, austerity, veracity, forgiveness, patience,

[1] YS., YBh., i, 19, 24-25.

[2] YS., i, 26; YBh., i, 24, 26-27, 29; TV., i, 24 & 29; YV., i, 24.

creative power, self-knowledge, and superintendence. His creative act is moved by compassion for the bound souls. Their liberation is the motive of His creation. He is supremely merciful to the creatures. He creates or reveals the Vedas in the beginning of each world-epoch for the souls' enlightenment and liberation. He is the promulgator of moral codes. The Vedas prescribe right and wrong actions. God is the Supreme Teacher. He was the teacher of the ancient sages, who were limited by time. God, unlimited by time, was their teacher.

God favours the aspirants who are devoted to Him, and fulfils their desires. Repeated practice of devotion to Him removes all obstacles to yoga—disease, inactivity of mind, doubt, inadvertence, laziness of body and mind, craving for enjoyment, illusion, non-attainment of the condition of ecstasy, and instability of mind even in ecstasy. Pain, mental excitement, bodily restlessness, and irregularity of breathing accompany the distractions. All these are removed by repeated practice of concentration on one principle. Repeated concentration on God also removes all these mental and bodily distractions, and enables the mind to attain trance and liberation. Devotion to God and dedication of all actions and resignation of their fruits to Him facilitate the attainment of yoga through His grace. He is expressed by the mystic syllable *Om*. He is revealed to a person who constantly recites it and meditates on Him.[1]

The relation of God to prakṛti and souls is not inseparable and organic. He is not the creator, preserver, or destroyer of prakṛti which is eternal, though mutable. He does not energize it to activity, but He merely upsets the equilibrium of prakṛti and removes all obstacles to the effectuation of material causes, sattva, rajas, and tamas. He indirectly helps evolution and dissolution of the world. He is not the immanent Spirit in it realizing His purpose in it. He is loosely connected with the world. He is not the creator or destroyer of the souls, which are eternal and all-pervading, uncaused and indestruc-

[1] YS., i, 23, 26-28, 30-32; ii, 1; YBh., i, 23, 25 & 28; iii, 6; ii, 1; TV., i, 23, 25, 30 & 32; YV., ii, 1; i, 23.

tible. They are entangled in empirical life owing to ignorance. They can work out their own salvation unaided by God. He is not their indwelling Spirit. God is not organically related to them. But if they are devoted to Him or dedicate all their actions and their fruits to Him, He removes all their distractions and helps them attain liberation. He is loosely connected with the souls.

THE STAGES OF THE MIND (CITTABHŪMI)

Vyāsa mentions five stages of the mind : (1) distracted (kṣipta), (2) infatuated (mūḍha), (3) occasionally steady (vikṣipta), (4) one-pointed (ekāgra), and (5) restrained (nirūddha). (1) The distracted mind, being overpowered by rajas, becomes extremely unsteady and extraverted and flits constantly from one object to another, which is the source of pleasure or pain. (2) The infatuated mind being overpowered by tamas, is fixed on unrighteous actions under the influence of anger and other violent emotions. It loses the power of distinguishing between right and wrong, sinks into listlessness, drowsiness and sleep under the influence of tamas, and has dispersed attention or absolute inattention. (3) The occasionally unsteady mind being influenced by sattva, though unsteady for the most part, becomes occasionally steady, withdraws itself from painful objects, and fixes itself on pleasurable objects. Its persistent unsteadiness is either natural or due to physical or mental distractions. These three stages of mind are unfit for concentration. (4) The one-pointed mind, under the influence of pure sattva, is withdrawn from all other objects and focussed on one object, either physical or mental, and has an unflickering cognition of it. There is complete introversion in this stage. The restrained mind, under the influence of pure sattva, arrests all mental functions, and retains only subconscious dispositions according to Vācaspati. Vijñānabhikṣu also holds the same view. But Bhojadeva opines that there is complete suspension of all mental modes and subconscious dispositions in the restrained stage of mind. Complete arrest of mental functions (yoga) is possible in the last two stages.

All mental modes are attended with pleasure, pain, and delusion, and should be suppressed.[1] The Yoga enjoins the complete suppression of all mental modes and eradication of all mental dispositions by rigid discipline of the body, the vital forces, and the mind, and moral practices.

THE PATH OF YOGA

Patañjali defines yoga as complete suppression of all mental modes. Vyāsa defines it as absorptive concentration, and regards it as a universal attribute of the mind. All persons can attain yoga by repeated practice and detachment. The distracted, infatuated, and occasionally steady minds are not fit for yoga. The one-pointed and restrained minds are fit for it. The yogin only knows the nature of yoga, and can attain it by servere mental discipline. Yoga generates occult powers, clairvoyance, clairaudience, thought-reading, thought-transference, and the like. If the yogin is infatuated with them, he falls from yoga. If he is indifferent to them, he will delight in yoga for ever.[2] The yogic practices only can lead the yogin from a lower stage to a higher stage. The art of yoga is a matter of constant practice and discipline of the body, the vital forces, and the mind. It is pre-eminently an art of mental discipline.

The Yoga enjoins the practice of restraints (yama), observances (niyama), bodily postures (āsana), breath control (prāṇāyāma), withdrawal of the sense-organs (pratyāhāra), fixation of attention (dhāraṇā), meditation (dhyāna), and absorptive concentration (samādhi) as aids to yoga (yogāṅga).[3]

(1) The first discipline of restraint consists in non-injury, truthfulness in thought and speech, non-stealing, sexual restraint, and non-acceptance of unnecessary gifts. These are negative virtues. Non-injury consists in the absence of cruelty to all creatures in all possible ways and at all times. It is tenderness, good will, and kindness for all living beings.

---

[1] YBh., TV., YV., RM., i, 1.
[2] YS., i, 2 & 12 ; YBh., i, 1 ; RM., i, 2.
[3] YS., ii, 29.

Non-injury is the root of all other negative and positive virtues. So absolute non-injury is prescribed by the Yoga system. Animal sacrifice for a religious purpose is forbidden. Truthfulness consists in the harmony between true thoughts and words in conformity with the good of all creatures. The words should be spoken for the good of all creatures, and not for doing harm to others. If they are spoken for the purpose of doing harm to others, they cannot be regarded as true and righteous. Truthfulness in violation of the good of others amounts to falsehood. It should be in harmony with the walfare of the sentient creation. Absolute truthfulness regardless of the welfare of humanity and animal kingdom is forbidden. Truthfulness involves harmony of thoughts with facts which must be guaranteed by the speaker. A truthful person should vouch for the truth of his words. He ought to state what he has perceived, or inferred, or derived from a reliable authority. If his words deceive the hearer, or produce error in him, or are unintelligible to him, they are not true. A truthful person should have valid thoughts in his mind, speak them out correctly, excite similar thoughts in the hearer's mind, and his words should be conducive to the welfare of all creatures.[1] Truthfulness involves harmony of the speaker's thoughts with facts, harmony of his thoughts with his words, harmony of his words with the welfare of the sentient creation. Veracity should be consistent with the welbeing of humanity. If its consequence is injurious to others, it is not real veracity, but a semblance of it. Hypocrisy, flattery, deceit, and truthful words injurious to society are falsehood. Theft is immoral misappropriation of others' possessions. Non-stealing consists in not merely misappropriating the property of others, but also in the lack of greed. Sexual purity consists in restraint of the sexual organ and all other sense-organs with regard to the object of sex-gratification. Recollection of the sexual act, talk about it, sport and secret conversation with a woman, watching her limbs, sexual desire, and resolution to indulge in sexual

[1] YS., YBh., RM., ii, 30

pleasure, and overt sexual act are the eight kinds of sex-gratification. Sex-restraint consists in restraining the sex-organ and all other sense-organs with regard to its object. The Yoga enjoins absolute sexual continence. Non-acceptance of gifts consists in abstaining from acquiring objects of enjoyment. It consists in non-acquisition and non-possession. A person devoid of greed realizes that acquisition, preservation and expenditure of wealth are tainted with the faults of attachment and violence or exploitation. Hence he eschews wealth and other objects of enjoyment. Non-acceptance of gifts consists in accepting nothing but what is absolutely necessary for one's bare subsistence. These are the negative virtues, which are unconditionally obligatory, and which are not limited by time, place, caste, or purpose.[1] The fishermen earn their livelihood by killing and selling fish. A person may resolve that he will not kill a living creature in a place of pilgrimage. Or he may resolve that he will not kill life on an auspicious day. Or he may resolve that he will not kill life except for gods and Brahmins. Kṣatriyas kill only in the battle field. All these acts of killing are absolutely forbidden. Non-killing, truthfulness, non-stealing, sexual restraint, and non-acceptance of anything but what is absolutely necessary for bare subsistence ought to be observed unconditionally and universally, unlimited by profession, place, time, and purpose without any exceptions. They are the great vows which are universally obligatory. They ought to be observed in all spheres, in all possible ways, with regard to all objects.[2]

(2) The second discipline of observance consists in cleanliness, contentment, austerities, study of the scriptures, and dedication of all actions to God. Cleanliness is of two kinds, external and internal. The former is cleanliness of the body by means of water and other purifying articles. The latter is cleanliness of the mind by purging it of all impurities—attachment, aversion, pride, conceit, envy, and the like by cultivating good will, compassion, and cheerfulness. Contentment consists in the lack of desire to acquire anything but what comes of

[1] YS., ii, 31; YBh., TV., YV., RM., ii, 30.

[2] YBh., ii, 31.

itself without exertion and what is absolutely necessary for bare livelihood. Austerities consist in the habit of enduring hunger and thirst, heat and cold, sitting and standing, non-speaking, non-communication of desires even through gestures, and observance of vows involving physical hardships. Study of the scriptures includes reciting the mystic syllable *Om* and meditating on God. The observances are positive virtues limited by time, place, and other circumstances.[1]

Sins are counteracted by thoughts and habits of opposite virtues. Vicious habits are broken by cultivating opposite virtuous habits. Sins are of three kinds : they are either done, or caused to be done, or approved. They are actuated by greed, anger, and delusion and counteracted by the constant thought that they produce infinite pain and false knowledge. They cannot be overcome by fixing our thoughts on them but on the opposite virtues. The mind is purged of its impurities by cultivating good will for all happy beings, compassion for all distressed creatures, cheerfulness towards all virtuous persons, and indifference to all vicious persons. Attachment and aversion also are overcome by good will or friendliness. Good will, compassion, and cheerfulness are the three thoughts. By focussing the mind on them powers of good will, kindness, and cheerfulness are acquired. Focussing the mind on these three thoughts brings about absorptive concentration. Concentration generates these powers unfailingly. Indifference to vicious persons is not a thought. The mind cannot be focussed on it. So it cannot bring on absorptive concentration and cannot produce power of indifference. Afflictions are overcome by the thought of opposite excellences. False knowledge is overcome by right knowledge ; egoism, by discrimination of the self from the not-self ; attachment and aversion, by indifference ; and fear of death, by fearlessness.[2] Bad emotions are overcome by good emotions. This is a great psychological truth discovered by the Yoga system long ago. It is a commonplace of modern Ethics.

---

[1] YBh., YV., ii, 32.

[2] YS., ii, 33 ; YBh., ii, 34 ; iii, 25 ; TV., ii, 4.

(3) The third discipline is bodily posture. It is a steady and pleasant posture of the body. It should not be painful, and distract the mind. There are many kinds of postures, which can be learnt form experts. The various postures of the body are the means of controlling it and keeping it healthy and fit. They tone up the nervous system. The control of the body is the basis of the yoga discipline.

(4) The fourth discipline is breath control. It consists in controlling natural breathing and subjecting it to a definite law. It consists in slow and deep inspiration, retention of breath, and slow expiration. These three functions should be performed for definite periods. The time of inspiration, the time of retention of breath, and the time of expiration should be in the proportion : 1, 4 and 2. The vital forces move the body. The mind has desire and will which are expressed in bodily actions. So regulation of the vital forces leads to control of the mind. Breath control is conducive to concentration of mind. It removes the crust of affliction from illumination of the sattva of the mind and removes the demerit which obscures discriminative knowledge. Breath-control is the supreme austerity, which purges the mind of impurities and generates illumination of knowledge. It can be learnt only under the guidance of experts.

(5) The fifth discipline is withdrawal of the external sense-organs from their objects due to withdrawal of mind from them. If the mind is withdrawn from external sensible objects, the external senses are automatically withdrawn from them. They do not follow their objects, but they follow the mind. They are fixed on those objects only on which the mind is fixed. The restraint of the external senses depends upon the restraint of the mind. It can be acquired by repeated practice, resolute will, and sense-control.[1]

The five disciplines of restraint, observance, bodily posture, breath-control, and sense-control are the external aids to yoga. The last three disciplines, fixation of mind, meditation, and

[1] YS., YBh., ii, 46, 49-50, 52-54.

absorptive concentration are the internal aids of yoga. They directly lead to conscious trance.

(6) The sixth discipline is fixing the mind on a particular object. The object is either intra-organic or extra-organic. The mind is fixed on the navel, the heart, the tip of the nose, the tip of the tongue, the middle of the eye-brows, the throat, and the like. Or it is fixed on an external object, the idol or image of a deity. Bodily posture controls the body ; breath-control regulates the vital forces ; and withdrawal of the senses from their objects controls the senses ; fixation of attention controls the mind. It requires withdrawal of the mind from other objects, and prepares it for meditation.

(7) The seventh discipline is meditation. It consists in the continuous flow of the same cognition of the object of attention undisturbed by any other cognition. Fixation of attention on an object to the exclusion of other objects leads to meditation, if the cognition produced by it continues unbroken for a long time. There is a continuous stream of similar cognitions of the contemplated object undisturbed by dissimilar cognitions.

(8) The eightth discipline is absorptive concentration or trance. It is the manifestation of the object of meditation only devoid of the cognition of meditation.[1] Dhāraṇā is fixation of attention on an object undisturbed by the cognition of any other object. Dhyāna is unbroken flow of the same cognition for a long time. There is manifestation of the object, meditation, and the self in it. In trance the self and the act of meditation are not manifested, but only the object of meditation is manifested. If such trance continues for a long time, it is called conscious trance. When there is no manifestation of the object also, it is called superconscious trance. Fixation, meditation, and absorptive concentration on the same object are the internal aids to conscious trance, while restraint, observance, bodily posture, breath-control, and withdrawal of the senses from their objects are the external

---

[1] YS., iii, 1-3 ; YBh., iii, 1 & 7 ; RM., iii, 2.

aids to it. But they are the external aids to superconscious trance.[1]

The performance of the eightfold aids to yoga, external and internal, purges the mind of its afflictions, manifests right knowledge, which goes on increasing with the gradual removal of impurities, and culminates in discriminative knowledge of the true nature of the pure self as distinct from prakṛti and its evolutes, body, sense-organs, and mind (citta). When the impurities of affiictions—false knowledge, egoism, attachment, aversion, and the will-to-live—are completely destroyed, the pure sattva of the mind attains perfection, and is modified into discriminative knowledge. The performance of the aids to yoga is the cause of dissociation of afflictions from the mind. It is the cause of attainment of discriminative knowledge.[2]

Patañjali says that penance, regular study of the scriptures, or dedication of all actions to God, repeatedly practised for a long period, exhausts the afflictions gradually and generates concentration. When the afflictions are attenuated by the performance of actions, the mental modes afflicted by pleasure, pain, and delusion should be arrested by meditation on discriminative knowledge till they become incapable of producing effects almost like burnt seeds. The manifest modes of afflictions can be arrested by continuous human effort of meditation. But their subtle dispositions are destroyed only when the mind in which they subsist is destroyed or merged in cosmic egoism. Dispositions are modes of the mind. When the substance is destroyed, its modes are bound to be destroyed. When the mind attains liberation, it is merged in its cause. When the mind is merged in cosmic egoism, all subtle dispositions of afflictions, feelings, emotions, and passions are destroyed.[3]

KINDS OF SAMĀDHI

Vyāsa defines yoga as concentration, which is a universal property of mind, and can be acquired by all. The distracted,

[1] YS., YBh,. iii, 4, 7-8 ; YMP., iii, 3.
[2] YBh., ii, 28. [3] YS., ii, 2, 10-11 ; YBh., TV., YV., ii, 10-11.

torpid, occasionally steady states of the mind are unfavourable to concentration. The one-pointed and restrained states are favourable to it. Samādhi is either conscious (samprajñāta) or superconscious (asamprajñāta). The former manifests the real nature of an object, wears off afflictions, loosens the ties of bondage in the shape of merit and demerit and inclines the mind to the restrained state. The latter consists in the suppression of all mental functions. In the former the mind is concentrated on an object and indentifies itself with it. In the latter the mind is not concentrated on an object, and all mental modes and dispositions are suppressed.[1]

Conscious trance is of six kinds. (1) Savitarka samādhi is the concentration in which the mind identifies itself with a gross object together with its name and cognition. In it the object is not manifested to consciousness in its pure form but associated and identified with its name and cognition, though the object, the name, and the cognition are quite distinct from one another. It is called savitarka, for its object appears in trance-consciousness as associated with the determinations of its name and cognition. (2) Nirvitarka samādhi is the concentration in which the mind identifies itself with a gross object devoid of association with its name and cognition. In it the object is manifested to trance-consciousness in its pure form free from the recollection of its name and the cognition of the object. This kind of conscious trance is free from all determinations. (3) Savicāra samādhi is the concentration in which the mind identifies itself with subtle essences (tanmātras) associated with the notions of time, space, and causality, and endued with manifest qualities, which are apprehended by one cognition. (4) Nirvicāra samādhi is the concentration in which the mind identifies itself with subtle essences devoid of qualities, and yet capable of being endued with them, and free from associations with time, space, and causality. Subtle essences are manifested to trance-consciousness in their true nature devoid of all determinations and cognitions.[2] The subtle

[1] YBh., i, 1; YS., i, 46 & 51.
[2] YS., YBh., i, 42-43.

objects of concentration are not only the subtle essences, but also egoism, intellect, and prakṛti. (5) Ānandānugata samādhi is the concentration in which the mind identifies itself with the gross sense-organs, the products of egoism in which sattva with its bliss predominates. The mental mode 'I am happy' is manifested to trance-consciousness as a direct and immediate apprehension. It does not admit of two kinds, sānanda and nirānanda. (6) Asmitānugata samādhi is the concentration in which the mind identifies itself with egoism which is identified with the self. There is a direct and immediate apprehension of the mental mode 'I am' identified with the pure self. It does not admit of two kinds, sāsmita and nirasmita.[1]

Savitarka, nirvitarka, savicāra, and nirvicāra samādhis are called sabīja samādhi. They are concentration on objects which are their basis. The first two are concentration on gross objects. The last two are concentration on subtle objects. They are kinds of conscious trance. They are called sabīja also because they contain seeds (bīja) of bondage. They are devoid of discriminative knowledge which dispels false knowledge.

Nirvicāra samādhi or concentration on subtle objects free from all determinations of time, space, and causality, purges the mind of the impurities of rajas and tamas and makes it translucent owing to the predominance of sattva. It enables the mind to acquire intuition which clearly apprehends objects in their real nature without temporal order. The intuition (prajñā) of the yogin whose mind is pure and translucent and purged of all afflictions and impurities apprehends only truth (ṛta). So it is called ṛtambharā prajñā. It is free from all taint of falsehood, and directly apprehends all particular qualities of subtle, hidden, and remote objects, and souls. It is different from the knowledge derived from inference and testimony which apprehend generalities only.[2]

Superconscious trance is called nirbīja because it is objectless and devoid of ignorance (avidyā) which is the seed of bondage. It arises from the complete suppression of conscious trance and its dispositions. The dispositions of superconscious

[1] YS., YBh., i, 45 ; TV., YV., i, 17. [2] YS., YBh., i, 46—49.

trances overpower and counteract the dispositions of conscious trances. The dispositions of superconscious trances are destroyed along with the mind which is marged in prakṛti. When the mind is destroyed, the pure self abides in its essential nature and is said to be liberated.

Superconscious trance is objectless, in which there is complete suppression of all mental modes. But their dispositions are left in the mind. This kind of trance can be brought about by supreme detachment which is its means. Steadfast practice of supreme detachment makes the mind objectless, since all desires for objects are extirpated. When the mind is no longer modified into objects, it ceases to have modes. When its modes are destroyed, it seems to be destroyed. This is superconscious trance which is objectless and free from cognitions, feelings, and conations, but not free from dispositions. It cannot be brought about by inferior detachment which is not absolutely free from all attachment to objects. Inferior detachment can generate conscious trance. Superior detachment can generate superconscious trance.

The superconscious trance of disembodied souls and persons whose minds are merged in prakṛti is due to false knowledge (avidyā). Their minds are not destroyed, but they persist with their dispositions and cling to the souls. There is a semblance of apprehension of complete freedom or isolation. There is no extirpation of ignorance in them. They attain these supernatural conditions by concentrating their minds on prakṛti and its evolutes. They attain inferior release resembling heavenly bliss. They may fall from this condition and be born again.[1]

The superconscious trance of the yogins is due to faith, power, recollection of truth, concentration, and intuition. Faith is purity of mind, which protects the aspirant and does him great good. Desirous of discriminative knowledge he makes efforts. These generate meditation on truth. Meditation gives rise to conscious trance. The trance generates discriminative intuition. Steadfast practice of this intuition

[1] YS., YBh., i, 18—19 & 51.

and dispassion for its objects generates superconscious trance. Thus conscious trance is an aid to superconscious trance.

Samādhi can be attained by single-minded devotion to God also. The grace of God falls on His devotee who meditates on Him with extreme devotion. So His devotee attains it without his own efforts. All distractions of attention are completely overcome by devotion to God[1]. The Yoga recognizes the path of devotion to God.

LIBERATION (KAIVALYA)

In empirical consciousness the self wrongly identifies itself with mental modes which assume the forms of objects, and in which it is reflected. But in liberation the self remains in its eseential condition. There is a beginningless relation between the self and the mind (buddhi) due to ignorance on account of which the self erroneously identifies itself with the mind, and is entangled in bondage. Life is full of pain. All is pain to the discriminating person. The threefold pain is due to ignorance. It can be destroyed by right knowledge. Just as medical science treats of diseases, the cause of diseases, the cure of diseases, and the medicines for diseases, so the science of liberation treats of the empirical life of bondage (saṁsāra), the cause of embodied existence, liberation, and the means of liberation. Saṁsāra abounding in misery is to be avoided ; the conjunction of self with prakṛti is the cause of the avoidable saṁsāra ; the absolute extinction of their conjunction is avoidance ; right knowledge is the means of avoidance. Future pain is to be avoided. The conjunction of self with the mind is its cause. Ignorance is the cause of the conjunction. When it is destroyed, the conjunction is destroyed, and the self is liberated and exists in its essential condition. When the self realizes its intrinsic nature, it is liberated.[2]

Discriminative knowledge untainted by ignorance is the means of liberation. When afflictions and their seeds or dispositions are burnt by discriminative knowledge, and are made incapable of producing their effects, the sattva of the

[1] YS., YBh., i, 20, 23 & 29. [2] YBh., i, 3-4 ; ii, 15-17, 23-25.

mind becomes predominant and translucent, and the stream of discriminative knowledge becomes pure and untainted. This is the means of achievement of liberation. When the potencies of afflictions are burnt up, they cannot produce their effects. When they are destroyed along with the mind, the pure self does not suffer threefold pain. When the mind (manas) is merged in prakṛti with its sattva, rajas, and tamas, the self is completely dissociated from the guṇas, and realizes its essential nature as transcendental consciousness. When the self shakes off attachment even to the discriminative knowledge of itself, it attains absolute freedom or isolation. This is the culmination of supreme detachment. When the self acquires supreme dispassion for even discriminative knowledge of itself, it acquires a continuous flow of discriminative knowledge. It destroys all afflictions, actions, and merits and demerits with their dispositions. When they are destroyed, the discriminating self becomes liberated, even while living an embodied life. This is called embodied release. When the dispositions of all mental modes, afflicted and unafflicted, are destroyed, the self acquires superconscious trance. When all mental modes and their dispositions are completely arrested, the self is disentangled from the meshes of prakṛti, becomes pure and isolated, shines forth with its light of intrinsic transcendental consciousness, and becomes omniscient. When the guṇas are merged in prakṛti after accomplishing the purposes of the self, experience and liberation, the self attains disembodied release. It consists in abiding in its essential nature or transcendental consciousness free from empirical consciousness due to mental modes.[1]

The self is eternally pure and liberated. It is said to be entangled in bondage and liberated from bondage in relation to prakṛti. When mental modes are attributed to the self, it is said to be bound. When they are completely destroyed or merged in their cause, prakṛti, they are no longer attributed to the self, and it is said to be liberated. Bondage and liberation of the self are not real.

---

1 YS., YBh., ii, 16, 27 & 50; iv, 29-31, 34 & 55.

CHAPTER XII

THE MĪMĀṀSĀ PHILOSOPHY

Jaimini (400 B.C.) was the author of the *Mīmāṁsā Sūtra*, and the founder of the Mīmāṁsā system. Śavarasvāmin (300 A.D.) wrote a commentary called *Śavara-Bhāṣya*, in which he criticized the views of the different schools of Buddhism. He started his views on the principal philosophical topics, and raised the Pūrva Mīmāṁsā to the status of an independent system. Kumārila Bhaṭṭa (700 A.D.), the founder of the Bhāṭṭa school of Mīmāṁsā, wrote *Ślokavārtika*, *Tantravārtika* and *Tupṭikā*. *Ślokavārtikā* has great philosophical importance. Sucarita Miśra wrote a commentary entitled *Kāśikā* on it. Pārthasārathi Miśra (900 A.D.) wrote a commentary known as *Nyāyaratnākara* on it, *Nyāyaratnamālā*, *Tantraratna*, and *Sāstradīpikā*. Vācaspati Miśra (1000 A.D.) wrote *Nyāyakaṇikā*, a commentary on Maṇḍana Miśra's (680-750 A.D.) *Vidhiviveka*, and *Tattvabindu*. Prabhākara Miśra (700 A.D.), the founder of the Prābhākara school of Mīmāṁsā, wrote a commentary entitled *Bṛhatī* on *Savara-Bhāṣya*. Sālikānātha Miśra (800 A.D.), wrote a commentary known as *Ṛjuvimalāpañcikā* on *Bṛhatī* and *Prakaraṇapañcikā*. The third school of Mīmāṁsā was founded by Murāri Miśra whose works are lost.

The Mīmāṁsā is called the Pūrva Mīmāṁsā, while the Vedānta is called the Uttara Mīmāṁsā. The former is earlier than the latter in the sense that it deals with rituals, while the latter is concerned with knowledge. The performance of rituals leads to the knowledge of the reality. So the Pūrva Mīmāṁsā, called the Mīmāṁsā, is logically prior to the Uttara Mīmāṁsā or the Vedānta, the former being concerned with Dharma, and the latter, with Brahman.

The Mīmāṁsā is called Karma Mīmāṁsā. It mainly deals with the Vedic injunctions about rituals, the rules of interpretation of the texts, which remove the apparent contradictions among them, and harmonize them with one another, and the philosophical justification of the beliefs underlying ritualism.

It believes in the reality of the external world, the reality of the individual souls, and the Law of Karma. It believes in transmigration, heaven and hell, and liberation. It believes in many gods, who are worshipped through sacrifices, and rejects the notion of one God, who creates, preserves and dissolves the world. It frankly advocates atheism, and emphasizes the importance of ritualism. It believes in the eternality and infallibility of the Vedas, and rejects their divine authorship.

INTRINSIC VALIDITY (SVATAḤPRĀMĀṆYA) OF KNOWLEDGE, AND EXTRINSIC INVALIDITY (PARATAḤ APRĀMĀṆYA) OF KNOWLEDGE

Kumārila regards a cognition as a means of valid knowledge (pramāṇa) because it is apprehension. Prabhākara also regards apprehension, which is distinct from recollection, as a means of valid knowledge. Kumārila regards cognizedness (jñātatā) produced by a cognitive act as its result. But Prabhākara identifies pramāṇa with valid knowledge (pramā), and regards a cognition as manifesting itself, and not as inferable from cognizedness of its object. According to him, all cognitions as cognitions are valid, and their invalidity is due to their disagreement with the real nature of their objects, so that wrongness does not belong to the cognitions themselves, but to the objects cognized. Kumārila also regards apprehension as valid knowledge, which can be set aside by its disagreement with the real nature of its object. He regards novelty, non-contradiction and correspondence with the object as the tests of truth. He regards recollection as invalid, because it apprehends what was apprehended already by perception. Prabhākara also excludes recollection from valid knowledge, which is in the nature of apprehension.[1]

Kumārila recognizes the intrinsic validity and the extrinsic invalidity of knowledge. The validity of knowledge arises from the essential nature of its causes untainted by defects, and is known by the knowledge itself. It does not arise from

[1] ŚV., ii, 53 ; ŚD., p. 45 ; Bṛ., p. 103 ; TNR., pp., 2 & 5.

any special excellence in the causes of knowledge, and is not known by any other subsequent knowledge of fruitful action, or of the absence of a contradicting knowledge. Knowledge is valid in itself, and is not validated by any other knowledge. Intrinsic validity of knowledge consists in its being generated by the complement of causal conditions of the knowledge itself, and not by extraneous conditions besides them. The knowledge of validity also is generated by the same aggregate of causal conditions which make the knowledge known. But the invalidity of knowledge arises from defects in the causal conditions of the knowledge, and is known by the knowledge of them, and the knowledge of a contradicting knowledge.[1]

The Nyāya regards both validity and invalidity of knowledge as extrinsic due to excellence and defects of the causes of knowledge, and determined by the knowledge of a fruitful action and a fruitless action respectively. Kumarila criticizes this view. If validity and invalidity of knowledge were due to extraneous conditions, then prior to the knowledge of its validity or invalidity, the knowledge would be neutral and devoid of any logical value. But we never experience neutral knowledge, but only valid knowledge or invalid knowledge. If the validity of a knowledge depended upon the knowledge of excellence of its causes, or the knowledge of its agreement with its object, or the knowledge of a fruitful action, then the validity of the second knowledge also would depend upon some other knowledge, and so on to infinity. If the second knowledge is valid in itself, the first knowledge also is intrinsically valid. The Nyāya regards the validity of knowledge as due to the excellence of its causes. But the so-called excellence of the sense-organs and the like is not known through any means of valid knowledge. The validity of perception is generated by the essential nature of the sense-organs untainted by any defects, but not by any special excellence of them. If there were neutral knowledge, valid knowledge, and invalid knowledge, they would be due to the essential nature, excellence, and defects of its causes respectively. But, in fact,

[1] ŚV., ii. 53, 54, 35 & 187; NRM., p. 51.

we experience only valid knowledge and invalid knowledge. Invalid knowledge arises from causes tainted with defects. So valid knowledge must be held to arise from the essential nature of its causes untainted by defects.[1] The invalidity of knowledge is produced by a deficiency in its causes. It is held by some to be due to the knowledge of its deficiency, and not to its nature.[2]

The validity of knowledge cannot be determined by the knowledge of any special excellence in its cause, or the knowledge of its harmony with the real nature of its object, or the knowledge of a fruitful action. It is determined by the knowledge itsel No special excellence of the causes of knowledge except their essential nature is perceived. Nor can the validity of knowledge be determined by the knowledge of its harmony with the real nature of its object. Validity or truth is harmony of a knowledge with the real nature of its object. The valid knowledge itself cognizes the real nature of its object by its very nature. It does not depend upon another knowledge of harmony to manifest its object, because it does not differ from the first knowledge. Nor can the validity of knowledge be determined by the knowledge of a fruitful action, for unless its validity is determined, it cannot determine the validity of the first knowledge. If it is determined by another knowledge of a fruitful action, it will lead to infinite regress. If it is determined by the first knowledge, then there is mutual dependence : the validity of the first knowledge is determined by the second, and that of the second knowledge is determined by the first. If the latter is determined by itself, the former also should be regarded as determined by itself. Nor can the validity of knowledge be determind by the knowledge of the absence of a contradicting knowledge, since it cannot be exhaustively known by us, because we are not omniscient. Further, it is known either at the time of ascertaining the validity of a knowledge or at a subsequent time. It very often appears at a subsequent time, and hence the knowledge of it

1. ŚV., ii, 35-36 & 44 ; YSP., pp. 21-22.
2. NRM., pp. 48-49 NYR., p. 49.

cannot determine the validity of an antecedent knowledge Hence valid knowledge is produced by the essential nature of its causes untainted by defects, and known by itself. Invalid knowledge is produced by causes tainted with defects, and known by the knowledge of the defects or the knowledge of a contradicting knowledge.[1]

PERCEPTION (PRATYAKṢA)

Kumārila recognizes six pramāṇas, *viz.*, perception, inference, comparison, testimony, presumption, and non-apprehension. Prabhākara rejects negation as an independent category, and non-apprehension as the means of knowing it.

Jaimini defines perception as the knowledge produced in the self by the right intercourse of the sense-organs with existing objects. It is produced by real objects existing at present and acting upon the sense-organs. When there is a right intercourse of the sense-organs with their objects, valid perception is produced. Kumārila says, "Right intercourse is the intercourse of the sense-organs untainted by defects with real objects." Illusions are produced by wrong intercourse. The Mīmāṁsā theory of perception is similar to the Nyāya theory. Only the latter regards the auditory organ as ether limited by the ear-hole, while the former regards it as space limited by the ear-hole.

The Prābhākara defines perception as direct apprehension which relates to an object, the self, and cognition.[2] In every perception of an object, the self, the cognition, and the object are perceived. This is Prabhākara's doctrine of triple perception. In regard to objects, there is the perception of substances, qualities, and universals due to the intercourse of the sense-organs with them. Cognitions are self-manifest. But the self and an object are not self-manifest, but are manifested by a cognition, which is self-aware and which is not manifested by any other cognition.[3]

---

[1] NRM., pp. 52 & 58 ; TNR., pp. 5-7 ; ŚV., NR., ii, 34-37 ; ŚD., YSP., pp. 21-23.

[2] MS., i, 1, 4 ; ŚBh., i, 1, 4 ; ŚV., iv, 38-39, 60, 63, 83-85 ; ŚD., pp. 35-36 ; PP., p-51 ; TNR., p. 9.

[3] PP., pp. 52 & 57.

Kumārila and Prabhākara both recognize two stages of perception, *viz.*, indeterminate perception and determinate perception. Kumārila defines indeterminate perception as simple apprehension of an object, pure and simple, similar to the apprehension of a baby or a dumb person. It apprehends neither the specific characters nor the generic characters, but an individual object only, which is their substrate. It cannot apprehend the generic characters as generic and the specific characters as specific.[1]

Prabhākara defines indeterminate perception as a simple apprehension of the bare nature of an object. It apprehends a substance, a quality, and a genus as bare existences unrelated to each other just after the sense-object-intercourse. Its existence is proved by its self-awareness. It apprehends generic characters and specific characters, but it cannot cognize them as generic and specific, since it is devoid of recollection of other similar and dissimilar objects.[2]

Kumārila defines determinate perception as apprehension of the generic characters of an object as generic, and of its specific characters as specific. It contains an element of recollection of similar and dissimilar objects, and apprehends the community of its object with other similar objects and its distinction from other dissimilar objects. It apprehends an object and its generic and specific properties in a subject-predicate relation. Prabhākara also regards determinate perception as the apprehension of the generic characters and the specific characters of an object as generic and specific respectively. It apprehends its object and its properties in a subject-predicate relation. It apprehends its object as a substance endued with particular qualities and belonging to a certain genus. It contains an element of recollection produced by subconscious impressions. It is immediate apprehension produced by the sense-object-intercourse aided by subconscious impressions.

Kumārila recognizes the validity of indeterminate and determinate perception both. Indeterminate perception reveals

[1] ŚV., iv, 112-13. [2] PP., pp. 54-55; TNR., p. 10.

the bare nature of an object. It is direct apprehension or distinct cognition of an object in itself, unrelated to other objects. Its validity consists in its directness and immediacy; it yields new knowledge not acquired already. Though it is devoid of subject-predicate relation, it is valid. Determinate perception also is valid, since it is direct and immediate knowledge of an object and its properties as related to each other, which is produced by the sense-object-intercourse aided by subconscious impressions. Prabhākara also regards indeterminate perception as valid, since it is sensuous apprehension of an object unrelated to other objects and devoid of recollection, and since its validity is proved by self-awareness. He regards determinate perception also as valid, because it apprehends the subject-predicate relation between its object and its properties, substance, quality and genus, which is not apprehended by indeterminate perception.[1]

INFERENCE (ANUMĀNA)

Śavara defines inference as the knowledge of an unperceived object, which is not present to a sense-organ, from the perception of another object, when a uniform relation has been known to subsist between them. Kumārila explains the relation as invariable concomitance of a sign or reason with a predicate, the former being pervaded by the latter, and being the indicator of the latter, which is indicated. The sign is called vyāpya because it is coextensive with, or narrower than, the predicate in time and place. The predicate is called vyāpaka because it is coextensive with, or wider than, the sign in time and place. The unperceived predicate is inferred from the sign perceived in the subject on the ground of the uniform relation between them known already in similar instances. Smoke was perceived to be accompanied by fire in a kitchen and other similar instances at certain times and in certain places. Smoke is subsequently perceived in a hill exactly in the same form. So the existence of a fire in the same form in

[1] ŚV., iv, 120-125; PP., pp. 54-56; TNR., pp. 10-11; ŚD., pp. 38-39.

a hill is inferred from it. The sign or reason proves the existence of the predicate. The predicate alone (*e.g.*, a fire) is not the object of inference because it is already known. The subject (*e.g.*, a hill) as qualified by the predicate (*e.g.*, a fire) is the object of inference. The subject alone unrelated to the predicate cannot be the object of inference. Nor can the subject and the predicate, singly or collectively, be the object of inference, independently of the other The subject as qualified by the predicate is inferred from the sign perceived in it.[1]

The invariable concomitance, according to Kumārila, is known by repeated observation of concomitance of the two general properties of the reason and the predicate, and sometimes of two particular objects denoted by them, strengthened by the non-observation of contrary instances of their non-concomitance. The observation of concomitance of the reason and the predicate in numerous instances and the non-observation of non-concomitance between them are the means of knowing invariable concomitance. Invariable concomitance is known by induction by simple enumeration.[2]

Does inference involve the fallacy of *petitio principii*? Kumārila regards novelty as an essential characteristic of valid knowledge. It consists in not being apprehended already. It is objected that inference contains the recollection of invariable concomitance, which apprehends what has already been apprehended, and thus invalidates inference. Kumārila argues that though the concomitance of smoke and fire in a kitchen and the like is certainly known in a general way, yet the relation between the present subject (*e.g.*, a hill) and the predicate (*e.g.*, a fire) is not already known. The hill was not already known, far less its fieriness. What is the novel factor, which was not already apprehended, in the inference? The fieriness of smoky objects is already known in a general way. The generic character of fire is already known. The hill is perceived. But

[1] ŚBh., p. 90; ŚV., Anumāna, 4-6, 11-12, 27-28, 47-48; NR.
[2] Ibid, 12; NR.; ŚD., p.62.

the hill as qualified by a fire was not already known by an means of valid knowledge.[1]

Prabhākara slightly amends Śavara's definition of inference He defines it as the knowledge of a predicate in a subjec from the perception of a sign or reason on the ground o the knowledge of a uniform relation between them, if th knowledge is not contradicted by another knowledge The uniform relation may express inherence, coinherenc in the same substance, causality, and the like. Th causal relation between smoke and fire is invariable. Th relation between smell and earth is invariable. The relatio between taste and colour, which inhere in the same substanc is invariable. But the relation between colour and taste is nc invariable. Whenever there is taste, there is colour, for ins tance, in water. But wherever there is colour, there is n taste, for instance, in light. An invariable relation is th ground of inference.[2] Prabhākara also regards induction b simple enumeration as the ground of invariable concomitance He considers inference to be valid, since the knowledge of th predicate existing in the subject is in the nature of appreher sion, though it is produced by the perception of the sign an the recollection of the invariable concomitance.[3]

Prabhākara admits inference for oneself and inference fo others. Both consist of three members, *viz.*, (1) the thesis c proposition, (2) the minor premise which states the reason and (3) universal major premise which states the uniforr relation illustrated by an example. The proposition should b stated first, but the major premise and the minor premise ma be stated in any order. Either the reason or the applicatio may be stated. The conclusion follows necessarily from th general principle of relation between the sign and the predicate A heterogeneous example is needless, since a homogeneou example is enough to illustrate the general principle.[4]

Śavara admits two kinds of inference, *viz.*, pratyakṣatc

---

[1] ŚD., pp. 62-63. [2] PP., pp. 64 & 68 ; TNR., p. 11 ; Bṛ., pp. 90-9

[3] PP., 70-71 ; TNR., pp. 11-12.

[4] TNR., pp. 12-13 ; PP., p. 85.

ṛṣṭasambandha and sāmānyatodṛṣṭasambandha. Kumārila calls
iem dṛṣṭasvalakṣaṇaviṣaya and adṛṣṭasvalakṣaṇaviṣaya. Pra-
hākara calls them dṛṣṭasvalakṣaṇa and adṛṣṭasvalakṣaṇa. In
ie former there is the invariable concomitance between objects
which are perceptible, as smoke and fire. In the latter there
s the invariable concomitance between a perceptible object and
n imperceptible object, as motion of the sun is inferred from
ts change of position in the sky. Prabhākara regards motion
s imperceptible.[1]

COMPARISON (UPAMĀNA)

Śavara defines comparison as the knowledge of similarity
ubsisting in an unperceived object (*e.g.*, a cow) on the per-
eption of a similar object (*e.g.*. a wild cow). Kumārila defines it
s the knowledge of similarity subsisting in a remembered
bject (*e.g.*, a cow) with an object (*e.g.*, a wild cow) perceived.
The cow which was perceived by me in the past in a town is
imilar to this wild cow perceived in a forest at present'. This
s an example of comparison. The Prābhākara also defines
omparison as the knowledge of similarity subsisting in a
remembered object, which arises from the perception of simi-
larity. A person, who perceived a cow in a town in the past,
perceives a wild cow in a forest, perceives its similarity with
the cow, and then knows the similarity of the remembered
cow with the perceived wild cow. The knowledge of slmilarity
of the remembered cow with the perceived wild cow is com-
parison. Prabhākara's view of comparison identical with
that of Kumārila. Both regard similarity as an object of com-
parison. Both regard similarity of a remembered object with
a perceived object as known by comparison.[2]

Comparison is not perception, since its object known to be similar (*e.g.*, a cow) is not in contact with a sense-organ. Nor is comparison inference, since it does not depend upon the knowledge of invariable concomitance between the two objects, which are similar to each other. It may be reduced to an

---

[1] ŚBh., pp. 90 & 100 ; PP., pp. 78-79 ; ŚD., pp. 64 & 69.

[2] ŚBh., i, 1, 5 ; p. 107 ; ŚD., p. 74 ; PP., p. 110.

inference in the following manner. 'The cow is similar to the wild cow, because it is the substrate of similarity with the wild cow, and whatever is the substrate of similarity with another object is found to be similar to it, as one of the twins is similar to the other'. This is wrong, because the cow and the wild cow, which are similar to each other, were never perceived together in the past. So comparison is not inference. Nor is it testimony, since it does not depend upon verbal authority. So it is an independent means of valid knowledge.[1]

PRESUMPTION (ARTHĀPATTI)

Śavara defines presumption as the assumption of an unperceived fact without which inconsistency among perceived facts cannot be reconciled. If we know that Devadatta is alive, and perceive that he is absent from his house, we cannot reconcile his being alive with his non-existence in his house, unless we assume his existence outside his house. The assumption of this unperceived fact which reconciles two apparently inconsistent well-known facts is presumption. It is also called postulation or implication.[2] Kumārila and Prabhākara differ from each other in their views on presumption. Prabhākara maintains that there is an element of doubt in presumption, while Kumārila denies its existence in it. There is doubt, according to Prabhākara, as to the truth of the two perceived facts which cannot be reconciled with each other. The assumption of another fact removes the doubt, and reconciles the apparently inconsistent facts. We know that Devadatta is living, and perceive his absence from his house. This perception generates a doubt about our knowledge that he is living. In order to remove this doubt we assume that he must be outside his house. This presumption removes the doubt as to his living, and reconciles the two apparently inconsistent facts of his living and non-existence in his house.

The element of doubt, according to Prabhākara, distinguishes presumption from inference. There is no element of

[1] ŚD., pp. 75-76; TNR., p. 13; PP., p. 111.

[2] ŚBh., p. 110; ŚD., p. 76; PP., p. 113.

doubt in inference. From the undoubted perception of smoke we can infer the existence of fire. The sign is free from doubt. But the perceived absence of Devadatta from his house leads to the presumption of his living outside his house only when it has made the fact of his living doubtful. Thus there is doubt in presumption, while there is no doubt in inference. Presumption removes doubt, and reconciles two apparently inconsistent facts, and cannot be regarded as inference.

There is no element of doubt, according to Kumārila, in presumption. We perceive the absence of Devadatta from his house. We know for certain that he is alive. In order to reconcile these two well-known and undoubted facts we assume that he has gone out of his house. Without this assumption the apparent inconsistency between his being alive and his absence from his house cannot be reconciled. If the knowledge of his living were doubtful, it could not be the sound basis of presumption.[1] It removes the mutual inconsistency of two well-ascertained facts. The presumption of a third fact reconciles the two well-known facts perceived, which appear to be inconsistent with each other.

NON-APPREHENSION (ANUPALABDHI)

Kumārila regards non-apprehension as the means of knowing the non-existence of an object, which cannot be known by perception, inference, comparison, testimony and presumption. Non-existence is real and apprehended by non-apprehension. The non-existence of curd in milk is prior non-existence. The non-existence of milk in curd is posterior non-existence. The non-existence of a horse in a cow is mutual non-existence. The non-existence of horns in a hare is absolute non-existence. If non-apprehension were not recognized as an independent means of knowledge, there would be the existence of curd in milk, of milk in curd, of a jar in a piece of cloth, and of horns in a hare. Non-apprehension is non-production of perception and the like, but it is a cognition or a modification of the self. It is a means of valid knowledge, since it cognizes non-existence

---

[1] PP., pp. 113-15; ŚD., pp. 77-79.

which cannot be known by any other means of valid knowledge. How is the non-existence of a jar on the ground cognized? First, the ground, which is the locus of the non-existence of a jar, is perceived. Then the jar, the counter-positive entity of the non-existence, is remembered. Then a purely mental cognition of the non-existence of the jar, which is independent of the sense-object-intercourse, produced. A person first perceives the bare ground, then remembers a jar which existed on it. Then he cognizes the non-existence of the jar on the ground by means of non-apprehension.[1]

Non-apprehension being negative in character, cannot cognize positive existence. Perception, inference, comparison, testimony and presumption being positive in character, cannot cognize non-existence. Non-apprehension is their negation which cognizes the non-existence of their objects. Non-existence is cognized by a means of knowledge similar to itself, or negative in character.[2] It is an object of appropriate non-apprehension.

But Prabhākara does not recognize non-apprehension as an independent means of valid knowledge. Nor does he recognize the category of non-existence which may be cognized by non-apprehension. He rejects both non-existence as an ontological reality, and non-apprehension as a distinct mode of knowing it. When we perceive the existence of a jar on the ground, we perceive the existence of the ground as related to the existence of the jar. But when the jar is absent, we perceive the bare ground only. The non-existence of the jar is nothing but the existence of the mere locus, the ground. The perception of the mere locus is erroneously called non-apprehension by Kumārila. The so-called non-apprehension of the non-existence of the jar on the ground is nothing but perception of its mere locus, the bare ground. The perception of the bare ground is a positive cognition due to the contact of a sense-organ with the ground. It is not of a negative character and in the nature

[1] ŚV., Abhāva. 1, 2-5, 11 & 27 : ŚD., pp. 12, 17, 26-28.

[2] Ibid, 46-47, 54-55 ; ŚD., pp. 83-87.

of non-apprehension. Every kind of valid knowledge is invariably accompanied by an object. There is no distinct object of non-apprehension, and, consequently, no distinct means of knowing it. So non-apprehension is not an independent means of valid knowledge.[1]

Non-existence is not cognized by perception, since there is no intercourse of a sense-organ with it. Nor can it be said to be cognized by indeterminate perception at first, and then remembered by determinate perception. The non-existence of an object can never be cognized by indeterminate perception, since it is non-relational apprehension. So it cannot be remembered by determinate perception. Nor can non-existence be inferred from the knowledge of a sign, because the invariable concomitance between them is not known. Further, no sign pervaded by non-existence is known. Nor is non-existence known by testimony, comparison and presumption, because in the knowledge of non-existence there is neither knowledge of a verbal statement, nor knowledge of similarity, nor knowledge of inconsistency between two perceived facts which may be reconciled by presumption. It is known by appropriate non-apprehension, which is a distinct means of valid knowledge.[2]

TESTIMONY (ŚABDA)

Kumārila defines testimony as the knowledge of objects, which are supersensible, derived from sentences by comprehending the meanings of the constituent words. Testimony is verbal authority. He divides testimony into human and superhuman. The former is the testimony of trustworthy persons, while the latter is the testimony of the Vedas. The former is valid, if it is uttered by persons of trustworthy character, while the latter is valid in itself. Again, testimony may either give us knowledge of existing objects, as 'a jar exists'; or, it may direct us to perform an action, as 'bring a jar'. The former gives us the knowledge of existential propositions, while the latter gives us the knowledge of injunctive

[1] P.P., pp. 118, 122-23, 125, 128-32; TNR., p. 18.

[2] ŚD., pp. 86-87; TNR., p. 17.

propositions. Vedic testimony gives us the knowledge of duties. Dharma is supersensible, and cannot be perceived through the sense-organs. Inference, comparison, presumption and non-apprehension also cannot yield the knowledge of Dharma, since they presuppose perception. The knowledge that the performer of the Agniṣṭoma sacrifice will go to heaven cannot be given by them. Vedic testimony is the only source of our knowledge of duties relating to supersensible entities. The Vedic texts which enjoin us to perform certrin actions which lead to beneficial results are authoritative. Injunctive sentences in the Vedas are authoritative, and prohibitions are injunctions in disguise. The other Vedic texts are authoritative in so far as they help persons perform their duties.

Kumārila maintains that human testimony is valid, if the sentence is uttered by a person of trusworthy character, and that it is invalid, if it is spoken by a person of untrustworthy character. Human testimony has no intrinsic validity. It may be vitiated by carelessness, deliberate desire to cheat, and other defects of the speakers. But Vedic testimony has intrinsic validity, since the Vedas are impersonal and eternal, and not human compositions tainted with the defects of the speakers. Non-contradiction is a test of truth. A knowledge, which is contradicted by a subsequent valid knowledge, is invalid. But the Vedic injunctions are never contradicted by any subsequent valid knowledge. The objects denoted by them can never be known by perception, inference and other means of valid knowledge. Hence Vedic testimony is valid in itself.[1]

A word consists of letters which are eternal. It denotes a class or genus, and not an individual. It denotes an individual indirectly through a class denoted by it. A word has a permanent relation to an object, which is impersonal. It is neither created by God nor by persons. It is only learnt from the speech and actions of the elders acquainted with the meanings of words.[2]

Prabhākara regards testimony as the knowledge of super-

[1] ŚV., Śabda, 109 ; ŚD., pp. 72, 87-88.

[2] ŚV., Ākṛti, 4 & 18 ; ŚD., p. 117.

sensible objects depending on the knowledge of words. There is no other testimony than scriptural testimony. The supersensible object is Apūrva, supersensuous Ought, Categorical Imperative, or Duty. The entire Vedas are the means of knowing Apūrva or Duty. Apūrva or the moral command is the object of Vedic testimony, which cannot be known by any other means of valid knowledge.[1] The Vedas are not composed by any person, human or divine. The sentences in the Vedas manifest their meanings by their inherent powers. They enlighten us on Apūrva, which is incomprehensible by the human reason. Vedic sentences are intrinsically valid, and always yield valid cognitions, since they are impersonal and devoid of human origin. The entire Vedas which prescribe the Moral Law are intrinsically valid. The Moral Law is Ought or Duty, which is realizable by human volition.

Prabhākara includes human testimony in inference. Sentences uttered by persons cannot by themselves guarantee the real existence of objects which they mean. They often contain great falsehood and are not in harmony with real objects. The validity or the invalidity of a sentence spoken by a person is inferred from the trustworthy or untrustworthy character of the person who utters it. The knowledge of the person is the cause, and the sentence uttered by the person is the effect. The effect is inferred from the cause. So human testimony is included in inference.[2]

Words denote their objects by nature. Their denotative power is natural and permanent, and not determined by convention, human or divine. The Nyāya maintains that God fixes the meanings of words by convention. But the Mīmāṁsā does not believe in the conventional meanings of words. They have natural and eternal relations to the objects denoted by them. Prabhākara regards the meanings of proper names as fixed by convention, but does not consider the meanings of common words to be determined by convention, which are independent of human agency.

---

[1] PP., 17, 91 & 94 ; Br.; p. 106.

[2] PP., pp. 95-97, 105.

The Vedas are neither created by God nor composed by seers; they are unproduced and eternal. The words in the Vedic texts denote their proper objects by their very nature. Their denotative power does not depend on any convention determined by God or men. The Vedas are self-sufficient and independent of all personal agency. They mainly enjoin the performance of certain duties, which generates an apūrva, an invisible subtle potency, leading to a desirable result. No person can have any knowledge of duties independently of the Vedas. Hence the denotative powers of the Vedic words are eternal and independent of conventions, human or divine.[1]

Both Prabhākara and Kumārila maintain that a word denotes a class, and indirectly refers to an individual through it. All injunctions would be meaningless, if words did not refer to classes. The word 'cow' denotes the class 'cow'. The generic idea of 'cow' represents the class 'cow'. A word cannot denote a single individual, an aggregate of individuals, or all individuals. If a single individual only were denoted by it, there could be no eternal relation between it and its object, and no action would be possible, since one could not make sure which individual was meant by the word. Nor can it denote an aggregate of individuals, since all the individuals cannot be known, and, consequently, their aggregate cannot be known. Even if it could be known, the meaning of the word would constantly change, since some individuals are born and others perish. Nor can a word denote all individuals, since they can never be known, and, consequently, its meaning can never be fully comprehended. Hence a word denotes a class at first, then an individual through it.[2]

THEORIES OE ERROR: PSYCHOLOGY OF ILLUSION

Kumārila regards an error or illusion as a false perception or misperception of one object as a different one, and advocates the doctrine of Anyathākhyāti or Viparītakhyāti

---

[1] PSPM., pp. 54-56; PP., pp. 90-91, 93, 99, 161-70.

[2] NRM., p. 121; NYR., p. 123.

like the Nyāya. In the illusion 'this is silver' 'this' or the brightness of a nacre, which it has in common with silver, is perceived owing to its intercourse with the visual organ ; then 'silver' is remembered owing to the revival of the subconscious impression of silver. The nacre then is *perceived* as silver owing to some defect, though it is remembered. He regards the illusion as a single false perception. He regards it as positive false knowledge due to false identification of the remembered element with the perceived element, or false perception of identity of the remembered element with the perceived element. The cognition of identity of the nacre present to the visual organ with the silver remembered is of the nature of perception due to its intercourse with the visual organ, which does not cease to function at the time.

Kumārila maintains that an illusion as a cognition *per se* is valid, but that its validity is destroyed by the subsequent knowledge of its disagreement with its object and of defects in its causes. If a defect in its cause cannot be found even after a careful search, or a sublating cognition does not contradict it, a cognition is valid. But if a cognition is contradicted by the knowledge of the contrary nature of its object, or superseded by the knowledge of some defect in its cause, it is invalid. But an invalid cognition is valid as cognition *per se* : its intrinsic validity is destroyed by the extraneous conditions mentioned above.[1]

Prabhākara advocates the theory of Vivekākhyāti or Akhyāti. In the illusion 'this is silver' 'this' is perceived, and 'silver' is remembered ; there is non-discrimination of the two psychoses from each other. Non-discrimination is non-apprehension of distinction. The distinction between the perceived element 'this' and the remembered element 'silver' is not apprehended. Non-apprehension of the distinction leads to the illusion 'this is silver'. It is not a single psychosis of false perception of one object as another as Kumārila maintains. The two elements of perception and recollection

1 ŚD., pp. 49-50 ; ŚV., ii, 53.

are not distinguished from each other owing to lapse of memory. When a nacre is perceived as silver, only the common quality of them, *viz.*, brightness, is perceived, since it predominates over the peculiar qualities of the nacre. Then the perception of brightness revives the subconscious impression of silver owing to similarity. But the recollection of silver does not appear to be recollection owing to obscuration of memory due to a defect of the mind. Though silver is remembered, it is not remembered as 'that'—something perceived in the past owing to lapse of memory. The illusion is not experienced as 'this is *that* silver', but as 'this is silver'. Non-distinction prompts the self to put forth an effort to appropriate the illusory silver. When the illusion is said to be contradicted by a sublating cognition, the distinction between the two elements is apprehended, and, consequently, the self does not put forth any effort to appropriate the silver.

Prabhākara defines valid knowledge as apprehension, and regards all apprehension as valid. In the illusion 'this is silver' the perception of 'this' is valid, since it is not contradicted, and the recollection of 'silver' is invalid, because it is recollection and contradicted by a sublating cognition.[1] But a cognition, which is found to disagree with the real nature of its object, *as* cognition, is valid. Prabhākara does not recognize error as error. He does not distinguish between truth and error from the logical point of view. But he distinguishes between them from the practical point of view. Knowledge is subservient to practical action. The knowledge that leads to successful action is true, and that which leads to unsuccessful action is false. We cannot speak of truth or falsity of knowledge prior to action prompted by it. We cannot brand a knowledge as false until it leads to unsuccessful action. True knowledge is not the knowledge that apprehends the real nature of its object, but it is the knowledge which is capable of a fruitful action. When the object that is manifested to

[1] PP., pp. 43 & 82.

consciousness is attained by an action prompted by it, it is regarded as true.[1] Thus Prabhākara distinguishes between truth and error from the standpoint of practical utility.

KUMĀRILA : THE CATEGORIES

Kumārila divides categories into positive and negative. He recognizes four positive categories, *viz.*, substance, quality, action, and community. He admits four kinds of non-existence, *viz.*, prior non-existence, posterior non-existence, mutual non-existence, and absolute non-existence. He rejects the Vaiśeṣika categories of particularity and inherence.

A substance is the substratum of dimension and quality. A substance and a quality are produced at the same moment, and non-different from each other, since both of them are produced by the same causal conditions taken together. They are produced at the same moment and found to be related to each other as cause and effect.[2]

Kumārila admits eleven substances, *viz.*, earth, water, fire, air, ether, self, mind (manas), time, space, darkness, and sound. Earth has smell. The sense of smell is made of earth. The body is made of earth. Water has natural fluidity. The sense of taste is made of water. Fire has touch. The visual organ is made of fire. Air has touch, but no colour. Darkness has colour, but no touch. It has black colour, which is manifested in the absence of light. It can be apprehended by the visual organ only. Ether is one, eternal, partless, and ubiquitous. Time and space also are eternal, partless, and indivisible. Time, space, and ether are perceptible, because they are ubiquitous, like the self, while they are not manas. Further, if they were not perceptible, then their existence would be disproved, because it cannot be proved by any other means of valid knowledge.[3] Time is perceived by the six sense-organs. 'It is morning'. 'It is evening'. These notions are

---

[1] PP., pp. 39 & 43.

[2] ŚV., Abhāva, 2-4 : MM., p. 148-50.

[3] MM., pp. 151, 155-56, 159, 186-87.

produced by the visual organ assisted by the sight of the sun-rise. Space too is perceptible, because the notions of east, west, up, down, forward, backward, etc., are produced by the visual organ, and have space as their content. Time and space are perceptible as qualifications of other substances. Space is one and ubiquitous. It appears to be many and limited on account of its limiting adjuncts. Ether is one and ubiquitous. But it appears to be limited on account of its limiting adjuncts. It is perceptible. The Nyāya view that darkness is the absence of light is wrong, because darkness has qualities and motions, and because it is perceived as existent. So it is certainly a positive entity.[1]

Earth, water, fire, air, and darkness are composed of atoms. The whole is distinct from the parts. The perception 'this jar is one and gross', which is valid and uncontra dicted, proves the existence of the whole distinct from the parts. The whole does not inhere in the parts, since there is no inherence. It is different and non-different from them. There is identity-in-difference between them. The whole is not a different substance from its parts. It is a different condition of them. Owing to a particular conjunction, they become one substance of a large dimension. As parts they are many, and as a whole it is one. A cloth is one, while the yarns are many.

The Bhāṭṭa Mīmāṁsaka maintains that composite things are made of atoms, which are of the dimension of motes in a sun-beam. They correspond to the traids of the Nyāya-Vaiśeṣika, which are perceptible. The minuter primary atoms of the Nyāya-Vaiśeṣika are non-existent, since there is no means of valid knowledge by which they can be known. Atoms of smaller size than motes in a sun-beam are not perceived.[2]

Sound is an eternal and ubiquitous substance, which is perceived by the auditory organ, and which has the genus of sound. It is self-existent and devoid of a substratum. It is directly perceived by the auditory organ through a direct relation. It is ubiquitous, because it is an intangible, partless

[1] MM., pp. 160, 163, 189-91 ; ŚD., pp. 140, 45-46.

[2] ŚD., pp. 105-07 ; MM., pp. 163-66,

substance, which is not a cause. It has a large dimension, since the same sound is simultaneously perceived by many persons in different places. It is not contradicted by any sublating valid knowledge. So sound is all-pervading. Sound is made manifest and unmanifest by the proximity and remoteness of a manifesting condition. It is eternal, for it is not produced. The vocal organs do not produce it, but only manifest it. Their activity is its manifesting agent. The audible sound manifests sound which is eternal. It has different degrees of loudness, and transfers these attributes to the sound manifested by it. Sound is an eternal and ubiquitous substance. There are two kinds of sounds, significant and non-significant. Audible sounds produced by beating a drum are non-significant. Letters manifested by the audible sound produced by the activity of the vocal organs are significant. A word is a collection of sounds, which signifies a single object. It denotes a genus directly, and an individual by implication. If sounds were not eternal, the Vedas, which consist of sentences, would not be eternal.[1]

The mind (manas) is the internal organ through which cognition, pleasure and other qualities of the self are perceived. It is all-pervasive and motionless.[2] It is not atomic in dimension as the Nyāya-Vaiśeṣika maintains. It is all-pervasive, because it is an intangible substance, which is neither a cause nor an effect, and because it is the substratum of a conjunction, which is the non-inherent cause of knowledge, like the self. It is all-pervading, and, consequently, motionless, like ether. Though it is all-pervading, it is limited by the entire body, and serves as the organ of internal perception. Both self and manas are all-pervading, and their conjunction is natural and not produced by an action.

A quality is distinct from action, has the genus of quality, and is not a material cause. There are twenty-four qualities : colour, taste, smell, touch, number, dimension, distinctness, conjunction, disjunction, remoteness, proximity, weight, fluidity, viscidity, cognition, pleasure, pain, desire, aversion,

[1] MM., pp. 218-28. [2] MM., p. 214.

volition, impression, audible sound (dhvani), manifestness (prākaṭya), and potency. Audible sound is a quality of air, which manifests sound. An object is the substrate of manifestness, which is its qualification called manifestation. It determines what becomes an object of knowledge. It is known by perception through the relation of identity with what is in conjunction. Though it abides in substances only, it abides indirectly in genus, quality and action owing to the relation of identity with them, and also in non-existence of which they are counter-positive entities. They become objects of knowledge through the manifestness of substances. Distinctness exists in all substances, eternal and non-eternal.[1]

Potency abides in substance, quality and action, and has the genus of potency. It is known by presumption and from Vedic testimony. It is empirical and scriptural. The first, *e.g.*, the power of burning in fire is known by presumption. The second, *e.g.*, the potency of a sacrifice to produce happiness in heaven is known from injunctions of the Vedas only. The potency of burning abides in a substance (*e.g.*, fire). Potency is a quality which is known by presumption. It is not a distinct category.

Action or motion abides in non-pervasive substances only, is perceptible, and the cause of conjunction and disjunction. It is of five kinds, *viz.*, upward motion, downward motion, contraction, expansion, and locomotion. Kumārila recognizes also action in the self. Physical motion is not the only form of action. Motion in a substance, which brings about conjunction and disjunction in space, is perceived.[2]

Kumārila admits the existence of generality which is the cause of the knowledge of non-difference among different individuals. 'This is a cow'. 'That also is a cow'. There is the genus of cow in different individual cows, which is common to them. Community is the ground of assimilation, while individuals are the ground of discrimination. There would be no assimilation, if there were no community in the

[1] MM., pp. 214-17, 256-57, 240, 242-43.

[2] ŚV., Ātmavāda, 74; MM., p. 277; ŚD., p. 71.

individuals. A single community subsists in many individuals. It cannot be said to subsist in them either in its entirety or in its parts, since it is devoid of parts. But we perceive it to subsist in them. There is no inherence between a universal and an individual, since there is no inherence. Further, inherence is said to be a relation between two inseparable entities, which is the cause of the notion 'this subsists in it.' But we have such a perception as 'this is a cow', and not as 'the genus of cow' subsists in this cow. There is identity-in-difference between the universal and the individual. The universal is not entirely different from the individual. Nor is it entirely identical with it. It is partly different from, and partly identical with, the individual. Generality and individuality subsist in the same locus the individual : this proves their non-difference or identity. 'The genus of cow' and the 'cow' are not synonymous : this proves their difference. Hence there is no contradiction between difference and non-difference between the universal and the individual.[1]

Kumārila denies the category of inherence. It is said to be a relation between two inseparable entities, substance and quality, substance and action, the whole and the parts, and the universal and the individual, which is the cause of the notion 'this subsists in it'. Kumārila regards inherence as essential identity (tādātmya). If it is different from the relata such as the universal and the individual, it cannot subsist as a relation between them. If, on the other hand, it is identical with them, they cannot be different from each other. Inherence is identity between two inseparable entities, and a particular phase of them. If it were an external relation between substance and quality, or the like, which related them to each other, then it would require another inherence to relate it to each of the two relata, and so on to infinity. This infinite regress can be avoided, if inherence is regarded as identity in essence. Further, inherence is said to be inseparable relation, which is

[1] ŚD., pp. 99-101 ; ŚD., Ākṛtivāda, 52-62 ; Vanavāda, 24, 32-34 ; MM., p. 229.

the absence of separable relation. Separable relation is either having separate movements or subsisting in different substrates. Parts of a whole can have movements, though the whole is motionless. The whole subsists in its parts, which subsist in their parts. They subsist in different substrates. The genus subsists in an individual, which subsists in its parts. So there is a separable relation between the whole and its parts, and the genus and the individual. There is no inherence between them.[1]

Kumārila rejects the categories of potency, number and similarity recognized by Prabhākara. Potency is an unperceived quality in a substance, which is inferred from its effect. It is generated along with the substance. Number is a quality. Similarity is a quality which consists in the possession of the same arrangement of many parts by two substances. It is not a distinct category, since it admits of degrees.[2] Thus potency, number and similarity are not distinct categories.

PRABHĀKARA : THE CATEGORIES

Prabhākara recognizes the eight categories of substance, quality, action, community, inherence, potency, number, and similarity. Substance is the substrate of qualities. There are nine substances : earth, water, fire, air, ether, self, manas, time, and space. Earth, water, fire, and air are visible and tangible. Ether is not visible, since it is colourless. It appears to be white owing to the particles of fire in it, and appears to be dark at night owing to the absence of light. It is imperceptible, but inferred as the substratum of sound. Air is perceptible. It is neither hot nor cold, but it appears to be hot owing the particles of fire in it, and appears to be cool owing to the particles of water in it. Earth, water, fire, and air are perceptible in the non-atomic state. But ether, time, space, and manas are only inferable. Darkness is not a substance, but mere absence of light.[3] There are twenty-two qualities :

[1] ŚV., NR., iv, 146-50 ; ŚD., p. 100.
[2] MM., pp. 258-63, 240 ; ŚD., p. 104.
[3] PP., pp. 143-45, 77-78 ; TNR., pp. *20-21*.

colour, taste, smell, touch, dimension, distinctness, conjunction, disjunction, remoteness, proximity, weight, fluidity, viscidity, impression, sound, cognition, pleasure, pain, desire, aversion, volition, and merit. Action or motion is imperceptible ; it is inferred from a series of conjunction and disjunction.

Generality subsists in the individuals entirely, and is distinct from them. It is perceived by the sense-organs. It is common to many individuals which are different from one another. It is the ground of our conception of non-difference among different individuals. It is the basis of their assimilation. The genus is different from the individuals in which it inheres. There is a relation of subsistence (paratantratā) or inherence between them. When an individual is born, a new relation of inherence is generated, which relates it to the genus which subsists in the other individuals of the same class. When an individual dies, the relation of inherence between it and the genus is destroyed. Prabhākara admits the generalities of substance, quality and action. But he denies the reality of the highest genus or beinghood, which is recognized by the Vaiśeṣika. An individual thing has its specific existence, but no mere existence or beinghood. So Prabhākara denies the existence of the highest genus or beinghood.

Prabhākara admits the reality of subsistence or inherence which is the relation between two inseparable entities. It is eternal in eternal substances, and non-eternal in non-eternal substances. There are many inherences. Inherence is produced, when an effect is produced, which inheres in its material cause. It is not perceptible, but always inferred.[1]

Prabhākara recognizes the category of potency or power. It is the imperceptible energy which produces an effect and inferred from its effect. Fire has the power of burning, which either overpowered or destroyed by a fire-extinguishing gem, a charm, or an unguent, when it does not burn. When the effect is never destroyed, the causal power is destroyed. When it is produced on removal of these counteracting agents, the causal power is overpowered. It is eternal in eternal substances, and

[1] TNR., p. 21-23 ; PP., p. 17.

non-eternal in non-eternal substances. It is generated along with the transient substances in which it subsists. Potency differs from velocity in that the latter is transient in eternal things also, and dependent on other causes in transient things[1].

Number is not a substance, since it subsists in qualities. There are two odours, three touches, and the like. The subsistence of number in qualities cannot be said to be figurative, since its subistence in them in a primary sense is not contradicted. The argument that it cannot abide in them because it is a quality is wrong, since its being a quality cannot be proved. It is not a quality of a substance, since it abides in many substances like a genus. Nor is it a movement, since it is perceptible, unlike a movement. Nor is it a generality, since it is non-eternal. Hence number is a distinct category.

Similarity is not a substance, since it abides in qualities and motions. An odour is perceived as similar to another odour, and a motion is inferred as similar to another motion. So it is neither a quality nor a motion. Nor is it a generality, for it is not the cause of the experience of being common to many entities. It subsists in generalities, but a generality does not exist in generalities. We know similarity between the genus of a cow and that of a buffalo. So similarity is different from generality.

Inherence is a kind of relation between a substance and its quality or motion, the genus and the individual, and a material cause and its effect. So similarity is not inherence. It is a distinct category which is perceived in perceptible things through the perception of the qualities, actions, and parts as common to two or more things. It is inferred in imperceptible things from many common features.[2]

Prabhākara rejects the Vaiśeṣika category of particularity, which is said to abide in an eternal substance, that distinguishes it from another eternal substance possessing common qualities and actions. But distinctness can distinguish an eternal substance from another eternal substance having similar

[1] PP., pp. 81-82 ; TNR., p. 23.

[2] TNR., pp. 23-24 ; PP., pp. 110-11.

qualities and actions. So particularity is not different from distinctness, and so not a distinct category.[1]

Both Kumārila and Prabhākara recognize the reality of the external world independent of our cognitions. The Mīmāṁsā does not believe in the periodic creation and dissolution of the world by God. Production and destruction of things are constant. The parts of the world have an origin and an end, but the world, as a whole has no origin and an end in time. There is no creator or destroyer of the world.[2]

KUMĀRILA : THE NATURE AND KNOWLEDGE OF THE SELF

Kumārila regards the self as different from the body, the sense-organs, and cognitions. It is ubiquitous, eternal, incorporeal, immaterial and transmigrating. It is a knower, enjoyer, and active agent. It is the substrate of cognition, pleasure, pain, desire, aversion, volition, impression, merit and demerit, which are its modes. It undergoes modifications, and is yet eternal. Its modal changes do not compromise its eternal nature. Cognition is an action or a modal change of the self, which is not perceptible, but inferable from cognizedness (jñātatā) or manifestness (prākaṭya) of the object. In deep sleep there is no cognition, but there is a potency of cognition. There is no pleasure in deep sleep. The so-called recollection of pleasure during deep sleep on waking from it is due to the absence of pain. The self is of the nature of potency of cognition.

Kumārila sometimes speaks of the self as self-illumined. It is cognized by itself, and not by others. Sometimes he speaks of it as an object of 'I'-consciousness. When it is spoken of as imperceptible, it means that it is apprehended by itself, and cannot be perceived by others. Thus Kumārila regards the self as both self-illumined and an object of 'I'-consciousness, which always points to the mere existence of the self, which is of the nature of pure consciousness. But Pārthasārathi Miśra, a follower of Kumārila, regards the self as

[1] PP., p. 110 ; TNR., pp. 22-23.

[2] J. Sinha : *Indian Realism*, Ch. VI ; ŚV., Sambandhākṣepaparihāra, 42-60, 113-16.

an object of 'I'-consciousness or mental perception. He denies its self-luminosity on the ground that it is not manifested in dreamless sleep. So it is an object of mental perception. 'I'-consciousness is mental perception.[1]

But how can the self be subject and object at the same time? The self, according to Kumārila, is a conscious substance; as conscious, it is the subject,, and, as a substance, it is the object.[2] It is the knower through the conscious part, and the object of knowledge through the unconscious part.[3] It is transformed into cognition, pleasure and the like through it.

The self is distinct from the body, which is its organ of experience. It is material and unconscious, and cannot act by itself. It can act only when it is supervised by the conscious self, and realize its ends. The self is immaterial and devoid of physical motion. It assumes a particular body in accordance with its merits and demerits acquired in the past birth, and directs its actions. When the unseen potencies are exhausted, it ceases to have any body and direct its actions, and attains liberation. Though the self is devoid of physical motion, it can transmigrate into another body, since it is ubiquitous. It can produce physical motion through its body.

Kumārila cites the Sāṁkhya arguments for the distinction of the self from the body. The former is pure, simple, incorporeal, immaterial, and disembodied, while the latter is impure, complex, corporeal, meterial, and embodied. The body is an aggregate and an arrangement of parts, which exist for a conscious self, and realize its purpose. The self is a conscious knower, which has experience through its body with a particular arrangement of parts to realize its ends. It is ubiquitous, eternal, conscious and active, while its body is limited, perishable, unconscious and inactive. The former is the knower, while the latter is a known object. The former is imperceptible to others, while the latter is perceptible to them. So the self is distinct from the body. Its identification with the body is due to false knowledge.

---

[1] ŚV., Ātmavāda, 7, 8, 20, 22, 29, 107, 110, 126, 142-43, 147; Tantravārtika, E. T., p. 516; ŚD., p. 122-24; MM., p. 80.

[2] NM., p. 430 [3] Siddhāntavindu.

Pleasure is inferred from a beaming face, which may be said to be a quality of the body. But it is not its quality, since it is not perceived inside the body when it is dissected. We can perceive the colour of its interior, but we cannot perceive pleasure. But pleasure is a quality, which must abide in a substance, and the substance in which it abides is the self. Similarly, cognition, desire, volition and the like are the qualities of the self, which is their substrate. Further, consciousness cannot be a quality of the material elements of the body either distributively or collectively. Earth, water, and the other elements separately do not possess consciousness, and, consequently, cannot possess it collectively. If consciousness belonged to all the elements of the body, then all being equal could not be related to one another. If it belonged to one of them, the other elements would be subordinate to it, which is contradicted by experience. Hence consciousness cannot be a quality of the body, which cannot be a knower. Life is not a quality of the body, since it is destroyed when the body is not destroyed, or a contradictory quality is not produced in it. So life must be due to an effort of the self which guides the body. It has life so long as it is animated by the soul.

The self is distinct from the sense-organs. It is the conscious agent of them, which are its unconscious instruments. They cannot function without its guidance. Even on the destruction of a sense-organ, the self can remember objects perceived in the past through it. It can synthesize the sensations derived through the different sense-organs. It is eternal and all-pervading, while they are perishable and of limited magnitude. The mind (manas) cannot be the knower, since it is the internal organ by which the self can perceive its qualities. It is an unconscious instrument of the self which is its agent. So the self is distinct from the manas and the external sense-organs.[1]

PRABHĀKARA : THE NATURE AND KNOWLEDGE OF THE SELF.

Prabhākara regards the self as distinct from the body, the sense-organs and cognitions. It is eternal, ubiquitous and

[1] ŚV., Ātmavāda, 7, 73, 74, 76-79, 94-101, 111-14, 125-28, 147 ; ŚD., pp. 119-24.

manifold. There is a distinct self in each body. It is manifested in all cognitions of objects. It is unconscious, since consciousness does not constitute its essence. It is known as the substrate of the cognition 'I know', but not as of the nature of consciousuess. The self is a substance, which is not of the nature of consciousness, but a substrate of consciousness. Cognition is not a modification of the self, as Kumārila maintains, but its quality. The self is manifested as the knower of all cognitions of objects. It is a knower or subject, and apprehended as such and never apprehended as an object.

The self has nine special qualities, *viz.*, cognition, pleasure, pain, desire, aversion, volition, merit, demerit, and impression, which are produced by its conjunction with manas, the internal organ. Cognition is self-aware. It is apprehension and recollection. Pleasure, pain, desire, aversion and volition are apprehended by mental perception. Pleasure is a positive feeling, and not a mere negation of pain. Impression is a peculiar quality of the soul, which is the cause of recollection. It is imperceptible but inferable from recollection. Unseen power is merit and demerit, which are known from Vedic testimony. The self is the substrate of these nine specific qualities.[1] Prabhākara's conception of the self resembles the Nyāya-Vaiśeṣika view.

Prabhākara regards the self as the inherent cause of cognitions, which depend upon the conjunction of the self with manas as the non-inherent cause. This mind-soul-contact is generated by a movement of the mind (manas) due to the effort of the soul or its merit and demerit produced by its previous actions. These efforts and merits and demerits are the effects of previous mind-soul-contacts and so on without a beginning. The action of the mind is not the inherent cause of cognitions, since it will require another action of the mind as its non-inherent cause. So the self is the inherent cause of cognitions which inhere in it, and the mind-soul-contact is their non-inherent cause.

---

[1] PP., pp. 141 & 149 ; Siddhāntavindu.

The manas is the internal organ of the self, which is of atomic dimension. It is the organ of the perception of pleasure, pain, desire, aversion, and volition. It supervises the functions of the external sense-organs. It is eternal and capable of quick movement. Its conjunction with a soul depends upon its beginningless merits and demerits.

The self is the enjoyer ; the body is the vehicle of enjoyment ; the sense-organs are the instruments of experience ; the external objects and pleasure, etc., are the objects of experience ; enjoyment is a feeling of pleasure, and suffering is a feeling of pain. These five kinds of entities exhaust the reality. The self is neither atomic nor coextensive with the body, but ubiquitous. It is the inherent cause of all its qualities, while the mind-soul-contact is their non-inherent cause. This conjunction subsists in the soul and the manas which cannot exist apart from the body. The qualities of the soul are not perceived apart from the body which is animated by it. The body is capable of movement, but the soul is motionless, and comes into contact with all things without movement. So it is all-pervading. But though it is ubiquitous, it can experience its qualities in connection with its own body which it has acquired by its merits and demerits. The sense-organs are parts of the body. The soul can have experience through its own body and sense-organs only, which are the fit media of its experience. It cannot have experience through others' bodies and sense-organs.[1] Though it is ubiquitous, it comes into contact with the atomic manas and produces cognitions. If the manas were ubiquitous like the soul, there would be no contact between them. Two ubiquitous substances devoid of parts cannot come into contact with each other. The atomic manas comes into contact with the different sense-organs by its quick movement, and generates different cognitions in quick succession. They are never simultaneous, but appear to be so owing to the quick movement of the manas and its rapid contacts with the soul and different sense-organs. The mind-

[1] PP., pp. 149,151, 157-59.

soul-contacts are due to the soul's merits and demerits acquired by its past actions.[1]

There are many souls. Their experiences are different. They acquire different merits and demerits by their different voluntary actions. Their different lots and pleasures and pains are due to the variety of their merits and demerits. If there were one soul only, there would be no variety of merits and demerits. If there were no variety of them, there would be no variety of enjoyments and sufferings, which is a fact of experience. So there are many souls, one in each body. Oneness of the soul would lead to oneness of experience, which is contradicted by experience. There is an irreducible plurality of souls with unique experiences. They are moral agents experiencing diverse objects in accordance with their moral deserts. The Advaita Vedānta doctrine of oneness of the soul flatly contradicts the testimony of consciousness and undermines morality. Just as the actions of my body are due to the volitions of my soul, so the actions of other bodies are due to the volitions of other souls, and not to those of my soul. I experience the volition of my soul producing actions of my body. But I never experience the volition of my soul producing actions of other bodies. So I infer that they must be due to the volitions of other souls. I have inferential knowledge of other souls. I infer them from the actions of their bodies produced by their volitions. One soul cannot be perceived by another soul.[2]

The soul is neither produced nor destroyed. It is devoid of origin and end. It is uncaused and indestructible. It is immortal and eternal. It achieves its non-empirical, pure and transcendental condition by exhausting its merits and demerits. This is the state of liberation.

The self is not self-luminous, and does not apprehend itself. But a cognition is self-luminous, and apprehends itself. The self is known as the subject or knower in all cognitions of objects. Objects are not apprehended, unless the self

[1] PP., p. 149.

[2] PP., pp. 155, 158-59.

apprehending them is apprehended. It is not apprehended in the absence of cognitions of objects. Cognitions manifest themselves, the objects which produce them, and the self in which they exist. The self is apprehended as the knower of objects, and manifested as the subject in all cognitions of objects. It cannot be the subject as well as the object of a cognition, since it is self-contradictory. The self is always the agent of knowledge, and never its object.

The self cannot be an object of mental perception as Kumārila maintains. It is self-contradictory to hold that the same self is the knowing subject and the known object. In the cognition, 'I know the jar' the self-luminous cognition manifests the jar as an object, and the self as its subtrate. The self is apprehended as the knower of objects ; it is always manifested as the subject or knower of object-cognitions ; it is never known as an object.[1]

KUMĀRILA'S THEORY OF KNOWLEDGE OR INFERENCE OF COGNITION FROM COGNIZEDNESS OF ITS OBJECT (JÑĀTATĀ)

Kumārila regards a cognition as an act of the self, which is inferred from the cognizedness (jñātatā) of its object. A cognitive act produces cognizedness or manifestness (prākaṭya) in its object. If there were no cognition, then we could not, in any other way, account for the cognizedness of an existing object ; so after the object has been cognized, we know the existence of the cognition as a means of knowing the object.[2] (1) The act of cognition is the cause ; cognizedness is the effect. The cognitive act as the cause is inferred from cognizedness as the effect. The objects of knowledge are either perceptible or inferable. Perceptibility and inferability are produced by sense-perception and inference respectively in their objects. A cognition is imperceptible but inferable from cognizedness. (2) A cognition is inferred from the relation between the self and the object, which is apprehended by mental perception. The self is the knower, and the object is

[1] PP., pp. 148, 151-53.   [2] ŚV., v, 182, p. 318 ; NR.

known. The self can know the object when it is related to it; and the relation between them is brought about by a cognition, which relates them to each other. From the specific relation between the self and the object brought about by the cognition which is an adventitious condition we infer the existence of the cognition. The relation is known by mental perception. Hence a cognition is inferred from the specific relation between the self and an object. (3) A cognition is inferred from the peculiarity produced by it in its object. Manifestation is produced in the object by the cognition. It is cognizedness from which the cognition is inferred. A perceptual cognition produces cognizedness in a present object. An inferential cognition produces manifestation or cognizedness in past, future and remote objects. So the cognition is inferred from the manifestation of objects. Hence a cognition is inferred from manifestation or cognizedness of its object, which is a peculiar property produced by it in its object, or the specific relation between the self and the object.[1]

PRABHĀKARA'S THEORY OF KNOWLEDGE : THEORY OF TRIPLE PERCEPTION (TRIPUṬĪPRATYAKṢAVĀDA)

Prabhākara holds that perception apprehends the self, its object, and itself. Perception is direct apprehension, which cognizes these three factors. This view is called the doctrine of triple perception. Cognition is self-luminous, and manifests itself. It is not manifested by any other cognition. But the self and the object are not self-luminous, and do not manifest themselves. They are manifested by a cognition. In walking condition both the self and the object are manifested. But in dreamless sleep both are unmanifest, though they continue to exist during the period, since they are recognized on waking from sleep. If they were self-luminous, they would be manifested during deep sleep. They are not manifested at the time, because there is no cognition to manifest them. So they are not self-luminous, but they are manifested by a cognition which is self-luminous.[2] The self is directly

[1] ŚD., pp. 56-57. [2] PP., pp. 57 & 127.

manifested by every cognition presentative or representative. There can be no cognition of an object apart from that of the self. In every cognition of an object there are a consciousness of the self, a consciousness of an object, and a consciousness of the cognition. In the cognition 'I know the jar' there is a triple consciousness, a cognition of the jar, a cognition of 'I' or the self, and a self-conscious cognition.

According to Prabhākara, the self is always cognized as the knower, a cognition, as a cognition, and an object, as a known object. The self is a knower, and can never be known as an object. A cognition can never be known as an object, but as a cognition. It is self-manifest or self-aware. If it were cognized by another cognition, it would not be self-luminous. If it were cognized as an object of another cognition, it would require another cognition to cognize it, and so on to infinity. So a cognition is self-conscious awareness and apprehends an object. But, though a cognition is apprehended by itself, its existence is inferred from the apprehension of its object.[1] We infer the existence of the cognition from the apprehension of its object.

Prabhākara refutes Kumārila's doctrine of inferability of a cognition. There is no reason or mark from which it may be inferred. The existence of an object cannot serve as the mark of inference, since it is not invariably accompanied by a cognition. The cognition of an object cannot be the mark of inference. It cannot be a mark as soon as it is produced ; but it can be so only when it is mainifested to consciousness. If it is not manifested, it cannot be distinguished from an object-cognition which has not yet come into existence. A cognitive act canot be inferred from non-manifestation of the object-cognition. The manifestation of the object-cognition does not depend upon any other cognition, since it is not known to exist. Thus, there is no mark from which a cognition can be inferred. Hence the cognition of an object is self-illumined. The so-called cognizedness or manifestness

[1] Bṛ., i, 1, 5, p. 82 ; ŚBh., i, 1, 5 ; pp. 80-81 ; NM., p. 432 ; PSPM., p. 26.

of an object is nothing but the cognition of the object, which is self-luminous. A self-cognized cognition manifests an object.[1]

DHARMA

Jaimini defines Dharma as a good which is of the nature of a command. Śavara defines it as an utterance which prompts the self to act and carry it out. It is a command which leads it to the attainment of the highest good. It is a prescription of the Vedas, which indicates the nature of good and evil, and impels the self to realize the highest good. Dharma can be revealed by the Vedic prescriptions only ; it is not apprehended by perception, inference, comparison or any other means of knowledge. Dharma is non-temporal and supersensuous Duty or Moral Law, which is revealed by the Vedas, and impels the self to obey it. Kumārila regards the Moral Law as a Vedic prescription or command which impels the self to act. What leads to the attainment of the good is dharma. The good is the happiness of the self. The performance of sacrifices and other rites and ceremonies prescribed by the Vedas is conducive to its happiness. Certain substances, qualities and actions are the material of these rites. So Kumārila regards the acts enjoined by the Vedas and all the ingredients necessary for them as dharma. External acts prescribed by the Vedas and the substances, qualities, and actions which are required for them constitute dharma. The latter are regarded as dharma, because they are means to the performance of duties, though they are perceptible. The conduciveness of the acts and the auxiliary substances, qualities and actions to the highest good is always known from the Vedas.[2] Kumārila regards the external acts prescribed by the Vedic injunctions and prohibitions as dharma. He advocates the ethics of ritualism and ceremonialism. He propounds an external and legalistic view of morality. The Moral Law is of the nature of an impersonal command, and not the command of God.[3]

---

[1] PP., p. 63.

[2] ŚBh., i, 1, 2 ; ŚV. Codanāsūtra, 1-7 ; NR., 3, 11, 13-14, 190-92.

[3] Ibid, 210, 213-15, 242-43.

Kumārila recognizes two kinds of duties, secular and scriptural or non-temporal. The secular duties fulfil perceptible secular ends. The scriptural duties fulfil imperceptible supersensuous ends. They are of two kinds, *viz.*, conditional duties and unconditional duties. The former are empirical duties for the realization of desired ends. The latter are obligatory daily duties *e.g.*, morning and evening prayers, and obligatory occasional duties *e.g.*, bath in the Ganges on the occasion of the solar eclipse and the lunar eclipse. The performance of conditional duties leads to happiness ; the performance of Jyotiṣṭoma sacrifice produces happiness in heaven. The non-performance of unconditional duties produces sins of omission and consequent sufferings. But the performance of them does not produce merits and consequent enjoyments ; nor does it produce demerits and consequent sufferings. It purifies the mind, generates the knowledge of the self, wipes off past sins, and prevents sins which would accrue to the self from the omission of unconditional duties. The conditional duties are obligatory when there is a desire for a particular end, but the unconditional duties are unconditionally obligatory. The scriptural duties are positive or negative : they are either injunctions or prohibitions. The former enjoin the performance of right actions, while the latter prohibit the commission of wrong actions.[1]

Prabhākara holds that Apūrva or the supersensible Moral Imperative is conducive to the highest good,—which is indicated by the Vedic injunctions. A moral law is of the nature of duty. A duty is Apūrva because it is incomprehensible by any other means of knowledge than Vedic testimony. It is a command or Imperative because it impels a person to accomplish it ; it is realizable by an action, which is its means. The supersensible Ought is the end of our moral actions ; there is a permanent relation between Apūrva and its accomplishment by a voluntary action. When there is a volition, there is the accomplishment of Ought ; and when there is no volition,

[1] ŚD., YSP., pp. 25-31 ; EH., pp. 19-20.

there is the absence of its accomplishment. Volition is an effort of the self, which aims at the realization of Ought through a voluntary action. Thus Dharma is Apūrva or supersensible Ought revealed by the authoritative suggestion produced in the self by the Moral Imperative. It is an objective category. But it is not an external act enjoined by the Vedas as Kumārila holds. A person who performs the sacrifices enjoined by the Vedas is said to be virtuous because he executes the Moral Imperative. He cannot be said to be virtuous, if he does not execute it. The accomplishment of the Moral Imperative is inferred from the performance of the sacrifices enjoined by the Vedas. The ceremonial acts are the contents of duty in that they fulfil the Moral Imperative which is a transcendental verity revealed by the Vedic injunctions. They do not derive their authoritativeness from their conduciveness to any ulterior end or good, but from their intrinsic validity as self-revealing, transcendental Moral Law. It is revealed by moral obligation produced by the moral imperative in the self.[1] It is revealed to the self by the unique feeling of moral obligation which is different from physical compulsion and psychical impulsion. Moral obligation is a self-revealing experience. The prescribed duties do not derive their authority from the Vedas, as Kumārila thinks, but from Apūrva or the moral imperative which is indicated by the Vedic injunctions. It is an impersonal Law which has intrinsic validity—a transcendental verity of the moral order, which is self-revealing and self-authoritative.[2]

Prabhākara recognizes two kinds of duties, *viz.*, conditional duties for the fulfilment of ends, and unconditional duties which are obligatory in themselves. Unconditional duties are obligatory daily duties and obligatory occasional duties. Both of them ought to be done out of the sense of duty. They are authoritative because they embody Moral Imperatives indicated by Vedic injunctions. Their authoritativeness is not due to

[1] TNR., pp. 66-67, 81-82; PP., pp, 180-81, 188, 195-96.

[2] NM., p. 347.

their conduciveness to any ulterior end or consequences. They ought to be performed for their own sake.[1]

APŪRVA

The acts enjoined by the Vedas produce their fruits. The performance of the Jyotiṣṭoma sacrifice produces happiness in heaven. The enjoined action is performed at one time and the fruition of the act follows much later. The performance of prescribed acts generates an unseen agency (apūrva) which produces their fruition at a later time. The deferred fruition of the performance of duties is due to the mediation of Apūrva. Kumārila posits Apūrva as a third entity between the prescribed acts and their deferred fruition. It is an imperceptible potency in the principal action, or in the self, which did not exist before the performance of the action.[2] Before the prescribed acts are performed, there is an incapability in them for producing happiness in heaven, and there is an incapability in the self for attaining heaven. Both these incapabilities are removed by the performance of sacrifices, which creates a positive power (apūrva), by virtue of which heaven is attained. The imperceptible power called Apūrva is known by presumption. The hypothesis of Apūrva removes the apparent inconsistency between the performance of the prescribed sacrifice at one time and the attainment of heaven at a later time. The performance of the act produces directly a certain potency in the agent, which persists in him, and produces happiness in heaven after the death of his body. The causal relation between the prescribed act and its fruition cannot be explained without such an intervening potency, which is generated by the act in the self, and is the immediate cause of the final result. Kumārila regards Apūrva also as an objective potency of the prescribed act itself.[3]

Prabhākara rejects Kumārila's view. A prescribed act, which is transient, cannot bring about its final result, the attainment of heaven, at a subsequent time. The Apūrva, or

[1] PP., pp. 171-201 ; EH., Ch. II.

[2] Tantravārtika, ET., p. 504. [3] PSPM., pp. 166-67.

Ought, or Duty, which is different from the transient act, which is indicated by a Vedic prescription, and which is aimed at by a volition, generates the fruit. The volition is called bhāvanā, because it generates a voluntary action, which executes the Ought.[1] The Moral Imperative (Niyoga) prompts the agent to put forth volition and exertion to accomplish the act. But it is difficult to explain how the Niyoga or Apūrva can lead the self to attain the final result of the prescribed act done by it without producing a potency or disposition in the permanent self. Śālikānātha, a Prābhākara, thinks that the Niyoga produces an effect in the self in the form of a disposition which inheres in it, and cannot be known by any other means of knowledge except moral obligation. The act is not permanent, but the self's disposition is permanent, which can bring about the accomplishment of the final result.[2]

LIBERATION (MOKṢA) AND ITS MEANS

Kumārila and Prabhākara consider the nature of liberation and the means of its attainment. Kumārila regards liberation as negative in character, and, consequently, eternal. If it be a state of positive happiness in heaven, it cannot be eternal. It is of the nature of negation, and therefore eternal. But negation cannot be the result of any action. Liberation is due to absolute extinction of merits and demerits. When they are completely destroyed, the body, which is the vehicle of experience, is destroyed. When no traces of them are left, no cause is left for the production of the body. The self attains liberation on the destruction of the present body and the non-production of any future body. It is a state of absolute negation of all experience of cognition, pleasure, pain, desire, aversion, impression, merit and demerit. It is the natural transcendental condition of the self free from empirical contents. It does not consist in enjoyment of happiness. If it did, it would be synonymous with heaven, and therefore perishable. Heavenly happiness is not eternal. When merit is worn off, it is succeeded by rebirth and bondage due to

[1] PP., p. 197. [2] PP., p. 187.

merits and demerits and connection with a body. Liberation is negation of this connection due to extinction of merits and demerits.[1]

Kumārila regards action and knowledge both as necessary for the attainment of release. An aspirant for release should refrain from forbidden acts which produce suffering, and prescribed acts which generate happiness here and hereafter. But he should continue to perform daily obligatory and occasional duties in order to avoid sins which accrue from their non-performance. Prescribed acts for the realization of selfish ends produce happiness on earth and in heaven. Forbidden acts generate sins and sufferings. They lead to transmigration and rebirth for the experience of the resulting enjoyments and sufferings. The knowledge of the self wipes off all traces of merits and demerits with the aid of the performance of obligatory daily and occasional duties, and prevents further accumulation of them. But mere knowledge of the self is not adequate to effect final release. It impels the self to perform enjoined duties, and must be accompanied by the performance of obligatory duties. Thus action and knowledge both are necessary for release.[2]

Prabhākara describes heaven as unalloyed bliss free from pain. He defines release as the absolute cessation of merits and demerits and the consequent total destruction of the body. It is absolute cessation of the sufferings of empirical life consequent on the complete destruction of the self's contact with the body and the sense-organs, which are destroyed by the complete disappearance of merits and demerits. Consciousness is an accidental quality of the self, due to its conjunction with manas and a body. When manas, the body and the sense-organs are completely destroyed on the destruction of merits and demerits, the self is divested of cognition, pleasure, pain, desire, aversion, volition, and impression, and becomes unconscious. Release is absolute cessation of merits and demerits and the consequent pleasure and pain. It is

---

1 ŚV., Sambandhākṣepaparihāra, 105-09, NR.

2 Ibid, 110, 103; ŚD., p. 103; MM., p. 89.

negative in character, and consists in the complete destruction of the specific qualities of the self. It is the natural transcendental condition of the self free from empirical contents as an eternal and ubiquitous substance ; it is not a state of positive bliss, but a negative state of absolute extinction of pain.[1] The nature of release is the same according to Prabhākara and Kumārila.

Prabhākara, like Kumārila, regards action and knowledge both as necessary for release. Abstention from all prescribed acts for the avoidance of sins, and the performance of obligatory duties together with rigid moral discipline are the means to release. But action alone is not sufficient for the attainment of release. It must be supplemented by the knowledge of the self, which stops further accumulation of merit and demerit, and completely destroys the body, which is the vehicle of experience. Knowledge of the self is not subservient to action. Aided by sense-restraint, control of mind, sex-restraint, and other auxiliaries, it leads to release.[2]

ATHEISM

The Mīmāṁsā teaches ritualistic morality and religion, and enjoins the performance of sacrifices to gods. But they are not objects of worship, and do not give the rewards of the offerings. The deities are only Beings to whom offerings are to be made, and who have existence beyond the spatio-temporal world. At the time of making an offering to a deity, a person has to think of his form. So the Mīmāṁsā believes in polytheism. But its belief in many gods is not serious, since they have no function. The later Mīmāṁsā denies their existence except in the mantras, and regards the references to them as mere praises of sacrifices. The performance of sacrifices generates an unseen potency (apūrva) in the self, which generates their fruits without the intervention of gods. The Apūrva is the intermediate agency between the performance of sacrifices and the attainment of heaven. Heaven is

---

PP., pp. 102-03, 156-57, 153.

unalloyed happiness for a long duration, which is terminated by the exhaustion of merits.[1]

Prabhākara and Kumārila deny the existence of God. The Mīmāṁsā believes in polytheism but not in theism. It does not believe in the existence of God as the creator, preserver, and destroyer of the world, or the apportioner of rewards and punishments, or the author of the Vedas. Its belief in many gods does not serve any useful purpose. They have no relation to the world and the finite souls. They are not organically connected with the Mīmāṁsā system. Hence this system is as atheistic.[2]

Kumārila and Prabhākara have a realistic and naturalistic view of the world, and regard it as composed of atoms which are perceptible. External objects are real and permanent substances, which are not mere aggregates of qualities. A substance is permanent, though its qualities change.[3] Kumārila rejects the notion of a substance as a self-identical unit devoid of difference. He advocates the doctrine of pariṇāmavāda or satkāryavāda, which regards an effect as a real modification of a cause. He regards the relation between cause and effect as identity-in-difference. He rejects the relation of inherence between them. Kumārila and Prabhākara deny the periodical creation and destruction of the world, but they believe in the constant process of its parts coming into existence and passing away. Both deny the existence of God as the creator of the world, the supervisor of merits and demerits of the individual souls, the apportioner of rewards and punishments, and the author of the Vedas and moral laws.

Kumārila offers the following arguments against the reality of God. If God is the creator of the world, He must have a body. He cannot have desire to create without a body, since desire is produced by the contact of the soul with its manas and sense-organs. If God had a body before creation, it could not be created by Himself, but by another God, whose body was created by another, and so on to infinity. If the body of God were eternal, it could not be material, since there

---

[1] ŚV., E.T., Introduction, p. xliv ; PP., pp. 184-86.

[2] KM., Ch. IV ; PSPM., pp. 85-88. [3] ŚV., Upamāna, 32-33.

were no earth and the like prior to creation. Again, if His body were material, it could not be eternal. If it were eternal, our bodies also must be eternal, since both are material. His body must have been produced by a cause, since it was composed of parts like our bodies. If God were the creator of His own body, then He created it without a body. But bodiless God, like a released soul, could not exercise any control over His body. Just as a jar is found to be made by an intelligent potter, who is perishable, so the body of God was made by an intelligent maker, who was perishable. If God had no body, He could not exert His will on the atoms. If He did not act on the unconscious atoms, they could not follow His will. The insentient atoms could not combine with one another, and from various substances under the guidance of the will of God. Similarly, they cannot separate from one another, and bring about destruction of the world under the guidance of the divine will.[1]

The Nyāya holds that God creates the world out of the atoms with the aid of the individual souls' merits and demerits, keeps them in abeyance during dissolution, activates them again at the time of creation, and creates the world in accordance with them for the souls' enjoyments and sufferings. Kumārila criticizes this view. All actions are destroyed with their effects, merits and demerits, when the world is destroyed. God cannot activate the souls' merits and demerits at the time of the next creation. If He is omniscient and omnipotent, He can create the world by His will without the aid of their merits and demerits. If He depends upon them for creation, He is not independent and omnipotent. If they are subject to the will of God, they are needless. Kumārila does not deny that the diversity of the world is due to the diversity of the souls' merits and demerits. But he denies the reality of God as the creator of the world.

Kumārila argues that there is no evidence for God's creative activity. No one can testify to the creation of the world by God. The first creatures could not know how they were born. Nor could they know the state of things prior to

[1] ŚV., Sambandhākṣepaparihāra, 45-49, 77-82, NR.

the creation of the world by God. If they relied on the assertion of the Creator, they might be deceived. God might not create the world and yet tell them that He did so in order to show off His powers. So God cannot be regarded as the creator of the world. Similarly, there is no evidence to prove that God is the destroyer of the world. There is none to testify to the fact that He destroys the world. So God is neither the creator nor the destroyer of the world.[1]

Further, God has no motive for creating the world. Compassion for living creatures could not be His motive, since there were no living creatures before creation, for whom He could feel compassion. Moreover, if He were moved by compassion to create the world, He would create only happy beings. But the world is full of suffering and misery. God, who is benevolent, cannot create so much suffering in the world. If He cannot create a world free from evil, He is not omnipotent. If He is omnipotent, He can certainly create a world free from evil. If He depended on moral laws and natural laws and instruments, His independence would be compromised. If He created the world without a motive, then He is not intelligent. Even a fool does not act without a motive. If God created the world for amusement, He would not be perfectly happy and contented, and creation would involve Him in wearisome toil. God is completely fulfilled and cannot, therefore, realize any end in creation. If compassion is the motive for creation, it cannot be the motive for destruction. The same cause cannot produce contradictory effects—creation and destruction. Hence God is not the creator or destroyer of the world.

God is not the author of the Vedas. Even if they were created by Him, they are doubtful. They are not a sure proof for His existence. If they existed before creation, they could not be connected with the objects created. If they speak of creation as made by God, they are mere praises of certain injunctions about sacrifices. The Vedas are self-revealing, authoritative and eternal. They contain injunctions and

[1] ŚV., Sambandhākṣepaparihāra, 57-60, 67, 72, 75, NR.

prohibitions which embody positive and negative duties. God is not the author of the Vedas and the promulgator of moral laws. We can know dharma from the Vedas. Both Prabhākara and Kumārila regard the Vedas as eternal and self-revealing.

Prabhākara argues that there is no evidence for the creation and destruction of the whole world at the same moment, though its parts are produced by the conjunction of their constituent atoms, and destroyed by their disjunction. All animals and men are born of their parents, and do not owe their existence to the intervention of God. Similarly, all things in the world are produced by their causes, and do not owe their existence to God. All effects are produced by their natural causes, and no supernatural causes are necessary for them.[1]

The Nyāya argues that God is the supervisor of the individual souls' merits and demerits. They are unconscious, and so cannot produce their results without the guidance of a Being possessed of supreme intelligence. Omniscient God is the supervisor of the souls' merits and demerits. Prabhākara urges that the finite souls may supervise their own merits and demerits. If they cannot supervise them because they have no knowledge of them, then God also cannot supervise them because He has no knowledge of them. He has no sense-organs through which He can perceive them. He cannot perceive them through manas, since it cannot perceive external objects without the aid of the external sense-organs. He has no merit and demerit which are the causes of a body, the sense-organs, and the contact of manas with the sense-organs. So He cannot perceive the souls' merits and demerits through the sense-mind-contact, and, consequently, cannot supervise them. His knowledge is not uncaused and eternal, since knowledge is always found to be caused and transient. So God's supervision of the souls' merits and demerits is unintelligible. He cannot supervise them without being related to them. His relation to them is either conjunction or inherence. It is not conjunction, since it holds between two substances only. God is a substance; but merits and demerits are the souls' qualities. There

[1] Ibid, 52-56, 61-63; ŚD., YSP., pp. 116-17; PP., pp. 137, 139-40.

can be no conjunction between a substance and a quality. So there can be no conjunction between God and merits and demerits. Nor can there be inherence between them, Merits and demerits inhere in the individual souls, and cannot inhere in God, who is distinct from them. A carpenter's supervision of his tools consists in his contact with them. But God's supervision of the souls' merits and demerits does not consist in His contact with them. He cannot act upon their merits and demerits, because they are qualities, and so cannot surpervise them. Hence God cannot create the world out of the atoms with the aid of the souls' merits and demerits.

It cannot be argued that God acts upon the atoms, even as the soul acts upon its own body by virtue of merits and demerits, because the atoms are not the body of God, on which He may act and create the world out of them. Even if God is supposed to have a body, His action on the body is due to volition. But there is no cause of His volition. If the divine volition were eternal, creation would be unceasing. Further, God cannot supervise the unconscious atoms, because He has no motive in doing so. There is no need of a supramundane creator of the world. The existence of God is an unwarranted hypothesis.[1]

The earlier Mīmāṁsakas did not believe in the reality of God, and regarded the world as self-existent and self-evolving. They looked upon effects as modifications of their causes under the influence of the souls' merits and demerits, which are the supernatural agents in their production. They are otherwise due to purely natural causes. But the later Mīmāṁsakas smuggled the concept of God into the Mīmāṁsā system, and conceived Him as the supervisor of the Law of Karma, the apportioner of rewards and punishments, and the Moral Governor of the world. Laugākṣi Bhāskara recognized the reality of God as the creator, preserver and destroyer of the world, the inner guide of the souls, and the Moral Governor. Vedānta Deśika brought the theistic tendency to the fullest development.[2]

---

[1] PP., pp, 137-40. [2] Arthasaṁgraha, pp. 1-2 ; Seśvara Mīmāṁsā.

CHAPTER XIII

THE ADVAITA VEDĀNTA OF ŚAṀKARA

Śaṁkara (788—820 A.D.) was the greatest philosopher among the Indian thinkers in intellectual eminence. He was relentless in his criticism of the other systems, and zealous and untiring in the exposition of his own system of Absolute Idealism (advaitavāda). He defeated many rival eminent contemporary philosophers in philosophical discussions. He wrote commentaries on the principal Upaniṣads, the *Brahmasūtra*, and the *Bhagavad Gītā*. He wrote commentaries on Kena, Kaṭha, Īśa, Praśna, Muṇḍaka, Māṇḍukya, Chāndogya, Bṛhadāraṇyaka, Śvetāśvatara, Aitareya, and Taittirīya Upaniṣads. His commentary on the *Brahmasūtra* is called the *Śārīraka Bhāṣya*. Vācaspatimiśra (1000 A.D.) wrote a commentary on it called *Bhāmatī*. Amalānanda (1300 A.D.) wrote a commentary on *Bhāmatī* called *Kalpataru*. Appayadīkṣita (1600 A.D.) wrote a commentary on *Kalpataru* called *Kalpataruparimala*. Govindānanda wrote a commentary on Śaṁkara's *Śārīraka Bhāṣya* called *Ratnaprabhā*. Padmapāda wrote an elaborate gloss on the first four sūtras of the *Brahmasūtra* called *Pañcapādikā*. Prakāśātman (1200 A.D.) wrote a commentary on it called *Pañcapādikāvivaraṇa*. Vidyāraṇya (1400 A.D.) wrote a gloss on it called *Vivaraṇaprameyasaṁgraha*. Śrī Harṣa's *Khaṇḍanakhaṇḍakhādya* (1200 A.D.) is the greatest work on Advaita Vedānta dialectics. Dharmarājādhvarīndra's *Vedāntaparibhāṣā* is an important work on Advaita Vedānta Logic.

Śaṁkara emphasizes the monistic tendency in the Upaniṣads and develops it into a systematic Advaitavāda. He emphasizes the reality of the unconditioned and unqualified (nirguṇa) Brahman, and regards God, the individual souls and the world as appearances due to an indefinable principle called cosmic nescience (Māyā) which is neither real nor unreal, but indefinable. God is

Brahman associated with Māyā in its excellent aspect. The empirical self is Brahman associated with Māyā (avidyā) in its inferior aspect. It is, in essence, identical with Brahman or Ātman. Brahman is one, eternal, pure, transcendental consciousness. It transcends the duality of subject and object, and the empirical categories of space, time, substance, causality, change, and the like. The world is an appearance of Brahman, which is non-different from it. Ignorance is bondage. True knowledge is liberation. Bondage is due to nescience which generates a false sense of individuality. Liberation is pure intuition of Brahman—integral experience of identity. Śaṁkara admits the empirical reality of God, the individual selves and the world-appearance. But he admits the ontological reality of Brahman only.

HIGHER KNOWLEDGE (PARĀ VIDYĀ) AND LOWER KNOWLEDGE (APARĀ VIDYĀ)

Śaṁkara distinguishes between the ontological reality and the empirical reality. The former is known by higher knowledge (parā vidyā), while the latter is known by lower knowledge (aparā vidyā). Higher knowledge is true knowledge (vidyā), while lower knowledge is false knowledge (avidyā). The former transcends the distinction between the knower and the known, while the latter involves it. Brahman is known by higher knowledge. It is trans-empirical subject-objectless consciousness, which is not conditioned by space, time, and causality, which are empirical categories. The spatio-temporal world bound by causality is known by lower knowledge through the categories of space, time, and causality. True knowledge is intuition, which is supra-intellectual integral experience, while false knowledge is discursive, intellectual, categorized, empirical, fragmentary, knowledge. Higher knowledge is absoute knowledge of identity, while lower knowledge is relative and pragmatic knowledge of difference. Though they are opposed to each other, relative knowledge is a step to absolute knowledge—intellect is a means to intuition.[1]

SCRIPTURAL AUTHORITY, REASON AND INTUITION

The knowledge of Brahman is first acquired from the scripture, which is confirmed by reasoning which culminates in intuition. The scriptural authority, which is self-certifying, bears testimony to the existence of Brahman. Hearing, reflection, and meditation lead to intuitive apprehension of Brahman. The scripture must be admitted to be the means of knowing Brahman. Brahman or God (Īśvara) is the cause of Śruti. The identity of the Ātman with Brahman cannot be known by any other means than the scripture. The knowledge of Brahman is the result of reflection on the meaning of the scriptural texts regarding it. It cannot be derived from inference and the other means of valid knowledge. The scripture is authoritative because it embodies intuition.[2]

Śaṁkara does not abjure reason, but he subordinates reason to the scripture. Hearing must be followed by reflection which includes reason. Reasoning in conformity with the scripture is conducive to the intuition of Brahman, and therefore should be employed. Reason unaided by the scripture never leads to absolute truth, because it deludes us. Inference in harmony with the scripture is a valid means of knowledge of the ontological reality. Reason must be admitted to be auxiliary to the scripture.[3] Perfect knowledge culminates in perfect intuition of Brahman. Reasoning which follows the scripture can prove the existence of God as the material cause and the efficient cause of the World. But reasoning cannot prove the existence of indeterminate Brahman, which is inscrutable, and which can be known from the scripture only.[4]

The perfect intuition of Brahman is immediate, integral

---

1 SB., Māṇḍ. K., iv, 1 ; iii,, 43 ; i, 12 ; ii, 32 ; iii, 25 ; SB., Muṇḍ. Up., ii, 1, 1 ; SB., Īśa Up., 11.

2 SBS., i, 1, 2-4 ; ii, 1, 1 & 4 ; iii, 2, 24.

3 Ibid, ii, 1, 6 ; i, 1, 2 ; ii, 1, 11.

4 SBS., ii, 1, 11 ; ii, 1, 4 ; ii, 1, 31 ; i, 1, 4.

experience (anubhava), which annuls avidyā, and reveals the nature of Brahman. It does not depend upon the act of a person, but it depends upon the existence of Brahman, which is apprehended by it. Brahman reveals itself to intuitional consciousness. Intellectual knowledge involves the distinction of subject and object. Brahman is one and known by perfect intuition. Intuition is the knowledge of identity which annuls the intellectual knowledge of duality. God can be known by meditation which involves the duality of the deity and the devotee. But Brahman is one and can be realized by intuition. The perfect knowledge of Brahman is non-different from its object, the ontological reality. The Ātman or Brahman reveals itself to intuitional consciousness, which is immediate and indeterminate.[1]

TRUTH

Śaṁkara recognizes non-contradiction (abādhitatva) as the test of truth. The knowledge of the non-dual Ātman is valid, since it is not contradicted. Vācaspati defines truth as uncontradicted, novel, and undoubted knowledge. Dharmarajādhvarīndra defines truth as novel, uncontradicted knowledge of an object. Novelty is the given element in knowledge which was not acquired already. Harmony or coherence is the test of truth. Śaṁkara emphasizes this idealistic test of truth, but he recognizes correspondence and practical efficiency also as tests of truth. Correspondence is the realistic test, and practical efficiency, the pragmatic test. The truth of the knowledge of objects depends upon them. Perception, inference, and the other pramāṇas depend upon their objects for their validity. Correspondence is the test of empirical truth.[2] Valid knowledge is produced by the means of knowledge, which has for its object the real nature of an existent object. It cannot be made or unmade by the empirical self. It is determined by the object, and does not depend upon the

[1] SBS., i, 1, 4 ; SB., Māṇḍ, K., iii, 1 & 33.

[2] SBS., ii, 1, 14 ; Bhāmatī, SBS., i, 1, 4 ; VPB , p. 20.

command of the self. The knowledge which corresponds with the real nature of its object is valid. Correspondence is the test of absolute truth also. Brahman ought to be known by valid knowledge because it is the highest Good. The knowledge of Brahman is valid, since it corresponds with its real nature. Integral experience is determined by the real nature of Brahman. The scripture gives the knowledge of Brahman, which dispels nescience (avidyā). Though the validity of the scripture is self-certifying, it can be known by the pragmatic test of its fruitful consequence. Dharmarājādhvarīndra defines valid knowledge as uncontradicted knowledge of an object or as the knowledge of an object as it really is, which is conducive to fruitful activity. This definition applies to apprehension and recollection alike. It recognizes correspondence, practical efficiency, and coherence as tests of truth.

Dharmarājādhvarīndra recognizes intrinsic validity of knowledge as to its origin and knowledge. Validity of knowledge arises from the general conditions of knowledge untainted by deficiencies. It is not due to special proficiencies as the Naiyāyika maintains. It is directly known by the Winess Self (sākṣin), which apprehends the knowledge. It is not known from adventitious conditions. Invalid knowledge arises from the general conditions of knowledge vitiated by deficiencies, is due to extraneous conditions, and known from fruitless activity prompted by it.[1]

PERCEPTION

Śaṁkara recognizes perception, inference, scriptural testimony, comparison, presumption, and non-apprehension as the sources of valid knowledge. Dharmarājādhvarīndra also discusses six kinds of pramāṇas, which yield empirical truth.[2]

There is one eternal consciousness or Brahman. When it is determined by the internal organ, it is called the subject-consciousness. The empirical self is the subject-consciousness.

---

[1] SBS., i, 1, 2 ; iii, 2, 21 ; i, 1, 2 ; iv, 1, 7 ; i, 1, 4 ; VPB., pp. 19-20, 332-38.

[2] SBS., iii, 1, 11 ; SB., Muṇḍ. Up., 1, 2, 12 ; SB., Bṛ. Up., iii, 3, 1.

When the eternal consciousness is determined by mental modes, it is called the knowledge-consciousness. When it is determined by an empirical object, it is called the object-consciousness. In external perception the mind (antaḥkaraṇa) goes out to an empirical object through a sense-organ, and is modified into its form. This mental mode assuming the form of the object is called vṛtti. So the knowledge-consciousness or consciousness determined by the mental mode coincides with the object-consciousness. There is identification of the apprehending mental mode with the object; the mental mode conforms to the empirical object. In external perception the mental mode and the object occupy the same position in space. This mark distinguishes perception from inference. The perceptive process and the object occupy the same point of time at present. The memory of pleasure is not perception. Memory is a present mental mode. But pleasure remembered is past. The apprehending mental mode and the apprehended object occupy different time-positions. The object should be capable of being perceived. Fitness for being perceived is a mark that distinguishes perception from scriptural testimony, which apprehends supersensible objects like merit and demerit. In the bare perception of an object there is only identification of the knowledge-consciousness with the object-consciousness. But in the perception of the object *as object* there is not only identification of the knowledge-consciousness with the object-consciousness but also identification of the knowledge-consciousness with the subject-consciousness. The apprehending mental mode is referred to the empirical self and identified with it. In internal perception of pleasure the apprehending mental mode is identified with the mental mode of pleasure, or the knowledge-consciousness coincides with the object-consciousness.

Perception is indeterminable or determinate. Indeterminate perception is non-relational apprehension. 'That thou art': this verbal knowledge is indeterminate perception, since there is no subject-predicate relation in it. Determinate perception

24

is relational apprehension. 'I know the jar' : this is determinate perception, since there is subject-predicate relation in it. Perception is either sensuous or non-sensuous. Perception through the sense-organs is sensuous. Mental perception is non-sensuous, since the manas is not a sense-organ. In sensuous perception the mind goes out to an external object through a sense-organ, and is modified into its form. In mental perception the mind does not go out to an object. Mental modes of pleasure, pain, and the like are perceived in it. Perception, again, refers to an object or a cognition. An object is perceived through the medium of a mental mode. A cognition is directly perceived by the self without an intervening mental mode.[1]

In the illusory perception 'this is silver' the visual organ perverted by a defect comes into contact with a nacre, and generates a mental mode in the form of 'this-consciousness' The consciousness of 'this' is perception. There is identification of 'this-consciousness' with the knowledge-consciousness and the subject-consciousness. The mental mode goes out through the visual organ to the bright object ('this'), and is modified into its form. This is perceptive process. Then nescience (avidya) in the form of nacre in the object-consciousness which is identified with the subject-consciousness, is transformed into the objective illusory silver and the subjective illusion of silver with the aid of the subconscious impression of silver revived by the perception of brightness, which is common to the nacre and the silver, and a defect in the visual organ. The illusory silver, which is a modification of nescience, exists in 'this-consciousness' subsisting in nescience. All effects are modifications of nescience, and subsist in it. The consciousness of 'this' is valid perception ; the consciousness of 'silver' is a memory image. But illusion fuses them into a unitary psychosis, which is perceptual. Illusory silver has illusory reality, while real silver has empirical reality. Illusion is contradicted by right perception. Illusory silver is neither existent nor

[1] VPB., Ch. 1 ; IPC., pp. 128-39.

non-existent, but indefinable. The Advaita Vedānta advocates the theory of Anirvacanīyakhyāti.[1]

INFERENCE

Inference is produced by the knowledge of invariable concomitance of the probans with the probandum as such. The knowledge of vyāpti is its instrumental cause of inference. The residual impression of it is the intermediate function which generates inference. The Nyāya regards the knowledge of the existence of the probans, pervaded by the probandum, in the subject of inference as the instrumental cause of inference. But the Advaita Vedānta does not regard it as a cause of inference, far less an instrumental cause. Vyāpti is the co-existence of the probans and the probandum in all the substrata of the probans. It is known by observation of concomitance of the probans with the probandum and non-observation of their non-concomitance. The number of instances is not material to inference. Concomitance may be observed once or many times. Observation of concomitance only is the ground of inference. Vyāpti does not depend upon the agreement in absence between the probans and the probandum. Inference is of one kind. It is Anvayi and depends upon the agreement in presence between the probans and the probandum. It is founded on their positive concomitance. There is no Anvaya-vyatireki inference, which is said to be based on agreement in presence and agreement in absence between the probans and the probandum since knowledge of vyatirekavyāpti, agreement in absence, is not a cause of inference. There is no Kevala-vyatireki inference, for knowledge of negative concomitance of the absence of the probandum and the absence of the probans cannot generate inference. What is called Kevalavyatireki inference is presumption. Thus the Advaita Vedānta rejects the three kinds of inference, Kevalānvayi, Kevalavyatireki, and Anvaya-vyatireki, which are recognized by the Navya Nyāya. There are two kinds of inference, inference for oneself and inference for others. The former is generated by the sub-conscious impression of vyāpti. The latter consists of three

[1] VPB., pp. 121-37 ; IPC., p. 284.

members only, proposition, reason, and example, or example, application, and conclusion. Three members can show vyāpti and existence of the probans in the subject of inference. The two other members of the Nyāya syllogism are redundant.[1]

COMPARISON

Comparison is the means of the knowledge of similarity. A person, who has perceived a cow in a town, goes to a forest, and perceives a wild cow. He has an apprehension 'this animal is similar to a cow' owing to the intercourse of his eyes with the animal. Then he has an apprehension 'my cow is similar to this animal'. This knowledge of similarity of a cow with a wild cow is acquired by comparison. The knowledge of similarity existing in a wild cow with a cow is the instrumental cause of comparison. The knowledge of similarity existing in a cow with a wild cow is the result. This knowledge of similarity cannot be acquired from perception, since the cow is not present to the eyes. Nor can it be acquired from inference, for similarity existing in a wild cow with a cow cannot serve as a mark of inference as follows: 'my cow is similar to this wild cow; because she is the correlate of similarity existing in this wild cow; whatever is the correlate of similarity with another thing is similar to it, as Caitra, the correlate of similarity existing in Maitra, is similar to Maitra.' The Advaita Vedānta contends that the reason or mark must exist in the subject, but that the reason 'similarity existing in a wild cow with a cow' does not exist in the subject 'my cow'. Therefore, it cannot prove the existence of the probandum 'similarity existing in my cow with a wild cow'. Therefore the knowledge of similarity existing in my cow with a wild cow cannot be acquired from inference. It is acquired from comparison, which is neither perception nor inference, but a distinct means of valid knowledge.[2] The Advaita Vedānta view of comparison is similar to the Mīmāṁsā view.

PRESUMPTION

Presumption is the assumption of a fact to account for another inexplicable fact. The postulation of a hypothesis to

[1] VPB., Ch. ii. [2] VPB., Ch. iii.

explain the inexplicable fact is called arthāpatti. It is presumption, postulation, or implication. The knowledge of the fact to be explaind is the instrumental cause of presumption. The knowledge of the fact that explains is the result. A person is known not to eat in the day time, and yet gets stout. His stoutness is to be explained. It cannot be explained without postulating his eating at night. In the absence of his eating at night his stoutness cannot be explained. Eating at night explains the unintelligible fact. This assumption of a hypothesis is called presumption.

Presumption cannot be regarded as an inference, since the universal major premise cannot be based on positive concomitance. Negative concomitance is not admitted by the Advaita Vedānta. The Kevalavyatireki inference based on negative concomitance is nothing but presumption.[1]

NON-APPREHENSION

Non-existence is known by non-apprehension. It cannot be known by the other means of valid knowledge. Non-apprehension is the unique pramāṇa which cognizes non-existence. The non-existence of a jar on the ground is known by non-apprehension. When the jar is removed from the ground, we perceive the ground, the locus of the non-existence of the jar, but we do not perceive the non-existence itself. We know the non-existence by non-apprehension. Though the locus of non-existence is perceived, the non-existence itself is not perceived. Non-existence is known by non-apprehension. It can never be known by perception. The perceptive process is directed only to the locus of the non-existence, but not to the non-existence itself. The non-existence is known by appropriate non-apprehension. The object, which is absent, must be fit for being perceived. If it is not capable of being perceived, its non-existence cannot be known by non-apprehension. A jar is capable of being perceived. If the jar had been present, it would have been perceived. Merit and demerit are supersensible and cannot be perceived. So their non-existence

[1] VPB., Ch. v.

cannot be known by non-apprehension. The thing that is absent, must be of the same order of reality as its locus which is perceived. The negation must not be absolute negation, but it must be the negation of something perceptible.[1]

TESTIMONY

A sentence refers to an objective relation. That sentence is a valid source of knowledge, which refers to an objective relation, which is not contradicted by any other means of valid knowledge. A sentence must fulfil four conditions in order to convey a meaning. It must have syntactical connection among its essential parts. The verb must demand a subject, a transitive verb an object, and the like. A sentence must have fitness or compatibility of meaning among its parts. The objective relation conveyed by a sentence must be free from contradiction. It must be harmonious. 'He wets the ground with fire': this sentence is meaningless The objective relation conveyed by it is self-contradictory. A sentence must have proximity of its parts. If the words 'bring', 'a', and 'cow' are uttered at the interval of one hour each, they do not form a sentence, and convey any meaning. They must be uttered in close succession to form a sentence. A sentence must have an objective intention. '*Saindhavam ānaya*'. It means either 'bring a horse' or 'bring salt'. If a person utters the sentence while taking his meal, it obviously means 'bring salt'. Fitness is the formal compatibility of meaning. Intention is compatibility in a material reference. It is correspondence of the subjective intention of the speaker with the objective relation conveyed by the sentence.

A sentence is composed of words. The Nyāya maintains that words denote individuals, connote the genus, and suggest configuration, or that words denote individuals endued with the genus and configuration. But the Advaita Vedānta maintains that a word denotes a genus, and not individuals, since individuals are infinite in number. How, then, can it denote an individual ? The genus and the individual are apprehended

[1] VPB., Ch. vi.

by the same cognition produced by a word at the same time.[1]

THE ĀTMAN

The Ātman, according to Śaṁkara, is the universal Self. It is Brahman, the Absolute, the supreme reality. The jīva is the individual or empirical self. It is the Ātman limited by the body, the sense-organs, manas, buddhi, and the like, which are its limiting adjuncts. The Ātman is the transcendental, metaphysical self. The jīva is the empirical, phenomenal self.

The Ātman is the reality in the empirical self. It is the foundational consciousness which sustains the empirical self. Its existence cannot be denied. Every person knows the existence of his self ; he never knows its non-existence.[2] Whoever denies it affirms its existence. The self is always present ; it is present even in the act of denial of its existence. The Ātman is self-proved : it cannot be proved by the means of valid knowledge which cannot function without it. The Ātman is the foundation of all means of valid knowledge, which prove the existence of those things which are not self-proved. The Ātman exists prior to all means of valid knowledge. Śaṁkara starts with the existence of the Ātman which is self-proved.

The Ātman is of the nature of undifferentiated consciousness which reveals the empirical self. It is subject-objectless universal consciousness. It is trans-empirical or non-phenomenal and of the essence of consciousness and bliss. It is devoid of enjoying nature and activity, but it appears to be an enjoying and active agent owing to its limiting adjuncts.[3]

The Ātman is one, eternal, homogeneous consciousness in its essential nature. It is the witness or seer of all cognitions. Its essence consists in the mere power of consciousness. It is pure, transcendental, undifferentiated, eternal consciousness devoid of origin and destruction. Presentations appear and disappear ; but the Ātman is the eternal principle of consciousness which reveals and apprehends them. It is the universal

---

[1] VPB., pp. 239-60, 369. [2] SBS., i, 1, 4.

[3] SBS., ii, 3, 7 ; Bhāmatī, i, 1, 1.

consciousness, which is self-luminous ; it is not revealed by any other consciousness. It reveals all cognitions and objects which cannot reveal themselves. It is neither subject nor object. It is the eternal consciousness which is present in the adjunct of the internal organ, and reveals all its modes. The distinction of subject and object is due to nescience. When nescience is destroyed, the distinction vanishes. The internal organ apprehended as the self appears to be subject and object. The Ātman is non-dual and beyond subject and object.[1]

The Ātman is of the nature of pure consciousness. It is eternally pure, conscious, and liberated. It is the eternal, unchangeable, absolute, formless, one, supreme reality. It is different from the empirical self. But the empirical self is not different from it. The Ātman is its reality.

The Ātman is not an enjoying and active agent. It is devoid of merit and demerit and does not enjoy and suffer. It is inactive, since it is immutable. It is not subject to birth and death. Transmigration is due to nescience because it is empirical existence. The Ātman has non-empirical, transcendental existence. When it is limited by the adjuncts of buddhi and the like, it becomes an enjoyer.[2] The Ātman is devoid of activity. If it were active, it would be changed by its acts, and be non-eternal. It is unchangeable and eternal and consequently cannot be the abode of its own activity or activity of any other thing. Activity is due to egoism which is the adjunct of the empirical self. It is an active agent, which performs duties and bears responsibility. The Ātman is not naturally active. If it were so, it would not be liberated. Activity is of the nature of pain. The Ātman is of the nature of bliss which is always revealed in it. So it cannot be active. The empirical self is not of the nature of bliss. Activity is a quality of buddhi, which is superimposed on the Ātman, and

---

1 SB., Māṇḍ. K., iv, 60 & 92 ; iii, 30 & 35 ; SB., Īśa Up., 6 ; SB., Kena Up., ii, 4 ; SB., Praś. Up., vi, 2 ; SB., Muṇḍ. Up., i, 6 ; ii, 6.

2 SBS., i, 3, 19 ; i, 1, 4 ; i, 2, 11 & 12 ; ii, 3, 19 ; SB., Kath. Up., i, 3, 4.

attributed to it. Activity and power of feeling pleasure and pain are due to nescience.[1]

The Ātman is neither an agent nor an object of activity. It is beyond space, time, and causality. It is one but appears to be many empirical selves owing to nescience. Pleasure, pain, desire, aversion, volition and activity appear and disappear, and belong to the empirical self. They do not belong to the Ātman. If they belonged to it, it would be non-eternal like them.[2] These are due to the adjunct of buddhi.[2]

The Ātman cannot be related to manas, which is dissimilar to it. So knowledge cannot be its accidental quality due to its conjunction with manas. It constitutes its essence. The Ātman is of the nature of the eternal light of knowledge which never lapses. It is the witness of all cognitions. It is not the individual self but the universal Self or Brahman.[3] Thus Śaṁkara refutes the Nyāya view.

The Ātman is not the agent of the act of knowledge. It is of the nature of eternal knowledge. Empirical Knowledge is produced and destroyed. When it is produced, the Ātman is modified by the act of knowledge, and becomes determinate and qualified. When knowledge is destroyed, the Ātman is divested of knowledge, and becomes a mere indeterminate and unqualified substance. Thus it becomes composed of parts, modifiable, non-eternal, and empirical. The Ātman is eternal, self-luminous knowledge, which is devoid of the distinction of the knower and the known. Thus Śaṁkara refutes Kumārila's view.[4]

The Ātman is Brahman. The transcendental Self is the Absolute. The psychic principle is the cosmic principle. The Ātman is the eternal consciousness, which is the foundation of the empirical universe.[5]

THE EMPIRICAL SELF (JĪVA)

The Ātman is the supreme, universal Self. It is non-dual or one, partless and omnipresent like space. The empirical

1 SBS., i, 1, 4, 16 & 19 ; ii, 3, 33 & 40 ; SB., Muṇḍ. Up., ii, 7, 8.
2 SB., Praś. Up., vi, 3 ; SB., Māṇḍ. K., iii, 5.
3 SB., Kena Up., ii, 4. 4 SB., Māṇḍ, K., iv, 1, 99, 53 & 60.
5 SB., Kena Up., i, 5.

self or ego is the Ātman limited by the adjuncts of the body, the sense-organs, manas, buddhi, and ahaṁkāra—the psycho-physical organism. The Ātman is one, but appears to be many individual selves owing to its limiting adjuncts. The Ātman is the universal self, while the jīva is the individual self. The Ātman is the transcendental self, while the jīva is the empirical self. It is neither a part nor a modification of the Ātman, but its appearance. The adjuncts of the body, the sense-organs, manas, buddhi, and the like are creations of nescience, and not real. So the jīva is a construction of nescience. When nescience is destroyed, the jīva remains in its essential nature as the Ātman, which is its reality.[1]

The empirical self is the knower, enjoyer and active agent. It acquires merits and demerits, and experiences their fruits. It is subject to transmigration, lives an embodied life in the empirical world, and is capable of bondage and liberation. Though it is non-different from the Ātman, the supreme Self, and immortal in its essential nature, mortality is attributed to it owing to its actions due to nescience. The difference between the empirical self and the Ātman is not real, but phenomenal due to the limiting adjuncts caused by nescience. The origin of the empirical self from the Ātman is not real, because it is a limitation of the latter. The origin of the limiting adjunct of the mind-body-complex is said to be the origin of the empirical self. On the destruction of the psychophysical organism the empirical self merges in the Ātman, the supreme Self.[2]

The relation of the Ātman to the adjunct of buddhi is due to false knowledge which is dispelled by right knowledge. It does not cease until the knowledge of identity of the empirical self with Brahman dawns upon it. The empirical life of the individual self is annulled by right intuition of the Ātman. The empirical self is not an ontological reality but an imaginary construction of the adjunct of buddhi. It has no existence apart from buddhi which is the individuating principle. There is no ontological difference among the empirical selves,

[1] SBS., i, 2, 6 & 20 ; ii, 3, 32 ; SB., Māṇḍ. K., iii, 3, 7 & 15 ; i, 3.

[2] SBS., i. 2, 11, 17 & 27 ; SB., Māṇḍ. K., iii, 3, 4.

which owe their empirical difference to the adjuncts of the mind-body complexes, even as there is no real difference among the limiting spaces, there being only one all-pervading space.

The empirical self is the embodied self. It has a gross body, a subtle body, and a causal body. The gross body is composed of the five gross elements, the sense organs, and the vital forces. The subtle body is made of the seventeen elements, *viz.*, the five organs of perception, the five organs of action, the five vital forces, manas, and buddhi. The empirical self transmigrates with its subtle body which is the basis of its moral equipment. The causal body is made of nescience or false knowledge of the not-self as the self. The empirical self is the conscious ruler of the body, and the sustainer of its vital forces.[1]

The waking self knows external objects through the sense-organs. The dreaming self knows dream-cognitions through the manas with the aid of subconscious impressions, when the external organs cease to function. The sleeping self is one homogeneous mass of consciousness and bliss. The intuitive self is the Ātman, which is unconditioned, non-dual, homogeneous, distinctionless, devoid of genus and species, quality and activity, non-objective, non-empirical, unchangeable, unprovable, and indefinable. It is present in the waking, dreaming, and sleeping self. It is the ultimate reality, the universal self, the eternal consciousness, which apprehends all.

The empirical self is an object of I-cognition, while the Ātman is the witness which reveals the empirical self. The Ātman is the pure Self, which is self-luminous. The empirical self is its limited form, though there is ontological identity between them. The Ātman reveals I-cognition, which cannot reveal it, because it is a mental mode which is unconscious. Mental modes have origin and destruction, but the Ātman is eternal, immutabte, and indestructible. The empirical self is

---

1 SBS., ii, 3, 30 ; SB., Māṇḍ. K., iii, 6 ; SB., Iśa Up., 8 ; SBS., i, 1, 6.

is an object of I-cognition, while the transcendental self is apprehended by supra-intellectual intuition.[1]

BRAHMAN

Brahman is the only ontological reality. It is the supreme, perfect, absolute reality. The existence of Brahman is proved as the Self of all beings. Every one knows the existence of his own self. The existence of the Self (Ātman), which is self-existent and self-proved, proves the existence of Brahman. The Ātman is the ontological reality in the empirical self. It is the foundational consciousness, which is the transcendental ground of the empirical self and which is the transcendental ground of the empirical universe. The Ātman is Brahman. There is one, eternal, universal consciousness which is the only ontological reality.[2] Śaṁkara gives this ontological proof for the existence of Brahman.

Brahman is existence, knowledge, and bliss. It is the only ontological being, infinite, eternal, supreme knowledge, and infinite, eternal, supreme bliss. Existence is knowledge; knowledge is existence; they cannot be sundered from each other. Being *is* consciousness. Consciousness *is* Being. Brahman is infinite, immortal and imperishable. It is not limited by time, space, and objects. It is eternally fulfilled and of the nature of bliss. Existence, knowledge, and bliss are its essential characters, and neither its parts not its properties. They distinguish Brahman from the world-appearance which is unreal, non-intelligent, and of the nature of pain.[3]

Truth is freedom from contradiction, which is never sublated. Absolute truth can never be contradicted. It is constant and unalterable existence. Brahman is absolute existence, while appearance is relative existence. The world-appearance is not constant and invariable, since it is sublated by the knowledge of Brahman. It has contingent existence; it can be thought

---

[1] SB., Mānḍ. K., iv, 60 & 92; SB., Mānḍ. Up., i, 3-7; SB., Mund. Up., i, 6; ii, 6; SB., Īśa Up., 6; SBS., i, 1, 1; Bhāmatī, i, 1, 4.

[2] SBS., i, 1, 1; SB., Tait. Up., ii, 6.

[3] SB., Tait. Up., ii, 1, 1; Bṛ. Up., iii, 9, 28.

away. But we can never think away existence itself. Brahman is absolute, independent, eternal existence. Therefore it is one, pure, transcendental, trans-empirical being. It is absolutely positive, absolutely simple, absolutely indeterminate. It is free from negation and limitation, change and mutation. It is not limited by any conditions and determinations.[1]

Brahman is non-spatial, non-temporal, non-causal, and trans-empirical existence. It transcends the past, the present and the future, and causes and effects, which are empirical phenomena. It transcends all empirical existence. It is free from all differences of space, time, substance, attribute, action and the like. It is one attributeless and indeterminate real being. Though it is devoid of phenomenal qualities, it appears to persons of dull intellect to be possessed of attributes. Brahman is devoid of all adjuncts and determinations such as genus, quality, activity, and other determinations. The higher Brahman (para brahma) is devoid of phenomenal attributes and determinations. It is the supreme reality.[2] It is noumenal and immutable and transcends all phenomena. Indeterminate Brahman is apprehended by intuition.

Brahman only is the reality. All else are a mere false appearance. Brahman, expanded in the form of effects, appears as mere names and forms. It is the ground of the entire universe of phenomenal appearances. This entire universe is Brahman itself. Brahman is one. One eternal Brahman appears to be manifold appearances owing to nescience. One partless Brahman cannot be differentiated into the manifold world and a plurality of empirical selves. If it does, it ceases to be partless and imperishable. So duality or plurality is not metaphysically real. Brahman is immortal by nature. It can never be divested of its nature, even as fire can never lose its heat.[3] Brahman is the ontological ground of the manifold empirical world.

---

[1] SBS., i, 3, 9-10 ; Pañcadaśī, iii, 29 ; Bṛ. Up., ii, 1, 20 ; ii, 3, 6.

[2] SB., Kaṭh. Up., i, 2, 14 ; SB,, Chānḍ. Up., viii, 1, 1 ; SB., Kena Up. i, 3 ; ii, 1 ; SB., Praś., Up., v, 2 & 7.

[3] SB., Muṇḍ, Up., ii, 2, 12 ; SB., Māṇḍ, Up., i, 19 & 21.

Brahman is devoid of all difference, homogeneous, heterogeneous, and internal. There is no other reality similar to it, from which it may differ. There is no other reality dissimilar to it, from which it may differ. There are no other realities within it, which differ from one another, as branches, leaves, flowers, and fruits differ from one another in a tree. Brahman is absolutely undifferentiated pure identity.

Brahman is limitless and infinite. It is limitless in space and omnipresent. It is limitless in time, since it is not an effect which is limited in time. It is limitless in relation to objects. One object is limited by another different from it; but there is no difference in Brahman. So it is infinite. It is the cause of all phenomena in the sense that it is their substratum, which are non-different from it. They are effects which are unreal, and which do not really exist apart from their cause. There are no other realities except Brahman. Hence it is the infinite, non-spatial, non-temporal, non-causal, trans-empirical reality.[1]

Brahman is of the nature of existence and consciousness. Existence *is* consciousness. Consciousness *is* existence. Brahman is of the nature of eternal knowledge. It is not different from its knowledge. Brahman is eternal knowledge or consciousness devoid of subject and object. It is the eternal, transcendental consciousness devoid of the distinction of knowledge, known, and knower.[2] It is subject-objectless consciousness, which has no relation to empirical objects. It is the Inner Self of all creatures. The Ātman of all knowers is Brahman. Therefore it cannot be known by knowers or empirical selves. It can be known by superconscious intution.[3]

Brahman is impersonal or supra-personal, since personality implies distinction between self and not-self. Brahman is devoid of distinction. It is not the knower, but eternal knowledge. It is not the will, since the will implies becoming, change, mutation. It is not an active agent, since activity

---

[1] SB., Tait. Up., ii, 1; SBS., iii, 2, 21.

[2] SB., Tait. Up., ii, 1; SB., Māṇḍ. Up., iv, 1; i, 37.

[3] SB., Māṇḍ. Up., i, 39; SB., Kena Up., ii, 1.

would make it mutable and non-eternal. It is not an experiencer of joy and sorrow, since it is devoid of merits and demerits. It is supermoral and transcends virtue and vice.

Brahman is the eternally fulfilled and accomplished reality. It is the perfect reality and cannot be divested of its perfection. It is the infinite reality and so essentially blissful. Infinitude is bliss, while finitude is limitation and misery. Brahman is infinite, eternal, transcendental bliss. Finite creatures feel the bliss of Brahman tainted by nescience. They feel empirical joy, which springs from the relation of subject and object. But the subject-object-distinction is due to nescience. When nescience is destroyed, the distinction of subject and object vanishes, and the Ātman or Brahman shines forth in its essential nature of infinite bliss, which is transcendental and eternal.[1]

Brahman is the eternally accomplished being. It does not change, increase and decrease, grow and develop. It is eternally perfect and does not acquire perfection. It is immutable and unchangeable. It is not dynamic, but static, inactive and immobile. It is non-teleological and does not realize an end or purpose, external or immanent.

INDETERMINATE BRAHMAN AND DETERMINATE BRAHMAN

The Upaniṣads speak of the higher Brahman (para brahma) and the lower Brahman (apara brahma). The former is unconditioned, indeterminate and attributeless, while the latter is conditioned, determinate, and qualified by attributes. The former is trans-empirical and non-phenomenal, while the latter is empirical and phenomenal. The former is transcendent, while the latter is transcendent and immanent. Existence, consciousness, and bliss constitute the essence of the indeterminate Brahman. Brahman conditioned by cosmic nescience (māyā) is the Lord, who is the creator, preserver, and destroyer, of the empirical world, and moral governor. God is the determinate Brahman—a phenomenal appearance

[1] SB., Kaṭh. Up., i, 2, 14 ; Chānd. Up., vii, 23, 1 ; SB., Māṇḍ. K., iii, 47 ; SBS., i, 1, 13 & 16 ; SB., Tait. Up., ii, 7 & 8.

of the indeterminate Brahman or Absolute which is free from all conditions and determinations. Indeterminate Brahman is the indefinable and inexpressible Witness of all known phenomena, and therefore itself unknown. It is imperceptible by the sense-organs, incomprehensible by the manas, and inexpressible by speech. It is known by right intuition. Brahman, in its essential nature, transcends all empirical life. But it appears to be the Lord of the empirical selves and the empirical world of phenomena, when it is conditioned by cosmic nescience, which is neither real nor unreal but indefinable, through its undifferentiated and differentiated empirical names and forms. Indeterminate Brahman transcends the duality of the worshipper and the worshipped. It is the transcendent essence of God, devoid of all determinations and attributes. It is the substratum of all, which appears as empirical phenomena of names and forms. Creation is an unreal appearance due to cosmic nescience. It does not affect the identical nature of Brahman. God (Īśvara) is the determinate Brahman. He is the omniscient and omnipotent creator, preserver, destroyer, and moral governor of the world.[1]

Brahman is not both indeterminate and determinate. It is indeterminate in itself, but appears to be determinate owing to the limiting adjunct of cosmic nescience and its products. Brahman is indeterminate and undifferentiated, and cannot assume different forms. It is in itself non-different, but appears to be different—God and the individual self, the worshipped and the worshipper, for the sake of prayer. The difference is due to adjuncts of cosmic nescience. The empirical reality of the worshipper and the worshipped depends upon difference which is apparent due to nescience. Their duality is an empirical appearance due to ignorance. It is destroyed, when nescience is dispelled by right knowledge. One Brahman free from limiting adjuncts is the object of intuition, and the object of worship when it is conditioned by the limiting adjuncts. Phenomenal God (Īśvara) is the object of worship, but the

[1] SBS., iii, 2, 23 ; ii, 1, 27 & 28 ; i, 1, 20, 22-23 ; i, 1, 4 ; SB., Br. Up., ii, 2, 1.

indeterminate Brahman is not the object of worship, since it is beyond actor and activity. When the knowledge of the identity of Brahman dawns, all knowledge of duality vanishes. Indeterminate Brahman is realized by supra-intellectual intuition. In this sense, twofold Brahman is known, Brahman free from all adjuncts and Brahman qualified by the adjuncts of empirical names and forms.[1]

GOD (IŚVARA)

God is the determinate Brahman. He is not the unconditioned, indeterminate, attributeless Brahman. He is the personal Lord. He is Brahman conditioned by cosmic nescience (māyā). Though Brahman is attributeless, it is said to be endowed with empirical attributes for the sake of prayer. Brahman is one and devoid of the duality of the ruler and the ruled in it. It appears to be the omniscient and omnipotent creator, preserver, and destroyer of the world owing to the differentiation of the seeds of empirical names and forms due to nescience. The empirical names and forms projected by nescience are the seeds of the entire world of phenomena (prapañca). They are neither real nor unreal, but indefinable. They are the magic power of God, who is different from them. But they are non-different from Him. God is Brahman conditioned by the adjuncts of empirical names and forms due to cosmic nescience. Without them Brahman cannot appear to be God. He is ontologically one, immutable, eternal, pure consciousness (Brahman). But He appears to be the creator of the world owing to cosmic nescience. But He is not, in reality, different from Brahman. Omniscience, omnipotence, and lordship depend upon the limiting adjunct of cosmic nescience, which is not ultimately real. When it is destroyed by right knowledge, the distinction of the ruler and the ruled vanishes, and one Brahman shines forth. God is a phenomenal appearance. He is eternal, pure, conscious, free, and omniscient. But He is conditioned by the adjunct of pure essence (sattva)

[1] Bhāmatī, i, 1, 2; SBS., iii, 2, 11 & 12; i, 2, 4; i, 1, 11; i, 1, 4 & 11.

of māyā. He is not an enjoyer, but an indifferent spectator. He is the eternal Witness of the individual souls and their objects of enjoyment and suffering, and their inner guide. He guides them by merely witnessing them. His mere knowledge is enough for their guidance.[1]

God is omnipresent, independent, unequalled, unexcelled, and one. He is the inner Self of all, the controller of the entire world, and of the nature of pure consciousness. But He produces multiform objects with the aid of the different impure adjuncts, of names and forms[2] by dint of His inconceivable power. He is self-subsistent, subsisting in His own greatness, and omnipresent. He is non-different from Brahman, though it is different from Him. Brahman is the pure eternal consciousness, while God is the witness or knower of the empirical world. Brahman is unconditioned, while God is conditioned by the pure essence of māyā, and creates the world of phenomena. He is the material cause and the efficient cause of the world. He is inactive in His essential nature, but active in association with cosmic nescience. He is omniscient, because His knowledge is unobstructed by nescience. It is nonsensuous, intuitive, and independent of the body and the sense-organs. He illumines the universe.[3]

God is the creator, preserver, and destroyer of the world (tajjalān). The world is born out of Him, sustained by Him, and absorbed in Him. He is immanent in the world as the inner Self of all. He is the Moral Governor and awards fruits to the individual souls in accordance with their actions. He is the Lord of the Law of Karma. He creates empirical objects for the enjoyment and suffering of the individual souls according to their merits and demerits. He is devoid of merits and demerits, and does not feel joys and sorrows which are due to false knowledge. He is omniscient and devoid of false knowledge. The empirical selves enjoy and suffer under the influence of nescience. God is a mere spectator and makes them enjoy

---

[1] SBS., ii, 1, 14 ; i, 3, 19 ; SB., Muṇḍ. Up., iii, 1.

[2] SB., Kaṭh. Up., ii, 2, 12.

[3] SBS., i. 1, 20 ; ii, 1, 11 ; ii, 2, 7 ; i, 1, 5.

and suffer.[1] He is free from all taint of sins and imperfections. He is the founder of the moral order, harmonizer of the conflicting members of the society, sustainer of the moral organism, and protector of all creatures.

God is omnipresent and immanent in all. Though He is omnipresent, He becomes gracious to the devotee who worships Him as residing in His heart. Though He is formless, He assumes various forms of His own accord to favour His worshippers.[2]

THE ABSOLUTE (BRAHMAN) AND GOD (ĪŚVARA)

The Absolute (Brahman) is the pure, trans-empirical, unconditioned, indeterminate, eternal, subject-objectless consciousness. God (Īśvara) is Brahman conditioned by cosmic nescience (māyā). He is reality and appearance. He is non-different from Brahman, the reality in Him. Brahman is the impersonal or supra-personal foundational knowledge or consciousness. God is the supreme person, the empirical Lord of the world of phenomena. He is the intermediate principle between Brahman and the empirical world. He is the knower of the world, which is the object of His knowledge. Even before creation of the world, the undeveloped seeds of names and forms are the objects of His knowledge. He creates the world by differentiating the seeds of empirical names and forms, which are of the nature of nescience, which are neither real nor unreal, but indefinable. They are the seeds of the phenomena of the empirical world, which are the power of God, which is called māyā or prakṛti.[3] So God depends upon the adjuncts of names and forms caused by nescience, and is different from them. He controls and guides the empirical selves which depend on the adjuncts of the body, the sense-organs, manas, buddhi and the like in their empirical life,

---

1 SBS., i, 1, 5, 20-21 ; i, 2, 8-9, 11 & 13 ; i, 2, 1 ; iv, 1, 3 ; SB., Ait. Up., i, 3 ; SB., Chānd. Up., iv, 14, 2-4.

2 SBS., i, 1, 20 ; i, 2, 7 & 13 ; SB., Chānd. Up., iv, 14, 2-3 ; SB., Bṛ. Up., iv, 4, 22.

3 SBS., ii, 1, 14.

which are the products of nescience. His Lordship, omniscience and omnipotence depend on the limitation of the empirical names and forms which are of the nature of nescience. All these adjuncts are destroyed by the right knowledge of Brahmaṇ. The difference between the Lord and creatures is not real. God is real in empirical life only. He is a phenomenal appearance devoid of ontological reality. In trans-empirical life there is neither creator nor creation. One Brahman, free from adjuncts, is realized by intuition. Limited by adjuncts, it is worshipped as the Lord. So God has no reality apart from Brahman. Intuition of Brahman leads to embodied release at once. But worship of God leads to gradual liberation. Brahman is pure Being, while God is Becoming. Brahman is the causal Brahman, while God is the effect Brahman. Brahman is inactive, while God is active. He wills, creates, preserves, and destroys the world, maintains the moral order, creates the Vedas, and promulgates the moral laws. His oneness is not affected by creation of the many appearances.[1]

GOD (IŚVARA) AND EMPIRICAL SELF (JĪVA)

Both God and individual self are empirical realities. But God is the ruler, whereas empirical selves are the ruled. God is limited by the excellent adjunct of the pure essence (sattva) of māyā. But empirical selves are limited by the impure adjuncts of nescience, the mind-body-aggregate. So God rules the empirical selves. They are related to each other as master and servant. Individual selves are favoured by God, while He is their benefactor. They are parts of God, as it were, while God is devoid of parts. Individual souls cannot be His real parts. Pure consciousness is the common element in both; Brahman is the reality in both. God and the individual souls are phenomenal appearances. Brahman is limited by the pure essence (sattva) of māyā, and appears to be God. It is limited by the impure adjuncts of avidyā, psychophysical organisms, and appears to be individual selves. God is non-different from Brahman. Individual selves also are Brahman in their essential

[1] SBS., ii, 1, 14 ; i, 1, 11 ; SB., Bṛ. Up., v, 1, 1 ; SB., Chānd. Up., vii, 14, 1.

nature. But God is not deluded by the influence of māyā, and therefore not subject to empirical life, and consequent misery. Individual selves, on the other hand, feel misery of empirical life owing to non-discrimination between Self and not-self or its adjuncts. Individual selves are neither the supreme Self, nor different entities, but its reflections. Though God and individual selves are appearances of Brahman, they are not identical with each other. God is the Lord and creator of the empirical world of names and forms, while individual selves are devoid of lordship and cannot create the world of phenomena. God is omniscient, omnipotent, and perfect, while individual selves have finite knowledge, limited powers, and imperfections. God is eternally enlightened and liberated, while individual selves are bound, and liberated by right knowledge. Though God is the inner ruler of all beings, His powers are manifested in different degrees in the individual selves according to the different degrees of purity of their minds which are their limited adjuncts [1]. God is the directive cause of human actions and enjoyments and sufferings, while individual selves do right and wrong actions, acquire merits and demerits, and feel joys and sorrows. He is free from merits and demerits, and joys and sorrows. He is perfect and not affected by their enjoyments, since He has right knowledge. He is omniscient, devoid of false knowledge, and not subject to empirical life, while the individual selves have false knowledge, and so undergo miseries of empirical life. They are Brahman in their essential nature, but their imperfection is due to their limiting adjuncts. Their divine nature is manifested when the right knowledge of their identity with Brahman dawns upon them. So the difference between God and individual selves is not real, but apparent due to false knowledge.[2]

THE PROOFS FOR THE EXISTENCE OF GOD

Śaṁkara gives the cosmological, teleological, and moral arguments for the existence of God. Determinate Brahman

[1] SBS., ii, 3, 43, 46 & 50 ; ii, 4, 20 ; ii, 1, 9 ; i, 1, 22.

[2] SBS., i, 2, 11 ; i, 2, 8 & 11 ; i, 3, 19.

or God is the cause of the origin, subsistence, and dissolution of this world of appearances or differentiations of names and forms, which includes many agents and enjoyers, which is the abode of fruits of their actions, and which is determined by space, time, and causality. Omniscient and omnipotent God is the material cause and the efficient cause of the world. The undifferentiated names and forms, which are the seeds of phenomena of the empirical world, which are of the nature of cosmic nescience constitute the nature, as it were, of God. They are the cause of the subtle essences of the elements. So God is the material cause of the world. He is also its efficient cause ; He differentiates the undifferentiated seeds of names and forms, creates the subtle essences of the elements out of them, combines them with one another in definite proportions, and produces the gross elements. So He is the material cause and the efficient cause of the world. He is the omniscient Witness of the world, and wills the world into existence—His immediate knowledge being the cause of creation. Non-intelligent prakṛti cannot create the world, but God creates, preserves, and dissolves the world.[1] He is the uncaused cause of the world, since He cannot spring from any other cause. He is pure being and cannot spring from another pure being, since the cause must be superior to the effect. He is homogeneous, and cannot therefore spring from a differentiated being. Nor can he spring from non-being, since non-being is a non-entity, and an entity cannot spring from a non-entity. Nor is He a modification or effect. If He were an effect, His cause would be produced by another, and so on to infinity, and thus would lead to infinite regress. He is the uncaused cause or the First Cause. This is the cosmological argument for the existence of God. The hypothesis of many Lords is useless, since One Lord is enough to create the world.[2]

The world is full of unity, order, and harmony. Its

[1] SBS., i, 1, 4-5, 11 & 22 ; i, 2, 1, 10, 21-23 ; i, 3, 10-11, 16 ; ii, 1, 14 & 21.

[2] Śvet. Up., vi, 9 ; SBS., ii, 1, 4, 6, 8-9 ; ii, 2, 44 ; ii, 3, 9.

arrangement is inconceivable even by the mind. There are adjustments and adaptations in the world which can be adequately explained by God only. Non-intelligent things without being guided by an intelligent being cannot serve the purposes of human beings. Houses, palaces, beds, seats, pleasure-gardens and the like, which are adapted to the attainment of pleasure and avoidance of pain, are contrived by intelligent artists. So the entire world adapted to the enjoyment of fruits of various actions of individual souls, including the elements and the bodies of the different species with a definite arrangement of organs capable of being the vehicles of enjoyment and suffering, is contrived by omniscient and omnipotent God. The arrangement of the world including adjustments of the organs in various kinds of organisms cannot be even conceived by the most intelligent artists. So it must be contrived by God who is the intelligent designer of the world. Non-intelligent prakṛti cannot account for it. Just as clay is made into a pot by a potter, so prakṛti also must be shaped into the world by an intelligent being—God, the designer of the world. He acts upon the undifferentiated seeds of empirical names and forms, which constitute cosmic nescience (māyā), and fashions them into a definite arrangement.[1] This is the teleological argument for the existence of God.

God is the omnipresent, omniscient, and omnipotent Self of all beings. Though He is devoid of activity, He can incite all to activity through the influence of cosmic nescience which projects the names and forms or empirical objects to be acted on. He acts on them, and creates a particular arrangement in the empirical world. Non-intelligent prakṛti cannot be transformed into the world, and dissolve it into itself. But God can create and destroy the world, since He is omniscient, omnipotent, and endowed with the power of cosmic nescience. God is inactive in His essential nature, but active in association with cosmic nescience. Therefore

---

[1] SBS., i, 1, 2 ; ii, 2, 1-2 ; SB. Ait. Up., i, 3.

omniscient and omnipotent God possessed of the power of cosmic nescience is the cause of the world.[1]

God is the Lord of the Law of Karma, and awards fruits to the individual selves in accordance with their merits and demerits. He creates various objects for the enjoyments and sufferings of the individual selves according to their merits and demerits, since He knows them and the place and the time of their fruition. God is the directive cause of the souls' actions and their merits and demerits produced by them. Actions are destroyed in a moment, and cannot produce their fruits in future. Actions cannot be said to produce their fruits before they are destroyed, which are enjoyed by the individual souls in future. This is not tenable, because fruits are fruits when they are enjoyed by the individual souls. Joys and sorrows related to them and experienced by them are the fruits of their actions. The Mīmāṁsaka holds that actions produce an unseen power (apūrva) which produces the fruits in proper time. This view also is wrong, because apūrva is non-intelligent. It cannot act and produce any effects without the guidance of an intelligent agent. So God produces the fruits of actions.[2] This is the moral argument for the existence of God.

God is the source of the scriptures which reveal injunctions and prohibitions constituting the moral laws. He is the promulgator of them. His will is the moral standard ; whatever is enjoined by Him is right, and whatever is forbidden by Him is wrong. These prescriptions of God are embodied in the Vedas which are breathed out by Him.[3] This also may be regarded as the moral argument for God's existence.

The proofs are inadequate to prove the existence of God. Inference and other means of valid knowledge cannot prove His existence. The Śruti is the only means of knowing His existence. Reason is subordinate to it, and strengthens its verdict.[4]

---

[1] SBS., ii, 2, 2, 4 & 7 ; ii, 1, 37.

[2] SBS., i, 1, 4 ; i, 2, 13 ; ii, 3, 41 ; iii, 2, 38 & 41.

[3] SBS., i, 1, 3. [4] SBS., i, 1, 2-3.

Śaṁkara regards God as the material cause and the efficient cause of the world. God is Brahman conditioned by māyā with its pure sattva as its limiting adjunct. Māyā is the power of God, His nature, as it were, and the matrix of undeveloped seeds of names and forms. God differentiates them into subtle elements, quintuples them into the gross elements and transforms them into the world. It is the appearance (vivarta) of Brahman, but the transformation (pariṇāma) of God, though He is immutable in His essential nature. He is immanent in the world-appearance, and transcendent of it. But Brahman transcends all empirical phenomena.

BRAHMAN AND THE EMPIRICAL SELF (JĪVA)

Āśmarathya regards the empirical self as partly different and partly non-different from Brahman, even as the sparks are partly different and partly non-different from a fire. As the sparks issuing from a fire are not absolutely different from it, because they both are of the nature of fire ; and, on the other hand, are not absolutely non-different from it, because in that case they could be distinguished neither from it nor from one another ; so the empirical selves also are neither absolutely different from Brahman, because they both are of the nature of consciousness, nor absolutely non-different from Brahman, because in that case they could be distinguished neither from Brahman nor from one another, and if they were identical with Brahman and omniscient, instruction to them would be useless. Hence the individual selves are different and non-different from Brahman.

Auḍulomi regards the individual self as different from Brahman, when it becomes impure in contact with the adjuncts of body, sense-organs, manas, and buddhi. But he regards it as non-different from Brahman, when it is divested of the limiting adjuncts by right knowledge and meditation. The bound self is different from Brahman, while the liberated self is non-different from Brahman. The self loses its individuality, and realizes its identity with Brahman in the state of liberation.[1]

[1] Bhāmatī, i, 4, 20 ; SBṢ., i, 4, 21.

Kāśakṛtsna regards the empirical self as identical with Brahman. The empirical self is not different from immutable God or Brahman. Though Āśmarathya regards the empirical self as different from Brahman, he seems to hold that they are related to each other as effect and cause, since the former depends upon the latter. Audulomi looks upon difference and non-difference of the empirical self from Brahman as due to different conditions. It is different from Brahman in the state of bondage, and non-different from Brahman in the state of liberation. Kāśakṛtsna's view accords with the Śruti which says: 'That thou art'. The empirical self is identical with Brahman. It is not a modification, since if it were so, it would be merged in prakṛti or māyā in dissolution, and would not be immortal. So the names and forms, which subsist in the adjuncts, are attributed to the empirical self. Its origin from Brahman like that of the sparks issuing from fire is really the origin of its limiting adjuncts.[1]

Śaṁkara adopts Kāśakṛtsna's view. There is no ontological difference between the individual self and Brahman. Their difference is empirical due to the limiting adjuncts of body, senses, manas, and buddhi produced by nescience. The purity of indeterminate Brahman is the real nature of the empirical self whose enjoyments, sufferings, and the like are its accidental nature due to its limiting adjuncts.

The empirical self is not a part of Brahman, since Brahman is devoid of parts. It is not a modification of Brahman, since Brahman is unchangeable. Brahman, the eternal, transcendental consciousness, is the substratum of the empirical selves and the entire empirical universe, which cannot exist apart from it. The empirical self limited by the adjuncts of body, vital forces, senses, and the like subsists in Brahman which is its reality. It cannot exist without Brahman. One, eternal, self-luminous consciousness exists in the heart of the empirical self. On meditating on it the empirical self is liberated. Just as the space limited by a jar is non-different from the infinite space, so the empirical or individual self is non-different from the

[1] SBS., i, 4, 22.

pure universal self or Brahman. The difference is due to the limiting adjuncts. Non-difference of the empirical self from Brahman is primary, while their difference is secondary.[1]

MĀYĀ : AVIDYĀ

Śaṁkara uses the two words synonymously. Brahman conditioned by māyā is Īśvara. Māyā is His power or energy, the source of the names and forms, which are modified into the phenomena of the world, and which are neither real nor unreal, but indefinable. They are the seeds of phenomena of the empirical world, and constitute the nature of God, as it were. He depends upon the limiting adjuncts of these names and forms which spring from cosmic nescience. Omniscience and creatorship depend on the manifestation of the seeds of the world in the form of names and forms which are of the nature of His cosmic nescience. God is the omniscient knower ; He knows the entire universe, which is the object of His knowledge. Even before creation, the unmanifest seeds of names and forms. which are developed by God into the world, are the objects of His knowledge. His omniscience, omnipotence, and Lordship depend on the limiting adjuncts produced by cosmic nescience. He knows, creates, and rules over the empirical world of names and forms. He Himself imagines different forms in Himself through His own cosmic nescience. He Himself creates subtle essences and gross elements out of the seeds of names and forms. They are of the nature of God, but He is different from them. He is eternal, pure, conscious, and free in His nature. Names and forms are like the foam of transparent water. He manifested the unmanifest names and forms, which are His own self, and created the entire world. So names and forms do not exist apart from God ; they are His nature or His energy. Brahman is the only reality. So names and forms, in all conditions, are of the nature of Brahman. But Brahman is not of the nature of names and forms. Names

---

[1] SBS., i, 4, 22 ; i, 3, 19 ; iv, 3, 14 ; SB., Māṇḍ. K., iii, 13-14 ; SB., Māṇḍ. Up., ii, 2, 1 ; SB., Muṇḍ. Up., ii, 2, 2 ; SB., Kaṭh. Up. ii, 2, 1.

and forms are germs of the empirical world. They are not real in themselves but their reality is Brahman. But Brahman is not empirical, but absolutely trans-empirical. One, uncaused Brahman is real, but the world appears to be born owing to cosmic nescience. It is an imaginary construction of cosmic nescience.[1] Brahman cannot be defined by a name and known by any form ; it is devoid of names and forms. Creation is not real, but an appearance—a creation of cosmic nescience. One eternal, immutable Brahman appears to be the manifold world owing to cosmic nescience. Duality of empirical selves and empirical objects is not ontologically real. Brahman, the ontological reality, is not touched by names and forms. Pure consciousness is common to them ; they are of the nature of pure consciousness, and essentially Brahman. Brahman is neither a substance, nor a non-substance ; and so it cannot be a cause or an effect. All empirical objects are generated by cosmic nescience. They are created and destroyed from the empirical standpoint ; but they are eternal Brahman from the ontological standpoint. Production of empirical objects is due to cosmic nescience. Māyā is avidyā. Avidyā is mentioned in the Upaniṣads. Production is unreal like māyā. Māyā is neither being, nor non-being, but indefinable. Brahman is the ontological reality. It is formless, but it assumes diverse forms owing to its limiting adjuncts. It is one in itself, but it appears to be manifold owing to limiting adjuncts. Brahman is real, while māyā is unreal. There is no relation between them.[2] How is Brahman related to māyā is an illegitimate question. The differences of empirical objects are mere appearances, which do not affect the immutability and transcendental identity of Brahman. They are not metaphysically real. Brahman is, in itself, changeless and non-empirical. But it appears to be modified into the empirical world through indefinable

---

[1] SBS., ii, 1, 14 ; i, 1, 5 ; SB., Māṇḍ. K., ii, 12-13 ; iii, 24 & 27 ; SB., Ait. Up., i, 1, 2 ; SB., Bṛ. Up., i, 4, 7 ; SB., Tait. Up., ii, 6.

[2] SB., Māṇḍ. K., iii, 36 & 19 ; iv, 57-58 ; i, 7 ; SB., Chānd. Up., viii, 14, I ; SB., Kena Up., ii, I ; SB., Ait. Up., iii, 23.

names and forms. Brahman is not modified into the world. The Śruti regarding modification of Brahman into the world really conveys the identity of the world-appearance with trans-empirical Brahman. The world is not a modification of Brahman, but its mere appearance. A modification is transformation of a cause into an effect of the same order of reality. But an appearance is perversion of a cause into an effect of a different order of reality. The world is a perversion of Brahman—its mere appearance; its reality is Brahman. Brahman is devoid of all determinations, and cannot have infinite powers. The multiplicity of appearances is a construction of cosmic nescience.[1]

Māyā is cosmic nescience. It is an indefinable principle. It is ontologically unreal, since Brahman is the only ontological reality. But it is not absolutely unreal like a hare's horn; it is real enough to project the multiple world of appearances. They are modifications of names and forms, which are creations, constructions or modifications of cosmic nescience. But they are appearances of Brahman.

Māyā is not an independent principle like prakṛti of the Sāṁkhya. It is dependent on God. It is His energy and contains the unmanifest seeds of names and forms, which are transformed into the subtle essences and the gross elements.

Māyā is called unmanifest (avyakta), because it cannot be defined as real or unreal, and also because it consists of subtle essences of the elements which exist in an unmanifest condition in it. They exist as unmanifest names and forms or as seed-potentialities of appearances.[2] The empirical world consists of manifest names and forms. Māyā is the subtle condition of the world prior to creation. It is of the nature of nescience or false knowledge. It is non-apprehension of the reality or misapprehension of it as manifold appearances. It is the beginningless cause of saṁsara. It exists in the form of seeds of actions in the souls. Avidyā veils the nature of

[1] SBS., ii, 1, 27, 7 & 31; VPB., p. 141.

[2] SBS., i, 1, 4 & 17; i, 2, 22: i, 3, 19; ii, 1, 22, 27, 31 & 33; ii, 2, 2; i, 4, 3.

the Ātman or Brahman. The soul subject to nescience cannot know its inner Self, Brahman, within it. Māyā consists of sattva, rajas, and tamas. Pure sattva not overcome by rajas and tamas is the adjunct of God. Māyā is the sumtotal of causal powers of all effects. It subsists in God, and is permeated by Him. Māyā is cosmic nescience subsisting in, and dependent on, God, in which bound empirical selves, ignorant of their essential nature, sleep. This is the state of dissolution prior to creation. God creates the world out of this state of cosmic nescience. The bound souls also are reborn at the time of creation to exhaust the store of merits and demerits.[1]

The later Advaitavādins distinguished between māyā and avidyā and regarded the former as cosmic nescience and the latter as individual nescience of an empirical self.

THE WORLD-APPEARANCE (PRAPAÑCA)

The empirical world is the unfoldment of undifferentiated names and forms, which are the objects of nescience. It is the abode of empirical agents, acts, and their fruits and consists of formed and formless objects constructed by nescience. It is superimposed on the Ātman or Brahman, which is different from empirical names and forms. Though it is one, eternal, pure or trans-empirical, conscious, and free, it appears to be the manifold world of appearance variegated by differences of agents, acts, and fruits. Intuitive knowledge of Brahman dispels nescience, which is the seed-potentiality of attachment, aversion, and actions. The world is the scene of retribution where the empirical selves experience the fruits of their actions done in the past. The empirical objects are the material of their enjoyments and sufferings.

Duality which infects the world-appearance is mere appearance. Non-duality or Brahman is ontologically real. Duality is the object of nescience, while non-duality is the object of intuition. When nescience is destroyed by intuition,

---

[1] SBS., i, 4, 2-3 ; SB., Māṇḍ. K., i, 16 ; SB., Iśa Up., 3 ; SB., Muṇḍ. Up. iii, 1, 7 ; iii, 1, 1 ; Kaṭh. Up., 1, 3, 11.

duality vanishes, and non-dual Brahman shines forth. When Brahman is known, duality does not exist. Empirical selves and empirical objects are not metaphysically real, but appearances. When the mind is purged of the taint of nescience in trance, it no longer perceives subjects and objects, but it becomes one, pure undifferentiated consciousness or Brahman.[1]

The world-appearance is false—mere Māyā. Both external objects and mental modes are unreal, like the illusory snake in a rope, and the like. But though the world-appearance is unreal, it is not absolutely unreal like a hare's horn, or a barren woman's son. The world has not illusory reality. Even illusions are not objectless, because they have foundation in empirical objects. The illusory snake is existent in the rope, which appears to be a snake owing to nescience. A rope is an empirical object which is mistaken for a snake. An illusion cannot exist separated from the empirical object, which is its substrate. It is unreal in comparison with its substrate.[2] The empirical objects in the world are unreal in comparison with Brahman, which is the only ontological reality. They have relative or pragmatic reality, and are objects of empirical knowledge and practical use.. They are real in comparison with illusory objects. Illusory objects are unreal, because they do not serve practical needs. But empirical objects have pragmatic reality, because they serve the practical purposes of life, and because they have fixed laws. When the empirical self realizes its identity with Brahman, it is no longer deluded by the apparent plurality of the world. But until the intuition of Brahman is attained, the objects of practical use, have empirical reality.

It is entirely erroneous to suppose that Śaṁkara treats the world as illusory, or as absolutely real. He recognizes the

[1] SB., Bṛ. Up., i, 1, 1 ; SB., Ait. Up., i, 1, 1 & 3 ; SB., Chānd. Up., iii, 16, 1 ; iv, 1, 1 ; vi, 3, 3 ; SB., Māṇḍ. K., i, 17-18, 29 ; iii, 18-19 ; ii, 1 ; iv, 72 & 80 ; iii, 35.

[2] SB., Māṇḍ. K., i, 6, 17-18, 27 ; ii, 31-32, 38 ; iv, 17 ; iii, 29 ; SB., Māṇḍ. Up., i, 7.

relative, empirical, or pragmatic reality of the world. He accords more reality to it than to illusions which are false, and less reality to it than to Brahman, which is the only ontological reality. Illusions are more real than ideas of absolutely unreal things like hare's horns, because they subsist in empirical objects. The world-appearance is false in comparison with Brahman. Just as illusions subsist in empirical objects, which are their reality, so the world-appearance subsists in Brahman, which is its reality. Brahman is the substratum of the world-appearance.[1]

Brahman is the substratum of the world-appearance, even as a rope is the substratum of the illusion of a snake. It is the reality of formed and formless things, which cannot exist apart from it. All beings subsist in the eternal consciousness, which is real, while the beings subsisting in Brahman are unreal. Brahman alone is true, and all its apparent modifications are false. That is the essence of a thing which does not depend upon any other thing; it is its reality. That is not the essence of a thing which depends upon some other thing, since it does not exist in its absence. The essence of a thing consists in its immutability, for it does not depend upon another thing. So the essence of empirical things is Brahman, and their mutations are unreal appearances. The world of mutations is unreal; it is nothing but Brahman; there is no reality called the world other than Brahman.[2]

There is causation in the world of empirical objects, but no causation in Brahman, the ontological reality. There is ontological non-difference of the empirical world from indeterminate Brahman. But there is causation in the world of empirical objects. Empirical causation is mutation, modification, or transformation, and the world is the modification or evolute of cosmic nescience, power of God. God, determinate Brahman, is the material cause and the efficient cause of the

[1] SB., Tait. Up., ii, 6; SB., Kaṭh. Up., ii, 3, 2; SB., Māṇḍ. K., ii, 18 & 32; VPB., Ch. i.

[2] SB., Muṇḍ. Up., ii, 1, 1-2; ii, 2, 1-2, 12; SB., Tait. Up., ii, 8; SB., Muṇḍ. Up., ii, 1, 10.

world, because He is an appearance of Brahman. But there is non-difference between indeterminate Brahman and the empirical world. Ontological non-difference is the truth of empirical causation. The world is the appearance of indeterminate Brahman, but not its modification. It is the ground of the world-appearance. Śaṁkara advocates Vivartavāda from the ontological standpoint, and Pariṇāmavāda from the empirical standpoint.

An effect does not exist apart from its cause, and so it is its unreal appearance. Gold ornaments are non-different from gold, but gold is not of the nature of gold ornaments. Though effect and cause are non-different from each other, the effect partakes of the nature of the cause, but the cause does not partake of the nature of the effect. The effect is non-different from the cause. The entire world is an effect or appearance of Brahman, and so it is non-different from Brahman. The world-appearance cannot exist apart from Brahman, its ground and reality. It has only empirical reality, and its ontological reality is Brahman.[1]

Creation is real from the empirical standpoint, and unreal from the ontological standpoint. Texts relating to creation of the world by Brahman aim at proving its non-difference from, or identity with, Brahman. The differences in the world are not due to creation. They are products of nescience, mere names and forms,—empirical appearances. Creation is not ontologically real.[2] A thing composed of parts is modified into a different thing owing to mutation of its parts. But one, uncaused, partless Brahman cannot be modified into the manifold objects of the world. One immutable Brahman appears to be the multiform world owing to cosmic nescience; it does not really become the manifold world. Brahman is eternal and immutable, devoid of

[1] SBS., ii, 1, 9, 14 & 20 ; SB., Tait. Up., ii, 1.

[2] SBS., ii, 1, 33 ; SB., Māṇḍ. K., iii, 15.

cause and effect, and so connot be really modified into the world.[1]

SPACE, TIME, AND CAUSALITY

Brahman is non-spatial, non-temporal, and non-causal. The empirical world is spatial, temporal, and determined by causality. Space, time, and causality are categories of empirical knowledge. They imply plurality which is a construction of nescience or empirical knowledge. Space implies coexistence of a plurality of objects ; time, succession of a plurality of events ; and causation, sequence of causes and effects. The space-time-cause world is an object of empirical knowledge, and not an object of higher knowledge. Only Brahman is known by right intuition. Space, time, and causality have empirical reality, which apply to empirical objects only. Empirical objects are many, caused, divisible, composed of parts, and have inside and outside. They are therefore spatial. They are limited in time, produced by their causes, and produce effects. Whatever is limited in space, is limited in time, and produced by a cause. Therefore empirical objects are spatial, temporal, and caused.[2]

There is no causality from the ontological standpoint. Brahman is the ontological reality, and not subject to causality. It is neither a cause nor an effect. Brahman is the cause of the world-appearance in the sense that it is its ground or substrate. Causation implies distinction of cause and effect, their temporal sequence, and modification of cause into effect. But Brahman is distinctionless, non-temporal, and immutable, and so not a cause in the empirical sense. Brahman is the substratum of the world-appearance, even as a rope is the substratum of an illusory snake. Brahman is not transformed into the world, for it is unchangeable and unmodifiable. The world

---

[1] SBS., ii, 1, 14 ; SB., Māṇḍ. K., iv, 14.

[2] SB., Māṇḍ. K., ii, 14 & 32 ; iii, 2, 19-20, 24, 27 & 38 ; iv, 14, 22, 38, 40 ; SB., Muṇḍ. Up., ii, 2, 6 ; SB,, Kaṭh. Up., i, 2, 4 & 14 ; SBS., ii, 2, 41.

is an appearance of indeterminate Brahman and non-different from it. Identity is the truth of causality, which has only empirical reality.

CREATION

God is the creator, preserver, and destroyer of the world. Māyā is the matrix of the seeds of names and forms, which is dependent on God. When the world is created, it remains non-different from God. When it is destroyed, it remains in the form of seed-potentialities of names and forms, non-distinct from māyā, the power of God. It exists in an effect state after creation, and in a causal state after dissolution. Dissolution is the reverse order of creation.[1]

God created ether, air, fire, water, and earth in due succession. Ether is one, infinite, imponderable, inert, and all-pervasive. It is a positive entity, which is inferred from the quality of sound. It is an effect of cosmic nescience. Air is generated from ether ; fire, from air ; water, from fire ; and earth, from water.[2] The subtle elements are different from the gross elements. From māyā of God, the matrix of unmanifest names and forms, is generated the subtle essence of sound, which is the subtle element of ether, and which has the quality of sound only. The subtle element of air is generated from it, and its essence is touch. The subtle element of fire is generated from them, and its essence is colour. The subtle element of water is generated from them, and its essence is taste. The subtle element of earth is generated from them, and its essence is smell. Ether has sound ; air, sound and touch ; fire, sound, touch, and colour ; water, taste in addition to these ; and earth, smell in addition to these. Gross elements are generated from the subtle elements by quintuplication. Each subtle element is divided into half. Each half is divided into four equal parts. Each half of a subtle element is combined with $\frac{1}{8}$ of each of the other elements, and thus a gross element is produced.

---

[1] SBS., ii, 3, 15 ; SB., Ait. Up., i, 2.

[2] SBS., ii, 2, 22 & 24 ; ii, 3, 8-13.

Gross ether = $\frac{1}{2}$ ether essence + $\frac{1}{8}$ air essence + $\frac{1}{8}$ fire essence + $\frac{1}{8}$ water essence + $\frac{1}{8}$ earth essence.

Gross air = $\frac{1}{2}$ air essence + $\frac{1}{8}$ ether essence + $\frac{1}{8}$ fire essence + $\frac{1}{8}$ water essence + $\frac{1}{8}$ earth essence.

Gross fire = $\frac{1}{2}$ fire essence + $\frac{1}{8}$ ether essence + $\frac{1}{8}$ air essence + $\frac{1}{8}$ water essence + $\frac{1}{8}$ earth essence.

Gross water = $\frac{1}{2}$ water essence + $\frac{1}{8}$ ether essence + $\frac{1}{8}$ air essence + $\frac{1}{8}$ fire essence + $\frac{1}{8}$ earth essence.

Gross earth = $\frac{1}{2}$ earth essence + $\frac{1}{8}$ ether essence + $\frac{1}{8}$ air essence + $\frac{1}{8}$ fire essence + $\frac{1}{8}$ water essence.

Śaṁkara recognizes triplication also of the subtle elements. Triplication is the combination of the three subtle essences of earth, water, and fire. Ether and air cannot combine with the other elements. Gross fire = $\frac{1}{2}$ fire essence + $\frac{1}{4}$ water essence + $\frac{1}{4}$ earth essence. Gross water = $\frac{1}{2}$ water essence + $\frac{1}{4}$ fire essence + $\frac{1}{4}$ earth essence. Gross earth = $\frac{1}{2}$ earth essence + $\frac{1}{4}$ fire essence + $\frac{1}{4}$ water essence. Thus the gross elements are compounds of the subtle elements. Gross ether has manifest sound ; gross air, sound and touch ; gross fire, sound, touch, and heat and light ; gross water, taste in addition to these qualities ; and gross earth, smell in addition to these.[1] The subtle elements possess them in an unmanifest condition. The gross elements possess them in a manifest condition. The gross elements produce the different kinds of substances by transformation. They produce compounds, which possess like qualities with the constituents ; or they produce compounds, which possess unlike qualities. The cosmic system is composed of the gross elements with the excess of tamas in various forms of integration and disintegration. God Himself creates the subtle and gross elements out of His mayā by volition. In dissolution earth becomes water ; water, fire ; fire, air ; air, ether ; and ether is reabsorbed in God's māyā.[2]

The physical organism is made of all the five gross elements.

[1] SBS., ii, 4, 20 ; SB., Chānd. Up., vi, 3, 3 ; SB., Praś. Up., vi, 4 ; SB., Muṇḍ. Up., ii, 1, 3 ; VPB., pp. 356 & 362 ; VSR., p. 41 ; PSAH., p. 88.

[2] PSAH., pp. 89-90 ; VSR., p. 42 ; VPB., pp. 364-65 ; SBS. ii, 3, 13-14.

It is the gross body ; its different constituents form different parts of the body. The chief prāṇa, the cosmic life, which is the energy inherent in all natural forces, is a creation of God. Life is the energy inherent in the physical organism. It is a subtle physical force pervading the organism. It is prior to the senses, and regulates the development of the organism. It is subtle and pervades the body. The five organs of knowledge—ears, skin, eyes, tongue, and nose—arise from the five subtle elements individually with the excess of sattva, which manifests objects. The five organs of action—vocal organ, hands, feet, excretive organ, and generative organ—arise from the subtle elements individually with the excess of rajas, whose function is activity.[1] The external sense-organs are physical.

Manas, buddhi, ahaṁkāra, and citta are the internal organs. Assimilation and discrimination are the functions of manas ; determination is the function of buddhi ; and self-sense is the function of ahaṁkāra. Recollection is the function of citta. The internal organs also are physical, and arise from the five subtle elements collectively with the excess of sattva. The subtle body is composed of the five subtle elements, the five organs of knowledge, the five organs of action, the five vital forces, manas and buddhi, and clings to the empirical self till it attains liberation. It helps it transmigrate from one body to another.[2] The causal body is the cause of the subtle body and the gross body. It is the individual nescience, which is an appearance of the eternal consciousness. It is destroyed by the intuition of the identity of the Ātman with Brahman. The entire aggregate of effects and organs is of the nature of names and forms which are assembled to serve the ends of individual selves.[3]

Śaṁkara recognizes the empirical reality of the world. He recognizes different degrees of reality in it. Though eternal and immutable, God is one, who is modified into the empirical world. There are degrees of reality which manifest His

[1] SBS., ii, 4, 9 & 13 ; SB., Kaṭh. Up., ii, 3, 6.

[2] VSR., pp. 17-18 ; VPB., pp. 357-58 & 363.

[3] SB., Iśa Up., 8 ; SB., Praś. Up., iv, 8 ; SB., Kaṭh. Up., ii, 2, 5.

powers in different degrees. He is immanent in all living creatures. But they can comprehend His powers in different degrees owing to different degrees of nescience perverting their minds. The inorganic, organic, and psychic worlds are higher and higher stages through which God reveals His nature. There is a gradual diminution of knowledge, power, and the like in the series of beings from men down to blades of grass. There is a gradually increasing manifestation of knowledge, power, and the like in the series of beings from men up to Hiraṇyagarbha. There are different degrees of manifestation of bliss in men, gandharvas, and gods.[1] Though Śaṁkara recognizes different degrees of reality in the empirical world, he does not treat them as ontologically real; he accords them only relative or empirical reality.

BONDAGE

The pure, transcendental, universal self or Ātman is the reality of the empirical self which is really one, eternal, universal consciousness. It is eternally liberated. Its bondage is due to ignorance which generates the psychophysical organism, which limits the universal consciousness, and makes it appear as the individual self. Thus ignorance or intellectual knowledge infected with the duality of subject and object is the cause of bondage. Ignorance is removed by intuition of the identity of the Ātman with Brahman. Integral experience of the Ātman or Brahman leads to liberation. Bondage is ignorance (avidyā). Liberation is higher knowledge (vidyā).

False knowledge is the knowledge of difference between the individual self and God due to non-discernment of the accidental nature of the empirical self owing to its limiting adjunct of the psychophysical organism. It is the cause of bondage and suffering, and destroyed by the knowledge of the Ātman or Brahman. The mind-body-complex, attachment, aversion, delusion, enjoyment, and activity constitute the empirical nature of the individual self, which is due to nescience. When

[1] SB., Ait. Up., SB., Tait. Up., ii, 4; SBS., i, 1, 12; i, 3, 30.

nescience is destroyed, its intrinsic pure divine nature is known, even as the real nature of rope is known when the illusion of a snake is destroyed. Integral experience uproots nescience, which is the root cause of birth and death. It destroys rebirth due to conjunction of the Ātman with the mind-body-complex. The Ātman is eternally liberated, but its intrinsic freedom is not known because it is veiled by nescience. Liberation is not an achievement, but a discovery.[1]

Śaṁkara repeatedly speaks of avidyākāmakarma. Avidyā is the cause of desire (kāma) which takes the forms of attachment and aversion. These are called faults or afflictions which are due to intellectual disorders. They are the springs of action and produce actions (karma). Actions are either righteous or unrighteous. Righteous actions produce merits, and unrighteous actions produce demerits. Merits and demerits are residual impressions, potencies, or dispositions of righteous and unrighteous actions. They are also called karmas. They produce their fruits in the shape of joys and sorrows in the present life or in a future life. They are the cause of rebirth or transmigration. Until the merits and demerits, which are the seeds of actions, are completely burnt up by the fire of integral experience of the Ātman or Brahman, the wheel of birth and death continues to revolve. When they are exterminated by true insight transmigration ceases, and liberation is attained.[2]

Śaṁkara believes in the transmigration of the empirical self. The self is distinct from the body and does not perish with the death of the body Birth is union of the soul with a body, and death, separation of it from the body.[3]

Śaṁkara maintains that the empirical self transmigrates with a subtle body. It is subtle in its essence and dimension,

[1] SBS., i, 1. 4-5 ; i, 3, 19 ; ii, 3, 46 ; SBG., xiii, 26 ; SB., Bṛ. Up., ii, 1, 20.

[2] SB., Tait. Up., Introduction ; SB., Chānd. Up., vi, 15, 2 ; SB., Ait. Up., ii, 1 ; iv, 1 ; SB., Māṇḍ. Up., 1, 4 ; SB., Muṇḍ. Up., i, 1, 8 ; i, 2, 7 & 12 ; iii, 3, 1-2.

[3] SBS., ii, 3, 16.

and capable of movement. It is transparent, irresistible, and invisible, and has infra-sensible touch and colour. It contains the seed of a future body in the shape of merits and demerits. The kind of body to be assumed on rebirth is determined by the merits and demerits acquired in the previous births. Knowledge, character, and impression of past experience pursue the empirical self during transmigration.[1]

LIBERATION (MOKṢA)

The experience of Brahman is the supreme end, because it completely destroys nescience, which is the root cause of the round of birth and death. The Ātman is the reality of the individual self, which is the eternal existence, consciousness, and bliss, and identical with Brahman. The experience of the identity of the Ātman with Brahman is the highest good, because it destroys all afflictions. Brahman is an eternally accomplished fact, and cannot be acquired by actions. It can be experienced by intuition only.[2]

The Ātman is eternally liberated. Liberation is its essential nature. It is unchangeable, eternal, omnipresent, unmodifiable, eternally fulfilled, undivided, self-luminous, supermoral, non-temporal, and disembodied. It is hidden by nescience. When nescience is removed by true knowledge, liberation is realized. It is life eternal and absolute, and consists in existence in the essential condition of the Ātman or Brahman. The individual self, which knows Brahman, attains eternal peace and rest and becomes Brahman.. Liberation is extinction of the individual self in the Absolute. Individuality is due to nescience. When it is destroyed by true knowledge, the individual self is merged in the Absolute and reailzes its intrinsic transcendental and absolute nature. The transcendental Ātman is the highest Good, because it transcends duality. Non-duality is good and free from fear.[3] Saṁsāra is empirical life infected with duality of subject and object.

---

[1] SBS., iv, 2, 9 & 21 ; iii, 4, 11 ; ii, 1, 5-8.

[2] SBS., i, 1, 1 & 4.

[3] SBS., i, 1, 4 ; SB., Muṇḍ. Up., iii, 2, 6 & 9 ; SB., Māṇḍ. K., ii, 32 ; iii, 40 ; i, 12.

Liberation is not produced, but eternal. So it does not depend upon bodily, verbal, and mental actions. It is not modifiable, because if it were so, it would be non-eternal. It is the essential nature of the Ātman and so cannot be attained. The Ātman is omnipresent, and so its liberation is eternally present in it. Liberation does not admit of refinement. Refinement consists in producing excellence in the object refined, or in removing its defects. Liberation is the essential nature of Brahman and does not admit of production of any excellence in it. It is the essential nature of Brahman, which is eternally pure, and does not require any purging of imperfections. It cannot be said to be hidden in the Ātman, which is manifested by an activity, since the Self cannot be an object of activity. If it were modified by activity, it would be non-eternal. It is neither an object of its own activity nor activity of any other agent and so cannot be refined by activity. Activity can lead to production, attainment, modification, and refinement. Liberation is not in the nature of any of these, and cannot therefore be brought about by activity.

The individual self is identical with God. Divinity is its essential nature, and its bondage is due to its ignorance of its divine nature. Its liberation is due to its knowledge of its divine nature. The divinity of the individual self is hidden by the veil of nescience, which is destroyed by the grace of God, when it meditates on Him, and makes strenuous efforts to know its essential divinity. Divine knowledge and sovereignty are hidden by nescience in the empirical self, and it appears to be different from God owing to its connection with the mind-body-complex. When nescience is completely destroyed, there is no more rebirth. Bondage is due to the adjuncts which are generated by nescience. When they are destroyed, the empirical self realizes its intrinsic liberation.[1]

Perfect knowledge is of one kind, since it depends upon its object, Brahman, which is identical with its nature. Identity

[1] SBS., i, 1, 4 ; SB., Tait. Up., i, 11 ; SB., Bṛ. Up., iii, 3, 1 ; SB., Muṇḍ. Up., i, 2, 12 ; SBS., iii, 2, 6, 9 & 11.

of the Ātman with Brahman is natural. The identity consciousness is the consciousness of all as identical with the Ātman. When the intuitional consciousness of the identity of the whole universe with the Ātman or Brahman is attained, the empirical self is purged of all desires for any other objects, since they are non-existent. The intuitional consciousness of identity is not illusory, since it results in the cessation of nescience, and since is not contradicted. Release is a state of desirelessness. When Brahman is known, there remains no duty to be performed. The sense of duty is transcended. Liberation is the supreme state of beautitude or blessedness—a supermoral state of fulfilment.[1] Virtue and vice both are causes of bondage. Virtue leads to heaven. Vice leads to hell. True knowledge destroys both, and puts an end to transmigrations. True knowledge is superior to virtue, and destroys all merits and demerits, and leads to liberation after death.

Actions are useless in achieving liberation. Release is a state of actionlessness. It is existence in the essential state of the Ātman, which is a state of inactivity. Activity belongs to the empirical self, and does not pertain to the trascendental Self. It is the effect of lower knowledge, and possible in the empirical world of duality and plurality, where there is a distinction of the agent, action, object, and fruit, means and ends. It is not possible in the realm of the eternal, absolute, transcendental, non-dual reality or Ātman.[2]

He, who has realized the Ātman as the reality of the universe, is delighted in it, sports with it, is united with it, and filled with supreme bliss, and becomes autonomous. Eternal bliss is the essence of the Ātman, which is hidden by the limiting adjuncts of the psychophysical organism due to nescience. When nescience is destroyed by integral experience, the transcendental bliss of the Ātman manifests itself. The bliss arising from the intuition of the Ātman is supreme, transempirical, self-luminous and ineffable. It springs from the realization of the Ātman as the essence of the whole

[1] SBS., ii, 1, 11 & 14; i, 1, 4.

[2] SBS., iv, 1, 4; ii, 3, 40; SBG., iii, 1 & 4: SB., Muṇḍ. Up. i, 2, 11.

universe, and transcends all relation to empirical objects, avidyā, desires, and actions.[1]

The knower of the Ātman has integral experience of the whole universe. He does not cease to have cognitions of external objects. But his cognitions of them are not tainted by attachment, aversion, delusion, and other imperfections. He knows them as non-different from Brahman. His desires are withdrawn from external objects, and turned inward to the Ātman. He does not dissolve the empirical world of plurality, but he destroys the sense of plurality. His knowledge of plurality is transmuted by the intuition of Identity. He throws off the sway of empirical objects.[2]

Śaṁkara recognizes gradual liberation and liberation in embodied life. The person who meditates on the mystic syllable *Om*, the symbol of Brahman, goes to Brahmaloka or heaven after death. He retains his personality there, and gradually acquires integral experience of Brahman. This is gradual release. Worship of determinate Brahman or personal God leads to gradual release. Indeterminate Brahman cannot be comprehended by persons of dull intellect. But the person, who acquires intuition of indeterminate Brahman, realizes his infinitude and absoluteness in the embodied state. He is purged of nescience, desires, and actions, virtue and vice, and becomes infinite and eternal spirit.[3] The knower of Brahman becomes omnipresent spirit, and realizes absoluteness here and now. Release is not production of anything new but mere cessation of bondage owing to annulment of nescience. It is the complete cessation of birth and death; it is beginningless, endless, unageing, undying, immortal, fearless, pure, and faultless.[4]

THE MEANS TO LIBERATION : MORALITY AND KNOWLEDGF

Śaṁkara is the staunchest advocate of knowledge as the only means of liberation. Liberation is attained by integral

[1] SBS., iii, 2, 35 ; SB., Kaṭh. Up., ii, 2, 12 ; iii, 1, 4.

[2] SB., Chānd. Up., vii, 26, 2 ; SBS., iii, 2, 21 ; SBG., iii. 29.

[3] SB., Chānd. Up., viii, 12, 1 ; SBS., iii, 2, 21 ; SB., Kena. Up., iv, 5 ; SB., Kaṭh. Up., ii, 2, 1 ; ii, 3, 14-18 ; SB., Muṇḍ. Up., iii, 2, 9.

[4] SBS., iv, 2, 14 ; iv, 4, 2 ; SB., Muṇḍ. Up., i, 11, 1.

experience. It is the experience of all beings in the Ātman and the experience of the Ātman in all beings. It is the experience of the identity of the Ātman with Brahman without any distinction. The person, who has acquired integral experience, remains in the highest condition of Brahmanhood. Integral knowledge of the Ātman is the highest good. It can be attained by total extinction of all desires for external objects of enjoyment. It can be acquired by meditation on Brahman by the concentrated mind free from all taint of attachment, aversion, and the other afflictions, and withdrawn from external objects of enjoyment. It can be attained by the extirpation of all desires for enjoyment and false egoism, and the cultivation of universal good will, amity, and compassion.[1]

Liberation cannot be produced by works, which spring from ignorance. Works are antagonistic to knowledge. True knowledge is the knowledge of one undifferentiated Ātman. Works are due to the false knowledge of difference of actors, actions, fruits, means and ends. They are due to egoism or confusion of the Self with the body. Knowledge of Brahman results in realization of all-selfness. Desires cannot spring from it. When avidyā is destroyed by Brahmavidyā, nothing but the Ātman exists.[2] Works can never lead to the knowledge of Brahman, since they are antagonistic to each other like light and darkness. Works devoid of knowledge spring from desires due to nescience, and therefore give rise to misery.[3]

Knowledge combined with works cannot lead to liberation, since they are antagonistic to each other. Knowledge is vidyā ; works are avidyā. When vidyā dawns, avidyā is dispelled ; they cannot co-exist with each other. Release can be attained by knowledge only. Knowledge dispels nescience, and ends in liberation. Liberation is the eternal reality—the essential nature of Ātman or Brahman. It cannot be produced by knowledge or works, or both together, but it is only revealed

---

[1] SB., Māṇḍ. K., iv, 2 ; SBG., x, 10.

[2] SB., Tait. Up., i, 11 ; SB., Bṛ. Up., ii, 1, 20 ; i, 4, 10 ; i, 5, 2 ; ii, 4, 14.

[3] SB., Māṇḍ. Up., i, 1, 12 ; SB., Muṇḍ. Up., i, 1, 7.

by knowledge. It is not produced by voluntary actions motived by desire for an end. Knowledge of identity of Ātman with Brahman cannot be combined with works even in dream. Karma is the path of action. Knowledge is the path of renunciation of action.[1]

Śaṁkara prescribes niṣkāma karma for purification of mind, which is necessary for the attainment of true knowledge. But it cannot directly lead to liberation. Duties performed without attachment, aversion, and desire for fruits are niṣkāma karma. They are not actuated by egoism, and devoid of the sense of 'I' and 'mine'. They are dedicated to God, and done for the good of mankind. They produce purification of mind and aid the production of true knowledge.[2]

Śaṁkara advocates ethics of asceticism. Extirpation of all primal egoistic desires is indispensable for achievement of eternal and absolute life. Desire for sons, desire for wealth, and desire for enjoyment here and hereafter must be extirpated. Destruction of all desires due to nescience is auxiliary to the realization of identity of the Ātman with Brahman.[3]

The liberated souls, who have acquired integral experience, renounce all actions for egoistic ends, and engage in actions only for the good of humanity without attachment and desire for fruits. Their actions are, in reality, not actions because they spring from integral experience of the Ātman or Brahman. Those, who perform actions for solidarity of mankind, are not bound by them, because they are selfless acts and unmotived by nescience and egoism.[4]

---

[1] SB., Iśa Up., 2, 9 & 18 ; SB., Tait. Up., i, 11 ; SB., Bṛ., Up., iii, 5, 1.

[2] SBG., ii, 11, 47-48 ; iii, 19-20 ; iv, 14 ; v, 11-12.

[3] SB., Kena Up., i, 2 ; SB., Kaṭh. Up., ii, 1, 2 ; ii, 3, 14 ; SB., Bṛ. Up., i, 4, 17.

[4] SBG., iv, 19-20 & 24 ; SBG., v, 7 ; SBS., ii, 3, 48.

CHAPTER XIV

THE PHILOSOPHY OF VIŚIṢṬĀDVAITA

Rāmānuja was the chief propounder of the doctrine of qualified monism (viśiṣṭādvaitavāda). He criticized Śaṁkara's monism, and established the ontological reality of God, the individual souls, and the world and regarded the souls and the world as attributes or modes of God. The germs of theistic Vedānta are found in the theistic Upaniṣads, the Nārāyaṇīya section of the *Mahābhārata*, the *Bhagavad Gītā*, and the *Pañcarātra Āgamas*. Rāmānuja refers to Bodhāyana, Taṅka, Dramiḍa, Guhadeva, Kapardin, and Bhāruci as his predecessors who propounded qualified monism. Bodhāyana's *Vṛtti* on *Brahmasūtra* has been lost.

Yāmunācārya, a teacher of Rāmānuja, wrote *Siddhitraya*, an important work. Rāmānuja (1017 A.D.—1137 A.D.) wrote a commentary on the *Brahmasūtra*, known as the *Śrībhāṣya*, a commentary on the *Bhagavad Gītā*, *Vedāntadīpa*, *Vedāntasāra* and *Vedārthasaṁgraha*. Sudarśana wrote *Śrutaprakāśikā*, a sub-commentary on *Śrībhāṣya*. Lokācārya's *Tattvatraya* is an important work on the Viśiṣṭādvaita ontology. Veṅkaṭanātha's (1300 A.D.) *Nyāyasiddhāñjana*, *Tattvamuktākalāpa*, and its commentary, *Sarvārthasiddhi* are useful works on ontology. Śrīnivāsācārya's (1700 A.D.) *Yatīndramatadīpikā* is a valuable work. *Śrībhāṣyavārtika* is a summary of *Śrībhāṣya* in verse.

BRAHMAN : GOD

Brahman is the Supreme Person endowed with innumerable supreme and auspicious qualities and devoid of all impure qualities. He is the infinite reality by nature and qualities ; there is no other supreme reality. He is possessed of truth or reality, knowledge, and bliss. He is the eternal and changeless reality. He is self-luminous and not manifested by any other agent. He is infinite and not limited by time, space and other objects. Brahman is the determinate whole. All qualities coinhere in the divine substance. Brahman is identical with

God. There is no distinction between the indeterminate Brahman and the determinate Brahman. There is no indeterminate Brahman. Brahman is said to be attributeless because He is devoid of the impure qualities derived from prakṛti. The supreme Brahman is eternal, omnipresent, subtle, immanent in all, inexhaustible, omniscient, omnipotent, and endowed with many auspicious qualities. He is the creator, preserver, and destroyer of the world, its material cause and efficient cause, and the ground of all. He is the giver of the supreme ends of life, and of the fruits of actions. He is the Lord of Karma and the refuge of His devotees. He is of the nature of infinite knowledge and bliss. His auspicious qualities are eternal, unlimited, innumerable, unconditional, flawless, unequalled, and unexcelled. He is the inner guide, and inner Self of unconscious matter and conscious souls, and their ground, controller, and principal. He is immanent in them and transcendent of them. He is worshipped and attained by the souls. He is the bridge that leads them to immortality. He is infinite and exists in His own greatness. He is the First Cause of all effects. He is the eternal, unborn, immortal, infinite, identical in essence, and immaculate. He is the infinite in the sense that He is eternal and immanent in all conscious souls and unconscious matter, and their inner controller, but He is not tainted with their impurities.[1] He is possessed of supreme knowledge, power of creating, preserving, and destroying the world, strength or absence of fatigue in creating and sustaining it, lordship, capacity for regulating all objects and spirits, or independence, virility or unchangeability in the midst of changes in his body, or immutability in spite of His being the material cause of the world, and self-sufficiency or power of acting without auxiliary conditions. He gives knowledge to the ignorant, power to the powerless, forgiveness to the guilty, mercy to the miserable, tenderness to the impure, honesty to the dishonest, straightness to the crooked, goodness to the vicious, solace to the bereaved, and fruition to the aspirant. He is the

[1] RBS., i, 1, 1 ; TT., pp. 85-9 ; VD., p. 1 ; i, 1. 30-31 ; i, 2, 1, 4-5, 12, 19 & 25 ; i, 3, 1-2 ; i, 3, 8 ; VAS., pp. 11, 16, 25, 32, 134, 183, & 185.

Lord of all, the chief of all, the cause of all effects, the soul of all souls and unconscious objects, and the object of worship through all actions dedicated to Him. He controls the entire universe of conscious souls and unconscious matter which are His powers, parts, manifestations, forms, attributes, or modes. They are His body, and He is their soul. They coinhere in Him, their ground and substance. He is different from His attributes or modes. There is inseparable relation (apṛthaksiddhi) between them. There is unity in plurality in Him. The nature of God is inconceivable. Though one only as the ruler, He enters into the multiplicity of souls and unconscious objects as their inner Self, and makes the former do many actions freely, and makes the latter assume various forms. He assumes multiform nature in spite of His unity, and does not lose His integrity in the midst of diversity of His manifestations. He abides in them as the supreme Lord.[1] He is devoid of homogeneous difference and heterogeneous difference : there is no other reality like Him or unlike Him. But there is internal difference in Him. There is no contradiction between His unity and internal diversity. He is different from all, the ground of all, and has infinite powers. He can assume infinite forms and retain His identity by His infinite wonderful power. He harmonizes all multiplicity in His all-embracing unity. He is one in many. He is one in the sense that He is the inner Self of all which coinhere in Him. He is devoid of plurality in the sense that plurality of souls and material objects are His body, attributes, or modes. He is different from them, that are the creations of His manifold powers. God is perfect and creates the world in sport out of His fullness. He does not realize any extraneous end in creating the world. He creates the creatures with unequal lots in accordance with their merits and demerits and adjusts the manifold world to their moral deserts.[2]

Matter and souls are attributes, modes, or parts of God. They are accessory to Him. There are changes in His parts or

---

[1] TT., pp. 95-96 ; VAS., pp. 11, 27, 34-35 & 127 ; YMD., p. 37.

[2] VAS., pp. 129 & 134 ; VD., ii, 1, 31-33 ; RBS., ii, 1, 33-34.

modes, but He remains unchanged in them. There is no change in the divine substance. The conscious and unconscious modes constitute His body and He is their soul. There is an inseparable relation between them, and they are controlled by Him. They are means to Him, who is their end. He is identity-in-difference ; He remains identical in the midst of diverse modes, and harmonizes the plurality of modes within His unity. He is their Lord, chief ground, and inner Self. He is perfect, immutable, and different from them.

The text 'That thou art' means that the individual soul is identical in essence with God. The soul presiding over a body is a mode of God ; it is His body and cannot exist apart from Him. It is not a mere appearance, but an eternal reality, an eternal part of Brahman. It is finite and dependent, while God is infinite and independent. He is perfect, unchangeable, and endowed with all auspicious qualities. The soul is identical in essential nature with God. The souls and God both are real and distinct. The souls coinhere in the same ground or substance. God is an organic whole of different souls and material objects. He is a synthetic whole of interrelated modes or parts. He is a determinate whole. He is not an undifferentiated unity or indeterminate Absolute. He is the Supreme Person, and not the sumtotal of finite persons. All souls are co-eternal members with him. He is the Soul, Lord, Controller, and Chief of the community of finite souls. He is immanent in them and transcendent of them. Though He is immanent in them, He is not affected by their joys and sorrows, since He is devoid of merits and demerits. The souls experience them as fruits of their actions. God is unaffected by modifications of matter and imperfections of the souls. Matter and souls are dependent on Him as His inseparable attributes.[1]

THE SELF (JĪVA) AND CONSCIOUSNESS

The jīva is the individual self. It is different from the body, life, the sense-organs, mind and intellect ; it is different from the psychophysical organism. It is the knower, enjoyer

[1] RVS., i, 1, 2 ; pp. 35, 41 & 116 ; ii, 1, 14 ; RBS., ii, 1, 9.

and active agent. It is self-luminous and manifests itself without the aid of knowledge. It is the abode of knowledge, and has attributive consciousness. It is the substrate of consciousness and of the nature of bliss. It is eternal, and persists in all times. It is unborn, immortal, and not affected by birth and death. Birth is its union with body, and death, its disjunction from body. The self is atomic or monadic, resides in the heart, and pervades the world with its knowledge, even as the light of a lamp pervades a room. It cannot be perceived through the sense-organs. It cannot be thought as similar to matter. It is an ego, and cannot be thought as a non-ego. It is not composed of parts ; it is a simple, immaterial spirit. It remains identical with itself without undergoing modifications. The body changes, but the self does not. The self is said to be of the nature of knowledge, since it manifests itself without knowledge. Knowledge is its essential property. The self is controlled by God ; its freedom is subject to the divine will. The self is grounded in God and sustained by Him. It cannot exist apart from Him, for it is His attribute or mode and inseparably related to Him. There is a relation of a master and a servant between a self and God. The self is an accessory to God, who is the Lord.

Self-luminosity, consciousness, selfhood, and agency are common to the self and God. The self manifests itself to itself, and is the conscious substrate of knowledge. It is embodied in an organism, and an active agent. These are the general characteristics of the self. It is a spiritual monad, an accessory to God, subsists in Him, and is dependent on Him. These are its special characteristics. It is permanent, since it recollects its past experiences. It is a soul in relation to its body, but it is a body in relation to God. It is self-luminous and endued with attributive knowledge. Consciousness, atomicity, purity, and the like are its essential properties. The self is of the nature of knowledge, bliss, and purity. Ignorance, pain, and impurity are due to its connection with prakṛti or its product, the mind-body-complex. Its essential properties are not due to its merits and demerits due to its connection with prakṛti.

od exists in all selves in His essence, free from all taint of nperfections due to connection with prakṛti. All souls have e essential properties of knowledge and bliss. They are omogeneous, accessory to God, controlled by Him, subsist in Iim, and constitute His body. Their bondage is due to their onnection with prakṛti due to their merits and demerits.[1]

The self's birth is due to ignorance (avidyā), which is false dentification of the self with the body. Ignorance is beginning-ess, generates merits and demerits, and obscures the essential ature of the self and its affinity with God. When it is destro-ed by meditation on God. its essential nature is manifested, nd it experiences the infinite bliss of God. Rāmānuja recog-izes avidyā in the selves, which veils their essential nature nd kinship with God. But he does not admit avidyā which rojects the plurality of world-appearance.

Knowledge and bliss constitute the essence of the selves. The differences among them are due to their bodies, which are nodifications of prakṛti. They are due to merits and demerits vhich are due to avidyā. When it is destroyed, the selves are livested of these differences due to modes of prakṛti, and xperience their essential knowledge and bliss. They are ommon to all selves. They have similarity with God in their iberated state.

The self acquires avidyā, actions, dispositions, and desires n connection with unconscious matter. When connection with t is destroyed, avidyā and its products are destroyed. The self experiences pleasure and pain owing to its actions. Its plea-sures and pains are not due to its connection with the body. God is devoid of them, and so does not experience pleasures and pains. The self is of the nature of bliss. Knowledge in its manifest condition is pleasant. All objects partake of the nature of God. So they are essentially agreeable. Their disagreeable nature is due to false identification of the self with the body.[2]

The selves are subordinate knowers. God is the principal

---

[1] TT., pp. 5-15, 22-26; VAS., p. 124; YMD., pp. 31-32, 125-26.

[2] VAS., pp. 7 & 9; TT., pp. 29, 38-39; VD., i, 2, 8; ii, 1, 14.

knower. The knowledge of the selves is eternal, immaterial and blissful. It is an attribute of the self, and yet it is a substance, since it contracts and expands. The essence of the self neither contracts nor expands. The self manifests itself to itself. But knowledge, which is its attribute, does not manifest itself but manifests an object. It is pervasive and subject to contraction and expansion. Some selves always have pervasive knowledge ; others always have non-pervasive knowledge ; others sometimes have pervasive knowledge. The self's knowledge is eternal, but it appears to be produced, when it issues through the sense-organs and apprehends objects, and it appears to be destroyed, when it withdraws from objects. One eternal knowledge appears to be many cognitions because it expands to different objects. Knowledge is a substance because it is the substrate of quality and activity, and because it manifests objects. It does not manifest objects in deep sleep and swoon, for it does not extend to objects at that time because it is overcome by inertia (tamas). Knowledge manifests itself when the self in which it subsists apprehends objects. But it is not manifested in deep sleep because it is obscured by inertia and because the self does not apprehend objects. The self experiences the whole body through its knowledge, even as a gem manifests a large area through its light.

The self is the substrate of consciousness. Consciousness abides in the self, and apprehends an object. Śaṁkara recognizes subject-objectless consciousness. But Rāmānuja denies its existence and maintains that there is no consciousness which does not apprehend objects, since such consciousness is never perceived. The self is not mere manifestation or consciousness. It is a conscious knower of objects. It is self-luminous in the sense that it manifests objects. Consciousness is the manifestation of an object to its substrate, the self, through its own being. Self-luminousness consists in manifestation of consciousness to the self, its abode, through its own being.[1] Manifestation prompts

[1] TT., pp. 35-38 ; RVS., ii, 3, 26 ; RBS., i, 1, 1

mpirical use. 'I know a jar': here the knowledge manifests a ar to the self through its own being. The self is the vitness of all objects. It is the agent of the cognitive ct or knowledge. A thing is an object of the cognitive act vhich cannot be its own object. The self is the subject of nowledge, while a thing is an object of knowledge. Knowedge is a particular property of the self. Cognitions appear nd disappear; they have origin, existence, and destruction. But the self, which is their witness, is permanent. It remembers nd recognizes the objects of its past experience; therefore it nust exist in the past as well as the present. Memory and ecognition presuppose the existence of the permanent self. I perceived this in the past.' This recollection shows that the elf is the knower, and not mere knowledge. There is no onsciousness without a self and without an object, since it s absolutely unknown. The self is the subject, and not an bject of knowledge. To argue that the self, the subject of nowledge, is the object of knowledge is as absurd as to argue hat one's mother is a barren woman. The self is always a ubject, ego, or knower, and never an object of knowledge. t is self-luminous, and manifests itself to itself and is not nanifested by any other agent. Consciousness is its ssence which constitutes its self-luminous nature. What is elf-luminous is not manifested by any other agent. The self nanifests itself and other objects, even as a lamp manifests tself and other objects.

Śaṁkara maintains that subject-objectless consciousness ppears to be the knower owing to illusion. Rāmānuja ontends that this view is wrong, since there is the apprehension I know'; but never 'I am knowledge'.[1] Knowledge subsists n the knower. There is no mere knowledge, but a knowing elf that has knowledge. Knowerhood is not a false appearance. f the knower is false, the knowledge also is false. If the nowledge is not false, the knower cannot be false. The nowlegde is uncontradicted and valid. So the knower must xist. Śaṁkara argues that the knower is the agent of the act

[1] RBS., i, 1, 1.

of knowledge, and that the self, which is unmodifiable, cannot be the agent of the cognitive act. Activity belongs to egoism, an internal organ, which is non-intelligent, modifiable, and active. The self is inactive and immutable and can never be the agent of the act of knowledge. Agency is the quality of an object, like colour. If the self were the agent of the cognitive act, it would be a non-self, an object, and a non-intelligent being. But Rāmānuja urges that this argument is invalid. Inertness, being a modification of prakṛti. knownness, externality, being a means to the self's experience, and the like are the qualities common to the body and the internal organ of egoism. But knowerhood is a unique property of an intelligent knower or self. Egoism, which is revealed by knowledge, and which is an object of knowledge, can never be a subject of knowledge or knower. Further, knowerhood consists in being a substrate of the quality of knowledge and not in undergoing a change. The self is eternal, and so its essential quality of knowledge also is eternal. Knowledge constitutes its essence and naturally subsists in the self. It is of the essence of knowledge, and yet is the substrate of knowledge, even as a lamp is of the essence of light, and yet is a substrate of light. Though knowledge of the self is unlimited, it undergoes contraction and expansion due to actions during bondage. Contracted knowledge expands to objects through the sense-organs. The origin and destruction of knowledge are due to the operation or non-operation of the sense-organs. The self is the agent of the expansion of knowledge, while the sense-organs are its instruments. But this agency is not essential to the self, because it is due to actions. The self is, in its essence, immutable. Such knowerhood as does not involve any modification belongs to the self, which is of the nature of knowledge. It can never belong to the non-intelligent egoism.[1] Śaṁkara maintains that non-intelligent egoism becomes a knower owing to the reflection of consciousness due to proximity. Rāmānuja asks whether egoism is reflected on consciousness or whether consciousness is reflected on

[1] RBS., i, 1, 1.

egoism. Egoism cannot be reflected on consciousness, since Śaṁkara does not admit the knowerhood of consciousness. Nor can consciousness be reflected on egoism, since egoism is non-intelligent, and cannot be a knower. Both consciousness and egoism are invisible, and cannot be reflected on each other. Egoism cannot be a knower, for it is unconscious ; an unconscious entity cannot be conscious owing to proximity to consciousness. Consciousness cannot be said to be manifested by egoism. The self is self-luminous and cannot be manifested by non-intelligent egoism. Egoism is manifested by consciousness. But consciousness is not manifested by egoism. Hence the inner self is essentially a knower and not mere knowledge. If it were not a knower, knowledge also could not manifest objects. Knowerhood constitutes the essence of the self. In deep sleep it is not manifested as a knower because there are no objects of knowledge at that time. But it continues to be a knower in the state of liberation.

Śaṁkara maintains that consciousness is self-luminous, and that it is never an object of another consciousness. Rāmānuja disputes this view. When the self manifests an object, its consciousness is said to be self-luminous. But the self can apprehend its own past consciousness as its object, and also the consciousness of another person in that we infer the consciousness of another person from his speech and behaviour. When consciousness is apprehended as an object, it does not cease to be consciousness. The essential nature of consciousness consists in its manifesting itself to its substrate at the present moment through its own being, or in its manifesting its object through its own being. Consciousness does not lose its essential nature, when it becomes an object of another consciousness. Both unconscious things and consciousness are objects of consciousness. Thus Rāmānuja differs from Śaṁkara in his views of the self and consciousness.[1]

The self is a knower, enjoyer, and active agent. Agency and enjoyerhood are states of knowledge. Enjoyment is the experience of pleasure and pain—a state of knowledge. Volition

[1] RBS., i, 1, 1.

is due to desire to act, which is due to knowledge of end and means. So agency, which involves desire and knowledge, is a state of knowledge. The Saṁkhya maintains that the self is not active, but that buddhi composed of sattva, rajas, and tamas is active. But this view is not tenable. If the self is not free and active, it cannot acquire merits and demerits by doing right and wrong actions laid down in the Vedas, and experience pleasure and pain. But the activity of the self in the state of bondage is due to its conjunction with the guṇas, and not due to its essential nature. Its activity is dependent on God; human freedom is not absolute, but relative; it is subject to divine freedom. God permits the selves to do actions freely, and enjoy their fruits. He impels them to act freely, but He does not compel them to do so. God is the permitter and the jīvas are permitted and freely do right and wrong actions. Prakṛti or buddhi does not do the actions. But the free activity of the selves is subject to the permission of God. They experience the fruits of their actions. But God, who exists and shines in them, does not experience them. Rāmānuja insists on human freedom subject to the will of God.[1]

BONDAGE AND LIBERATION

The souls are either bound, or released, or eternally liberated. The bound souls are in bondage to empirical life. The released souls are liberated from bondage. Bondage is due to avidyā, karma, vāsanā, and ruci. Avidyā is ignorance of the soul's dependence on God. Karma is action prompted by ignorance. Vāsanā is the subconscious disposition produced by actions. Ruci is attachment produced by the dispositions. Avidyā and its products connect the soul with a mind-body-complex. They can be destroyed by the intuitive knowledge of the self as disconnected with the psychophysical organism. This knowledge can be attained by devotion, complete self-surrender to God, and moral discipline.[2] Devotion is steady recollection

[1] TT., pp. 18-20, 25; RVS., i, 2, 11; i, 1, 2; i, 3, 6; ii, 3, 40-41; RBS., ii, 3, 41.

[2] TT., p. 26; RBS., iv, 4, 2-3; YMD., pp. 33-34.

of God, which is a particular kind of knowledge. Meditation also is an uninterrupted stream of recollection which is aided by the performance of duties relating to castes and stages of life throughout life. Service and taking refuge in God are essential to devotion. Daily prayers and occasional duties ought to be performed. Sacrifices, charity, penances, truthfulness, cleanliness, straightforwardness, kindness, non-injury, strength, tranquillity, sense-restraint, and other virtues should be cultivated. Constant prayer, recollection, obeisance, worship, effort, chanting the name of God, hearing of His qualities, uttering them, and meditation on Him are necessary for liberation. Bondage and liberation depend on the will of God. The essential purity of the self is concealed by a beginningless series of karmas due to avidyā at the will of God. This is bondage. The veil of karmas is removed by devotion, meditation, and knowledge at His will. This is release which is community of nature with God, and not identity with Him. The self does not lose its identity in God in the state of release. It persists as a knower and its knowledge becomes infinite and is not contracted by karmas. It gets rid of karmas, and enjoys the infinite glory of God. It apprehends His nature, and enjoys His infinite bliss. Though it attains community of nature with God, it cannot create and govern the world. The released soul becomes autonomous and enjoys the infinite sport of God at will. God grants it release through His grace. He, pleased with its devotion and self-surrender, destroys its avidyā in the form of accumulated merits and demerits (karma), and releases it from birth and death. The manifestation of its essential purity, infinite knowledge and enjoyment, and existence in the eternal abode of God depend upon Him.[1]

The self is not identical with Brahman. The identity texts indicate the essential similarity between them. They are different from each other. Brahman is the creator, controller, preserver, destroyer, moral governor, ground, goal, and Lord. He is omniscient, independent, pure, and possessed of

[1] RBS., i, 1, 1 ; iii, 2, 4 ; iv, 4, 3, 15, 17, 19-20, 22 ; VAS., pp. 142-44 & 248.

auspicious qualities. The embodied soul is created, controlled, preserved, destroyed, and governed by God, and subsists in Him. It is ignorant, dependent, impure, possessed of inauspicious qualities, and accessory to the Lord. He is worshipped while the self is the worshipper. He is attained by the soul. Therefore the self is different from God. It is a part of God even as light issuing from a luminous thing is a part of it. A part constitutes one place of a thing. An attribute is a part of the thing qualified by it. A distinction between a qualified thing and a qualifying attribute is made. Though an attribute is a part of the qualified thing, there is a difference between them. The self is an attribute of God. It is a part of Him. There is a difference between a part and a whole. There is a difference between an attribute and a substance. So the self is different from God. There is inseparable relation between them.[1] God is not composed of parts. The souls cannot be cut out from Him. The text 'that thou art' does not show the identity of the self with God. It shows that God is the ground of the self. The subject and the predicate are distinct. They have identity of the ground and coinhere in the same substance. The selves are the attributes or parts of God.

MATTER : PRAKṚTI AND ITS MODES

Matter is an unconscious, mutable object of experience. It is of three kinds : pure sattva, mixed sattva, and matter devoid of sattva. Pure matter is unmixed with rajas and tamas and is eternal. It produces knowledge and bliss. It is of the nature of infinite effulgence. It is a very wonderful entity. Its magnitude cannot be known definitely by the liberated souls and God. It is modified into celestial palaces and various other objects by the mere will of God without any action. It constitutes His transcendental abode and eternal manifestation. Some call it matter, while others call it non-matter. It manifests itself without the knowledge of the eternally released souls, released souls, and God. It is not manifested to the bound souls. It is different from the self

[1] RBS., ii, 3, 42 & 45 ; iii, 2, 28 ; RVS., i, 1, 2.

and knowledge. It is not known as 'I', and so it is not the self. It is modified into the body, and manifests itself without objects. It possesses the qualities of sound, touch, and the like, and so it is not knowledge. It is pure matter different from the self and knowledge—pure sattva unmixed with rajas and tamas. It constitutes the body of God in His eternal manifestation. It is self-luminous and manifests itself to God and the liberated souls. It is transformed into instruments and objects of their enjoyment by the will of God. It is an object, but different from matter composed of sattva, rajas, and tamas. Therefore it may be regarded as immaterial.[1]

Prakṛti, avidyā, or māyā is mixed sattva or sattva mixed with rajas and tamas. It is eternal and the means of God's sport in empirical manifestation. Yet it is mutable and transformed into homogeneous and heterogeneous modifications in different times and places. Creation is the evolution of prakṛti from the homogeneous to the heterogeneous condition. Dissolution is the devolution of prakṛti from the heterogeneous to the homogeneous condition. Prakṛti obscures knowledge and bliss of the bound souls, and produces false knowledge in them. It is a kind of matter. It is called prakṛti because it produces modifications. It is called avidyā because it counteracts right knowledge. It is called māyā because it creates the manifold universe. Prakṛti is the substrate of sattva, rajas, and tamas—the equilibrium of three guṇas, which is thrown into disequilibrium by the will of God. It is called avyakta in a state of disequipoise ready to be transformed into effects.[2] Sattva, rajas, and tamas are the constituents of prakṛti. They are inseparably related to the essence of prakṛti. They are unmanifest in the state of prakṛti and become manifest when prakṛti is modified into cosmic intellect and the other categories. Sattva produces knowledge and pleasure, and association with them. Rajas produces attachment, desire, and action. Tamas produces false knowledge, inattention, laziness, and sleep. They are not

[1] TT., pp. 41-45 ; YMD., p. 24.

[2] RBS., ii, 2, 2 ; TT., pp. 45-46 & 48 ; YMD., p. 15.

substances because they are devoid of conjunction. They are non-eternal and pervade prakṛti. They overcome one another, and predominate over one another. They are fit matter for creation, maintenance and dissolution of the world by God.[1]

In dissolution prakṛti exists as a power of God, consisting of the subtle constituents in the causal state, abiding in Him. It is uncaused in this sense. In creation it issues forth from the body of God and assumes a gross or effected state. Prakṛti is the power of God, exists in Him, and depends upon Him. It is not an independent entity as the Saṁkhya maintains. Prakṛti, independent of God, is not the material cause of the world. God, in the causal state in which manifold objects are not yet differentiated, is its material cause. In this condition He is said to be non-existent or unmanifest. Prior to creation prakṛti exists in a subtle state devoid of diverse objects as the body of God. It assumes diversity of forms at the time of creation at the will of God. So God is the cause of Prakṛti. It is the body of God, His mode, and identical with Him in its essence. He is the Self of its modifications. God as the substance of prakṛti is immutable ; but as modes of prakṛti He is mutable. As substance He is the inner controller of prakṛti and its mutations. Prakṛti is subtle unconscious matter, which is impregnated by God with His conscious power. Prakṛti is unconscious and cannot act without being supervised by conscious God.[2]

Prakṛti is transformed into cosmic intellect (mahat, buddhi). Determination is its quality. It is threefold, sāttvika, rājasa, and tāmasa, according as sattva, rajas, or tamas predominates in it. Cosmic intellect is transformed into cosmic egoism which is sāttvika, rājasa, and tāmasa. Sāttvika egoism is transformed into the five cognitive senses, the five motor senses, and manas. Tamasa egoism is transformed into the five subtle essences which are modified into the five gross elements. Rājasa egoism aids sattvika egoism and tāmasa egoism to

[1] TT., pp. 51-52 ; YMD., p. 43.

[2] VD., i, 4, 10 & 14 ; RBS., i, 1, 1 ; i, 4, 10 ; ii, 1, 1 ; RBG., xiii, 2 ; VAS., pp. 113-14.

produce their effects. Sāttvika egoism produces mind (manas) without any auxiliary condition. It produces the cognitive and motor organs with the aid of the subtle essences. Space (dik) is not a separate substance. Ether (ākāśa) is the cause of occupation and has sound. Air is devoid of colour and smell and neither hot nor cold. Fire is bright and hot. Water has taste and cold touch and is devoid of smell. Earth has smell, taste, and touch. The Viśiṣṭādvaita Vedānta advocates the doctrine of quintuplication of the elements[1].

According to Lokācārya, time is eternal, devoid of sattva, and the cause of transformation of prakṛti and its mutations. It is the body of God and aids Him in His sport. It is the cause of all effects, and modified into moments, days and the like, due to conditions. According to Śrīnivāsa, time is a kind of matter devoid of sattva, rajas, and tamas. It is eternal, ubiquitous, past, present, and future. It is the cause of the use of simultaneity and succession, soon and late, and the like and an object of perception through the six sense-organs. It is eternal in the transcendental abode of God and non-eternal in the world.[2]

Unconscious material objects cannot act by themselves. They act under the supervision of God. They give pleasure or pain to the individual souls in accordance with their merits and demerits at the will of God in different times and places. They are the matter of the sport of God who controls them in various ways. God is free from merits and demerits. So physical objects cannot give Him pleasure or pain.[3]

CAUSALITY : SATKĀRYAVĀDA

Rāmānuja advocates the doctrine of Satkāryavāda. An effect pre-exists in its cause ; the cause and the effect both are real ; the effect is non-different from the cause. Production is modification of the cause into the effect and destruction is re-absorption of the effect in the cause. Production and

[1] TT., pp. 53-62 ; YMD., pp. 15-19.

[2] TT., pp. 74 & 79 ; TMK., i, 69 ; YMD., p. 23.

[3] RBS., ii, 2, 2 ; iii, 2, 12.

destruction are the different states of the causal substance. Production is modification, or rearrangement of the parts, of the causal substance. A jar is a modification of earth and destroyed and turned into earth. A gold ornament is a modification of gold and destroyed and turned into gold. Production, existence, and destruction are the different states of the causal substance, even as childhood, youth and old age are the different states of a person. There is essential identity or non-difference between cause and effect, both of which are real. If the cause is real and the effect is an unreal appearance, as Śaṁkara maintains, there cannot be identity between them, for there can be no identity between a reality and an appearance.[1]

CREATION

God is the world-soul. Unconscious matter and conscious souls in all states constitute His body.[2] God is the cause, and the entire unconscious world and conscious souls are the effect. The effect is non-different from the cause. Matter and souls are not separate entities from God. They are attributes of God which coinhere in Him. God invested with subtle or causal matter and souls is the cause. He invested with gross or effected matter and souls is the effect. He in the causal and effected condition with His body of conscious souls and unconscious matter is the whole reality. He is one in the unmanifest condition and manifold in the manifest condition. Subtle, unconscious, unmanifested matter and subtle conscious souls are the body of causal God. Gross, unconscious, manifested matter and individual souls with their manifest qualities are the body of effected God. Matter and souls are inseparable from God; they together with God immanent in them constitute the reality.

God is cause as well as effect. In the causal state He is invested with the body of subtle conscious souls and unconscious matter. In the effected state He is invested with the body of gross conscious souls and unconscious matter. So the effect is non-different from the cause. Though God is partless,

---

[1] RBS., ii, 1, 15-16. [2] VD., p. 3.

He can transform Himself into the manifold world owing to His omnipotence. One indivisible God can transform Himself into the manifold world of souls and matter, even as one partless universal can exist in many individuals without being divided.

God's creation consists in the transformation of matter into various objects and endowing souls with bodies and sense-organs and expanding their knowledge. Maintenance consists in His entering into created objects and conserving them all. Dissolution consists in His withdrawing them into Himself. Brahmā endowed with rajas is the creator; Viṣṇu endowed with sattva, the preserver; and Rudra endowed with tamas, the destroyer. They are different aspects of God. As the inner controller of created objects God creates, maintains, and destroys them.[1]

God is the material cause, efficient cause and auxiliary cause of the world. He creates the world by His mere will without any effort. Creation, maintenance, and dissolution are His mere sport. God freely transforms Himself or His power, prakṛti, into the world. So He is its material cause. Or, God as qualified by subtle conscious souls and unconscious matter, which are His attributes and which are not manifested as embodied souls and gross matter, is its material cause. He is its efficient cause because by His mere will He transforms His power or prakṛti into the world. He as qualified by knowledge, power and the like is its auxiliary cause. God as substance is immutable, because His essence does not undergo modification. But as qualified by the attributes of conscious souls and unconscious matter He is modified into the world. So there is no contradiction between His immutability and modifications. God as substance is not modified, but His attributes or modes of conscious souls and unconscious matter are modified. As qualified by the two attributes God, their controller, undergoes modification in the shape of being qualified by them. God is immutable and subject to change.[2]

---

[1] VD., pp. 3-4; ii, 1, 21 & 26; TT., pp. 112-15.

[2] TT., pp. 105-07, 109-11; RBS., ii, 3, 18.

Śaṁkara maintains that Brahman as cause is real, that the world as effect is unreal, and that the unreal effect is non-different from the cause. But Rāmānuja urges that there cannot be non-difference between a real thing and an unreal appearance. If there could be non-difference between them, Brahman also would be unreal and the world would be real. But this is absurd. So Śaṁkara's view is wrong.

God creates the world in sport out of His fullness to realize His internal end of sport. He does not create it to realize any external end. He is perfect and fulfilled and has no unrealized end. He creates the world of various objects of enjoyment in accordance with the moral deserts of the individual souls. He makes them happy or unhappy according to their merits or demerits. Otherwise He would be partial to happy creatures and cruel to unhappy creatures. So God, who is omnipotent and different from matter and souls, creates the multiform world with the aid of the souls' merits and demerits in order to realize His end of playful activity.[1]

REFUTATION OF ŚAṀKARA'S DOCTRINE OF MĀYĀ OR AVIDYĀ

Saṁkara maintains that one undifferentiated, indeterminate, self-luminous Absolute (Brahman) is real, and that God, souls, and the material world are unreal appearances due to some defect. The defect is beginningless cosmic nescience (avidyā). It is neither real nor unreal but indefinable. It conceals the real nature of Brahman, and projects the appearance of the multiform world.[2] It is not being, since it is illusory and contradicted by right knowledge. Nor is it non-being, since it is experienced and sublated by right knowledge. So Śaṁkara maintains that cosmic nescience (avidyā, māyā) is indefinable and inexplicable.

First, Rāmānuja contends that nescience must subsist in something. It cannot abide in the individual soul (jīva), since it is a product of nesience, an unreal appearance. It is Brahman limited by nescience or the mind-body-complex due

[1] VD., ii, 1, 32-33 ; RBS., ii, 1, 34-35. [2] RBS., i, 1, 1,

to nescience. Nescience cannot abide in Brahman, since it is self-luminous and of the nature of knowledge which is contradictory to nescience. Nescience is sublated by knowledge. Brahman is of the nature of pure knowledge which destroys nescience. Therefore Brahman, which is of the nature of pure knowledge, cannot be the locus of nescience. Nescience cannot abide in any locus.

Secondly, nescience cannot veil the self-luminous nature of Brahman, since self-luminosity which is its essence would be destroyed. Veiling the self-luminosity of Brahman consists in either obstruction of the production of manifestation of Brahman or the destruction of its existing manifestation. The manifestation of Brahman is eternal and not produced. So concealment of self-luminosity of Brahman amounts to the destruction of its manifestation. Hence nescience is incapable of concealing the nature of Brahman.

Thirdly, Śaṁkara maintains that the self-luminous subject-objectless consciousness apprehends itself as countless subjects and objects owing to some defect it itself. Rāmānuja asks whether this defect is real or unreal. It is not real, because its reality is not admitted, and because its reality contradicts monism. Nor is it unreal, for in that case it is either the knowing self, the known object, or knowledge. The knowing self and the known object are imaginary and unreal. Therefore their defect must be due to some other defect, and so on to infinity. This will lead to infinite regress. The defect cannot be of the nature of knowledge, since there is no distinction within knowledge itself. If Brahman itself is the defect, then it is eternal like Brahman, and it makes liberation of the self impossible, since the defect of nescience cannot be destroyed. If the reality of nescience different from Brahman be not admitted, the world-appearance cannot be regarded as false. So the reality of nescience is incapable of being proved.

Fourthly, nescience is indefinable. It is neither existent nor non-existent. Rāmānuja urges that all objects are known through experience. All experience is either of the existent or non-existent. There is no experience of anything which is neither existent nor non-existent. If such a thing, which is neither existent nor non-existent, were an object of experience, then any thing would be an object of any experience. So nescience cannot be indefinable.

Fifthly, Śaṁkara maintains that nescience is destroyed by the integral knowledge of the identity of Brahman and the Self. Rāmānuja urges that bondage is not apparent but real, and that it cannot be destroyed by the knowledge of one undifferentiated Brahman. Bondage is due to merits and demerits of the selves, which lead to embodied life and enjoyments and sufferings. Cessation of bondage can be acquired by devotion to and meditation on God through His grace. The duality of Brahman and the selves and the world is real and known by valid knowledge. The knowledge of identity contradicts the real nature of this duality, and is therefore false. It leads to increase of bondage. The knowledge of God, who is different from the selves, and who is their inner controller, is the means of liberation. The knowledge of identity is itself false, and cannot destroy nescience.

Lastly, there can be no cessation of nescience, since there is no knowledge which can destroy it. Nescience of the self is due to merits and demerits. It cannot be removed by the knowledge of the identity of the Ātman and Brahman as Śaṁkara maintains. Nescience is the knowledge of the independence of the self of Brahman. It can be destroyed by constant meditation on God, the true knowledge of the self, and disinterested performance of duties relating to castes and stages of life. So there can be no destruction of nescience by the knowledge of undifferentiated Brahman as Śaṁkara supposes.[1]

REALITY OF THE WORLD

Before creation the world exists in God in the form of prakṛti composed of sattva, rajas, and tamas in equilibrium. Prakṛti is a power of God. Individual souls also exist in God prior to creation, devoid of their bodies. Prakṛti and souls,

[1] RBS., i, 1, 1.

in a subtle condition, constitute the body of God. The manifest world and the embodied souls also constitute His body. Matter, souls, and God constitute the reality in their inseparable relation to one another. So the world is real and not an unreal appearance. God is the material cause, efficient cause, and auxiliary cause of the world. Both cause and effect are real. The effect is not an unreal appearance of the cause but a transformation of it. The world is a transformation of prakṛti which is a power of God. God is cause as well as effect. The world is effected God and cannot be condemned as a false appearance. The manifold world is apprehended by perception and inference. Both indeterminate perception and determinate perception apprehend objects qualified by difference. All means of valid knowledge prove determinate objects. There are no objectless cognitions. All cognitions abide in subjects and apprehend objects.[1] That cognition is false, which prompts unsuccessful activity. But the cognitions of various objects of the world do not lead to fruitless acts. The illusion of snake is contradicted by the perception of a rope. But the perceptions of jars, cloths, and the like are not contradicted by one another. They prompt fruitful activities. Perceptions of various objects cannot be said to be sublated by the testimony of the scripture, for their spheres are different. Perception apprehends sensible objects. The scripture bears testimony to the existence of God.[2] Objects of experience are not unreal because they do not persist. They may exist here and now, but may not exist at some other place and time. There is no contradiction between their existence in this place and time and their non-existence in some other place and time. The world is real, but its gross objects are not eternal. Distinctions are real, and identity also is real. Distincts are attributes or modes of identity. They are inseparable from, and not contradictory to, each other. They are not therefore unreal appearances. They are real and coinhere in God. They constitute the coherent whole in their organic unity.

[1] RBS., 1, 1, 1.

[2] VAS., pp. 87-88.

CHAPTER XV

THE DVAITAVĀDA OF MADHVA

Mādhva (1199-1278 A.D.) is the founder of Dvaita Vedānta. He is a staunch advocate of dualism. He recognizes the five distinctions of God and the individual soul, God and matter, the individual soul and matter, one individual soul and another, and one material thing and another to be eternal. This is the central teaching of Madhva's dualism. It is realism, and looks upon the world as real.

Epistemology

Pramāṇa is valid knowledge which is in accord with the real nature of its object. It makes an object known as it is in itself. It makes the object known either directly or indirectly through the medium of some other knowledge. The self possessing valid knowledge is the knower (pramātṛ). The object of valid knowledge is the known (prameya). Valid knowledge is pramā. There are two kinds of valid knowledge, *viz.*, kevalapramāṇa, direct and immediate intuition of objects, and anupramāṇa, the instrument or means of valid knowledge. There are four kinds of kevalapramāṇa: (1) the knowledge of the Lord; (2) the knowledge of Lakṣmī, his consort; (3) the knowledge of the yogin; and (4) the knowledge of an ordinary person. There are three kinds of anupramāṇa, *viz.*, perception. inference, and Vedic testimony.

Perception is the means of the apprehension of an object present here and now, which is proximate and unobstructed. Its range is limited to present time and space. There is no indeterminate perception. All perception is determinate. Inference is the means of the knowledge of objects which are not proximate, and which are past, future, remote, and obstructed. Vedic authority is an independent source of knowledge of innumerable objects. Perceptual knowledge is direct and immediate knowledge (sākṣātkāra). Inferential knowledge is indirect and mediate knowledge. Knowledge derived from testimony is verbal (śābda). Perceptual knowledge is of seven kinds: olfactory, gustatory, visual, tactual, auditory , mental perceptions, and intuition of the self (sākṣin). The sense-organs and the objects must be flawless. Perception is due to the four-fold contact of the self with the manas, of the manas with a sense-organ, and of a sense-organ with an object. The sense-organs are the instrumental cause (karaṇa); the sense-object-intercourse is the function or operation (vyāpāra); immediate knowledge is the result (phala) of the process of perception.[1]

Inference is flawless reasoning from a mark of inference to another property marked by it. The reason or mark of inference (liṅga) is the instrumental cause (karaṇa).The knowledge of the reason pervaded by the inferable property abiding in the subject of inference (parāmarśa) is the function or operation (vyāpara). The indirect knowledge of the property marked by the reason is the result (phala) of the inferential process. Inference depends on vyāpti. Vyāpti is invariable concomitance of the *probans* (*hetu*) and the *probandum* (sādhya): 'Wherever there is smoke, there is fire.' It is an unfailing relation between the *probans* and the *probandum*. Vyāpti does not mean their co-inherent in the same substrate (sāmānādhikaraṇya). There are three kinds of inference: (1) Inference from effects; (2) inference from causes; and (3) inference from events which are neither causes nor effects. When an effect is the reason of inference of its cause, there is an inference from an effect. We infer the existence of fire from smoke. When a cause is the reason of inference of its effect, there is an inference from a cause. We infer a rainfall from a dense mass of clouds. When a phenomenon, which is neither a cause nor an effect, is the reason of inference of another phenomenon, there is an inference from a phenomenon which is neither a cause nor an effect. We infer the existence of colour from the presence of taste. There is uniformity of co-existence between taste and colour. There is no uniformity of causation between them. Inference is of two kinds from another point of view: (1) Dṛṣṭa, inference of a perceivable object, as fire is inferred from smoke, and (2) Sāmānyatodṛṣṭa, inference of an unperceivable object, as the visual organ is inferred from the perception of colours. The Mādhvas reject the Naiyāyika division of inference into three kinds *viz.*, Kevalānvayi, Kevalavyatireki, and Anvayavyatireki. Invariable co-absence cannot prove the presence of the *probandum*. Inference is again of two kinds: (1) inference for oneself (svārtha) and (2) inference for others (parārtha). The former is the cause of self-conviction. The latter is intended for convincing others. It consists of five members: (1) thesis (pratijñā); (2) reason (hetu); (3) example (udāharaṇa); (4) application (upanaya); and (5) conclusion (nigamana). Vyāpti is of two kinds: (1) Anvayavyāpti, and (2)

[1] *Pramāṇacandrikā*, C.U., Ch. I.

Vyatirekavyāpti. The former is the pervasion of the *probans* by the *probandum*. The latter is the pervasion of the absence of the *probandum* by the absence of the *probans*.[1]

Testimony (*āgama*) is flawless verbal knowledge. There are two kinds of testimony: (1) personal (pauruṣeya); and (2) impersonal (apauruṣeya). The former is created; the latter is eternal. The Vedas are uncreated and eternal. They are revealed by God. They are self-evident. They are valid in themselves. They have intrinsic validity.[2] Personal testimony is not reliable. Reason is subordinate to Śruti. It cannot override the authority of the Vedas. It is of some help where Vedic statements appear to be conflicting.[3] Comparison, presumption, and non-apprehension are not independent means of valid knowledge.[4]

Knowledge is intrinsically valid. Its validity is produced by the causes which produce the knowledge. Its validity is known by the knowledge itself. The sākṣin is self-luminous; it makes itself and its validity known by itself. Invalidity of knowledge is due to adventitious conditions. The Mādhvas believe in intrinsic validity of knowledge and extrinsic invalidity of knowledge.[5]

Viśeṣa

Madhva recognizes the reality of viśeṣa. One thing is apprehended as manifold owing to its viśeṣa or particularity. Viśeṣa is the essence of a thing (vastusvarūpa). It is self-explānatory. It defines and specifies its own nature. There are as many viśeṣas as there are qualities in a substance. They do not require other viśeṣas to connect them with the substance. So there is no infinite regress.[6] The viśeṣas bind together the different qualities of a substance into a integral unity. The Mādhvas do not recognize inherence (samavāya) as the relation between a substance and its qualities like the Nyāya-Vaiśeṣika.[7] The Mādhva conception of viśeṣa is different from the Nyāya-Vaiśeṣika conception of viśeṣa which is the distinctive feature of eternal individual substances only. The viśeṣas of the Mādhva characterize eternal as well as non-eternal substances.

We perceive whiteness of a cloth. We do not perceive difference

[1] *Pramāṇacandrikā*, Ch. II.
[2] MBS., ii, 1. 4.
[3] MBS., ii, 1. 26, 28.
[4] *Pramāṇacandrikā*, C.U., Ch. III.
[5] *Pramāṇacandrikā*, C.U., pp. 165-66.
[6] *Nyānasudhā*, p. 106.
[7] HIP, Vol. IV. pp. 126-27.

between the cloth and the whiteness. We perceive a particularity (viśeṣa) of the cloth. If there were difference between the cloth and whiteness, then there would be difference between this difference and the cloth, and difference between it and whiteness, and so on to infinity. This would involve infinite regress. Therefore, the qualities are identical with the substance.[1]

God

Madhva recognizes two kinds of reality, independent (svatantra) and dependent (paratantra). God is the independent reality. Individual souls and the world are dependent realities. God is free from all imperfections. He is possessed of infinite, excellent, spiritual qualities.[2] He is not attributeless (nirguṇa). He is free from the attributes of prakṛti. This is the import of the texts speaking of nirguṇa Brahman. He has being (sat), consciousness (cit), and bliss (ānanda). He has six qualities of Lordship, infinite knowledge, infinite power, infinite strength, infinite rulership, infinite vigour, and infinite glory. There is no mutual difference among the qualities of God. There is non-difference among them. There is non-difference between God and his qualities which constitute his nature. Their co-inherence in him proves their identity with him. They constitute his determinate nature on account of viśeṣas.[3] He is the cause of creation, subsistence, dissolution, control, knowledge, nescience, bondage, and liberation.[4] He is the efficient cause (nimittakāraṇa) of the world. Prakṛti is the material cause (upādānakāraṇa) of the world. God is said to be indescribable because he cannot be completely comprehended. The highest and perfect Lord is Viṣṇu. He is called the Absolute (Brahman), the Supreme Self (Paramātman), and Bhagavān (Lord). He is the Inner Ruler (Antaryāmin). He is not all. But he is the ruler of all. He is the Supreme Person (Puruṣottama).[5] He is omniscient, omnipotent, perfect, eternal, extremely subtle, and immutable. He is the cause of all beings, and dwells in them. He impels men in their activities. He is the object of knowledge. He is the goal of attainment. He reveals the Vedas which embody eternal truths.[6] He has extraordinary and inconceivable powers. He can make the impossible

[1] *Tattvapradīpa* (edited by B. N. Krishnamurti Sharma), p. 11.

[2] SDS., v. 1.

[3] *Ibid.*, pp. 12-13; MBS., ii, 2. 30. 31.

[4] MBS., i, 1. 2.

[5] MBS., i, 1. 6. 7, 11, 12, 17, 29; i, 2, 1.

[6] MBS., i, 1. 1; i, 2. 1, 20; i, 2. 7.

possible. He is the controller of all. He is partless. He is devoid of body and sense-organs. He is not subject to prakṛti.[1] The Supreme Lord is Viṣṇu. He is immanent in the souls and the world. He transcends them all. He is both immanent and transcendent. He is the abode of contrary qualities.[2]

Prakṛti

Lakṣmī, the consort of Viṣṇu, is eternally blessed and absolutely accomplished. She eternally contemplates Viṣṇu. She is eternally related to the Lord. Lakṣmī and Viṣṇu rejoice in each other. They are eternally united with each other. Lakṣmī is dependent on Viṣṇu. In herself she is not.[3] She is intelligent Prakṛti. She has an eternal supernatural body. She is immortal.[4] Māyā is the eternal power or will of God, which is his essence. He creates all things by the power of his will.[5] Prakṛti is the material cause of the world. The Lord moulds various forms out of Prakṛti and exhibits himself in manifold ways. He enters into Prakṛti, and makes himself many.[6] The Lord's will is Prakṛti. He is the master of the will. His will is variously called Māyā, Avidyā, and Prakṛti. He is Puruṣa. His will is Prakṛti. He is the light. He is the support.[7] Prakṛti and the Lord (paramapuruṣa) co-exist in time and space. Prakṛti is eternally liberated. She is omnipresent, immutable, and eternal. Brahman is more subtle than Prakṛti. Knowledge, bliss, power, and authority of God are infinitely greater than those of Prakṛti. They are absolutely perfect in God. Prakṛti, like God, is all-pervading in time and space. She is absolutely free from bondage like him. Her freedom is dependent on God's grace. Prakṛti is ruled by the Lord who is absolutely free.[8]

The World

The Śruti has it: "All are known when one is known." When Brahman is known, all are known. When the cause, Brahman, is known, the effect, the world, is known. The cause and the effect both are real. Brahman is real, and the world is real. Śaṁkara is wrong in holding that Brahman is real, and that the world is an unreal appearance. This is a wrong interpretation of the text. One and all both are real. The effect is a real modification (vikāra) of

[1] *Ibid.*, ii. 1. 29-32. [2] *Ibid*, i. 3. 12.
[3] *Ibid*, iii. 3. 40-42. [4] SDS., v. 33.
[5] *Ibid*, iii. 2. 38. [6] *Ibid*, i. 4. 27.
[7] *Ibid*, i. 4. 25, 26. [8] *Ibid*, iv. 2. 7-10.

the cause which remains intact (avikṛta). The world is created by God out of prakṛti which is not a false appearance. Madhva asks: Is falseness of the world-appearance real or unreal? If it is real, monism is compromised. If it is unreal, then the world-appearance is real.[1] Creation is divine sport. It is the expression of God's overflowing bliss and mercy. He has no purpose in creating the world. Creative activity is his essential nature. He creates multiplicity of forms without undergoing modification.[2]

Reality of Difference

Śaṁkara maintains that Brahman is devoid of homogeneous difference (sajātīya bheda), heterogeneous difference (vijātīya bheda), and internal difference (svagata bheda). But Madhva recognizes difference in the Reality. Śaṁkara advocates absolute monism. But Madhva advocates pluralistic theism. He stresses the five kinds of difference which are real and beginningless. There is difference between God and the individual souls. There is difference between God and matter. There is difference between soul and matter. There is difference between one soul and another. There is difference between one material thing and another. These are the five kinds of differences.[3] Matter, soul, and God are irreducible to one another. Madhva gives a pluralistic universe with God as its Lord. The fivefold difference is not a mere appearance (māyāmātra), since Māyā is the will of God. Māyā or Prakṛti is the knowledge (prajñapti) of God which is characterized by bliss. This knowledge apprehends all, and saves all. It cannot therefore be a false appearance. Duality cannot be an imaginary appearance. God cannot have an illusory knowledge of all, since he is omniscient, and an illusion is false knowledge due to non-perception of particular qualities of an object. God is without an equal or a superior. Therefore Śruti says: "In reality, there is non-duality." It does not mean that duality or plurality is a false appearance.[4]

Difference is real. It is perceived. We perceive blue, yellow, and the like. We perceive that blue is different from yellow. Perception apprehends the difference between blue and yellow. The Advaitist contends that perception cannot apprehends difference. For it apprehends either difference only, or difference with the distinct entities. Perception cannot apprehend difference alone without apprehending the correlate (prati-yogi) of the difference. Diff-

---

[1]SDS, v. 36.
[2]MBS., ii, 1. 34; i, 3. 13.
[3]SDS., v. 22.
[4]SDS., v. 19-21.

erence is the distinction between two distinct entities. If the distincts are not perceived, the difference between them cannot be perceived. Perception cannot apprehend difference with the distincts. If it does, either it apprehends the distincts first, and then apprehends difference between them, or it apprehends both the distincts and their difference simultaneously. It cannot apprehend the distincts first, and then their difference. When perception apprehends the distincts, it ceases to function, and cannot apprehend difference between them. Difference is mutual non-existence of two things in each other. So it cannot be perceived without perception of the distincts. So distincts cannot be perceived without perception of their difference. Difference cannot be perceived without perception of the distincts. This involves mutual dependence or vicious circle. Perception cannot apprehend the distincts and their difference simultaneously. Cognition of cause and cognition of effect cannot occur at the same time. Cognition of an entity (*e.g.*, a jar) and cognition of its counter-entity (*e.g.*, a cloth) are the cause of the cognition of their difference. Therefore, difference cannot be perceived.[1]

But Madhva maintains that when we perceive objects, we perceive their relations, their difference, and their individualities in one and the same act of perception. Difference is the essence of the object itself. It is the essential feature of it. Essence, difference, and individuality are apprehended in the same act of perception. Perception of difference is not illusory, since even illusion is misinterpretation of sensory data. The Advaitist cannot mention any disturbing factors which are the cause of misinterpretation. Sensory data themselves are not illusory. Perception can apprehend objects and their difference. The Sākṣin or the I—awareness can apprehend the external order or material objects and individuals with their differences directly. Difference is real. It is the foundation of Madhva's pluralistic universe. It is not a subjective construction of the mind. It is constitutive of the universe. It is directly perceived by the Sākṣin.[2]

Madhva and Rāmānuja

Madhva agrees with Rāmānuja in holding that the Vedas are impersonal and eternal, that they testify to the existence and nature of Brahman, that perception, inference, and Vedic testimony

---

[1]SDS., v. 3.
[2]Nagaraja Sharma: *The Reign of Realism in Indian Philosophy*, pp. 51-53.

are the three kinds of valid knowledge, that knowledge has intrinsic validity, that Viṣṇu himself is the reciter of the *Pañcarātra Āgama*, which therefore has supreme authority, that the world is real, and that the jīva is atomic. But he differs from Rāmānuja in holding that God is different from the souls and the world, that God is not related to the conscious souls (cit) and the unconscious matter (acit) as the soul to its body. Two contradictory qualities of cit and acit cannot exist in God at the same time. Rāmānuja's doctrine resembles the Jaina doctrine in so far as he advocates the existence of contradictory qualities of consciousness and unconsciousness in God at the same time.[1]

The Jīva

The individual soul (jīva) is the knower, enjoyer, and doer. It is partless and eternal. It dwells in the body and the senses. It is subject to happiness and misery.[2] It is atomic in size, and yet it can experience sensations in its entire body, even as a lamp can illumine a room by its light. The soul is eternal; its birth and death are due to its connection with and separation from its body.[3] It has by nature perfect wisdom and bliss, but they are clouded by the influence of merits and demerits (karma). When they are worn off and its embodied existence ceases, its natural wisdom and bliss are manifested by the grace of God.[4] Though the soul is dependent on God, it is an active agent, performs right and wrong actions, and acquires merits and demerits. It freely adapts means to ends, and adopts various methods to achieve liberation. But its free activity is controlled by God. It has no absolute freedom. It is not an absolute agent. It is allowed relative freedom by its divine master. God guides the free actions of the jīvas.[5]

The jīvas are different from God. There can be no absolute identity between them. God is the worshipped master. The jīvas are his worshipping servants.[6] The Deity and the devotee are different from each other. God is omniscient, omnipotent, and perfect. The jīva has finite knowledge, limited power, and is absolutely dependent on God. God dwells in the soul. But he does not experience its joys and sorrows. He enjoys bliss only arising from its good actions. God is real; the soul is real; their difference is real.[7] One individual soul is not the ruler of another, since it would involve infinite regress.

---

[1]SDS., v. 1. [2]MBS., ii 1. 27.
[3]MBS., ii. 3, 24, 26, 19. [4]MBS., ii. 3. 31.
[5]MBS., ii, 3. 33-42. [6]MBS., i, 3. 5.
[7]MBS., i. 2, 8, 11, 12.

Prakṛti is not the inner ruler of the souls. God is their inner ruler.[1] The text 'Tat tvam asi' does not convey identity of the soul with God. It means that the soul has similarity in essence with God. Madhva reads 'Sa ātmā tat tvaṁ asi' as 'Sa ātmā atat tvam asi'. 'That ātman, thou art not'. The soul is not identical with God.[2] The jīva and God are always different from each other. The knowledge of difference between them liberates a person. He is the refuge of all liberated souls. They enjoy his companionship and bliss. He is their abode. He is their final goal.[3]

God is the Moral Governor. He dispenses the fruits to the souls in accordance with their good and bad actions (karma). So he cannot be charged with partiality and cruelty. There is a beginningless series of actions and their fruits. The souls freely do right and wrong actions, and reap their fruits. God, like an impartial judge, awards fruits to them in strict conformity with their merits and demerits. He is the Lord of the Law of Karma. He does not abrogate the Moral Law which follows from his nature.[4]

There are three kinds of souls: (1) eternally free (nitya) souls, like Lakṣmī; (2) liberated (mukta) souls, like gods, ṛsis, fathers, and men; (3) the bound (baddha). Among the bound souls some are eligible for liberation (muktiyogya), some are bound to saṁsāra for ever (nityasaṁsārin), and others are intended for hell (tamoyogya). Vāyu is the mediator between God and souls.

The jīva gets release through the grace of God. Release is the original state of purity. The liberated soul attains similarity with God. It never loses its identity in him. It enjoys a small measure of the infinite bliss of God through its śuddhasattva body. Its desires are not different from those of God. They are under his control. The released soul is liable to experience of miseries. It does not acquire power of creating, preserving, and destroying the world.[5]

Liberation is attained through knowledge of the excellence of the qualities of God. It cannot be attained through knowledge of its identity with God. It can be attained through the knowledge of its difference from and inferiority to him. It cannot be achieved without his grade. When a devotee surrenders himself to, and takes refuge in God, he grants him saving knowledge of difference, and

---

[1]MBS., i, 2. 17, 19, 20.

[2]SDS., v. 29-30; MBS., iii, 2. 18.

[3]MBS., i, 3. 1, 2; SDS., v. 31, 22, 34.

[4]MBS., ii. 1, 35, 36; iii. 2. 42.

[5]MBS., i. 3. 19; iv. 2. 16; iv. 4. 4, 5, 9, 15, 17; SDS., v. 17, 18.

liberates him.[1] Devotion, knowledge, performance of duties are the means to release. Truthfulness, study of the scriptures, charity, benevolence, compassion, desire for God, meditation, righteousness, faith, devotion, and worship of God should be cultivated. Yogic practices also are enjoined.[2] Bondage is due to ignorance. Release is due to knowledge. When the soul casts off its inessential forms, and is restored to its pure spiritual essence, it attains final release.[3] Until the karmas accumulated in the past births are completely worn off, the body continues. When they are exhausted, final release is attained[4].

The Categories

Madhva recognizes ten categories: substance (dravya), quality (guṇa), action (karma), generality (sāmānya), particularity (viśeṣa), qualified (viśiṣṭa), whole (aṁśi), power (śakti), similarity (sādṛśya), and negation (abhāva). These are twenty substances: God, Lakṣmī, souls, uncreated space, prakṛti, sattva, rajas, tamas, ahaṁkāra, buddhi, manas, the sense-organs, the elements, subtle essences (tanmātra), nescience (avidyā), uttered sounds, darkness, dispositions (vāsanā), time, and reflection (pratibimba). Uncreated space (avyākṛta ākāśa) is different from the element ākāśa (bhūtākāśa). It is eternal vacuum. It is not affected by creation and destruction. Time is co-existent with it. It is a direct product of prakṛti. It is the self-subsistent abode of all other substances. It is the generic cause of production of all things. Prakṛti is the material cause of the world. God produces sattva, rajas, and tamas out of prakṛti. Then Mahat is produced. Then Ahaṁkāra is produced. Then buddhi, manas, ten sense-organs, five tanmātras, and five elements are produced. A substance is the material cause of modifications and manifestations. Prakṛti is subject to modifications. But God are souls cannot undergo modification; they can be manifested only. Nescience (avidyā) veils the natural knowledge and bliss of the jīvas. Each soul has a specific nescience which veils its natural qualities, and causes its bondage. There is no generic nescience which veils the knowledge of all souls. The universals or generalities, according to Madhva, are eternal in eternal substances and non-eternal in non-eternal substances and limited to the individuals so long as

[1]SDS., v. 27, 39; MBS., iii. 2. 42.
[2]SDS., v. 16; MBS., iii, 3, 48, 51, 53, 54; iv. 1. 4, 5, 8, 9, 10.
[3]MBS., i. 1. 17.
[4]MBS., iii. 4. 51.

they last. He does not recognize the relation of inherence between a substance and its qualities and actions in order to avoid infinite regress. But he recognizes the category of the qualified (viśiṣṭa) which binds together a substance with its qualities and actions. There is no relation of inherence between the whole and its parts. The category of the whole connects its parts with one another inseparably. Power is a separate category. Inconceivable power as what abides in God, causal power, adventitious power, and power of words are the forms of power. There are four kinds of negation: prior negation, posterior negation, mutual negation, and absolute negation.[1]

Madhva's dualism is realistic. It admits the ontological reality of God, souls, and the world. It recognizes eternal distinctions between God and souls, God and matter, souls and matter, one soul and another, and one material thing and another. It is pluralistic theism. It gives a pluralistic universe with God as its creator, preserver, and destroyer. It gives three irreducible grades of reality, matter, souls, and God. It recognizes the uniqueness of God, and the individuality of each souls and material thing. This is the distinct contribution of Madhva. He does not sacrifice the many to one like Saṁkara. He does not regard the souls and manifold world as appearances. He treats them as ontological realities depending on God who is the supreme, absolutely independent reality. He creates the world of matter, and preserves and destroys it, and controls the souls and guides them to their destiny. God concedes relative freedom to the souls to work out their own salvation or perdition. Madhva reconciles knowledge, devotion, and action with one another as the means to release. His pluralistic theism is the antithesis of Śaṁkara's absolute monism. The Madhvas severely criticize Śāṁkaras theory of Ajñāna and falsity of the world-appearance.[2] Mādhva ascribes an inconceivable power to God by which he harmonizes the five-fold absolute differences with one another in an integral whole. He introduces the concept of viśeṣa which holds together differences within an undivided Being. Viśeṣa is self-determining and self-explanatory. It does not require the aid of any other thing. "Madhvites claim their position to be monistic. Though they accept infinite differences, still they accentuate the integrity of Being. Their doctrine of specific particulars (viśeṣa) does not

[1]HIP., Vol. IV, pp. 150-60.
[2]HIP., Vol. IV, pp. 204-304.

make the differences absolute, it seeks to assimilate differences in integrity. They deny differences. They accept distinctions. These distinctions are specific and cannot create division in integrity In this way Madhvites reconcile ineffaceable differences in the Absolute "[1] But dualism and pluralism cannot be reconciled with monism

[1]*Comparative Studies in Vendāntism*, pp. 50-51.

CHAPTER XVI

DVAITĀDVAITAVĀDA OF NIMBĀRKA

Nimbārka lived shortly after Rāmānuja. Nimbārka advocates the doctrine of dualistic monism (dvaitādvaitavāda) He insists on difference as well as non-difference or identity (bhedābheda) between Brahman and the individual souls and the world. He advocates the relation of identity-in-difference between them. He, like Bhāskara, advocates the doctrine of transformation of Brahman into the world (brahmapariṇāmavāda). The Bhedābhedavāda of Bhāskara and Yādavaprakāśa has already been discussed.

Brahman

Brahman is the greatest, Supreme Person (puruṣottama) possessed of infinite, inconceivable, natural essences, qualities, and powers. He is omniscient, omnipotent, and omnipresent. He is possessed of infinite excellent qualities. He is free from all taint of imperfections. He is the creator, preserver, and destroyer of the world of conscious souls (cit) and unconscious matter (acit). He is absolutely free and independent controller of all finite agents, and dispenser of the fruits of their actions. He has infinite knowledge, infinite bliss, and infinite will and power. He is infinite (bhūmā). He is self-subsistent and absolute. He has transcendental bliss and immortality. He is imperishable (akṣara). He is the ground of all effects in the past, the present, and the future. He is the support of the world. He is the cause of its stability and harmony. He is of the nature of eternal manifestation. He is transcendent as well as immanent. He transcends the world. He is immanent in the world[1] He is knowable through the Vedas only. He is the final goal of human attainment. He is the supreme end of the individual souls. They share in the bliss of God. He is the inner controller (antaryāmin) of the world and the souls. He is the knower and controller of all things and beings.[2]

Brahman is the material cause and the efficient cause of the world. He transforms himself into the world by his own extraordinary power without any accessory conditions, even as milk is

[1]VPS., i. 1. 1, 2, 3, 4, 13; i, 3. 8, 9, 10, 11, 13, 16, 22.
[2]VPS., i, 1. 4, 18; i, 2. 20; ii, 1. 21.

29

transformed into curd without any accessory conditions. God, who is omniscient and omnipotent, transforms himself into the world by his own power and will with his essential nature (svarūpa) unmodified (avyākṛta). He is unmodified in his essential nature and modified in his inessential nature.[1] It may be urged that if God be the material cause of the world, he, being devoid of parts, becomes entirely transformed into the world, and that if he partly transforms himself into the world, he ceases to be partless. But the Śruti says: "Brahman willed to become many; he created the world (sat) out of himself and yet remained transcendent (tyat), even as a spider spins out a cobweb out of itself." The omnipotent Supreme Lord can create the world out of himself, and yet remain transcendent.[2] The inconceivable creative power in God is the cause of the world. It is real. It is the will of God. It is not indefinable Māyā of Śaṁkara, which is neither real nor unreal. The world which is the transformation of Brahman is real. It is not a false appearance as Śaṁkara holds.

Effect is non-different from cause. It is not absolutely different from cause. When cause is perceived, effect is perceived. Effect is a transformation of cause. Hence, effect is non-different from cause. The effect that happens subsequently, pre-exists in the cause. If the effect were non-existent in the cause, then sprouts of barley would be produced from fire. The effect is the unfoldment of the cause, even as an unrolled cloth is the unfoldment of a folded cloth. Vital airs are inhaled and exhaled. So the effect is implicit in the cuse, and becomes explicit when it assumes the form of the effect. The world pre-exists in Brahman in an implicit condition, and becomes explicit after creation.[3] Cause and effect are partly different and partly non-different from the world. Brahman is transformed into the world, which is non-different from him. Brahman is the inner controller of the world. So there is no absolute identity between them.[4] Brahman is both different and non-different from the world of unconscious matter and conscious souls, even as the sea is different and non-different from its waves, and the sun is different and non-different from its rays. The world including formed and unformed existence, material things and spiritual beings, exists in its cause, Brahman, is the relation of identity-in-different. God is related to

---

[1]VPS., i, 4, 26; ii. 1. 23.
[2]VPS., ii, 1. 25-29.
[3]VPS., ii, 1. 14-19.
[4]VPS., ii, 1. 14, 21.

the world as a snake is related to its coiled form.[1] God remains unmodified in his essential nature, and only undergoes modification through his conscious energy (cit-śakti) and unconscious energy (acit-śakti).[2] This doctrine resembles Vallabha's doctrine of immutable transformation (avikṛtapariṇāma). God transcends his three natures as the world, souls, and even as God. In his pure and transcendent nature he is absolutely unaffected by changes and mutations of the world of phenomena. As noumenon he is immutable; as phenomenon he undergoes mutations. In his esoteric and essential nature he is immutable; in his exoteric and phenomenal nature he is mutable.[3]

The Jīva

The individual soul (jīva) is not born. It is eternal. Its birth and death are due to its connection with and separation from its body. It is the knower or ego which possesses the essential quality of knowledge. The relation of the soul to knowledge is that of the qualified (dharmin) to its quality (dharma). There is identity-in-difference between them. The soul and knowledge, though non-distinct from each other, are related to each other as substance and attribute. The soul is an enjoyer. It feels pleasure and pain, which are the fruitions of merits and demerits. It is an active agent. It has the power of doing right and wrong actions. Its activity is controlled by God. It strives to share in the infinite bliss of God. It is atomic. But it can experience pleasure and pain through its entire body. Its seat is in the heart. It has experience through its whole body, even as the light of a lamp illumines the whole room. It is a part of Brahman. It is both different and non-different from him.[4]

There is great difference between a soul and Brahman. The soul is subject to joys and sorrows (bhoktṛ). It experiences the fruits of its actions. But Brahman does not experience fruits of actions (abhoktṛ). Brahman is the worshipped while the soul is the worshipper. Brahman is known by the soul which is the knower. The soul strives to receive the infinite bliss of God who is the giver of bliss. Brahman is the inner controller of the soul which is controlled by him. So Brahman and the soul are different from each other.[5] But they are not absolutely different from each other. The soul is a

[1] VPS., ii, 1. 16; i, 1, 4; iii. 2. 27.
[2] *Vedāntakaustubhaprabhā*, iii. 2. 29; HIP., III, p. 416.
[3] VPS., i. 1, 2; HIP., iii, p. 413.
[4] VPS., ii. 3. 16-19, 23-28, 32, 48.
[5] VPS., i. 2, 8, 11, 12; i, 3. 7.

part of Brahman. It is identical with him in essence. Its natural knowledge and bliss are covered by nescience (avidyā) which is removed by the grace of God. The liberated soul acquires absolute equality with God, being purged of merits and demerits and becoming immaculate. But it does not lose its integrity in him.[1]

Brahman is not defiled by the limitations and imperfections of the souls, though he regulates their different states, waking, dream, sleep, and intuitive state. Their natural will-power is eclipsed by the superior will of God who guides them in all matters according to their past deeds. Their bondage and release are due to the will of God. He is absolutely pure in spite of his connection with their impurities. He is the inner controller of all; yet he does not undergo any limitation. Though he is omnipresent, he does not suffer from the limitations of the souls. Even as light reveals objects covered by darkness, so God reveals every thing, but is not affected by it. He abides in the souls, but is not affected by their changes. He is not infected with their impurities.[2] Brahman is both different from and identical with souls, even as the sun is both different from and identical with its rays for the sun and its rays are both light.[3]

Nimbārka and Bhāskara

Nimbārka, like Bhāskara, believes in the transformation of Brahman into the world (brahmapariṇāma). He recognizes, like him, the relation of identity-in-difference (bhedābheda) between Brahman and the individual souls. But Bhāskara emphasizes identity between them, their difference being due to limiting conditions (upādhi). Nimbārka stresses both identity and difference between them. His doctrine is dualistic non-dualism (dvaitādvaitavāda) which stresses identity-in-difference (bhedabheda) between God and the soul and the world.[4] Nimbārka condemns both monistic absolutism and dualism, and reconciles the identity texts with the difference texts in his doctrine of dualistic monism. The world and the souls are different from Brahman because they have real and distinct existence dependent upon him. They are non-different from Brahman because they cannot exist apart from him. 'Tat tvam asi', or 'That thout art' means that individual soul (tvam) is both different and non-different from Brahman (tat). There is non-difference or identity between them in their essential nature. There is difference between them because they are related to each other as part and

[1]VPS., i, 3. 2.
[2]VPS., iii. 2. 5, 11, 12, 15, 18; iii. 2. 20, 30.
[3]VPS., iii. 2. 28. [4]HIP., Vol. III, p. 413.

whole, the controlled and the controller, and the worshipper and the worshipped.

Nimbārka and Rāmānuja

Rāmānuja recognizes internal difference (svagatabheda) within Brahman. He regards Brahman as the qualified (viśeṣya) substance whose attributes (viśeṣaṇa) or modes (prakāra) are the unconscious world of matter (acit) and conscious souls (cit). Matter and soul are adjectives of the divine substance. They co-inhere in Brahman. Their co-inherence in Brahman shows their substantial identity. They constitute the body of Brahman who is the soul. They are inseparably related to each other like body and soul. There is inseparable relation (apṛthaksiddhi) between them. Rāmānuja stresses identity or unity more than difference. But Nimbārka emphasizes identity as well as difference. The world is the transformation of the conscious energies (cit-śakti) and the unconscious energies (acit-śakti) of Brahman. The individual souls are parts of Brahman. The world and souls are real and substantial; they are not mere adjectives of Brahman. He is immanent in them as their inner controller. But he transcends them, and is not affected by their changes and mutations. He is immutable in his essential nature.

CHAPTER XVII

ŚUDDHĀDVAITAVĀDA OF VALLABHA

Vallabha (1481-1533 A.D.) was the founder of the Suddhādvaita school of Vedānta. Vallabha advocates pure non-dualism.

Epistemology

Valid knowledge is determinate apprehension of the real nature of an object which was not known before.[1] Perception, inference, and Vedic testimony are the three kinds of valid knowledge. The Vedas are the highest authority. Reason is sub-ordinate to them.[2] Perception is immediate knowledge produced by the right sense-object-intercourse.[3] There is no indeterminate perception which is non-relational consciousness. The Vallabhite, like Madhva, admits only determinate perception. All perception is determinate, and involves subject-predicate relation. There are two kinds of determinate perception: (1) viśiṣṭabuddhi; and (2) samūhāvalambana. The former is the determinate apprehension of an object (*e.g.*, a jar) qualified by some properties. It apprehends the relation between the qualified and the qualities. The latter is the determinate apprehension of a collection of objects such as a jar, a cloth, and a pillar.[4] Inference is mediate knowledge. It is derived through the medium of some other knowledge. It depends upon the knowledge of in variable concomitance (vyāpti). Vyāpti is the unconditioned and universal co-presence and co-absence of the reason (hetu) and the probandum (sādhya). Wherever the reason is present, the probandum is present. Wherever the probandum is absent, the reason is absent. There are two kinds of inference: (1) kevalavyatireki; and (2) anvayavyatireki. Puruṣottama does not admit kevalānvayi form of inference. Inference is either for oneself (svārtha) or for others (parārtha). These are five members in a demonstrative syllogism: (1) thesis (pratijñā); (2) reason (hetu); (3) example (udāharaṇa); (4) application (upanaya); and (5) conclusion (nigamana).[5] Comparison (upamāna) is not a distinct pramāṇa. It is perception of similarity between to objects, (*e.g.*, a cow and a

---

[1]ABS., i. 1. 2, 3; PRK., p. 18.

[2]ABS., i. 1. 2. 3; ii. 1. 11; PRK., p. 38.

[3]PRK., p. 20.

[4]PRK., p. 13.

[5]PRK., pp. 138-39; 142-44.

wild cow) with the aid of recollection of the similarity indicated by authority, determined by the knowledge of the relation of the name to the thing named. It is included in perception.[1] Presumption (arthāpatti) is a kind of kevalānvayi inference.[2] Tradition (aitihya) is authority, the source of which is not known. Therefore, it is not valid knowledge. When its truth is definitely ascertained, it is included in authority. Gesture (ceṣṭā) is included in inference.[3] Non-apprehension (anupalabdhi) is not necessary to apprehend non-existence (abhāva) of an object. Non-existence is not admitted. It is identical with the locus. The so-called non-apprehension is perception of the locus.[4]

Brahman

Vallabha does not admit the reality of attributeless (nirguṇa) Brahman. He is called nirguna in the Śruti because he is free from the qualities of prakṛti. He is qualified (saguṇa) and determinate (saviśeṣa). He is one, formed, omnipotent, omniscient, cause of all, and possessed of being, consciousness, and bliss. He is the embodiment of bliss. He has six qualities of Lordship. He has inconceivable power of producing all things and ruling over them. He is the inherent cause (samavāyikāraṇa) and the efficient cause (nimittakāraṇa) of the world. He is the world itself. He is the direct Lord of prakṛti and souls. Prakṛti, the stuff of the world, is the power of God. The souls are eternal parts of God. They are his emanations. The universe and the souls are Brahman. Brahman is God. He is not an unreal appearance, a product of māyā. Māyā is a his power. It is his creation. He is a knower, enjoyer, and doer. He has no body. but he can ssume bodies for the benefit of his devotees in sport. He is the Supreme Person (puruṣottama). Pure Brahman is the only reality.[5]

Brahman possesses being, consciousness, and bliss. He voluntarily conceals and manifests his qualities. He conceals his bliss and qualities of Lordship in the individual souls. He conceals his consciousness also in matter. Matter is Brahman with bliss and consciousness suppressed. The Jīva is Brahman with bliss suppressed. Being, consciousness, and bliss are fully manifested in Brahman. The qualities of Lordship are manifest in God only.[6] Being is manifest in matter; consciousness is manifest in the jīva;

---

[1]PRK., p. 148. [2]PRK., p. 151.
[3]PRK., p. 153. [4]PRK., p. 121.
[5]ABS., i. 1. 2-4, 8, 20, 21; ii. 4. 23; iii. 3. 47; SAM., SAMP., 8, 18, 19.
[6]ABS., iii. 2. 5; ii. 3. 43.

bliss is manifest in the inner soul (antaryāmin) in the jīva; all these qualities are manifest in Brahman.[1] There are different degrees of reality. They represent different stages of the concealment and manifestation of the divine qualities of being, consciousness, and bliss. On account of the evolution (āvirbhāva) and involution (tirobhāva) of these qualities, matter, soul, and God are different from one another. But when consciousness and bliss are manifested by Brahman, they become Brahman. Matter and soul are identical with Brahman in their essential nature. But they are different from him, when his qualities are partly concealed in them. Creation of the world and emanation of the souls are partial self-concealment (tirobhāva) of God. Self-manifestation (āvirbhāva) of him is the fulfilment of the destiny of matter and souls. Self-concealment and self-manifestation are the unique features of Śuddhādvaitavāda. Manifestation or evolution consists in perceptibility of present things. Concealment or involution consists in their imperceptibility.[2] There is greater or less manifestation of the divine qualities in different degrees of reality. Matter, souls (jīva), and inner souls (antaryāmin) are parts of being (sadaṁśa), consciousness (cidaṁśa), and bliss (ānandāṁśa) of God respectively.[3]

God is one. He wills to become many to sport with them.[4] His creative act is an act of sport undetermined by an external end. It is a voluntary play. God conceals his consciousness and bliss and becomes the world. But he does not undergo any modification in creating the world. Creation is involution (tirobhāva). Dissolution is evolution (āvirbhāva). Creation is enfoldment. Dissolution is unfoldment. God willingly becomes the world, even as a serpent folds itself into a coil.[5] God becomes the world without undergoing any modification, even as gold is modified into various ornaments without changing its nature.[6] Vallabha advocates the doctrine of immutable transformation (avikṛtapariṇāmavāda).[7] The cause remains intact and unchanged (avikṛta), though it is modified into the effect (pariṇāma).[8] Brahman remains immutable, though he is expressed in the world. How can non-eternal material

[1] *Jaḍajīvāntaryāmiṣvekaikāṁśaprākaṭyāt.* ABS., i. 1. 4.
[2] SAM., SAMP., 11, 14, 16.
[3] ABS., i. 1. 4.
[4] ABS., ii. 1. 33.
[5] ABS., iii. 2. 27; SAM., 12.
[6] SAM., 13.
[7] M. N. Sircar: *Comparative Studies in Vedāntism*, pp. 100, 102.
[8] Avikṛtameva pariṇamate. ABS., ii. 4. 26.

things be regarded as Brahman? Vallabha answers that they are really eternal Brahman, but that they appear to be non-eternal because consciousness and bliss are suppressed in them[1]. Material things are directly produced by God. There is no physical causation. All causation is spiritual causation. What appears to be physical causation is direct divine causation. Plurality is due to the divine will. God is the abode of contrary qualities. Plurality and contrariety are reconciled in the unity of God.[2]

God has infinite supreme powers. He causes the inherent causal potencies (śakti) in the causes to manifest themselves in their effects. Production is manifestation or evolution (āvirbhāva) of the causal powers. God causes the causal potencies in the effects to conceal themselves in their causes. Destruction is concealment or involution (tirobhāva) of the causal potencies. In involution the effect exists in the cause in a causal state. In evolution the effect exists in itself in an effected state. A jar is produced out of clay. Clay exists in earth in a causal state. In production a cause manifested as an effect. In destruction an effect is absorbed in its cause. But in production and destruction the cause does not undergo modification in its essential nature.[3] There is a causal power (śakti) in the cause to produce an effect. This power is not its nature (svabhāva). It is not its essence (svarūpa). A thing can never be divested of its nature. Its essence can never be separated from it. The nature or essence of a thing is always present. So, if the causal power were the nature or essence of the cause, it would always produce the effect. Hence, the causal power different from its nature or essence must be admitted. The effect is real and non-different from its cause.[4] Vallabha's Avikṛtapariṇāmavāda is a form of Satkāryavāda. He does not believe in Asatkāryavāda.[5] He does not admit prior non-existence (prāgabhāva), posterior non-existence (pradhvaṁsābhāva), mutual non-existence (anyonyābhāva), and absolute non-existence (atnyantābhāva) recognized by the Vaiśeṣika. Prior non-existence is the causal state (kāraṇāvasthā). Posterior non-existence is absorption in the cause (tirobhāvaśakti). Absolute non-existence is concealment of the divine nature. Mutual non-existence is voluntary concealment of specific natures of God. He conceals his pot-nature in a cloth, and cloth-nature in a pot. He is the cause of all things. They are not new

[1] SAM., 14.
[2] ABS., i. 1. 4; iii. 2. 27.
[3] SAM., SAMP., 15.
[4] ABS., ii, 1. 14.
[5] ABS., ii. 3. 35.

emergences (ārambha). They pre-exist in Brahman. They are his manifestations.[1]

Reality of the World

Śaṁkara maintains that the world is a false appearance (māyika) produced by Brahman related to Māyā. Brahman unrelated to Māyā is not its cause. The world is an appearance (prapañca), a product of nescience (ajñāna). Avidyā is a form of Māyā. Pure sattva is the chief element in Māyā. Impure sattva is the chief element of Avidyā. Brahman reflected in, or limited by Maya, is God (īsvara). Brahman reflected in, or limited by Avidya, is the individual soul (jīva). God and jīvas are appearances. The world is a false appearance. Therefore, creatorship of Brahman is apparent.[2] Nirguṇa Brahman only is real. Saguna Brahman or God is an appearance.

The Vallabhite disputes this view. Nirguṇa Brahman is not real. Brahman is saguṇa or qualified, and possessed of being, consciousness, bliss, and the six qualities of Lordship. He is the creator, preserver, and destroyer of the world, and the Moral Governor. God is not an appearance (māyika). He is real. Therefore, the world created by him is real. The cause and the effect are equally real. God cannot be the cause of an unreal world-appearance. Nescience (ajñāna) is unreal (asat), and cannnot produce any effects. If ajñāna is real, it resides in Brahman. Then he becomes ignorant and qualified. Māyā is impure and unreal. Brahman is formless. So Brahman cannot be reflected in Māyā. If he is reflected in Māyā, he becomes determinate (saviśeṣa). If Brahman appears like the world, even as a rope appears as a snake, then he has a form. The world is real; it is a manifestation of Brahman. But his nature is not fully manifested in the world. It is apprehended by waking perceptions which are dissimilar to dreams apprehending unreal forms. Real objects are apprehended by waking perceptions. The jīva is said to be an appearance. It is destroyed when identity-consciousness dawns on it. So its liberation consists in its destruction. Jīvanmukti is impossible. When avidyā is destroyed by identity-consciousness, the body is destroyed.

Is Māyā produced or not produced? If it is produced, Brahman must be its cause. Then Brahman becomes determinate and qualified. If Māyā is not produced, it is an eternal reality besides Brahman. Then non-dualism is compromised, and occasional

[1] SAM., SAMP., 17. [2] SAM., SAMP., 22.

appearance and disappearance of the world cannot be accounted for. If Māyā is not produced, it cannot be destroyed. The doctrine of Māyā is irrational and untenable.[1]

The Vallabhite maintains that Brahman is pure and free from all relation to Māyā, and that pure Brahman unassociated with Māyā is both cause and effect. Pure Brahman is the cause of the world. The world is pure Brahman is the state of an effect. Māyā is the power of God, which is non-different from him. Jīvas are not apparent (māyika). They are pure Brahman with bliss concealed. They are real parts of Brahman. There is no Avidyā in Brahman. The world is real and identical with Brahman as being. Jīvas are real and identical with Brahman as consciousness. Their inner souls (antaryāmin) are real and identical with Brahman as bliss. Matter and souls are of the nature of Brahman.[2]

Madhva maintains that there is difference (bheda) between God and the world. Nimbārka maintains that there is real identity-in-difference (bhedābheda) between them. Bhāskara maintains that there is identity-in-difference between them due to adjuncts (upādhi). Madhva maintains that the jīvas are parts of God separate from him. There are two kinds of parts, one's own parts (svāṁśa) and separate parts (vibhinnāṁśa). The divine incarnations are God's own parts. The jīvas are his separate parts. A part is a fragment of a whole. Or it is similar to the whole, though it is separate from it. The jīvas are God's parts in the second sense. They can never have divinity in them. Nimbārka holds that there is identity between God and the jīvas owing to the similarity to consciousness. The Vallabhite maintains that there is identity (abheda) between them, and that the jīvas are God's own parts (svāṁśa). There is real non-difference or identity between the whole and its parts.[3] The world is identical with God in essence. But it is different from him as an effect. When it is dissolved, it remains in him in the causal state.[4] When consciousness of God dawns, there is no consciousness of anything else. There is consciousness of God in all things.[5] This is the doctrine of pure non-dualism.

God is the inherent cause (samavāyi kāraṇa) and the efficient cause (nimitta kāraṇa)[6] of the world. He is the direct ruler of

---

[1]SAM., SAMP., 22-24.
[2]ABS., i. 1. 4; ii. 3. 43; SAM. SAMP., 28, 29.
[3]SAM., SAMP., 36-39.
[4]SAM., 40.
[5]SAMP., 34.
[6]ABS., i. 4. 4; ii. 4. 23; SAM., SAMP., 72.

prakṛti and souls.[1] He creates the world, and emits the souls for his own sport. He creates dravya, karma, kāla, svabhāva, and jīvas. Māyā or prakṛti is the power of God. It is the stuff (upādanā) of the world.[2] It consists of sattva, rajas and tamas. God creates prakṛti and its guṇas. Sattva is in the nature of illumination and pleasure. It is a part of the divine being (sat). Rajas is in the nature of attachment and desire for objects. It is not in the nature of pain as the Sāṁkhya holds. It is a part of the divine consciousness. Tamas is in the nature of delusion due to the power of veiling. It is a part of the divine bliss. The guṇas are parts of God. They are created by him. In the Sāṁkhya system they are self-existent, and they overpower one another, and transform themselves into various modifications of prakṛti. They are not controlled and guided by, an intelligent agent. The Sāṁkhya doctrine involves naturalism (svabhāvavāda) and atheism (anīśvaravāda). But the guṇas are created by God according to Vallabha. God, devoid of the guṇas of prakṛti, creates them out of his nature. He assumes a lower nature at his will, and produces them as parts of his being, consciousness, and bliss. They are the material cause (upādāna kāraṇa) of the world. God is its inherent cause (samavāyi kāraṇa). If he were its material cause, he would undergo modification into the world. Therefore, a distinction is made between the material cause and the inherent cause of the world.[3] Prakṛti, mahar, ahaṁkāra, tanmātras, and mahābhūtas constitute the creative order. Māyā is the potency of consciousness and bliss in God. Avidyā is a part of Māyā. It is a part of divine consciousness, which deludes jīvas into the false knowledge of plurality.[4]

Karma is destiny. It is a pervasive action which can be manifested partially by right and wrong actions. It makes them produce their fruits in time. Adṛṣṭa is not a quality of the soul. It is not necessary to enable actions to bring about their fruits.[5] Karma, one general pervasive action created by God, does the functions of the specific unseen agencies (adṛṣṭa) in the jīvas.

Real time contains being, consciousness, and bliss in itself. But empirical time is a partial manifestation of sattva part to our experience. Time upsets the equilibrium of sattva, rajas, and tamas. Karma and svabhāva are parts of time.[6]

Svabhāva is the cause of transformation. Svarūpa is the will

[1]SAM., 18.
[2]PRK., p. 163.
[3]HIP. iv. pp. 327-30.
[4]PRK., pp. 161, 170-72, 176.
[5]PRK., pp. 168-69.
[6]PRK., pp. 165-66.

of God in a specific form. Twenty-eight categories are evolved from svabhāva or specific volitions of God. They are not evolved by the general will of God.[1]

The Jīva

Jīvas are parts of God. They are eternal and devoid of the guṇas of prakṛti. They are superior to prakṛti. They are conscious souls. They are self-luminous. They control their bodies, sense-organs, life, and internal organs. They are apprehended by self-consciousness (ahaṁvitti). They are devoid of natural qualities in their essential nature. But they assume relationships to nature, and can divest themselves of all connection with nature, and acquire fitness for liberation.[2] They are not generated by God. They spring out of him, as sparks spring out of fire. They are emanations of God.[3] They are his parts. They are spiritual atoms (aṇu) or monads. They possess the quality of consciousness which is subject to contraction and expansion.[4]

The soul is the knower, enjoyer, and doer. Its activity is dependent on God.[5] Though it is atomic, it pervades the body through its consciousness. It feels through all parts of its body, even as sandal-paste in one part of the body produces pleasure and coolness in the whole body.[6] The souls are different from one another. They are different parts of Brahman. They are different from him owing to the suppression of bliss. They are identical with him in their essential nature. They are not appearances. They are real.[7] 'That thout art'. 'Tat tvam asi.' The soul is identical with Brahman. It is Brahman's own part (svāṁśa). There is real identity between them. There is real identity (abheda) between the the whole and its parts.[8]

The souls are monads (aṇu). They are eternal. Their birth and death are in relation to the bodies ensouled by them. If they were created by God, they would be liable to destruction. They are not limitations of God by limiting adjuncts (upādhi). **There is no proof for the existence of the adjuncts. If they were omnipresent**

---

[1]PRK., p. 169.
[2]PRK., p. 173.
[3]ABS., ii. 2. 17.
[4]CP. Rāmānuja.
[5]ABS., ii, 3. 18, 25, 33-35, 39, 43, 45.
[6]ABS., ii. 3. 23.
[7]ABS., ii. 3, 50; SAM., SAMP., 10.
[8]SAM., SAMP., 39.

like Brahman, they would not be controlled by him. They are controlled by him because they are atomic. If they were omnipresent, they would share the experiences of one another. There are different inner controllers (antaryāmin) within different souls. They are parts of the bliss of God, whereas the jīvas are parts of his consciousness, and their bodies are parts of his being.[1]

Different souls have different lots. Some are righteous, and others are unrighteous. Their different lots are not due to their merits and demerits which are the results of their past actions (karma). If they were the cause of their different lots, God would be useless and lose his sovereignty. If God awards fruits in accordance with merits and demerits of the jīvas, then he would depend upon them, and lose his independence and Lordship. God is the directive cause (kārayitṛ) of the jīvas' actions. He concedes relative freedom to them to do right or wrong actions for his own sport. The jīvas are free agents. Their free activity is dependent on God (parādhīna). They freely follow the injunctions and prohibitions of the Vedas, which are the moral laws. But God is the ultimate directive cause (kārayitṛ) of their actions. Human freedom is a part of God's freedom and sportive activity. He impels them to do right or wrong actions freely for his sport (līlā). Vallabha would not compromise the free causality and sovereignty of God for the sake of human freedom. But he concedes a part of divine freedom to jīvas to preserve morality and religion.[2]

Saṁsāra is due to the soul's ignorance (avidyā) of its non-difference from Brahman. Avidyā is due to egotism (mamakara) or a false sense of individuality. Vallabha, like Śaṁkara, posits Avidyā in the mundane soul. Liberation is due to true knowledge of the non-difference (abheda) of the world and jīvas from Brahman. Ballabha agrees with Śaṁkara on this point. Avidyā is destroyed by the true knowledge of Brahman. The liberated soul is divested of its adventitious qualities of prakṛti, and it acquires its intrinsic purity. It acquires affinity with God. It does not lose its identity in Him. It does not becomes God. The means (sādhana) can never never be the end (sādhya). God, by his infinite grace, makes his own dependent soul attain affinity with him, and liberates it. Merciful God makes his own devotee enjoy his supreme bliss.[3]

There are three kinds of souls, pure, mundane, and liberated.

---

[1]PRK., p. 162.
[2]ABS., ii. 1. 34; iii. 3. 29; SAM., SAMP., 44.
[3]SAM., SAMP., 83, 89; ABS., i. 1. 4.

Bliss and six qualities of Lordship are concealed in the jīva. A pure jīva is devoid of any relation to Avidyā. Bondage is due to relation to Avidyā. It is beginningless. The bound soul acquires, through the grace of God, fivefold vidyā, dispassion, discrimination, yoga, austerities, and devotion, and attains liberation. Liberated souls acquire affinity with God. They do not acquire Lordship of God. They are either jīvanmukta or mukta. The former are liberated in embodied life. The latter enjoy disembodied liberation.

The souls are either godly (daiva) or demoniac (āsura). Godly souls are of two kinds. Some follow the path of maryādābhakti. Others follow the path of puṣṭibhakti. The former cultivate action (karma), knowledge (jñāna), and devotion (bhakti). They attain Akṣara Brahman. The latter cultivate pure love of God. They are free from desires ior all things except affinity with God. They attain the Puruṣottama, Supreme Person, through his grace.[1]

Vallabha is right in stressing the reality of qualified and determinate Brahman, the reality of the world and the jīvas, and in rejecting the indefinable Māyā of Śaṁkara, but he does not adequately inter-relate Brahman, the jīvas, and the world to interrelate Brahman, the jīvas, and the world to one another. His virtual denial of human freedom and exaggeration of divine freedom, sovereignty, and direct causation of all things tend to make his doctrine pantheistic. Evolution (āvirbhāva) and involution (tirobhāva) of the qualities of God are its unique features. Vallabha's Śuddhādvaitavāda is the anti-thesis of the doctrine of emergent evolution. According to Alexander, life emerges out of matter, mind emerges out of life, and deity will emerge out of mind. According to Vallabha, God conceals his bliss, and becomes the soul. He conceals his consciousness, and becomes matter. There is progressive involution of the divine qualities in the jīvas and matter. The lower categories of existence can be explained by the higher by the higher categories cannot be explained by the lower.

[1]ABS., iii. 3. 29; iv. 3. 17; *Prameyaratnārṇava*, pp. 7-9. 17.

CHAPTER XVIII

ACINTYABHEDĀBHEDAVĀDA OF CAITANYA

Kṛṣṇadāsa Kavirāja's Philosophy

Caitanya (1485-1533 A.D.) did not write any treatise. His philosophical doctrine is known from *Caitanyacaritāmṛta* written by Kṛṣṇadāsa Kavirāja (1616 A.D.) in Bengali. It is an authoritative biography of Caitanya, which enjoys immense popularity in Bengal. It contains the philosophy of the Caitanya school. It gives an account of Caitanya's discussion with Vāsudeva Sārvabhauma, which brings out his philosophical doctrine. God is the supreme reality. He is inconceivable. His inconceivable qualities and powers subsist in him. He is not formless and indeterminate. He is devoid of the qualities of prakṛti.[1] He is determinate (saviśeṣa). Being, consciousness, and bliss constitute his essence. He is the embodiment of bliss. He is possessed of the six powers of Lordship. He is not powerless. He is the creator, preserver, and destroyer of the world. He creates prakṛti and the material world out of it. He has supernatural mind, body, and sense-organs. He has cicchakti, jīvaśakti, and māyāśakti. They are called Viṣṇuśakti, Kṣetrajñaśakti, and Avidyāśakti. The first is the internal (antaraṅga) power. the second is the inessential (taṭastha) power. The third is the external (bahiṛnga) power. The six powers of Lordship are manifestations of his divine energy (cicchakti), which is his essential power (svarūpaśakti). It is superior to his other two powers. His divine energy consists of power of being (sandhinī), power of consciousness (samvit), and power of bliss (hlādinī).[2] God is the Lord of māyā. The jīva is subject to it. The individual soul is a power of God (jīvaśakti). The *Bhagavadgītā* admits it.[3] The jīva is different from God. They are not identical with each other. God is transformed into the world, though he does not undergo any modification by his inconceivable power.[4] The world is not an appearance (vivarta) of Brahman. It is real. But it is mutable and destructible. The *Brahmasūtra* teaches the doctrine of modification (pariṇāma). But Śaṁkara wrongly ascribes the doctrine of Māyā do it. It is a

---

[1]CP. Madhva.

[2]*Caitanyacaritāmṛta*, Madhyalīlā, Ch. VIII.

[3]BG., xv. 7.

[4]CP. Vallabha.

false doctrine taught by the Buddhist. God is determinate. The jīvas are real. The world is real. They spring from the nature of God. They are his powers. The jīvas spring from the jīvaśakti of God. The world is a modification of the māyāśakti of God. The former is a conscious power. The latter is energy of matter. Devotion of God is the highest good.[1]

Caitanya explains the means of attaining the highest good in course of his conversation with Rāya Rāmānanda. The performance of duties relating to castes and stages of life leads to devotion God. Complete dedication of all works to God is superior to the performance of works. Renunciation of one's specific duties and complete surrender to God are superior to it. Devotion mixed with knowledge is superior to it. Higher than this is pure devotion unmixed with knowledge. Devotion in the form of love is the best means to the Highest Good. Servitude, friendship, tender affection, and love of a wife for a husband are the best means to attainment of God. There are various means to it. There are various degrees of attainment of him. Different aspirants have different aptitudes for different kinds of sādhanā. They are the best for them. Wifely love contains the excellences of the other kinds of love for God. Complete attainment of God is possible through it.[2]

Kṛṣṇadāsa explains the philosophy of Caitanya in different parts of his biography. Kṛṣṇa is God. He is the embodiment of bliss. He is the quintessence of love. He is infinite bliss and love. All creatures become happy by partaking of his bliss. He is the cause of their happiness.[3] His being is made of pure sattva. Love is his essence. His power is identical with him. Lakṣmī is the divine power. It is expressed in the six powers of Lordship. Rādhā is the infinite power of Kṛṣṇa. He is the infinite possessor of power. There is no difference between power and the possessor of power. Kṛṣṇa is full of pure consciousness, infinite joy and bliss. He is the abode contrary qualities. He is infinite, and yet he incarnates as a finite mortal. He is absolutely independent, and yet he is subject to love. Sweetness of Kṛṣṇa attracts all men and women towards him by its inherent power. He constantly endeavours to make them taste the nectar of his infinite sweetness. Pure love (prema) binds man to God. It is unconditioned. It does not seek selfish pleasure.

[1]*Caitanyacaritāmṛta*, Madhyalīlā, Ch. VI.
[2]*Caitanyacaritāmṛta*, Madhyalīlā, Ch. VIII.
[3]*Ibid.* Ch. IV.

It seeks only the pleasure of God. The devotee has instinctive love for him. His pure love transcends all moral observances and rituals.[1]

Kṛṣṇa resides in the highest heaven which is beyond prakṛti. He is infinite, ubiquitous, and possessed of divine qualities. He is unconditioned (turīya) and free from all traces of māyā. He is manifested in Vāsudeva, Saṁkarṣana, Pradyumna, and Aniruddha. He has unconceivable power (acintyaśakti). He is in the world, and yet not in it. The world is in him, and yet not in him. He is transcendent and immanent. His powers are inconceivable.[2]

God is like the blazing sun. The jīva is a spark of him. The souls issue forth from his soul-energy (jivaśakti). He is the possessor of this power. The jīva is a power of God, and yet different from him. It is an eternal servant of him. It forgets its essential divine nature, and is entangled in bondage to māyā. Devotion (bhakti) to God only disentangles him from the bondage, and leads him to attain him. If a person surrenders himself to God completely, he breaks the fetters of māyā. The jīvas are parts of God different from him (vibhinnāṁśa). But the four Vyūhas and Avatāras are his own parts (svāṁśa) non-different from him.[3]

Virtue (dharma), wealth (artha), happiness (kāma), liberation (mokṣa), and love of God (prema) are the five ends of life. The first four are worthless in comparison with the last. Love of God is the fifth supreme end. It is the ocean of infinite bliss of God. The bliss of Brahman, the impersonal Absolute, is not even a drop of this ocean of love of God. It can be attained by reciting and chanting his name.[4] Ignorance (avidyā) of the jīva is destroyed by the grace of God, which reveals the nature of the reality. He can be known in his real nature by devotion. He can be known as Brahman only through knowledge. Brahman is an imperfect manifestation of God.[5] Karma, yoga, and knowledge lead to devotion. They cannot lead to attainment of God without devotion of him. Knowledge without devotion cannot lead to liberation. But devotion without knowledge leads to liberation. Knowledge without devotion is not pure.[6] Devotion is sweet. Knowledge is bitter. Devotion or love is the best means of the attainment of God. It is the essence of the bliss of God. A devotee does not want liberation or union with God. He wants to serve and love him for ever. God is the embodiment of transcendent beauty. He is the repository of all kinds of senti-

---

[1] *Ibid*, Ādilīlā, Ch. IV.
[2] *Ibid*, Ādilīlā, Ch. V.
[3] *Ibid*, Madhyalīlā, Ch. XXII.
[4] *Ibid*, Ādilīlā, Ch. VII.
[5] *Ibid*, Ādilīlā, Ch. I.
[6] *Ibid*, Madhyalīlā, Ch. XXII.

ments (rasāmṛta). He is the object of devotion of the different kinds of devotees.[1]

Kṛṣṇadāsa summarizes Jīva

Goswāmī's philosophy and Rupa Goswāmī and Jīva Goswāmī view of the different kinds of devotion to and love for God. So his account of Caitanya's philosophy may safely be taken to be his account of the philosophy of his followers.

[1] *Ibid*, Madhyalīlā, Ch. VIII.

CHAPTER XIX

ŚAIVISM AND ŚĀKTAISM

Vācaspati mentions four schools of Māheśvaras: Śaiva, Pāśupata, Kāruṇika Siddhāntin, and Kāpālika.[1] Mādhava describes three schools of Śaivism, Nakulīśa Pāśupata, Śaiva, and Pratyabhijñā system.[2]

The Pāśupata Philosophy

Appyayadīkṣita gives a gist of the five categories recognized by the Nakulīśa Pāśupatas. They are effect, cause, yoga, vidhi, and mokṣa. The effect are of ten kinds. They are the five elements of earth, water, fire, air, and ether, and the five qualities of smell, taste, colour, touch, and sound. The causes are of thirteen kinds. They are the five organs of knowledge, the five organs of action, and the three internal organs, manas, buddhi, and ahaṁkāra. Yoga is the relation of the soul to God through the mind. It is of two kinds. It consists in activity such as recitation of mantras, meditation, and the like. It consists in consciousness of God without any activity. Vidhi is the observance which achieves virtue. Austerities such as besmearing the body with ashes, lying on ashes, recitation of mantras, and the like are the observances.[3] Mokṣa is absolute extinction of pain. It is also attainment of superhuman powers of knowledge and activity. They are supernormal vision (darśana) of subtle, remote, and hidden visible and tangible objects, supernormal hearing (śravaṇa) of all audible sounds, knowledge (manana) of all intelligible objects, complete and undoubted knowledge of the scriptures (vijñāna), and the omniscience (srvajñatva) or knowledge of all principles taken individually or collectively. These are the supernormal powers of knowledge (dṛkśakti). There are three kinds of supernormal powers of activity, excessive quickness of movements (manojavatva), assumption of innumerable bodies and sense-organs and their control and guidance by sheer will without activity (kāmarūpitva), and sovereignty over objects without the aid of the sense-organs (vikaraṇadharmitva).[4]

---

[1] *Bhāmatī* on SBS., ii, 2. 37.

[2] SDS., ch. vi, vii, viii.

[3] SDS., vi. 11.

[4] SDS., vi. 7; *Kalpatarupārimala*, ii. 2. 37.

The Pāśupatas recognize the reality of God (pati), the individual souls (paśu), and the world. God is the Lord (pati). He has supreme power of knowledge and activity. He is the independent cause of the world. He creates it by his unrestricted and arbitrary will without the aid of karmas of the souls. His sovereignty is eternal. The soul's karmas are not useless. They bear fruits, if they are aided by the will of God. They cannot bear fruits, if they are not favoured by the will of God, even as the labours of a peasant do not bear fruits without the aid of rain.[1] God is eternally fulfilled. He does not realize any end through the karmas of the souls. It is urged that if God is the independent cause of the world, all effects would be produced simultaneously. But this argument is invalid. God has inconceivable unrestricted power or creating effects by mere will. So he may create effects gradually. His will is absolute. He is the First Cause or the cause of causes.[2]

God is independent. The souls are dependent. They are produced by him. They are eternal products[3]. They are called paśu because they are fettered by bonds (pāśa). The are either tainted (sāñjana), or untainted (nirañjana). The former are embodied. The latter are disembodied.[4]

The impurity (mala) defiling the souls is fivefold: false knowledge, demerit, attachment, causality, and lapse. It is the root of sin. It binds the souls to saṁsāra. Purity is complete extinction of the fivefold impurity. There are five means of removing impurity; observance, recitation of mantras, meditation on God, constant recollection of him, and achievement of fruits. Knowledge, austeri ties, constancy, stability, and purity are the five fold fruits.[5]

Mokṣa is not mere absolute negation of pain. It is also achievement of divine sovereignty. It is proximity (sāmīpya) of God, which puts an end to rebirth.[6] The souls tainted by impurities are incapable of vision of God. They can attain release by means of true knowledge of the principles derived from the Pāśupata Śāstras only.[7] The Pāśupatas are said to be the Gujerat school of Śaivism.[8]

The Śaiva Siddhānta

The South Indian School of Śaivism is called the Śaiva Siddhānta. Mādhava's account of the Śaiva Darśana is that of

---

[1] *Kalpatauparimala*, ii, 2. 37; SDS., vi. 15.
[2] SDS., vi. 15.
[3] SDS., vi. 5, 14.
[4] SDS., vi. 9.
[5] SDS., vi. 2-4.
[6] SDS., vi. 14.
[7] SDS., vi. 16.
[8] *Indian Thought*, 1912, p. 36.

the South Indian school. It is based upon twenty eight Śaiva Āgamas. Mādhava quotes from the *Mṛgendra Āgama*, the jñānapāda of the *Kāmikā*, the first of the South Indian Āgamas, the *Pauṣkara*, *Kiraṇa*, *Karaṇa*, and the other Āgamas.

There are three principles of reality: God (pati), the soul (paśu), and bond (pāśa).[1] God creates the world with the aid of karmas of souls.[2] Śiva is the Lord (pati). He is independent while the souls are dependent. He is conscious while bonds are unconscious. So God is different from the souls and their bonds. The souls and God are conscious. God is the supreme reality. The souls are dependent on him. Bonds abide in them.[3]

God is omniscient, omnipotent, uncaused, pure, and formless He assumes many forms to favour his devotees. Formless God cannot be meditated on and worshipped. But forms of God can be easily worshipped.[4] His acts are five-fold: creation, maintenance, and destruction of the world, concealment or embodiment, and liberation of the individual souls. He bestows grace on his devotees in the pure path. He breaks the bonds, which fetter their souls. He is benign and endowed with auspicious qualities.[5] Śiva is the efficient cause of the world. Śakti, his conscious energy. is its instrumental cause. Māyā is its mterial cause. Śakti is conscious energy. It constitutes the body of God. It is not independent of him. Māyā is the unconscious primal matter. It is omnipresent, indestructible, and possessed of manifold powers. The individual souls are eternal.

They are tainted by impurities, and become embodied. When they are purged of impurities, they attain absoluteness (śivatā). The world and the souls are real. They are inseparably related to God. They are his body. He is their soul.[6]

The causal-teleological argument for the existence of God is given. The world is non-eternal and composed of parts with a particular arrangement. It is an effect. So it must be produced by an intelligent agent endowed with knowledge of its constituents and their arrangement. It cannot be a finite being. So it must be God.[7] It may be objected that the world may not be produced by a cause just as a body is not bound to be produced by a cause. This

---

[1]SDS., vii. 1. 3.

[2]Karmādisāpekṣaḥ parameśvaraḥ kāraṇam. SDS., vii. 1.

[3]SDS., vii. 2.

[4]*Pauṣkara Āgama;* SDS., vii. 9.

[5]*Karaṇa;* SDS., vii. 10.

[6]CP. Rāmānuja.

[7]SDS., vii. 4.

argument is wrong. A body is composed of parts with a particular arrangement and non-eternal like a jar. So it is an effect, and must have an intelligent cause. The world has a particular arrangement of parts. It is non-eternal. So it must have an intelligent cause. It cannot be a finite being because it has no knowledge of its constituents, and cannot arrange them in this particular manner. So it must be God.[1]

God is not the independent cause of the world as the Pāśupatas maintain. He creates the world with the aid of karmas of the souls. It does not compromise his independence, since independence of an agent is not compromised by the use of instruments. If the agent is not directed by any other agent, he is independent. The use of instruments does not make him dependent. The king makes gifts through his treasurer, but he does not impair his independence God is the supreme Lord. He does not depend upon any other Being. He is absolutely independent. His dependence upon karmas of souls does not impair his independence. He creates the world with the aid of karmas which are his instruments.[2] God is omniscient and omnipotent. He knows the constituents of the world. He knows the karmas of the souls and their fruits. He arranges the constituents of the world into objects of their experiences in conformity with their merits and demerits. A finite being is incapable of this task with his finite knowledge and power.[3]

It may be objected that God cannot create the world because he is disembodied. A potter with a body can produce a pot. If God creates the world with a body, he is not omniscient, omnipotent, and free from afflictions like human beings. This argument is invalid. Even a disembodied soul can produce vibration in the body ensouled by it. So even disembodied God can create the world. He is devoid of a natural body because he is free from the web of taint and karmas. But he has a spiritul body created by his will. It is made of Śakti.[4] Sakti is the conscious energy of Śiva. It is the instrumental cause of the world. Māyā is its material cause. God is its efficient cause.

The individual soul is called paśu. It is a knower, enjoyer, and active agent. It is non-atomic. It is pervasive and eternal. It is not identical with the body as the Cārvākas maintain, since it cannot account for recollection of objects perceived in the past. It is not an

---

[1]SDS., vii. 5. [2]SDS., vii. 6.
[3]SDS., vii. 7.
[4]Śāktaṁ vapuḥ prabhoḥ. *Mṛgendra Āgama*; SDS., vii. 8.

object of mental perception as the Naiyāyika maintains, since it would lead to infinite regress. If the soul is manifested by knowledge, that knowledge would be manifested by some other knowledge, and so on to infinity. The soul is not co-extensive with the body as the Jaina maintains, since it is not limited by space. It is not a stream of momentary cognitions as the Buddhist maintains, since it is not limited by time. It is unlimited by space and time. It is not inactive as the Sāṁkhya maintains, since it attains infinite power of activity when it is purged of all impurities. It is not one, as the Advaita Vedānta maintains, since one soul cannot account for variety of enjoyments ans sufferings undergone by different souls. There is plurality of souls.[1] They are not created by God. They are eternal.

The soul is of the nature of knowledge and activity. It attains absoluteness when its bonds (pāśa) of impurities are broken.[2] It acquires infinite knowledge and creative power, which were obscured during bondage.

Bonds (pāśa) are of four kinds: (1) Mala or impurity due to the false notion of finitude (āṇavamala); (2) karma which unites the soul with a body; (3) māyā, the cosmic power which is the material cause of the world; (4) rodhaśakti, the power which conceals the real nature of the soul. Māyā unfolds the world in creation. It withdraws it in dissolution. The world is merged in māyā as a potentiality. It is manifested in creation.[3]

There are three kinds of souls: vijñānakala,pralayākala, and sakala. The first tainted by āṇavamala only; they are free from karma, māyā, and rodhaśakti. The second are tainted by āṇavamala, and karma. The third are tainted by āṇavamala, karma, and māyā.[4]

The souls are real. The world is real. God delivers the souls from their bonds. The world has a moral purpose. It is the field of objects, which afford enjoyments and miseries to the souls. God is its First Cause. He is the Moral Governor. He gives fruits of karmas to the souls. The Śaiva Siddhānta is realistic and theistic.

The Śaiva Siddhānta recognizes thirty six principles. There are five pure principles: (1) Śiva-tattva; (2) Śakti: (3) Sadāśiva;

[1]SDS., vii. 11, 12.
[2]Pāśānte śivatāśruteḥ. *Mṛgendra Āgama;* SDS., vii. 12.
[3]SDS., vii. 21-22.
[4]*Tarrvaprakāśa;* SDS., vii. 13-15.

(4) Īśvara; and (5) Śuddhavidyā. Śivattata is an evolute of mahā-māyā or pure māyā, as distinguished from impure māyā. Māyā is not an essential power of the Lord. He assumes this power (pari-grahaśakti). Śivattava is one, omnipresent, and eternal. Knowledge and action constitute its essential nature. It is the cause of the other pure principles. Neither Śiva nor Śakti is their cause, since neither undergoes any modification. So Śivatattva is not identical with Śiva. Śakti is an evolute of Śivatattva. It is conscious energy. Sadāśiva is an evolute of Śakti; It is the principle of being (Sadākhya), in which the power of knowledge and action are held in equipoise. Īśvaratattva is an evolute of Sadāśiva, in which the power of knowledge is subordinated to the power of action. Śuddhavidyā is an evolute of Īśvaratattva, in which the power of action is subordinated to the power of knowledge. The pure principles are timeless. Some maintain that there is pure time in the realm of the pure principles.

Impure māyā evolves into the five sheaths (pañca-kañcuka): time (kāla), destiny (niyati); limited creative power (kalā), limited knowledge (vidyā), and interest (rāga) in particular things. Time is manifold, non-intelligent, caused, and non-eternal. Time helps production. Destiny regulates the enjoyment of appropriate fruits of actions. It is non-intelligent and guided by the conscious energy of God (Śivaśakti). Kāla partly removes the darkness that envelopes the soul. It evolves into mūla-prakṛti, on the one hand, and into vidyā and rāga, on the other. Knowledge (jñāna) is non-intelligent. It is manifested by vidyā. Attachment (avairāgya) also is non-intelligent. It is manifested by rāga. They are actuated by Sivasakti, which is conscious energy. The puruśatattva or individual soul has experience of mūla-prakṛti as enveloped in the five sheaths. Impure (aśuddha) māyā, kāla, niyati, kalā, vidyā, rāga, and puruṣa are the seven intermediate mixed principles.

Then the twenty four impure principles of the Sāṁkhya are recognized. Prakṛti is the cause of the guṇas, sattva, rajas, and tamas. It is not mere equipoise of them. It evolves into Buddhi or cosmic intellect. Ahaṁkāra, the principle of individuation, is evolved from it. The five tanmātras are evolved from tāmasa Ahaṁkāra in which tamas predominates. The five gross elements of ether, air, fire, water, and earth are evolved from the tanmātras. Manas and the five organs of knowledge are evolved from sāttvika Ahaṁkāra, in which sattva predominates. The five organs of action are evolved from rājasa Ahaṁkāra, in which rajas predominates. Manas is the sensory-motor organ. Some recognize citta also as an internal organ. Thus, Saivism recognizes thirty six principles.[1] The Southern Śaivism is realistic.

The Pratyabhijñā Philosophy

Both Nakulīśa Pāśupata school and the South Indian school are realistic and theistic. But Kāśmīr Śaivism is monistic and idealistic. It is called the Pratyabhijñā system.

Vasugupta (800 A.D.) discovered *Śivasūtra*. He wrote *Spandakārikā*. Kallaṭa (900 A.D.) wrote a commentary on it. Somānanda's (900 A.D. *Śivadṛṣti*, Utpala's (1000 A.D.) *Spandapradīpika*, a commentary on *Spandakārikā*, Abhinava Gupta's (1100 A.D.) *Īśvarapatyabhijñāsūtravṛtti*, *Tantrasara*, and *Tantrāloka*, and Kṣemarāja's *Śivasūtravimarśini* are important works on the Pratyabhijñā system.

Parama Śiva is the only ontological reality. He is pure consciousness. He is the Ātman.[2] He is universal consciousness. He is objectless self-luminous consciousness. He is omnipresent, omniscient, omnipotent, independent, infinite, eternal, formless, and possessed of infinite attributes. Independence is his unique attribute. He is pure undifferenced consciousness, unlimited by space, time, and forms. He is pure consciousness unlimited by adjuncts (upādhi). He is the supreme Self (paramātman).[3] He is the Lord of the wheel of powers. He is the goal. He is the Highest Good. He is nameless and homogeneous. But he assumes various forms by volitions. He is non-different. There is no distinction of the worshipper, the worshipped, and worship in him. He is devoid of subject and object. He is self-luminous (svābhāsa). There is no distinction of pleasure and pain in him.[4]

God is the non-dual Self (advaya Ātman) possessed or consciousness, bliss, and activity. Knowledge, activity, and independence are his essence. His knowledge is not veiled by avidyā.[5] He is the self-proved Ātman. He cannot be proved by any pramāṇa, which depends upon him. He is self-luminous. He always manifests himself. He is known by one's own intuition.[6]

God is the foundational knowledge, which is the only reality. But it appears in the triple forms of the knower, the known, and

[1] Article on "The Philosophy of Saivism" in *The Cultural Heritage of India*, Vol. II, pp. 36-41; SDS., vii. 16-17.

[2] Caitanyam ātmā. *Śivasūtra*, i. 1.

[3] *Śivasūtravimarśinī*, i. 1. *Spandapradīpikā*, V.S.S., 1898, p. 3.

[4] *Spandapradīpikā*, pp. 3-5.

[5] *Śivasūtravimarśinī*, i. 1; *Vārtika*, i. 1.

[6] Eṣa eva svānubhavaikapramāṇaḥ. *Spandapradīpikā*, p. 3. *Śivasūtravimarśinī*, i. 1. Cp. *Śaṁkara*.

knowledge.[1] The Experiencer (pramātṛ) alone is real. The experienced objects are unreal. The world divided into subjects and objects is an appearance like a reflection in a mirror. External objects are unreal. They do not exist in themselves. They exist for knowledge. But knowledge exists for itself. External objects owe their existence to the knowledge that apprehends them. They derive their being from the knowing Self, on which they depend. They have no independent existence.[2] Internal cognitons are manifested as external objects. Cognitions and their objects are of the same nature. They are known together. So they are of the nature of consciousness. The world is of the nature of knowledge.[3] All is pure consciousness, which is self-luminous and subject-object-less.[4] An object cannot exist apart from a cognition. A cognition cannot exist apart from the Ātman. So the Ātman alone, which is of the nature of pure consciousness, exists. A cognized object does not differ from cognition. Cognition does not differ from the Ātman. So the Ātman alone is real. The difference of objects from the Self that knows them is not real.[5] This is an emphatic statement of Absolutism. The Pratyabhijñā system is idealistic monism (advaitavāda).

Parama Śiva is the only reality. He is the embodiment of self-luminous consciousness and supreme bliss. He is transcendent (viśvottīrna). He is immanent in the world (visvātmaka). It is non-different from him. There are no subjects or objects different from him. He is undifferenced. Yet he is manifested in the infinite variety of the universe.[6] The individual souls and the world are of the nature of consciousness. They are, in reality, Parama Śiva.[7] The world is expansion of his power.[8] His power (śakti) is of the nature of consciousness. It is his conscious energy. Its expansion consists in the manifestation (ābhāsa) of his creative power in the world.[9] It endures for some time as an external manifestation, depending on his knowledge. Its dissolution consists in its resting in the Ātman

---

[1]Jñātā jñeyam jñānam iti jñānasyaiva tridhā sthitiḥ. *Spandapradīpikā*, p. 39.
[2]Jñānādvaitam svato'sti, na jñeyasya sattā kvacit. *Ibid*, p. 39.
[3]Tattadrūpatayā jñānaṁ bahirantaḥ prakāśate. Jñānād ṛte, nārthasattā jñānarūpaṁ tato jagat. *Śivasūtravimarśinī*, iii. 30.
[4]Sarvaṁ śuddhaṁ nirālambaṁ jñānaṁ svapratyāyatmakam. *Ibid*, iii. 31.
[5]Jñānaṁ na bhavato bhinnaṁ jñeyaṁ jñānāt pṛthaṅ na hi. Ato na tvitarat kiñcit tasmād bhedo na vāstavaḥ. *Ibid*. iii. 2.
[6]*Pratyabhijñāhṛdaya*, p. 8.
[7]*Śivasūtravimarśinī*, i. 1.
[8]Svaśaktipra ayo 'sya viśvaṁ. *Śivasūtra*, iii. 30.
[9]*Śivasūtravimarśinī* iii. 10, 30.

of pure consciousness. Creation, maintenance, and dissolution are evolution, continuance, and involution of the creative power of the Lord.[1] Creation is its unfoldment or expansion (unmeṣa). Dissolution is its enfoldment or contraction (nimeṣa). The world is inseparable from him. It is non-different from him.[2]

Umā is the will or power of Śiva. She is the supreme and independent power of God. She delights in the sport of creation and destruction of the world.[3] The supreme power (parā śakti) is subtle, pervasive, spotless, divine, and of the nature of infinite bliss. It is the foundation of all powers. It is omniscient. It is the conscious will of God. It is the seed of the universe.[4] Parama Śiva manifests the world in himself by the sport of his own vibration.[5] It is the power of God. He is endowed with the power. The power is non-different from the possessor of power.[6] Siva is not devoid of Sakti. Śakti is not independent of Śiva. There is no difference betwen them. Śakti is the infinite conscious energy of Siva, which is non-different from him.[7]

God is called *spanda*. It is vibration excited by the power of the Ātman. and enlightened by its will.[8] It is the indeterminate condition of the motionless Absolute or Ātman and its readiness to function everywhere. It is the manifestation of the intuitive consciousness of the Lord, who is of the nature of infinite and eternal consciousness common to all objects.[9]

The world is the expression of the divine will or thought. Thought is always expressed in speech (vāk) before it is expressed in an external object. Speech is of the nature of thought. Logos intervenes between God and the world. Thought is expressed in Logos. Logos is expressed in the world. It is like a ray of light of the Ātman or all-manifesting pure consciousness.[10] It is pure consciousness that is expressed in speech through the principle of life. Speech is founded in consciousness. There is no consciousness without speech. All cognitions are interpenetrated with words. The

[1]*Ibid*, iii. 31.
[2]*Spandakārikā*, 1; *Spandapradīpikā*, p. 9.
[3]*Śivasūtra*, i. 13; *Śivasūtravimarśinī*, i. 13.
[4]*Ibid*, iii. 15, 27, 43, 44.
[5]*Ibid*, iii. 9.
[6]Sā ca tadabhinnaiva. *Spandapradīpikā*, p. 11.
[7]Parāśaktirūpā citireva bhagavatī śivābhinnā. *Pratyabhijñāhṛdaya*, p.2. No śivaḥ śaktirahito na śaktir vyatirekiṇī. *Śivadṛṣṭi*, iii, 2. 3. *Kaṣhmir Shaivism*.p. 43.
[8]Cidicchāśaktisambuddhaḥ spanda ātmabaleritaḥ. *Spandapradīpikā*, p. 37.
[9]*Ibid*, p.3.
[10]*Ibid*, pp. 9. 37, 52.

world is the expression of the thought of God. It is interpenetrated by his thought and speech.[1] The Ātman manifests all objects by sheer will without any material. They are manifested by the Lord. They exist in him; they cannot exist apart from him. They are external manifestations of his thoughts or volitions.[2] They are limited by space, time, activity, and forms. They are mere external manifestations of the infinite and eternal Ātman.[3]

The world of conscious and unconscious creatures is a manifestation (ābhāsa) of God.[4] The finite objects are not unreal appearances (vivarta). They are not absolutely non-existent. They are aspects (ābhāsa) of God.[5] The world is known by the Ātman. So it acquires the nature of consciousness. The pure consciousness is one and indivisible. There are no objects external to the knower. They acquire the nature of the Ātman, when they are known. Subjects and objects are one reality. Consciousness is the real nature of the world.[6] Consciousness is the foundation of the world. When it is known by the Experiencer, it becomes existent. An unconscious entity cannot produce the world, which contains conscious creatures.[7]

The jīva is, in reality, identical with the Ātman. It is the Self or Ātman of the universe. It is the creator of all objects. Śiva, the Experiencer, manifests himself as objects of experience. The jīva becomes Śiva, when it recognizes its identity with him. It is nothing but the Ātman, the Self of the universe. It is the universal Experiencer.[8] But it becomes an object of experience (meya) under the influence of avidyā, and does not apprehend its essential nature. Avidyā is false (anṛta). It is not real. It neither destroys a real object nor does it modify it. It cannot change the nature of the Ātman. It is bound neither by it own nature nor by any external condition. Its bondage is neither intrinsic nor extrinsic. It is bound by avidyā. It is liberated by extinction of avidyā.[9] Saṁsāra is due to ignorance (ajñāna). There is no bondage in reality. There being no bondage, there is no liberation. Both bondage and liberation

---

[1] *Ibid*, pp. 36-37.

[2] *Ibid*, p. 38.

[3] *Ibid*, p. 25.

[4] Ābhāsarūpā eva jaḍacetanapadārthāḥ. *Pratyabhijñāvimarśini*, iii. 1.

[5] *Kashmir Shaivism*, p. 55.

[6] Vedakaṁ vedyam ekaṁ tattvam. Caitanyaṁ viśvasya svabhāvah. *Śivasūtravimarśinī*, i. 1.

[7] *Spandapradīpikā*, p. 35.

[8] *Spandakārikā*, *Spandapradīpikā*, 28-29.

[9] Baddho 'vidyayā jīvo muktis tasya hi tatkṣaye. *Ibid*, p. 5.

are due to imagination (vikalpa). When the jīva realizes its essential purity and identity with God, it is liberated. Until it recognizes its identity with him, it is in bondage. Its power is contracted by avidya, which is a beginningless purity due to non-discrimination. It produces a desire for enjoyment. When the jīva is freed from the taint of avidyā and recognizes its innate divinity, it realizes its intrinsic omniscience, omnipotence, and independence.[1]

The finite souls are not ontologically real. They are, in their essential nature, pure consciousness. They have no differences in their essential nature. The pure consciousness is devoid of difference. It is not limited by time, space, and forms. The objects, body, sense-organs, manas, buddhi, and ahaṁkāra are unreal, when they are not manifested by conciousness. When they are manifested by it, they become identical with pure consciousness. The souls are tainted by avidyā, and become finite and embodied.[2] When they are purged of all taints, they become the Self of pure consciousness.[3] There is no plurality of souls. The Pratyabhijñā system is advaitavāda. It differs from the realistic Southern Śaiva Siddhānta.

Śāktaism

Śāktaism advocates a position intermediate between absolute monism and qualified monism. Śiva is the static Absolute. Śakti is is the conscious energy of Śiva. He creates the world through Sakti. Siva is one Ātman. He appears to be many jivas through the bodies. They are Brahman or Ātman. The world is constructed by the Māyā of Śiva. The jīva can attain embodied release through knowledge of its identity with Brahman. Śiva and Śakti are Brahman. They are inseparable from each other. They are non-different from each other. Śiva is static. Sakti is dynamic. Śiva is the Absolute. Śakti stands for God.

Śiva is the one supreme Being. He is Being, Consciousness, and Bliss. He is indeterminate (nirvikalpa), undifferenced (nirviśeṣa), pure consciousness (cinmātra). He is perfect and self-luminous. He is non-dual truth. He is immutable, immaculate, immobile, and inactive. He is omnipresent, omniscient, infinite, eternal, formless, and transcendent. He is suprarational, incomprehensible, indefinable, and inexpressible. He transcends the guṇas, sattva, rajas, and tamas. He is immanent in the world. He is its ungrounded ground. He is the universal consciousness (brahma-caitanya). He is the

[1] *Śivasūtravimarśinī,* iii. 13.
[2] *Ibid,* i. 1.
[3] *Ibid,* iii. 34.

witness of the universe. He is the Ātman of all beings. He pervades the universe. All things are inseparable from him.[1]

One pure consciousness appears to be knowledge, knower and known through māyā. They are unreal appearances. The Ātman alone is the reality. It appears to be subject and object.[2] The Ātman is Brahman. He is the ground of the false world-appearance.[3] Brahman alone is real. The world is an imaginary construction of māyā.[3]

Being, consciousness, and bliss are the essential characters (svarūpa-lakṣaṇa) of Brahman. He is the creator, preserver, and destroyer of the world. These are his inessential characters (taṭastha-lakṣaṇa).[4] He is the cause of the world. He is manifested in it (viśvarūpa). He is the ground of the world.[5] It is constructed by his māyā. He appears to enter into it, though he does not do so. The Ātman, the witness of all, always shines by itself.[6]

Śakti is the supreme energy (parā prakṛti) of Śiva, the supreme Self. It is conscious and omniscient. It is the fountain of all powers. It is the source of all knowledge. It is subtle and gross. It is manifest and unmanifest. It is formless and multiform.[7] Śakti creates, preserves, and destroys the world at the mere will of Brahman. Śiva creates, preserves, and destroys it through his Śakti. He is the unmoved mover or energiser of Śakti. He is the First Cause.[8]

The Ātman is homogeneous, pure consciousness. It is Brahman Śiva. It is unborn and immortal. It is one. But it appears to be many indifferent bodies through Māyā, even as one space appears to many spaces when it is enclosed in jars, or as the sun appears to be many, when it is reflected in water in earthen vessels. There is ultimately no plurality of souls.[9] The Ātman is calm and inactive. The buddhi infected with ignorance becomes restless and active. Its activity is attributed to the Self.[10] The jīva is the Ātman embodied in the organism. It is never free. It is directed by the Ātman dwelling in it as its inner ruler.[11] It can become Śiva through yoga.[12]

Brahman pervades the world. All things are inseparable from

[1] *Mahānirvāṇatantra*, ii. 34-30; iii. 36, 50, 59, 60, 62, 63, 74; x. 210; xiv. 115. 129.

[2] Jñānaṁ jñeyaṁ tatha jñāṭā tritayaṁ bhāti māyayā. Vicāryamāṇe tritaye ātmaivaiko' vaśiṣyate. *Ibid*. xiv. 137.

[3] Asat trilokīsadbhānaṁ svarūpaṁ bhahmaṇaḥ smṛtam. *Ibid*, iii. 7.

[4] *Ibid*., iii. 5, 6, 8, 60.

[5] *Ibid, iii*. 60, 63.

[6] *Ibid, xiv*, 127, 128.

[7] *Ibid*, iv. 10-15.

[8] *Ibid*, iv, 25-27; v. 1, 26, 27.

[9] *Ibid*, xiv, 129, 131, 133.

[10] *Ibid*, xiv. 132.

[11] *Ibid*, xiv, 122.

[12] *Ibid*, ii, 43.

him. He exists in them. They exist in him.[1] The world depends upon him. It subsists in him. All things are real with the reality of Brahman. The entire universe is interpenetrated with him.[2] He assumes its form. He is subtle and gross. He is manifested in the world.[3] He creates it through his energy (māyā). Māyā is prakṛti. It is embedded in Sakti, which is his supreme conscious energy. Though Śakti is formless, it assumes diverse forms through Māyā,[4] Mahat is evolved from prakṛti. Ahaṁkāra is evolved from majar. Manas, the ten sense-organs, and the five elements are evolved from ahaṁkāra.[5] Śāktaism combines absolute monism with the Sāṁkhya theory of evolution.

[1] *Ibid*, xi, 210, 212.
[2] *Ibid*, ii, 38, 39, 46.
[3] *Ibid*, v. 195.
[4] *Ibid*, siv. 127; iv. 34; v. 19.
[5] *Ibid*, v. 95-97; xi. 5-8.